DATE DUE

~~SET 0 00~~			

DEMCO 38-296

THE REGIONAL WORLD

A GUILFORD SERIES

Perspectives
on Economic Change

Editors

MERIC S. GERTLER
University of Toronto

PETER DICKEN
University of Manchester

The Regional World:
Territorial Development in a Global Economy
MICHAEL STORPER

Lean and Mean:
Why Large Corporations Will Continue
to Dominate the Global Economy
BENNETT HARRISON

Spaces of Globalization:
Reasserting the Power of the Local
KEVIN R. COX, *Editor*

The Golden Age Illusion:
Rethinking Postwar Capitalism
MICHAEL J. WEBBER and DAVID L. RIGBY

Work-*Place:*
The Social Regulation of Labor Markets
JAMIE PECK

Restructuring for Innovation:
The Remaking of the U.S. Semiconductor Industry
DAVID P. ANGEL

Trading Industries, Trading Regions:
International Trade, American Industry,
and Regional Economic Development

HELZI NOPONEN, JULIE GRAHAM, and ANN R. MARKUSEN, *Editors*

THE REGIONAL WORLD
Territorial Development in a Global Economy

MICHAEL STORPER

School of Public Policy and Social Research
University of California, Los Angeles (USA)
and
Faculty of Social and Human Sciences
Université de Marne-la-Vallée (France)

THE GUILFORD PRESS
New York   London

el Rétiveau
1948–1996

© 1997 The Guilford Press
A Division of Guilford Publications, Inc.
72 Spring Street, New York, NY 10012
www.guilford.com

Printed in the United States of America

This book is printed on acid-free paper.

Last digit is print number: 9 8 7 6 5 4 3 2 1

Library of Congress Cataloging-in-Publication Data

Storper, Michael.
    The regional world: territorial development in a global economy /
Michael Storper.
        p.   cm. — (Perspectives on economic change)
    Includes bibliographical references and index.
    ISBN 1-57230-258-5. — ISBN 1-57230-315-8 (pbk.)
    1. Regional economics.   2. Economic development.   3. Technological
innovations—Economic aspects.   4. Economic geography.   I. Title.   II. Series.
HT388.S78   1997
337—dc21   97-16062
                                                                        CIP

Acknowledgments

As with any such book, this one is a result of personal reflection and research that is inextricably intertwined with the colleagues and friends who think about similar topics. I particularly thank my American, French, Italian, Danish, Canadian, British, Australian, Brazilian, and Mexican colleagues, for these are the countries where I have spent some time or had close contacts and learned from people; but it goes without saying that my thanks are not limited to people in these nations.

My ability to think and work during the period in which this book emerged, and my intellectual sensibilities and aesthetic are, quite simply, owed to Michel Rétiveau. His incredible love, generosity, and support for me, coupled with his extraordinary independence and wicked humor, made whatever I accomplished due to him. Michel's standards of thought and learning were so much higher than my own that they always served as a beacon of inspiration, something to strive for, however unattainable they were for me. This book, while dedicated to him, in no way could possibly reflect the breadth and depth of his own culture.

This book draws on certain pieces that were written as articles and presentations to conferences, most of which have been substantially revised for this book, as the overall pattern of thought on the subject took shape and matured. Bits and pieces of empirical material in Chapters 6 and 8, and theory in Chapter 5, are to be found in another recent book (Storper and Salais, *Worlds of Production,* Harvard University Press, 1997), but here they have been developed for different but complementary purposes.

Acknowledgments to the originals are as follows:

Chapter 1 was prepared while I was a visiting scholar at the Institut de Recherches sur les Sociétés Contemporaines (IRESCO), within two of its research units, the Centre de Sociologie Urbaine and the Groupement de Recherches "Institutions, Emploi et Politique Economique," supported by the PIR-Villes Program of the French CNRS. I wish to thank, in particular, Francis Godard, Edmond Preteceille, Robert Salais, and Christian Topalov for their sponsorship of this visit. The chapter was presented at the Conference, "Cities, Enterprises, and Society at the Eve of the XXIst Century," Lille, March 16–18 1994, sponsored by PIR-Villes, CNRS. Earlier versions of this paper were presented at the International Seminar on "Geographies of Integration, Geographies of Inequality in Post-Maastricht Europe," Syros, Greece, September 1–4 1993; and at the Nordic Critical Geographers, Copenhagen, September 23–24, 1993. Portions of this chapter are based on an article originally published in *European Urban and Regional Studies, 2,* 3, 1995.

Chapter 2: An earlier version was presented as keynote address to the colloquium of the Association des Sciences Régionales de Langue Française, "Industrial Economics, Spatial Economics," in Toulouse, August 30–September 1, 1995; and to the *Sviluppo Locale* conference, organized by Fabio Sforzi and Professor Giacomo Becattini, in Artiminio, Italy, September 9, 1996.

Chapter 5: Earlier versions of this chapter were presented at the workshop "Systems of Innovation," organized by the European Economic Community (FAST/SPRINT/DG V), LATAPSES-Nice, and the Deptartment of Economics, University of Bologna, Bologna Italy, October 5–6, 1992; and the Society for the Advancement of Socio-Economics, Paris, July 1994. This chapter draws on research I carried out with Robert Salais (CNRS-INSEE, Paris), but the author is solely responsible for the content. A previous version was published in *Industrial and Corporate Change 5,* 3 (1996).

Chapter 6: The paper on which the chapter is based was originally presented to the Annual Meeting of the Association of American Geographers, Miami, April 16, 1991, in a session entitled "The Geography of Rationality and Collective Action." This chapter is based on research carried out while I was a Fellow of the German Marshall Fund, and the support of the Fund is gratefully acknowledged. Additional support came from the International Studies and Overseas Programs of UCLA and the Academic Senate of the University of California, Los Angeles Division, and the Center for German and European Studies at the University of California, Berkeley, the Commission for International Exchange of Scholars (Fulbright), the French Ministry of Research and Technology, and the Groupement de Recherche "Institutions, Emploi, et Politique Economique" (Paris). An earlier version was published in *Regional Studies 27,* 5: 433-455, 1992.

Chapter 7: A previous version was published in *The Swiss Review of International Economic Relations (Aussenwirtschaft)* special issue on the international economy, June 1995, edited by Alain Thierstein.

Chapter 8: An earlier version appeared in *Economic Geography 68,* 1: 60–93, January 1992.

Chapter 9: Written as a presentation to the Fifth Annual RESER (European Network on Services and Space) Conference, "Service Activities and Urban Development," Aix-en-Provence, September 13–15, 1995.

Chapter 10: Originally prepared for presentation at the Conference on Employment and Growth in the Knowledge-Based Economy, sponsored by the OECD and the Danish Government, 7–8 November 1994, Copenhagen. I wish to acknowledge the support of the Institute of Geography, University of Copenhagen, and in particular John Jorgensen, for support during the time this paper was prepared. Thanks are also due to the Danish Fulbright Commission for a fellowship at the University of Copenhagen in 1994.

Conclusion: Originally presented at the meeting of EMOT, European Management and Organization in Transition, University of Durham, June 1996, organized by Professor Ash Amin, and sponsored by the European Science Foundation.

Permissions are gratefully acknowledged from the following:

The Longman Group, for Chapter 1; Academic Press, for Chapter 2; *Industrial and Corporate Change* and Harvard University Press, for Chapter 5; *Regional Studies,* for Chapter 6; and *Economic Geography,* for Chapter 7.

Preface

For almost a century, economists have been pulled in two different directions. Mainstream economic thought has emphasized the forces that lead to convergence, normalization, and equilibrium in the face of change. Thus, we find its key concepts of perfect competition, diminishing returns, the generic nature of resources, their mobility, and the reversibility of processes. From time to time, however, doubts emerge about one dimension or another of this package: market imperfections, increasing returns, asset specificity, factors that are slow to move or are fixed, and the possibility of irreversibilities. When the latter group of forces is emphasized, the view of the world is one of creativity, disruption, and dynamics, rather than adjustment to equilibrium. There are rough equivalents of these cleavages in many other modern social sciences, notably, sociology.

Some of the founders of 20th-century economics were themselves quite unresolved about how to reconcile these different elements of the economic process. Alfred Marshall concentrated his energies almost equally on notions of perfect competition and on specificities in the economic process, such as his famous notion of "industrial atmosphere." In the 1920s, there was major debate on how to accommodate increasing and decreasing returns in the same model, so aware were economists that both seemed to exist simultaneously. Technological change, admitted by all to be a principal motor of economic dynamics, has been studied by some as a process of diffusion—hence, normalization—and by others as a source of violent upheaval.

These views have often become sedimented into deep theoretical controversies. Used as the basis of how to structure economic policy, they often become ideological litmus tests, one used to defend a free-market view of the world, the other a statist or interventionist view.

The premise of this book is that the standard theoretical oppositions are wrong, and, hence, lead us to caricatural empirical and political views of what is going on today. Marshall's intuition was correct that the modern economic process involves both perfect and imperfect competition, sameness and difference, tendencies toward mobility and toward stickiness, decreasing and increasing returns. The industries Marshall observed in Lancashire were characterized by all the entry and exit and competition and price formation that standard economics likes so much. But its industrial atmosphere at a regional level was not itself accessible to producers from outside the region in a perfectly fluid way. Inside the region, the economy looked quite standard; from outside, there were barriers to entry.

Of course, this point has been the center of reflection by a number of authors throughout the 20th century, and there is currently a real blossoming of work on it in the economics of technological change, evolutionary economics, growth economics, international economics, and other fields.

A particularly sharp way to focus our attention on these questions is economic geography, which is necessarily about this relationship between specificity and difference, divergence and convergence, mobility and immobility. Economic geography continues to be marked by the controversies alluded to above. Are the economies of particular regions or nations distinctive because of momentary frictions, or technical dimensions (such as technical economies of scale) of the normal, perfectly competitive economic process? Or are they distinctive because the normal economy is imperfectly competitive, shot through with increasing returns, asset specificities, and irreversibilities? Which view should we accept as our necessary destiny and, hence, how should we structure policy toward it? These seemingly arcane theoretical debates are, of course, now absolutely essential to the construction of today's global economy and trading system by policymakers. They have to know what economic process they are dealing with. In the symbolic sphere, too, the stakes are big: are we moving toward McWorld, dominated by a few big firms, or will cultural diversity and political independence survive this phase of globalization?

Two dimensions of economic specificity are at the center of this book's inquiry: knowledge as the basis of technology, and the human relations that are essential to many types of economic coordination. Both are simultaneously necessary to the operation of a normal, competitive adjustment process so favored by mainstream economic thought and yet they incessantly create and re-create imperfect competition and economic differentiation. I try to show that human relations, rules, and conventions are at the heart of the economic process today. They structure a competitive process that involves many elements at the heart of the mainstream paradigm, but they also cause it to differ in key respects from that vision. Some of these relations lead to the standard picture of globalization as placeless and increasingly homogenous flows of resources. Many of them are also the sources of place-specific kinds of knowledge and practice, and the specializations of cities, regions, and nations in a global economy. By looking at things this way, we can reformulate what it is that "globalization" means, differently from the usual conceptual categories used for this purpose. We can also rethink some of the purposes and tools of an appropriate economic policy and identify some of the dangers of the current era.

Contents

PART I

REGIONS AS RELATIONS AND CONVENTIONS

CHAPTER 1

The Resurgence of Regional Economies,[1] 10 Years Later

THE REDISCOVERY OF THE REGION AND ITS CRITICS

Something funny happened in the early 1980s. The region, long considered an interesting topic to historians and geographers, but not considered to have any interest for mainstream western social science, was rediscovered by a group of political economists, sociologists, political scientists, and geographers. Not that no attention had been paid to regions by social scientists before that: in regional economics, development economics, and economic geography, such topics as regional growth and decline, patterns of location of economic activity, and regional economic structure were well-developed domains of inquiry. But such work treated the region as an outcome of deeper political economic processes, not as a fundamental unit of social life in contemporary capitalism equivalent to, say, markets, states or families, nor a fundamental motor process in social life, on the same level as technology, stratification, or interest-seeking behavior. Economic geography was thus considered to be a second-order empirical topic for social science.

In the early 1980s, in contrast, it was asserted that the region might be a fundamental basis of economic and social life "after mass production." That is, since new successful forms of production—different from the canonical mass production systems of the postwar period—were emerging in some regions and not others, and since they seemed to involve both localization and regional differences and specificities (institutional, technological), it followed that there might be something fundamental that linked late 20th-century capitalism to regionalism and regionalization.

Certain images piqued the interest of social scientists: the dense vertically disintegrated industrial districts of Northeast–Central Italy, Toyota City, Silicon Valley, Orange County, Route 128, the *cité scientifique* of Paris, Toulouse, Baden–Wurttemburg, and Bavaria; and even such lesser-known and less high-tech cases as the London and New York financial districts, Los Angeles' garment district, the Hollywood entertainment industry, the craft industries of Jutland, the metalcutters of the Haute Savoie in France, Sakaki in Japan, as well as hundreds of others. All of these were said to be manifestations of a resurgence of the region as the center of "post-Fordist," "flexible," "learning-based," production systems—the emerging face of capitalist industry in this *fin de siècle*. On a larger scale, it became evident that even with increasing intensity of global trade and investment flows, national specificities in terms of products traded and technologies produced were increasing: in certain respects, integration was not bringing similarity, but specialization, a form of regionalization.

But how important is regionalization? Is the region somehow a necessary source of the dynamism of these production systems and, hence, of the developmental dynamics of contemporary capitalism itself? Or is regionalization merely an expression of, another interesting empirical dimension of, technological and organizational changes in successful production systems?

Surprisingly, a fairly large number of social scientists, and not just those whose professional specialty is the region, began to respond in the early 1980s that regionalization was very important, and that it might be more than merely another localization pattern: it might actually be central to the coordination of the most advanced forms of economic life today.[2] And so a lively debate was joined. Over a period of more than ten years, the initial propositions have been reexamined theoretically and empirically, and new propositions have emerged. The debate over regionalization in contemporary capitalism continues to generate fascinating propositions, and for the first time has been taken seriously by social scientists interested in such central topics as technological and organizational innovation and national competitive advantage in a world economy. The subnational region (including such variants as cross-border regions, which include parts of more than one country) is also increasingly regarded as a level of economic policy making for these reasons (and not simply as a way to buy political calm, the traditional reason in much of Europe for regional policy).[3] The stakes of these debates are big in both theoretical and practical terms.

Three main "schools" have participated in the debate: those interested in institutions, those focusing on industrial organization and transactions, and those who concentrate their attention on technological change and learning. Each has made strong claims about the bases of the new competition and the role of the region, and each has inspired empirical research and theoretical critique. A reprise of the debate will show that there is good reason for including the region as an essential level of economic coordination in capitalism. But none of the main schools in the resurgence of regional economies debate has come up with the correct formulation of why this is the case. The critics of each of these schools, while in no way dismantling the case for regional economies, have shown their attempts at formulating the basis for the resurgence of regional economies to be partial, although often very rich in insight. The purpose of this book is to argue that the most general, and necessary, role of the region is as the locus of what economists are beginning to call "untraded interdependencies,"[4] which take the form of conventions, informal rules, and habits that coordinate economic actors under conditions of uncertainty; these relations constitute region-specific assets in production. These assets are a central form of scarcity in contemporary capitalism, and hence a central form of geographical differentiation in what is done, how it is done, and in the resulting wealth levels and growth rates of regions.

INSTITUTIONS AND INDUSTRIAL DIVIDES: THE ILL-FATED DEBATE OVER SMALL FIRMS

From the mid-1970s, Italian scholars called attention to the different development model that characterized the Northeast–Center of their country, dubbed the "Third Italy" by Bagnasco in 1977.[5] In the English-speaking world, the industrial systems of that region were made famous by Piore and Sabel in 1984.[6] They were the first to capture them in the form of a model; flexibility plus specialization. Generalizing from Italy to certain other cases (notably German), they then placed the success of such forms of production in macroeconomic and historical context and postulated the possibility of an "industrial divide" separating a putative era of flexible specialization from that of postwar mass production.

Their account was both empirically rich and theoretically powerful. It incited a debate that centered mostly on the empirical material they adduced to support the theory. Yet it was the theory, and at that, the elements that were least picked up in the subsequent debate that makes, in my view, the lasting contribution to our understanding of capitalist development in general and the status of the region in particular. Piore and Sabel echoed and paralleled the work that had been going on in Florence under the direction of Giacomo Becattini, who had become one of the major contemporary students of Alfred Marshall. Piore and Sabel made an analogy between what was happening in Italy and Marshall's notion of "industrial districts" in late 19th-century England. Becattini's Florentine group engaged in a systematic elaboration of the concept of a "Marshallian industrial district," centering both on its economic characteristic (externalities lodged in a division of labor) and on the sociocultural supports to interfirm interaction within an industrial district, this latter both through theoretical work and through very detailed studies of the history and structure of Tuscan industrial districts, especially that of Prato, the woolen goods district next to Florence.[7]

There are several fundamental contributions of the Italian school, and the formulations of Piore and Sabel and others, to the study of contemporary capitalist development. These contributions consist in four points that remain unchallenged.

First, technologies of production and divisions of labor in production are not dictated by a movement toward a globally optimal, foreseeable "best practice" for each sector. They are, rather, the outcomes of institutional pressures and choices made at critical points in the histories of products and their markets, and the direction of development is thus not necessarily toward greater scale and integration, but can be the reverse.[8] It is thus possible that rather different, but still efficient, forms of organization will coexist in the same sector.[9]

Second, the flexible specialization school got something basically right in identifying flexibility and specialization as fundamental alternatives to mass production. From IBM to Modena, these principles have not been challenged, though we are learning that the specific ways they are organized into industrial systems frequently take us far from the ideal types of Italy and southern Germany. A consequence of both these observations is that the "industrial divide" postulated by Piore and Sabel has probably been crossed, in the sense that the postwar mass production economy is being replaced by one characterized by greater flexibility and specialization. The strength of the analytical insight regarding flexibility-plus-specialization is suggested by the fact that it has made its way into virtually every important theory of the firm and the production system in "post-Fordism," including the high-volume, lean production models of Japan,[10] and that the language of flexibility-plus-specialization is now employed openly by corporate managers themselves when they restructure (as in the case of IBM). Moreover, the statistical evidence supports the overall notion that post-Fordism has arrested the long-term trend toward increased vertical integration and, in some cases, reversed it. In the American economy, for example, total vertical integration declined from 30% to 21% between 1977 and 1987, and even manufacturing vertical integration decreased from 30% to 27%. In most of the specific sectors said to be increasingly flexibly specialized, these declines were even more dramatic.[11]

Third, though the original examples of regionalism were much too pure, it now seems clear that some of the most dynamic forces in contemporary capitalist development—especially advanced forms of technological learning—are both localized and territorially specific. This insight, too, has become common currency not just among regionalists, but among economists and students of technology and trade. The contribution of the flexible specialization school was to assert that this seemed to have something to do with regionalized and territorially specific institutions, though this was not stated as clearly as would have been desired ten years ago.

Fourth, the key texts of this school emphasize that appropriately institutionalized networks are essential to successful ongoing adaptation of a regional economy in the face of uncertainty (technological, market, etc). Something approaching a new orthodoxy has arisen in the academic business economics and management literature in recent years: a network paradigm for organizing production systems. Participation in such networks is akin to a new best business practice, in much of this literature, much in the way that mass production was best practice three decades ago. There are now detailed microeconomic analytics for such a production paradigm, from single firms to whole *filières* (commodity chains). They differ essentially from the main points of the flexible-specialization school, where there is little emphasis on a single best practice or on the notion of optimum.

The critics of the empirical account centered on the lessons of the "Third Italy." They took two different routes. The first and least powerful attempted simply to deny the characteristics attributed by Bagnasco, Becattini, Bellandi, Brusco, Russo, Sforzi, Solinas, Dei Ottati, Trigilia, Regini, and Piore and Sabel, to the industrial systems of NEC Italy. These failed attempts at criticism rested simply on either on a misunderstanding of the Italian systems, in empirical terms or of an overreading of the model, reducing it incorrectly to a model about small firms, rather than a model about systems or networks of flexible and specialized firms.[12] Not all the criticisms of the Third Italy/industrial districts/flexible specialization model were spurious however; much of the problem stems from Piore and Sabel's attempt to root their deep theoretical claims about institutions, the division of labor, and the possibility of industrial divides in a very specific notion of flexible-specialization, drawn from Italian and southern German examples: the generalizability of those cases is limited. Some of the criticisms include:

1. Production systems dominated by small firms, especially the exceptionally small firms of the Third Italy, are few and far between in this world; so it gives a wrong impression to base the possibility of an industrial divide on small firm examples;

2. A model of an industrial divide needs to cover a wide sectoral composition, and the Italian and German examples concentrated on traditional nondurables or on specialized supplier (e.g., metalworking) industries, or on luxury versions of mass production (e.g., German cars);

3. There are deep historical roots to the Italian and German examples, although none spring directly and continuously from history or tradition[13]; still, the critics asked how it could be expected that in other regions similar forms of industrial skill and coordination could be built de novo. If a balance of cooperation and competition was a particularity of the conventions of certain regions, what about other regions with more orthodox (i.e., Anglo-American) competitive norms?

4. Were these just "niche" producers, enjoying favorable market positions while mass producers would occupy the central terrain of their respective sectors? The critics said yes[14]; the flexibilists said that the center, too, was giving way to flexible, high volume, "lean" production systems.[15] Here, the valid critique of the initial "flexible *specialization*" thesis concerned its empirical cases; but to hold firm, the critics would have had to show that there was

no significant big-firm version of flexibilization. Some attempted to do just that, claiming that Toyota was not really much different from any other mass producer and that big firms like IBM were really where the action was. But the bulk of the analyses—from Ohno himself to both Japanese and foreign observers of Toyota—claimed the opposite, and the dramatic restructuring of IBM for greater internal decentralization and flexibility in the early 1990s threw a heavy shadow on assertions that flexibility is an affair at the margin of markets. Still, though Piore and Sabel did assert clearly that there was a convergence between big and small firms, they conflated a general flexibilization of production with the particular model of flexible specialization within vertically disintegrated, small firm industrial systems. To this day, one cannot have a debate about flexibility as a general characteristic of contemporary industrial systems without it being confused with the specific model of flexible specialization in the sense of Italy and Germany. And this is true even with attempts, such as that of Hirst and Zeitlin,[16] to distance flexible specialization from the empirical contours of Italy and Germany, by rebaptizing it an "ideal type," for the ideal type retains the strong image of small firm, cooperative, and regionalized input–output relations.

5. In drawing on the extreme case of localization, that of the Third Italy, the flexible-specialization school opened itself up to the obvious criticism that most competitively successful production systems do not approach that level of regional closure.[17] Toyota City is, considered in this view, to be merely another exception.

6. The most important criticism, but one that was least precisely formulated by the critics, is that the flexible-specialization model did not define, in analytical terms, precisely what it was that distinguished a technologically dynamic, regionally rooted system of firms from those systems of firms that did not share these characteristics, but still appeared to be flexible and specialized. They correctly understood that the flexible-specialization model was only interesting to the extent that such production systems were technologically dynamic and not highly territorially mobile, but the words flexibility and specialization did not necessarily correspond to these characteristics.[18]

Likewise, though it developed certain building blocks of a model of performance,[19] having to do with the importance of collaboration, competition, trust, and confidence, the flexible specialization school itself did not develop an analytical language about ongoing industrial adjustment—or what is now called "learning"—sufficient to capture in a generalizable way the nature of flexible and specialized industrial systems that have long-term survival capacity without wage–price reductions, from those which do not.

This book will attempt to redress these deficiences, but in so doing it will need to reframe certain debates about industrial change and its geography in recent years.

INDUSTRIAL ORGANIZATION, TRANSACTIONS, AGGLOMERATION: THE CALIFORNIA SCHOOL OF EXTERNAL ECONOMIES

What we might call, for lack of a better term, the "California school" came at the problem of new production paradigms and the region from a the perspective of different industries, and a different political–institutional setting, from those described above; as such, it is not surprising that they also chose a different theoretical route. In the early 1980s, Allen Scott was already theorizing the relationship between the division of labor, transactions costs, and agglomeration, in his initial studies of the women's clothing industry in Los Angeles.[20] Just shortly thereafter, with no real prior theoretical disposition, Susan Christopherson and I, in studying Hollywood's film and television industries, observed a strong process of vertical disintegration[21]; and Piore and Sabel's book appeared while we were interpreting our empirical results. Other investigations, many carried out by Scott and his students, followed, and both Scott and I continued this work with our own investigations in France and Italy in the mid- and late 1980s.[22] Other geographers and regionalists, such as John Holmes, took an early interest in the division of labor as well.[23]

The argument that emerged rooted flexibility in the division of labor in production, and linked that to agglomeration via an analysis of the transactions costs associated with interfirm linkages. In essence, it took what seemed to be fact in the Italian cases and created an economic model of the agglomeration process.[24] It assumed that certain exogenous or endogenous market conditions gave rise to uncertainty—shifts in market conditions, or movements along a technological trajectory, for example. This uncertainty is met by externalization (disintegration), in one case to minimize exposure to risks of overcapacity (both production and labor force hoarding), in another to maximize the benefits of specialization and minimize the danger of technological lock-in.

Disintegration of production, caeteris paribus, in turn raises the transactions costs of input–output relations. There are more transactions external to the firm, and these transactions are, in a number of the empirical circumstances identified, more frequent, less predictable, and more complex. This raises their costs with geographical distance, and the feasibility of carrying out substantively complex transactions drops for certain kinds of complexity (especially noncodifiable or tacit knowledge or where trust is required and full contingent contracting impossible). So agglomeration is an outcome of the minimization of these transactions costs, where such minimization outweighs other geographically dependent production cost differentials.

This organization and cost-related explanation holds that agglomeration is one element in the external economies that attach to interdependent production systems. Under the circumstances specified above, in the presence of

agglomeration the advantages of interdependence—flexibility, risk minimization, specialization—are increased. In the extreme case, without geographical
proximity, these advantages would be cancelled out by the increased costs or
difficulties of the intensified transacting. The advantages of agglomeration
are external economics because flexibility lowers input costs (by minimizing
factor hoarding) and increases throughput to each firm in the sense that a
greater number of external input–output interconnections raises the probability of successful sale or purchase, all other things being equal. (A technical issue debated by economists is whether these economies are truly external,
since we don't really know whether the production functions of firms are truly
interdependent and whether their returns to investment are uneven; all we do
know, with certainty, is that the ensemble of firms has cost savings due to interconnections and these cost savings are enhanced by geographical proximity
because it lowers the resulting transactions costs.)

   This analysis thus partakes of a major trend in the business economics
literature, shared by much economic sociology: the economics of network
forms of production.[25] This analysis seemed to have several advantages over
the institutionally inspired flexible-specialization school. First, it did not seem
to depend on thick and historical institutional contexts. Indeed, one of the
main claims it made had to do with the establishment of new industrial
spaces. It argued that new industries—those that emerge after technological
branching points—have input structures independent of older industries—
and hence enjoy what we labeled "windows of locational opportunity," in the
sense that they are not attached to old stocks of external economies.[26] But
once a group of firms begins to get ahead, the proliferation of external linkages gives them advantages that rapidly attract new entrants and hence, only
a few major new agglomerations can form in a given new industry. So it offered an explanation for new flexible production agglomerations such as Silicon Valley.

   Second, it argued that the reagglomeration of older industries, analogous to those found in the European cases, could be accounted for via the
process of externalization and interlinkage of firms—the story of Hollywood
(told in Chapter 4), going from its own version of "mass" production and spatial diffusion toward vertical disintegration and reagglomeration, was a case in
point. It averred that there could be many reasons for such switches in the organizational and geographical pathways of development—in Hollywood, it
was regulatory and technological changes that set the process in motion[27]; in
the Third Italy, it was a combination of long-standing civic cultures and the
events of the postwar period[28]; in the Los Angeles fashion industry, it was endogenous changes in fashion and the possibility of making distribution more
attentive to consumer demand, enhancing the number of collections per
year.[29] Another major case would be consumer durables industries, where
technological changes in production and distribution made possible more

rapid changeovers; once these possibilities were realized by the Japanese, all world competitors had to follow suit. The list could go on, ad infinitum.

The coverage of the model, in other words, was meant to be greater than the initial version of the flexible specialization model, in that it allowed any mix of firm sizes, any sector, any mixture of interlinkages. Indeed, the model was defined around three groups of sectors, which account for increasing proportions of employment and output in industry—high technology, revitalized craft production, and producer and financial services—thus extending its reach.

As the debate proceeded, however, we realized that the linkage-transactions cost model was incomplete. Toward the end of the 1980s, we became more sensitive to the possibility that the agglomeration was itself a *source* of industrial dynamics. We held that agglomerations, once in place, constituted industrial communities where endogenous dynamics of knowledge and technology development occurred, drawing on the example of technology development in Sassuolo documented by Russo,[30] and extending this to our own California cases. This account of technological innovation turns explicitly on user–producer relations—that is, on information transactions in an input–output system—and holds that localization and appropriate communication rules are important to innovation in some industries.

This latter brought us to the question of institutions. Though agglomerations could be theoretically accounted for as the way that potential external economies were realized, there was no assurance that markets alone, nor even various forms of contracts, could successfully coordinate the nexus of transactions in an industrial agglomeration.[31] Such transactions—in labor markets, in interfirm relations, in innovation and knowledge development—tended to have points of failure in the absence of appropriate institutions. In these two respects—evolution and institutions—we attempted to go beyond the initial Williamsonian framework to argue that the "institutional arrangements" of agglomerations[32]—that is, the nexus of transactions and their economic performance—were themselves outcomes of broader institutional environments, and themselves generators of future choices for pathways of development. So we came "full circle" to rejoin the initial authors of the flexible-specialization thesis (and the Marshallian theme of "atmosphere"), albeit with a somewhat different perspective on the role of institutions in development as a whole. And, as we shall see shortly, we came to realize the central importance of the new economics of technological change and its core notions of evolution and path dependency, for our problem of the role of the region in late 20th-century capitalism.

As with the flexible-specialization school, there were spurious criticisms and serious critiques. Among the latter we may count the following.

It seems as if the California school's analysis does apply to certain modernized craft or traditional industries as well as certain labor-intensive manufacturing and service sectors: in clothing, furniture, jewelry, cinema and television, some financial services and banking industries, as well as certain segments of the mechanical engineering industries, the density of local linkages is consistent with the account of agglomeration. In other words, the California school's successfully analyzed cases overlap very strongly with those of the flexible-specialization school. The critique does not attempt to deny existence of agglomerations, nor of their recent growth, in other industries, but observes that dense local input–output relations are not present in them in sufficient quantity to account for the existence of the agglomeration. The direct local input–output relationships between firms are not dense enough to account for either the size of the agglomeration or for a high proportion of what goes on in the sector. The examples where this seems most applicable are parts of high technology and certain parts of supplier-intensive sectors, such as mechanical engineering—that is, the capital-intensive, high-wage examples of flexible production.[33]

The critics have attempted a sort of counter theory, which has as its point of departure not the input–output system, but the *firm*.[34] The post-Fordist firm is, for them, a nexus for the management of vast flows of resources, the principal node in a set of shifting property and production networks. The means for the firm to manage these networks is a mixture of ownership, contract, and alliance,[35] and in general, this new flexibility of networks carries out all the functions that disintegration does in the flexible-production school's analysis. Rather than an economy of direct cost reduction, even for the most innovative activities, we are in an "economy of organization,"[36] where scale, over long distances, can reduce the time and cost of flexible adjustments of capacity and shifts in product mix. Flexibility is retained as a key, but now linked to scale and geographical dispersion. Much of the causality of the flexible-production school's analysis with respect to regions is reversed.

Their description of the large firm as a nexus of shifting relations, and of the industrial system as a nexus of nexuses, is at the heart of much of the contemporary empirical economics of the firm.[37] It is not clear, however, that this stands in as an explanation of innovation, agglomeration, or the geography of input–output systems. If the flexible economy were really contained in such dispersed large-firm networks, for example, why would such firms allow significant parts of their activity to be "trapped" in specific countries and regions? Pavitt and Patel,[38] and Dunning,[39] all show empirically that the core technological activities of the biggest firms are principally rooted in their home countries. Why, indeed, would a firm like IBM bother with the cost and inconvenience of Silicon Valley at all? Here, the economy of organizations school responds that big urban areas are general "basing points" for advanced (knowledge-intensive) activities with high levels of risk.[40] We are back to urbanization economies. There are two problems with this. The first is that such an explanation of big firm–big city interdependence is necessarily a transactions-based explanation, insofar as the reason invoked for big city location is proximity to factor markets due to the need for high levels of factor (read: labor) turnover in the presence of uncertainty. In countries with primate cities, such as France and Japan, what appear in the form of urbanization economies cannot be distinguished from multiple and overlapping localization economies present in Paris and Tokyo. The two ways of interpreting the problem would lead to radically different policy prescriptions. The second is that the economies of even the biggest of the big cities, but especially middle-sized cities, are not only urbanized, but have strong sectoral specificities. So urbanization economies are underpinned by localization. This localization involves *parts* of firms, those that are in certain technological or economic "spaces," in the sense defined by Perroux.

One suspects that the model of the firm they have evolved is applicable to the flexibilization of rather routine productive activities—precisely those where market uncertainty is manageable (for example in the mass-production segments of the clothing industry) or those where innovation is also gradual and manageable: this is the spatially extended economy of organization. The *parts* of these *same* big firms that are involved in those productive activities are *not* free of agglomeration *nor* free of uncertainty in the relevant parts of their input–output chains, and it seems unlikely that transportation, telecommunications, and formal institutional arrangements (that is, strategic alliances and contracts) are sufficient to obviate the need for proximity in these cases.

Another approach that takes on some of the same questions as the California school is the new geographical economics of Paul Krugman and various international trade theorists. They explain geographical concentration of productive activity via returns to scale. These scale economies affect both intermediate and final outputs, giving rise to an uneven pattern of market dominance—a geometry of imperfect competition—and hence to specialization and trade (especially intraindustry trade). The existence of pervasive scale-based market power reflects itself in place-based pecuniary externalities. This line of explanation intersects with that of the California school in that it focuses on why intermediate-goods producers might be found clustered in particular places.

But it seems unlikely that all clusters of intermediate-output producers reduce to market size; even if they did, we would need a theory to explain why and how they become so specialized that they must cluster near their few, specialized customers, and in Krugman's model this is not discussed. As we have noted, the interfirm division of labor, and its evolutionary dynamics, seem to be the drivers of specialization and, hence, of possible scale effects at the intermediate level. In terms of final outputs, the new geographical economics seems to take for granted the results of a long process of concentration of assets, but tells us little about how industries get there, or what space might have to do with this. For example, if big final-output producers concentrate in an agglomeration to be near their specialist suppliers, then the primary issue for a theory would be how the structure of specialist suppliers and the demand for proximity is created, not simply the decision to optimize in the face of these circumstances. Where the issue is access to final markets, scale seems hardly an explanation for detailed patterns of location and trade where output scale is very high, market linkages are the most standardized, and distance the least costly element in them. Finally, there is almost nothing in the new geographical economics about the potential geographical foundations of economic performance. Everything reduces rather axiomatically to fully efficient, though imperfectly competitive, clusters of producers who enjoy pecuniary externalities. There is, thus, no question of the good versus bad agglomerations, nor of a potential link between agglomeration and performance through the possible effects of agglomeration on innovation and knowledge development.

In any case, the problem staked out by the California school remains: what are the sufficient conditions for the existence of the observed agglomerations of productive activity, which grew so strongly in the 1980s? The California school came up with an explanation, but it was partial, and it sensitized us as to the importance, complexity, and geography of input–output relations. But the localization of such input–output relations, that is, the localization of traded interdependencies, is inadequate to the task of explaining the link between flexible production and the resurgence of regional economies in contemporary capitalism.

The California school's explanation also suffered from the same problem as that of the flexible-specialization school: the central aspects of its theory could not, in the end, distinguish between good regional economies and bad ones. Vertical disintegration, high transactions costs, and agglomeration could be found in both high-wage, technologically dynamic industries and in low-wage, technologically stagnant ones. Adding in institutions helps, in the case of traditional industries, to distinguish good versions from bad. But in technologically dynamic industries, agglomerations are often found without overwhelmingly dense local input–output linkages and without the kinds of explicit institutional coordination found in many European industrial districts. A different explanation was needed.

INNOVATION, HIGH TECHNOLOGY, AND REGIONAL DEVELOPMENT

The subject of innovation is prefigured in the schools of thought reviewed above, though innovation is seen in both as a consequence of the institutional or organizational frameworks of production. From the late 1970s on, students of regional development investigated the regionally uneven distribution of high technology industries and the apparently better propensity of some regions to develop "high-tech" economic bases than others.[41] Defined as such, their problem was not the same as that of the two schools of thought reviewed above: rather than a broad problem of a change in production paradigms—flexibility and its consequences—they defined their subject as that of the incidence of industries based on new technologies. The empirical subject matter nonetheless overlapped with the preceding schools in certain cases; Saxenian's work on Silicon Valley falls securely into the institutionalist flexible-specialization school,[42] and Scott and Storper and others argued that high-technology development could be understood from the standpoint of their theory of agglomeration and the division of labor.[43] What distinguishes the work reviewed here is that their point of departure was technology itself, mostly high technology.

In using high technology as the focal point of explanation, they attempted to isolate cases of "advanced" regional development. They assumed that by studying areas that had become centers of production for advanced technologies, there would be lessons for policy making (how to imitate these places), and—for some of these scholars—there would be Schumpeterian lessons about advanced economic development in general: what occurs to economic activities affected by waves of radical technological change?

Two branches of this work can be reviewed here. The American school of high technology regional development sought the conditions for growth in Silicon Valley and Route 128.[44] What was it that had set off and sustained growth in these places? The work identified many different factors said to have contributed to these processes, among which the single most discussed is the research university–spin off process. Drawing on the American interest in entrepreneurship (and a strongly American reading of Schumpeter), and on the key experiences of Stanford University–Silicon Valley, MIT–Route 128, an abundant literature on R&D and regional development was generated. To this was added a list of secondary factors said to be present in successful high-tech regions, among which were a "high quality of life," good infrastructure, and even climate. It does appear, from the American historical record, that there were decisive links between universities and founders of firms in the Massachusetts and California cases. The problems come when this is taken to be a universal logic of new technology-based infant industry development. The logic works only when innovation is strongly formal-science based, as in the early years of semiconductors. It was not true, for example, in the case of airplanes in the 1920s and 1930s, where no local research universities were strongly present in the leap forward of Los Angeles.[45] To this the high tech school responds: "that was then, this is now," for organized science has become more and more important in the development of new technologies.[46] So they predict that the university–production link will be critical in future technology-based industries, such as biotechnology.

Assume (for the sake of argument) that this is the case. The question is how to theorize what it is, specifically, that leads from research to the establishment of a regional production base. For there are many research universities, and even many that have generated lots of knowledge in semiconductors, but there is a much smaller number of Silicon Valleys and Route 128s. That which actually makes the interaction virtuous remains unexplained. The California school discussed above offered a partial response to this, by noting that what distinguishes nascent agglomerations from other early centers is the rate at which their external economies grow due to the proliferation of input–output linkages and this could, in principle, include university–firm linkages.[47] But this observation, while essential, is insufficient: it does not plug up the gap in knowing what it is about the kind of knowledge or its transfer to producers that makes R&D presence effective sometimes and not effective other times and places.

A second branch of the American school is what we might call the "regional politics" approach.[48] It arose in part as a critical reaction to the first branch. In the place of the lists of factors (which it systematically showed to be irrelevant), it holds that regional coalitions secure resources that push for the transfer of high technology resources: thus, Silicon Valley got ahead partially because of the Stanford connection, but also because its early industrialists were clever enough to commandeer resources from the military–industrial complex. Indeed, much of the "gunbelt" developed because of politics, especially its key complexes in New England and Southern California. Yet these important observations fall far short of a complete explanation. For one, the Southern California aerospace complex was incipient before the growth of the military–industrial complex: its roots were in the success of Douglass Aircraft's DC3 in the 1930s. The military followed that installed technological competence; it did not place it there in Los Angeles. For another, there are many places where politically motivated investments have taken place (Texas, Georgia, Toulouse, Nice) but nothing approaching a diverse and dynamic high technology agglomeration has been created. Politics alone is insufficient.

The problem, then, is that the second American school has not come up with a coherent theory of high technology development or any necessary link to regional development.

An alternative, European, approach has been developed by the GREMI group (*Groupement de Recherche Européen sur les Milieux Innovateurs*), principally Franco–Italian–Swiss regional economists. Their central theoretical notion is that of the *milieu*. There are many different branches of this approach, many of them very rich; I will attempt simply to summarize what I see as the central theme that encompasses them all, with apologies to those who feel that their work is inadequately distinguished from the whole.[49]

The milieu is essentially a context for development, which empowers and guides innovative agents to be able to innovate and to coordinate with other innovating agents. The milieu is something like a territorial version of what the American economic sociologist Mark Granovetter has labeled the "embeddedness" of social and economic processes.[50] The milieu is described, variously, as a system of regional institutions, rules, and practices that lead to innovation. Many of the milieu theorists use the "network" as their principal organizational metaphor. For some, the milieu is itself a network of actors— producers, researchers, politicians, and so on—in a region. For others, the network concerns the input–output system; it is this network that is embedded in a milieu, and the milieu provides members of the network what they need for coordination, adjustment, and successful innovation.

Milieu is suggestive of something interesting, which rejoins a key theme of the Marshallian school: that there is something intangible, "in the air" as Marshall would have it, that permits innovativeness to proceeed in some places and not in others.[51] The GREMI group, however, has never been able to identify the economic logic by which milieux foster innovation. There is a circularity: innovation occurs because of a milieu, and a milieu is what exists in regions where there is innovation. The following definition is exemplary, not exceptional:

> A territory is not a defined space of resources. It is the mode of establishment of a group, in the natural environment, which through the organization and localization of activities, generates prevalent conditions of communication-language and collective learning (the forms of cooperation that create technological and organizational rationalities).

and

> The milieu appears as the socioeconomic formation that, at one and the same time, generates the economic dynamic and constitutes itself in setting this dynamic into motion. In other words, milieux take form in organizing themselves and they do so even better insofar as they are territorialized. The emergence of organizational dynamism is correlative to the dynamism of local milieux.[52]

The milieu school returns, again and again, to the properties of milieux, but they do not specify the potential mechanisms and proceses by which such milieux function, nor precisely what the economic logic of a milieux would be—why localization and territorial specificity should make technological and organizational dynamics better. Thus, though they attempt to go beyond the input–output based models of the Californian school, they cannot seem to specify the logic or content of the intangible they are after. As such, they do not reveal what it is about regions in innovation that is essential to contemporary capitalist development.

Nonetheless, the GREMI group, and in particular the work of Perrin

(1993) has successfully reformulated the problem of what regional "science" should be all about, in calling for abandonment of regional analysis based on the two fundamental precepts of neoclassical economic science, that is, comparative statics (equilibrium), and the rational action paradigm for human behavior. Instead, they argue, the economic process is fundamentally about creation of knowledge and resources, and this "Schumpeterian" (and Marxian as well) process cannot be derived from the calculations of the rational actor on the margin. How economic actors reason and interact is, they argue, in large part a product of their context, and this context is likely to have—at least in part—territorial boundaries and specificities. So the process of economic creation by such actors should depend on their milieu.

How, then, to get beyond this impasse to define what this territorial context could consist of in generating the dynamic of economic creation—organizational and technological evolution —in capitalism?

TECHNOLOGY, PATH DEPENDENCY, AND UNTRADED INTERDEPENDENCIES

It was left to a group of nonorthodox economists and sympathizers in other disciplines—a group that was not principally interested in territoriality or regions—to develop the analytical tools which, appropriately adapted, now permit us to identify (at least theoretically, if not empirically) the intangible aspect of a territorial or regional economy that underlies innovative, flexible, agglomerations, of both the high- and low-tech variety.

The first insight came from the evolutionary economics pioneered by Nelson and Winter,[53] and refined for the case of technology by Dosi, Arthur, Soete,[54] and others. They claimed, essentially, that technologies develop along pathways or trajectories, which describe choice sets that are totally different from those of orthodox economics. In contrast to the standard model's key mechanisms of substitutability and reversibility in choice, where investments and returns can always be adjusted well to each other, they show that choices are characterized by strong irreversibilities; unlike the orthodox model, it is virtually impossible to predict outcomes from a starting point, even if actors are rational. The outcomes reflect no single optimum, but, at best, optima, which are continually redefined as choices are made and other choices are foreclosed. In evolutionary economics, what we do is path-dependent, that is, truly historical; it is not the result of a series of actions on spot markets, where the long term can be reduced to a series of disconnected instants.

All this is the case because technologies are the products of *interdependent* choices. For one thing, technologies are subject to a variety of user–producer and user–user interactions: every technology made by a producer must have a user, and as the number of users of a given technology rises, it tends to cut off the possibility of different patterns of use (and hence, production) for other users. This is an external economy that benefits those who follow suit in both cost and feasibility terms (the story told by Arthur is that we all drive on either the right or the left, even though there's no efficiency reason, because everybody else does and it would be costly and hazardous to change[55]; or David's story that we use the inferior QWERTY[56] keyboard because it got ahead of other models early). Interdependency means uncertainty, since we cannot determine exactly what others upon whom our choices depend will do.

Beyond these external economies-as-accidents-of-history, there are reasons why producers tend to follow certain pathways. There are significant *technological spillovers* in the economy: knowing how to do one thing is frequently consequent upon knowing how to do another, or key to doing certain other things.[57] This idea draws on the seminal work of François Perroux in the 1950s, who noted that an economy consists of "spaces" or fields of endeavor, in part having to do with the density of nontraded technological connections between them (for example, common types of knowledge or similar types of machines, or knowledge of how to work similar types of basic materials or inputs).[58] In some cases, these nontraded connections overlap with traded input–output relations, that is, using similar inputs such as raw materials or capital goods; but often—and this is critical—the connections are untraded. The new economics of technological change has suggested, in the 1980s, that there are knowledge or "common practice" spillovers such that technological excellence comes in packages or ensembles.[59] Since such excellence relies frequently on knowledge or practices that are not fully codifiable, the particular firms who master it are tied into various kinds of networks with other firms, through formal exchanges and untraded interdependencies. The latter include labor markets, public institutions, and locally or nationally derived rules of action, customs, understandings, and values.[60]

Technological trajectories of a given industry are, in certain cases, parallel or complementary to technologies in other industries. Firms thus depend on decisions made outside their borders by other firms or decisionmakers in the technological space.[61] When things are going well, external economies— interdependent production functions—create increasing returns for the ensemble of interdependent actors traveling down these pathways (and there is, in technical terms, no ambiguity about these effects being defined as true external economies).

⋅ Orthodox economics is mainly concerned with the way the market allocates resources and assumes that structural change and development follow from either the additive forces of this allocational process or from exogenous influences such as technological or demographic change. Evolutionary economics holds that technological change is an endogenous property of economic systems and that it is not principally the result of allocational adjustments but of interdependent actions in which signaling, knowledge development, and doing the best one can are central.[62]

The evolutionists reinterpret the effects of competition in capitalism via this distinction. Comparative advantages are had when the position of a firm or of a group of interdependent firms in a nation or region find a more favorable location along a given production function: they are allocational. This is familiar to everyone who has ever taken an economics class. But, claim the evolutionists, this isn't what drives the distribution of market shares or the composition of economic activities in many cases. Absolute advantages exist when a firm, nation, or region possesses superior technologies such that virtually no set of alternative factor prices (production costs, in essence) would incite geographical redistribution of shares or activities. And this, they claim, is an aspect of the dynamic of capitalist competition wholly overlooked by the orthodox theory of competition-as-allocation.

The evolutionary economists working on technological change, not surprisingly, discovered territory—nations and regions. In theoretical terms, they began to reason that the technological spillovers and their untraded interdependencies would be territorialized under certain conditions, notably where the technological trajectories were particularly open, that is, had wide margins of potential variation. This would increase the uncodifiability and tacitness of knowledge development and heighten the importance of communicational clarity and common interpretation in understanding information.[63]

In other words, the territorial specificity and differentiation of certain untraded interdependencies and spillovers, or the territorial differentiation of the same, by permitting actors to travel along superior technological trajectories (or to do so more rapidly than others) can confer on them absolute advantages that shelter them, at least temporarily, from Ricardian competition (that is, competition based on prices for factor inputs). This would show up as territorial specialization and differentiation in trade, whether between regions or at the international level.[64] Virtually all the systematic empirical investigations of the technological performance of nations suggest that high, and increasing, differentiation or specialization characterize the western economies since the late 1970s. The main studies include Dosi et al.'s study of international trade,[65] Patel and Pavitt's[66] many investigations over the last decade, Guerrieri's[67] interpretation of OECD statistics, and Dunning's study of multinational firms.[68] Both Dunning and Patel and Pavitt note, in contrast to the prevailing assumption that multinational firms are indifferent to territory or to local context, that the major multinational firms of the world locate virtually all their most advanced technological capacities in their home countries and that where there are exceptions, they are almost always explained by investment in a technological core capacity of the host country; that is, they are attracted to the local technological tissue of another country. Jaffe, in the United States, has shown empirically that technological overspills correspond strongly to the patenting activities of firms[69]; and Antonelli[70] in Italy has indicated, in a very preliminary way, that overspills are often geographically bounded (although the measurement problems remain considerable). Evolutionary economics has not, however, provided a secure analytical basis, via the theory of localization and agglomeration, for why such untraded interdependencies and the technological trajectories they underlie, should be territorially specific and differentiated.

Evolutionary economics alludes only indirectly to the counterforces to the territorialization process. Among them are technological imitation and selection, and the ongoing effort to transcend geographical distance in both the untraded interdependencies and input–output relations that are critical to technological learning. But those forces are very far from triumphing, or so it would appear from the empirical evidence.

In sum, the evolutionary approach is, if not incompatible with the transactions cost approach to agglomeration, then at least wedded to fundamentally different theoretical commitments about dynamic processes of capitalist development. The transactions-cost-based theory of the California school is about allocation through cost-minimization,[71] and this is because transactions cost economics is about traded input–output relations. The evolutionary approach is fundamentally not about cost-minimization; it is about the forces that allow the parameters of cost minimization to be altered and which get in the way of optimizing.[72] And in terms of the mechanism of territorialization, evolutionary economics opens up the field of untraded interdependencies, which does not figure prominently in transactions-based approaches. Even though one can argue that untraded interdependencies are rooted in transactions—though perhaps not *input–output transactions* and market or contract exchanges—the analysis of such transactions cannot be easily accommodated within transactions-*cost*-based theories.

An answer to the principal dilemma of contemporary economic geography—the resurgence of regional economies and of territorial specialization in an age of increasing ease in transportation and communication of inputs and outputs and of increasingly scientific organizational rationalities of managing complex systems of inputs and outputs—must be sought in two lines of reasoning. One is the tension between respecialization and destandardization of inputs and outputs, which, caeteris paribus, raises transactions costs associated with them.[73] The other is the association of organizational and technological learning with agglomeration, which in turn has two roots. The first, and more limited case, is that of localized input–output relations, which constitute webs of user–producer relations essential to information development and exchange, hence to learning.[74] The second and more general case is the untraded interdependencies that attach to the process of economic and organizational learning and coordination.[75] Where these input–output relations or untraded interdependencies are localized, and this is, as we have suggested, quite frequent in cases of technological or organizational dynamism, then we can say that the region is a key, necessary element in the "supply architecture" for learning and innovation. Theoretical predictions that globalization means the end to economies of proximity are therefore likely to be wrong, because they are deduced only from consideration of hard, traded input–output relations, those which are most prone to geographical dispersion at some point.

CONCLUSION

We have now traced the history of an intellectual debate over the resurgence of regional economies. The next step is to go at the subject in a more theoretically organized fashion: to reconstruct a theoretical framework for understanding the persistence of regional economic specificity in a global economy.

NOTES

1. This title is drawn, deliberately, from Sabel (1988).

2. See, *inter alia*, Sabel (1988); Scott (1988); Scott and Storper (1986); Becattini (1987).

3. Bianchi (1992); Bianchi et al. (1988); Best (1990); see also papers in *Research Policy*, special issue on "Networks of Innovators" (1990) and more recently, Tolomelli (1993); Lassini (1985); Bursi (1989).

4. I first became aware of this term in the work of Dosi (1984) and that of Lundvall (1988, 1990), though there are echoes of it in the writings of François Perroux and Tibor Scitovsky in the 1950s.

5. Bagnasco (1977); Becattini (1987); Brusco (1982); Piore and Sabel (1984); Bellandi (1986, 1989); Dei Ottati (1987); Russo (1986); Trigilia (1986).

6. Piore and Sabel (1984); see also: Sabel and Zeitlin (1985).

7. Beccatini (1978, 1987, 1991); Bellandi (1989); Dei Ottati (1987, 1991); Brusco (1982); Balestri (1982).

8. Even proponents of the thesis of a revival of certain principles of mass production, in the context of "lean production," readily admit this as a lesson of recent industrial history; see, for example, Coriat (1991); the best statements, in my opinion, are Dosi (1987) and Dosi and Orsenigo (1985).

9. Suggested, richly, in Sabel and Zeitlin (1985), but theorized in Nelson and Winter (1982).

10. The new "theory of the firm literature" is so vast that we can offer but a tiny sampling. Aoki (1989); Williamson (1990); Coriat (1991); Dosi et al. (1988); Dore (1987); Cohendet and Llerena (1989); Hakanson (1989); Best (1990); Porter (1990); Mariti and Smiley (1983).

11. See Pollard and Storper (1996).

12. Amin and Robins (1990).

13. The point that the districts draw some of their "social capital" from deep historical roots and traditions, but that they are not simple continuations of industrial history there, having reinvented themselves several times since World War II is found in virtually all the work of the Florentine school, such as Becattini (1978); Dei Ottati (1987, 1990, 1991); and, for the Emilian cases, Cappecchi (1990a,b). For a literature review, see de Maria and Scarpitti (1992). And for a clear theoretical argument about social capital, see Putnam (1993). Civic capital is treated in a theoretical form by Coleman (1988, 1990).

14. Harrison (1989) and del Monte and Esposito (1989) make a similar argument more formally. Empirical claims are made by Luria (1988).

15. Sabel et al. (1989); but also suggested by Best (1990); Aoki (1989); and much of the business economics literature, which is more attentive to change in the business environment for both small and big firms, implying that size is not the principal axis of the analysis. See, for example, Hakansson (1987).

16. Hirst and Zeitlin (1992).

17. See Gordon (1990); Leborgne and Lipietz (1992, 1993).

18. Gertler (1988); and in a more sympathetic vein, Castillo (1991).

19. On the theme of collaboration and competition: Piore and Sabel (1984); Dei Ottati (1987); Lorenz (1988); Sabel and Zeitlin (1985); Scranton (1985); Sabel (1993); Sabel et al. (1989); and on a theoretical level, see Axelrod (1984).

20. See Scott (1988a).

21. Christopherson and Storper (1986); Storper and Christopherson (1987.

22. See, for example, Scott (1986, 1988b, 1991); Storper and Scott (1989); Scott and Angel (1987); Scott and Storper (1987); Scott and Kwok (1989); de Vet (1990).

23. As collected in Scott and Storper (1986); see, especially, Holmes, in that collection.

24. Worked out in its fullest analytical form in Scott (1988a); see more recently, Scott (1993).

25. There is a vast literature on this subject to which I can do no justice here. See, for example, Powell (1990); Hakansson (1989); Aoki (1990); Foray (1990). See also Johansen and Mattson (1987).

26. Scott and Storper (1987).

27. Storper (1989); see also Chapter 4 of this book.

28. Becattini (1978); Brusco (1982); Cappecchi (1990a,b); Ritaine (1989).

29. Pitman (1992).

30. Russo (1986).

31. Cooke and Morgan (1990); Storper and Scott (1989); Scott and Storper (1991).

32. See references at note 31.

33. Gordon (1990); Veltz (1993).

34. See references at note 9. This is a spatial or geographical outgrowth of the strategic management literature's twist on the network thesis, that is, convergence, optimality, and deterritorialisation.

35. Badaracco (1988); Mytelka (1990); Mowery (1988); Cooke and Morgan (1991).

36. Veltz (1993).

37. Hakansson (1987).

38. Pavitt and Patel (1991).

39. Dunning (1988).

40. Veltz (1993).

41. Malecki (1984); see also Breheny and McQuaid (1988); Glasmeier (1986).

42. Saxenian (1988, 1991, 1994).

43. Scott and Storper (1987).

44. Markusen et al. (1986).

45. Gauthier (1993); Scott (1990); and chapters on aerospace in Storper (1982).

46. See my critique in Storper (1985).

47. Scott and Storper (1987.

48. Markusen (1986); Markusen et al. (1991).

49. Aydalot (1986); Aydalot and Keeble (1988); Camagni (1991); Maillat et al. (1990, 1993); Camagni (1992).

50. Granovetter (1985).

51. Marshall (1919).

52. Both quotes are from an excellent paper by Perrin (1993). My translations attempt to get the sense of the message. They read, in the original, a bit differently:

> Un territoire, ce n'est pas un espace délimité de ressources. C'est le mode d'établissement d'un groupe, dans l'environnement naturel, qui, dans l'organisation des localisations des activités, instaure et fait prévaloir les conditions de la communication–langage et de l'apprentissage collectif (des coopérations créatrices de rationalités techniques et organisationnelles).
>
> Le milieu apparaît comme la formation socio-économique qui, à la fois, génère la dynamique et qui se constitue en la mettant en oeuvre. En d'autres termes, les milieux prennent corps en s'auto-organisant et ils y parviennent d'autant mieux qu'ils se territorialisent. L'émergence de la dynamique organisationnelle a été correlative de celle des milieux locaux.

For another sophisticated treatment, see Dupuy and Gilly (1992).

53. Nelson and Winter (1982).

54. Dosi (1987); Dosi and Orsenigo (1985); Dosi et al. (1990); Arthur (1989).

55. Arthur (1989).

56. David (1975).

57. Tyson (1990).

58. Perroux (1950a,b).

59. Lundvall (1990); Lundvall and Johnson (1992); Beije (1991).

60. Dosi and Orsenigo (1985).

61. Young (1928) and Kaldor(1972) both tried to make these points early on; I tried to use their insights about interconnectedness in Storper (1989).

62. Dosi et al. (1990).

63. Lundvall (1990, 1992).

64. As noted in Porter (1990); Amendola et al. (1992); Patel and Pavitt (1992); and Storper (1992). See also Chapter 8 of this book.

65. Dosi et al. (1990).

66. Patel and Pavitt (1991).

67. Amendola et al. (1992).

68. Dunning (1988).

69. Jaffe (1986).

70. Antonelli (1987).

71. Most clearly explained in Scott (1988a).

72. Clearly brought out in Dosi et al. (1990); See also Johansen and Mattson (1987).

73. Scott and I have also argued that the ongoing process of product differentiation in capitalism destandardizes outputs (and hence inputs); this means that new inputs are necessary. The uncertainty attached to these new input–output relationships recreates the need for proximity in input–output transactions. We used the recent growth of financial services agglomerations as an example, that is, an industry where transport costs for the "product" are practically zero. See Storper and Scott (1989).

74. Lundvall (1990); Russo (1986); von Hippel (1987).

75. Our discussions of the substantive nature of untraded interdependencies in following chapters will refer to them as conventions (Lewis, 1969), and the inspiration for this is the French school of *économie des conventions*. References include: Eymard-Duvernay (1987); Thévenot (1986); *Revue Economique* (1989); Salais and Storper (1992, 1993); Storper and Salais (1997). This is by no means a complete list of what is a rapidly evolving literature.

CHAPTER 2

Regional Economies as Relational Assets

THE "HOLY TRINITY" OF REGIONAL ECONOMICS

Regional economics and economic geography, like much of economics as a whole, has in recent years seen a heterodox paradigm emerge in its midst. The heterodox paradigm breaks the problem of economic development in regions, nations, and at a global level into a series of substantive empirical and theoretical domains, and attempts to build up a multilayered explanation for it. The heterodox approach involves what we might call a new "holy trinity": technologies–organizations–territories (Figure 2.1).

Technology and *technological change* are now recognized as among the principal motors of changing territorial patterns of economic development; the rise and fall of new products and production processes takes place in territories, and depends to a great extent on their capacities for specific types of innovation. Technological change in turn alters the cost–price dimensions of production, including its locational patterns. *Organizations,* most importantly firms and groups or networks of firms tied together into production systems, are not only dependent on territorial contexts of physical and intangible inputs, but they have greater or lesser relationships of proximity to each other. *Territories,* whether peripheral regions or cores of sectors, may be characterized by either strong or weak local interactions and spillovers between factors, organizations, or technologies.

The heterodox paradigm integrates the significant theoretical advances that have been made in each part of the holy trinity in recent years. Technological change is no longer the black box it was once thought to be. It is now common practice to distinguish between standardized, scale-dependent technologies and unstandardized, variety- or flexibility-enabling technologies in production, those which are dedicated to particular products and those which may be redeployed among different outputs.[1] The problem of the territoriality of technological change and of the effects of technological change on territory is now well posed, if not resolved. The study of organizations has been revolutionized by the work of Coase and Williamson, showing that firms are, at least in part, transactional structures with fluid boundaries.[2] Others have

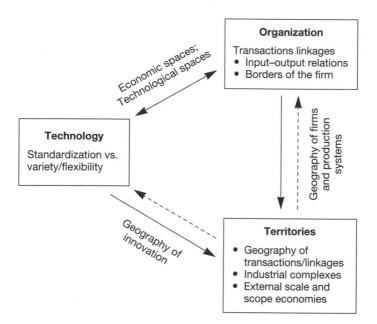

FIGURE 2.1. The holy trinity of the heterodox paradigm.

reconceptualized firms in terms of property rights and appropriability of assets; or as strategic growth-maximizing agents.[3] Territorial economics has in turn been revolutionized by integrating the insights of technology and organization studies. The effects of organizations on territorial economic patterns, presciently imagined by Perroux and the modern school of input–output analysis,[4] has been given new microfoundations by the application of transaction-cost economics to the geography of input–output relations.[5] As a result, the organizational foundations of agglomeration economies are now understood. We are well beyond the notion of external economies as simply scale-related; they are complex outcomes of interactions between scale, specialization, and flexibility in the context of proximity. Agglomerations also may enable dynamic processes, such as localized technological change.[6]

The emergence of this heterodox paradigm began in earnest in the 1970s, as regionalists and international economists attempted to understand the deindustrialization of old industrial regions[7]; it matured in the mid-1980s and early 1990s, as they attempted to understand the resurgence of regional economies, the emergence of high technology industries and regions, the ascendance of new Asian industrial tigers, and globalization. But new lacunae in the theoretical apparatus of regional or territorial development have also made their appearance. The heterodox paradigm has indeed defined the right holy trinity, but it has not yet fully seized the right content for the analysis of technologies, organizations, and territories. Heterodox regional economics, like economics in general, continues to be controlled by the metaphor of economic systems as machines, with hard inputs and outputs, where the physics and geometry of those inputs and outputs can be understood in a complete and determinate way. This focus on the mechanics of economic development must now be complemented by another focus, where the guiding metaphor is the *economy as relations*, the *economic process as conversation and coordination*, the subjects of the process not as factors but as *reflexive human actors*, both individual and collective, and the nature of economic accumulation as not only material assets, but as *relational assets*. Regional economies in particular, and integrated territorial economies in general, will be redefined here as *stocks of relational assets*.

This shift in guiding metaphors reflects new content for each of the elements of regional economics' holy trinity, content which goes beyond what is found even in the heterodox paradigm. Technology involves not just the tension between scale and variety, but that between the codifiability or noncodifiability of knowledge; its substantive domain is learning and *becoming*, not just diffusion and deployment. Organizations are knit together, their boundaries defined and changed, and their relations to each other accomplished not simply as input–output relations or linkages, but as untraded interdependencies subject to a high degree of reflexivity. Territorial economies are not only created, in a globalizing world economy, by proximity in input–output relations, but more so by proximity in the untraded or relational dimensions of organizations and technologies. Their principal assets—because scarce and slow to create and imitate—are no longer material, but relational.

REFLEXIVITY AS THE CENTRAL CHARACTERISTIC OF CONTEMPORARY CAPITALISM

In recent years, social scientists have been at pains to characterize the overall nature of the capitalism that began to take shape around the beginning of the 1970s. The economic capabilities of contemporary capitalism have undergone great expansion and deep qualitative change. Among the new "metacapacities" of modern capitalism, several are most important. First, the revolution in production, information, and communication technologies permits vast expansion of the *nature and spheres of control* of firms, markets, and institutions, involving deeper and more immediate feedbacks from one part of these complex structures to others than ever before, dramatic cheapening of many forms of material production, and great increases in the variety of material and intangible inputs and outputs. Second, there has been a vast *spatial extension and social deepening* of the logic of market relations, in part facilitated by the technological leap (especially through the cheapening of telecommunications and media as vehicles of market relations, and through the extension of physical infrastructure). Greater percentages of the population, and greater percentages of their relations than ever before, are involved in a market-based commodity production, and they are more and more tied into faraway places than ever before. This is, in one sense, a continuation of long-term processes of "modernization"; in another sense, it involves the crossing of a qualitative threshhold in terms of extent and depth. Third, and combining the effects of the first two processes, there has been a *generalization* of the "grid" of modern organizational methods, bureaucratic rule, and communicational processes to more dimensions of economic and noneconomic life than ever before. This does not mean the extension of a single, hierarchically administered regime to all peoples, but the sharing of certain general ways of life that are common to contemporary industrial-market society.[8]

The qualitative consequences of these metacapacities are more novel than the mere quantitative expansion of the capitalist market system. In the most general terms, they may be summed up as an enormous leap in *economic reflexivity*. This term refers to the possibility for groups of actors in the various institutional spheres of modern capitalism—firms, markets, governments, households, and other collectivities—to shape the course of economic evolution. They can do so because they can now reflect about the functioning of their environments in a way that is not limited by existing parameters, and where certain groups are explicitly wedded to shaking up such environments to their own advantage (innovation). This type of action goes well beyond correct anticipations of the actions of others (rational expectations). Instead, it involves critical distance from the traditional functioning of the spheres in which it takes place, such distance being facilitated by technologies and contemporary communicational practices that feed back information to actors in radically new ways. Interpretations and constructed images of reality are now just as important as any "real" material reality, because these interpretations and images are diffused and accepted and become the bases on which people act: they become real. Such interpretations and images are central to the organization and evolution of markets, prices, and other key economic variables. They are, in this sense, as real and material as machines, people, and buildings. The temporalities, the evolutionary trajectories, and the role of feedbacks of social and economic processes today make them fundamentally different from what social science has attempted to understand up to now.

Rules, institutions, and action frameworks have always been important, of course, as institutionalist social scientists have shown. But they were regarded principally as imperfections in modern capitalism, as in the notion of "states *versus* markets."[9] Fundamentally, they were viewed as noneconomic or premodern forces that did not permit full expression of modern capitalism, or by some as humane and socially necessary fetters on the rapacious tendencies of the market.[10] The ideological content of these theoretical disputes should no longer blind us to the new historical reality: in many ways, markets *were* once opposed to states, rules, and other institutions, but this is no longer largely the case. Ironically, however, the triumph of market capitalism in the West has not ended with a generalization of anonymous, standard, "perfect" capitalist markets, but instead coincides with a major new leap in the possibilities for reflexivity in that economy itself, generating enormous new variety within the market economy. In many ways, capitalist markets are more intertwined with "nonmarket" forces than ever before, with impulses from "civil society."[11] This is because the increasing dominance of capitalism also coincides with the development of the major new variety- and diversity-enabling metacapacities described above.

This in no way implies that such reflexivity is free from constraint. Instead, the old debate in the social sciences between determinism and free will, structure and agency, has been empirically left behind by the course of real socioeconomic evolution, in which the two sides of these traditional oppositions have become inextricably produced by each other. The metacapacities of contemporary capitalism, encompassing both of what Marx labeled the "forces" and the social "relations" of production, have developed and matured to a point where the variety of concrete empirical possibilities for the organization of markets, firms, and other institutional spheres of economic and social life have been vastly increased. On one hand, the empirical margins of what can happen within a given "structural" constraint have widened in these areas. On the other, the path-dependent nature of institutional evolution means that these innovations generated by agents can have long-lasting effects on "structures." Still, at any given moment, the possibilities for variety only become realities through the selection effects of competition, and through the mobilizing effects of rules, institutional routines, and collective action frameworks.

Moreover, new capacities and agency also involve the generation of new constraints, or "structures." Contemporary reflexive capitalism is a system that *manufactures new kinds of risks*[12] (economic, personal, ecological, psychological, social, etc.). In the economic sphere, these risks are expressed through the redefinition of competition—what it takes to win and how it is possible to lose. Winning has become a much more complex target, because the conditions which a firm, region, or production system must now satisfy in order to win are manufactured and remanufactured more thoroughly and more rapidly than ever before, creating a moving target for success and a shifting minefield of risks of failure. This is directly a consequence of the increase in the reflexivity of economic activity in the context of a generalized market system.

Theories of competitiveness have struggled to capture these phenomena over the last 20 years, developing many descriptive monikers for the new economy: postindustrialism, the information economy, flexible specialization, and post-Fordism.[13] Though each of these labels helps in understanding some dimensions of the contemporary economic process, the deepest and most general way to describe the logic of the most advanced forms of economic competition is that of "learning."[14] The notion that contemporary capitalism constitutes a "learning economy" was first advanced by Lundvall and Johnson in 1992. The argument is that such learning is the competitive outcome of heightened reflexivity. Those firms, sectors, regions, and nations which can learn faster or better (achieving higher quality or cheaper price for a given quality) become competitive because their knowledge is scarce and therefore cannot be immediately imitated by new entrants or transferred, via codified and formal channels, to competitor firms, regions, or nations. The price–cost margin of products they generate in this way can rise, while their market shares can increase; the resulting knowledge or technology rents alleviate downward wage or profit pressure. Learning-based activities are not immune to relocation or substitution by competitors. Once they are imitated or their outputs standardized, then there are downward wage and employment pressures. Firms or territorial economies must therefore be equipped to keep outrunning the powerful forces of imitation in the world economy. They must become moving targets by continuing to learn. *The learning economy is therefore an ensemble of competitive possibilities, reflexive in nature, engendered by capitalism's new metacapacities, as well as the risks or constraints manufactured by the reflexive learning of others.*[15]

The dimensions of the new economic reflexivity thus become principal concerns of any kind of economic analysis interested in developmental processes. These dimensions may be seized, at least in a preliminary way, by such keywords as "action," "created rules," "action frameworks," and "routines." Substantively, their study requires that we focus on how individual and collective reflexivity operate in the contemporary economy, through cognitive,[16] dialogic, and interpretative processes, with the substantive goal of understanding how *relations of coordination* between reflexive agents and organizations are established.

THE RELATIONAL TURN IN ECONOMIC ANALYSIS: TECHNOLOGIES, ORGANIZATIONS, AND TERRITORIES

In the field of regional economics and territorial development, the developments described above mean that the content of the theoretical holy trinity—technologies, organizations, and territories—must be redefined, from a series of machines, to a set of relations[17] and their constituent reflexive processes.

Technology

In orthodox economics, technology was considered to be a "black box,"[18] and theory assumed that rational agents, possessing full information, make optimal choices under strong constraint conditions. In contrast to this, the field of technological change economics has centered its attention on the generation of technological knowledge and its relationship to economic practice. Markets have notorious failures in this regard: prices are difficult to set because the seller does not give up the knowledge, possession is permanent, and the buyer cannot always do ex ante valuation.

The heterodox paradigm adapted the discoveries of technological change economics to the analysis of the *effects* of technological change on the geography of production, distribution and transport. In the geography of production, we now know that activities based on standardized technologies that permit economies of scale inside the firm can delocalize, while those based on nonstandardized technologies and economies of variety tend to locate in agglomerations. The former tend to be more vertically integrated and self-contained, or dependent on long-distance inputs, while the reverse is true for the latter. Hence, the heterodox paradigm better understood the spatiality of the input–output machine of the modern economy, and in so doing it revolutionized the theory of agglomeration.

The limits of the paradigm are found essentially in the analysis of the *causes* of technological change, and the geography of innovation and learning. The dominant postwar account of technological change[19] consisted of a linear input–output model, with scientific R&D upstream, innovation midstream, and commercialization and diffusion downstream. Diffusion was both economic (interfirm and interindustry) and geographical (from centers to peripheries) and at any given moment the spatial distribution of technologies takes the form of areas specialized in each of these phases. Though largely implicit in the early years, the notion of technologies emerging as rare and unstandardized innovations and then developing into increasingly standardized "mature" technologies, capable of exploiting economies of scale, became increasingly explicit through such models as the product cycle in industrial and development economics, and "spatial divisions of labor" in regional and international economics.[20] In many ways, this theoretical focus fit well with the interwar and postwar development experience of technology as the derived product of science, with the "problem" defined as its unequal spatioeconomic distribution,[21] a position shared not only by many developing-country economists, but also by many Europeans concerned with postwar reconstruction and modernization.

Experience since the 1970s, however, has radically called into question the assumption that the link between technology and development consists of a progression from invention/innovation to scale and standardization, where increasing factor productivity inside each firm or technology leads to greater wealth creation. It now appears that development, at least in wealthy countries and regions, depends, at least in part, on *destandardization* and the *generation of variety*. The increasing spatial integration of markets for standardized products bids away monopolistic rents, while automation takes away employment, and advantage accrues to low-wage, low-cost areas. The only way out of this dilemma is to recreate imperfect competition through destandardization, the source of scarcity.

This forces a complete reconceptualization of the technological innovation process in economic development: it now involves not only the gigantic formal organizations of research in laboratories, universities, and multinational firms, which correspond to our image of the process as hierarchical and linear, but the proliferation and dramatic complexification of relations among those institutions and between them and other elements of the economic environment. Paradoxically, the rise of bigger and bigger science and R&D has been accompanied not by its increasing isolation upstream, but by its increasing integration into a host of other economic and social processes. Within "big" R&D, for example, there are now more complex feedbacks between science and savoir faire in the high- and medium-technology industries than ever before,[22] while in many medium- or low-technology sectors, savoir faire is now subject to deliberate reflection, attempts at systematization, and appropriation of the results of science and engineering.[23] Research on technological change has documented the importance of user–producer relations (interfirm, interindustry and consumer–producer); science–production relations; interfirm relations in technologically cognate areas; and firm–government–university relations in technological innovation. It has also shown, importantly, that these relations are increasingly organized as nonhierarchical, networked, complex, and substance-filled communication and action processes.[24] Research on the proliferation of "flexibly specialized" industrial districts has shown, in addition, that the capitalisms of a number of very wealthy regions and countries are built around practical forms of technological innovation, involving relatively small or indirect roles for formal science or R&D, whereas complex relational feedbacks in the production systems are responsible for successful innovative performance.[25]

The technological enterprise that is so central to contemporary capitalism seems to involve a set of circular processes today. The increasing density and complexity of relations is the means to new forms of collective reflexivity, leading to a quantum leap in the possibility for generating technological variety, that is, to learning. This variety has two principal consequences. On one hand, it sets off traditional cycles of codification, standardization, imitation, and diffusion of knowledge. On the other, at any given time, there are innumerable "islands" of noncosmopolitan[26] knowledge in this variety-centered economy, where only those actors who are involved in the relations required to get access to the knowledge and, perhaps even more importantly, the relations required to *understand, interpret, and effectively use* the knowledge, will be able to deploy it in economically useful ways. In turn, these nodes of relationally linked actors may "spin off" new standardization and decodification processes, but they may also regenerate variety within their field of endeavor, prolonging the life of noncosmopolitan nodes of interaction. This is but one of the many new dynamics of an economy of reflexivity and its manufactured opportunities and risks.

In sum, the essence of the process of technological change is now the tissue of relations by which asymmetric, noncosmopolitan knowledge is generated, applied, and further evolved. The increase in variety is the result of the operation of these relations, in an economic environment radically different from that defined by orthodox theory: empirically, because of the qualitative jump in the communicational capacities of actors in modern capitalism, a historical phenomenon resulting from technological advances and the generalization of the organizational and communicational metamodels of modernity; and theoretically because (as evolutionary economics has shown) firms and other actors operate in "loose" rather than "tight" (Pareto-optimizing) selection environments for the consequences of their reflection and communication with others.[27]

For regional and territorial economics, this means a reorientation of the central issues posed by technological change: from standardization to *de-standardization and variety* as the central competitive process, from diffusion to *the creation of asymmetric knowledge* as the central motor force, and from codification and cosmopolitanization of knowledge to the organizational and geographical dimensions of *noncodified and noncosmopolitan* knowledge.

Organizations

The second element of the holy trinity is organizations, by which we mean, principally, firms and production systems.[28] In the postwar period, organizations have figured prominently in economics generally, and regional and industrial economics in particular. The theory of the firm—stemming from Coase and developed by transactions-cost economics—has defined, as its core subject, the functional boundaries of the firm, the division of labor between firm and market, and the relations or transactions between firms.[29] The theory of production systems got a major push in the late 1940s and early 1950s with the Perrouxian notion of economic spaces and industrial complexes, and was given greater generality and analytical power in Leontief's development of input–output models of the entire economy.[30] Regional economists made major efforts to use input–output theory and techniques in the modeling of regional economies.[31]

Transaction-cost economics, as developed by Williamson, provided a more precise understanding of the cost drivers for input–output structures, thus bringing the theory of the firm and that of the production system closer together.[32] In turn, the theory of industrial complexes and agglomeration was given new dimensions by consideration of the geographical dimensions of transacting. It was shown that geography figures in transactions costs in general, and hence influences the boundaries of the firm and production system (that is, geography influences the degree of internalization or externalization in the production system).[33] It was also shown that the geography of transactions costs helps explain agglomeration and spatial divisions of labor. Much of this work on spatial divisions of labor shared similar concerns with research on multilocational or multinational enterprise, with the first approaching the problem from the side of geography, and the second from the side of the firm, meeting around the subject of locational dynamics of complex production systems.[34] In addition, transaction-cost theory was extended to output markets and to labor markets on the input side, and both were integrated into geographical transaction-cost theory and modeling. Innovation theory, in many guises, has attempted to understand the transactional context for technological change and geographers and regionalists have claimed that this context has strong territorial dimensions; though still at an early stage,[35] it is an active area of work today, and its goal is nothing less than an integrated theory of economic space, consisting of the interrelations between organizational, technological, and geographical space. Finally, the new growth theory[36] has argued that organizational change in the division of labor is an outcome of Smithian–Stiglerian growth processes, whereas the new geographical economics[37] has reattached the theory of localization to market structure, arguing that spatially imperfect competition is widespread in modern capitalism because of scale economies in production, while the whole economy is subject to increasing returns due to the interrelationships of specialized producers and the accumulation of knowledge. Both are engaged in providing microfoundations for the work begun by Allyn Young in the 1920s.

It can be seen that great theoretical progress has been made in the last half century toward understanding economic organization, and its extension to location, and the geography of production systems. The fundamental concerns of theory and modeling, however, are focused almost entirely on the traded relations between firms and places (factor markets, institutions), on traded relations between firms (interfirm trade), or on exchanges between production units of big firms (intrafirm trade). The mechanism that accounts for organizational and geographical outcomes is the prices, quantities, and qualities of these *traded interdependencies*. This explanatory mechanism is similar, no matter which different underlying motor forces are privileged (technology, divisions of labor, neoclassical factor substitution, etc.) and no matter what kind of theoretical metanarrative is preferred (neoclassical rationality, Marxist drives for control, various brands of institutionalism).

The notion that such relations among economic actors ultimately are expressed in terms of direct and traded interdependencies, however, can no longer be sustained. There are many reasons why this is the case. First, there is a historical dimension. The rise of an economy where the most lucrative forms of competition occur around technological learning has pushed for the emergence of new forms of economic organization. Firms and production systems must be well-equipped to move resources around in order to implement what is learned: this is what has come to be known as the "flexibility" condition. Some kinds of learning necessarily involve highly focused attention of the learners, through divisions of labor: this is what has come to be known as the "specialization" condition. Both of these organizational attributes of learning contribute to the well-documented transformation of production organizations, away from the traditional managerial hierarchy typical of postwar mass production, in the direction of what we may (inelegantly) call the "quasiexternalization" or "deverticalization" of the division of labor. By this is meant the tendency for learning-based production systems to assume the form of networks based around an interfirm division of labor, or for large firms to mimic attributes of externalization, sometimes via interfirm alliances, sometimes via the introduction of price mechanisms inside the large firm, sometimes via increased reliance on external suppliers, and sometimes via a more decentralized internal system of organization of the firm.[38] These conditions, whatever the particular form they take, potentiate *organizational reflexivity*[39] and not merely bureaucratic control.

The second dimension is theoretical. All productive activity depends on actions by others which, if not forthcoming, will render our own actions inefficient or unproductive; economic activity is founded on the pragmatic necessity to coordinate one's actions with others. Yet virtually all such situations of action are beset by uncertainty—each of us faces uncertainty in deciding what we should do with respect to a given set of circumstances. Part of this uncertainty is "secondary," that is it comes from the fact that others upon whom we depend also face uncertainty on their side, so they do not know, with assurance, what they will do; part of it comes from our imperfect knowledge or their incomplete communication of their intentions. All this is another way of saying that productive activity is, of necessity, a form of collective action founded on the paradox of individual actions. Coordination among persons thus presents itself as the central problem of economic life.

The question is how actors manage to get themselves into successfully coordinated, forms of collective action. We now know that the solutions of most economic thought to this problem of coordination under uncertainty are partial. Much uncertainty in economic life cannot be resolved in price and contract terms, as transactions-costs economics has shown us. According to the latter, this is why there are firms (internalization = control + certainty). But it is also now clear that firms cannot successfully coordinate *merely* because they internalize transactions, because bureaucratic authority is frequently ineffective in the presence of high levels of uncertainty: either it fails to get things under control, or it does so by eliminating the necessary response to uncertainty, which is the organizational reflexivity required to learn and hence to compete.

Unlike transactions of standardized and substitutable goods, factor inputs, and information, transactions associated with many kinds of organizational reflexivity involve mutually consistent interpretation of information that is not fully codified, hence not fully capable of being transmitted, understood, and utilized independently of the actual agents who are developing and using it. Some kinds of information, for example, do not stand on their own: they require communication outside the formal structure of the information—as linguists have shown us—for people to come to a common agreement on what is being said. This is no less true for nonstandardized technical or economic information. It is also necessary for the political information in the economy, such as work rules, governmental rules, and forms of interfirm relations, to function smoothly. Moreover, for this communication-based interpretative convergence to occur, we have to have some level of confidence in what others are saying, or at least some confidence in how we interpret them. In the first case, some degree of trust is at hand; in the second, dense and multiple understandings of what is being transacted are required, that is, ways of reading between the lines, of verifying in multiple ways the possible meanings of what is an inherently uncertain formal content.

In all of these situations, the problem for actors is how other actors will deal with the uncertainties at hand, and how in turn, they should do so. Anglo-American social scientists are enamored of prisoners' dilemmas and uncooperative games which have, as a priori commitments and inevitable modeling outcomes, the difficulty or breakdown of nonmarket (institutional) coordination.[40] This is the microfoundation of "states versus markets." But even game theory has shown clearly, through the work of Axelrod,[41] that tit-for-tat cooperative games are both rational and feasible under most circumstances; and if the questionable assumptions of game theory that limit individual action to strict defense of interests are abandoned,[42] the circumstances under which nonmarket forms of coordination can be generated by actors increase dramatically.

The specific form and content of coordination will vary according to the product at hand, technologies, markets, etc., as well as other historical and structural factors impossible to inventory here, whose variation is as great as human life itself. There are two levels of this relational quality of transactions. In the first, personal contacts, knowledge of the other, and reputation are the basis of the relation.[43] In many other cases, however, transactions are not so completely idiosyncratic; they do have dimensions that can be reproduced or imitated by other agents. But transaction is by definition, mutual; so only those agents who are equipped to enter into the kind of relation that has come to be accepted as the norm for the particular learning process at hand (by the parties with whom they will transact) can do so. They are equipped when they possess faculties permitting them to take in, interpret, and use information in a way that is consistent with the other transacting party. Such faculties are, essentially, *conventions* that coordinate these productive agents. Conventions may be defined to include taken-for-granted mutually coherent expectations, routines, and practices, which are sometimes manifested as formal institutions and rules, but often not.[44] Most conventions are a kind of half-way house between fully personalized and idiosyncratic relations and fully depersonalized, easy-to-imitate relations (although even the latter do have conventional foundations, not natural or behaviorally universal foundations).

Conventional or relational (henceforth C-R) transactions affect many dimensions of production systems, but the nature and functions of such conventions differs from industry to industry, according to the nature of the product, the economic fluctuations associated with its markets and production processes, and the type of learning which is possible.[45] C-R transactions may be found in at least five principal domains: (1) interfirm "hard" transactions, as in buyer–seller relations that involve market imperfections; (2) interfirm "soft" transactions, as in the diffusion of nontraded information about the environment or about learning (e.g., through circulation of personnel through the same external labor market or through contact between producers); (3) in hard and soft intrafirm relations, as the bases for the functioning of large firms that are "internally externalized" in the way we noted above; (4) in factor markets, especially labor markets, which involve skills that are not entirely substitutable on an interindustry or interregional basis (i.e., where there are industry- or region-specific dimensions to workers skills); and (5) in economy–formal institution relationships, where universities, governments, industry associations and firms are only able to communicate and coordinate their interactions by using channels with a strong C-R content.

The C-R foundations of economic coordination do not refer to a stark contrast between internal ownership and externalization of production systems, or to hierarchies versus markets or external-embedded networks, but rather to the notion that manufactured opportunities and risks (respectively, learning or the competitive challenge of others' learning), carried out through organizational reflexivity, are becoming pervasive in contemporary capitalism. Every kind of production system has to cope with some form of fluctuations in markets, product design, available technology, and prices, which make difficult the full cognitive routinization of relations between firms, their environments, and employees.

Real systems of production reflect a wide range of conventional phenomena, from rules governing the labor market and work practices, to capital markets and investment practices, to forms of firm organization, to technological habits and propensities, and even to widely held ideas about the appropriate qualities of products. Evolutionary economics has shown that capitalist competition is a "loose" environment, where multiple pathways are possible at many different junctures, and therefore where the behavioral routines and patterns of agents become positively important. Conventions and relations "fill in" the space of this loose selection environment, giving it form and substance.[46]

Hence, a major additional focus in the analysis of organizations—firms and production systems—is now required. It has three principal components: attention to untraded interdependencies and not simply traded transactions as the cornerstones of the organizational question; the conventional and relational qualities of such untraded interdependencies; and the ways that conventions and relations organize and make possible many of the *traded* transactions of the contemporary economy.

Territories

Most social science has traditionally considered regional economies or, more generally, territorial economies at any subnational geographical scale to be derivative reflections of the more "basic" forces of technologies and organizations. Today, even national economies are being demoted, by many analysts, to the same secondary status traditionally assigned regions, due to the increasing reach of global technologies and global organizations. Thus, in the standard view, two elements of the holy trinity generate a set of outcomes in the form of the third: territory.

In contrast to this view, the apparent resurgence of regional economies and the growth of economic differentiation between major world trading economies has stimulated the notion that territorial economies make defining contributions to, and have important feedback effects on, technologies and organizations. Moreover, some branches of contemporary innovation theory, as noted above, propose a set of dynamic interrelations between technological, organizational, and geographical spaces. In these views, territory is a basic and not secondary element of the holy trinity.

The common way that economic analysis deals with geographical proximity and distance is by analyzing the geography of economic transactions—exchanges of goods, information, and human resources over geographical distance. Economic geography considers the price dimensions of transacting activity, to identify circumstances where geographical concentration is necessary to efficient transacting, and those where geographical dispersion of firms, consumers, workers, and institutions is consistent with it. In some analyses, agglomeration is the means to realization of superior pecuniary efficiencies of each transactor (i.e., firm).[47]

There is nothing inherent in transactions that makes geographical proximity necessary. Think, for example, of the counterfactual situation where everyone were equipped with magic carpets[48] and proximity could be had over any distance costlessly and instantaneously. Then any kind of community of interaction would be possible without propinquity, including those information transactions and interactions between persons that are the most subject to uncertainty, such as uncodified practices, informal understandings, as well as those transactions of goods most sensitive to the costs of covering distance. Our magic carpets in California could take fresh orange juice and midwinter flowers from the garden while on their way to pick up the morning's croissants from the boulangerie in Paris. A professor's students could come from all over the world and class could be held anywhere.

In the absence of such a technology of transacting, however, there are many circumstances in which distance is a barrier. The principal such circumstance is a high level of uncertainty, which impedes the planning that could facilitate long-distance repeated transacting (by reducing price and increasing certainty). Proximity in transacting is likely to be adopted in these circumstances. In what are such circumstances likely to consist? Though it is impossible to construct a complete list, many of them will probably concern technological change or learning, in both products and processes. Industries with ongoing product differentiation, for example, rely on informal and traditional knowledge and sensibilities, which are then recombined on short notice into new product designs. In advanced-technology industries, where the technological frontier has not been reached (the example here is not product redesign as in today's personal computer industry, but rather that of significant advances in microchip technology), it is difficult to reduce interaction entirely to projects and teams who can relate to each other with completely formal procedures and at great distances.

But even in the absence of technological change as a source of uncertainty, there are many circumstances where neither vertical integration (and its complement, the certainty of administrative procedures) nor vertical or horizontal disintegration coupled to full formal contracting (which should be indifferent to distance) are possible. The costs of covering distance rise greatly under these circumstances because interaction has to be frequent and sustained, and it often cannot be planned out in advance. These are situations involving high levels of substantive complexity in transacting between persons; in general they are circumstances which depend on interpretative interaction and require persons to achieve and reproduce confidence[49] in their relations, where external authority for the latter and codified rules for the former will not do.

What does this mean for the central problem of spatial economics, the tension between spatial concentration of production and its dispersion? The dominant account of the existence of geographically concentrated production systems, such as Silicon Valley (semiconductors), Hollywood (motion pictures and television), Manhattan (financial services), and the Connecticut River Valley (precision metalworking), is that they exist because many of their linkages, given existing technology of communication and transportation, are heavily reliant on geographical proximity. In this account, when linkages involve small scale or high levels of uncertainty, proximity reduces the actual cost of covering distance and allows uncertainty in turn to be attenuated by permitting producers to spread risks via increased access to other producers in the agglomeration. The law of large numbers is at work for them. An example is the subcontractor who gains access to more clients so as to offset the risks associated with relying on too few commands, in the absence of the possibility of having stable, large-scale orders from just a few clients. In practice, however, even transactional relations which are attributed to this kind of optimal economizing are resolved through the establishment of some rules of the game between the involved parties: even "market" linkages depend on specific conventions of market action[50] among actors, without which there is no coordination among them.

But this account is surely still inadequate in that it proposes just one model of motivation behind economizing through linkage—that of opportunism and moral hazard: the subcontractor is always afraid of getting cut off and the client is always afraid to be engaged.[51] Not only can uncertainty be resolved through means other than risk spreading through the law of large numbers in an agglomerated linkage system, it may be that risk spreading is itself inefficient, second best, or not possible—some linkages may do better when resolved through conventions other than those of markets and contracts. And regardless of efficiency concerns, we know that many linkages *are* in practice resolved through other principles of coordination. *The uncertainty which underlies geographical proximity is thus the same as that which, in the presence of proximity, is resolved through convention among actors, but the form of resolution is not determined by the uncertainty itself.*

The region is not merely a derived outcome of the informational or cognitive structure of transactions associated with technologies and organizations, however. For one, the conventions and relations which develop in association with particular production systems in a given region may affect the long-term evolution of technologies and organizations in those sectors, and the "loose" selection environment of contemporary capitalism suggests that there are many cases where such territorially specific forms of economic life are not washed out by a single best practice; territorialization and multiple equilibria go together.[52] In addition, the ensemble of conventions and relations that come into existence in a territorially defined economy may cut across the array of production systems and activities found there, affecting the evolutionary pathways of a variety of sectors in a regionally or nationally common way.

It is for these reasons that the proximity-inducing effects of conventions may "drag on" for long after the input–output (transactional) reasons that brought geographical concentration of the production system into being have disappeared or could be eliminated. They may also encourage ongoing geographical concentration even when the input–output system could permit deagglomeration. And they may differentiate the performances of superficial-

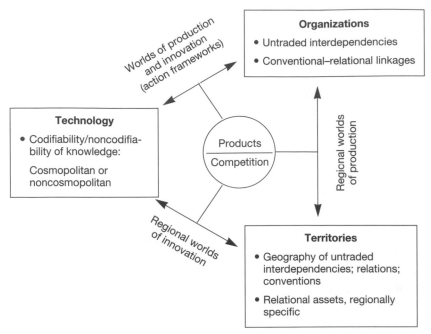

FIGURE 2.2. The holy trinity of the reflexive turn.

ly similar input–output systems, in terms of transactional coordination, product qualities, and evolutionary tendencies. Consider for example the aerospace industry in Southern California. While the large producers are surrounded by smaller job shops and input–providers, there is little way to explain, in strict input–output (transactional) terms, the geographical clustering of the large defense contractors. They could bring into being, almost anywhere, those local networks of input suppliers they require. The large skilled labor market may be then invoked as an explanation, except that skilled labor is highly mobile. At the same time, this skilled labor is industry- and even agglomeration-specific, not in terms of the content of this formal training, but because the persons involved learn much about the industry-specific production culture in the aerospace agglomeration of the region, as do managers and other company officials. These are conventional forms of asset specificity, in which human resources (assets) with generic characters *become* specific and maintain their specificity, and yet cannot be fully internalized within companies and moved around from region to region easily. The frameworks of action (ensembles of conventions) learned by actors constitute key forms of asset specificity in the economy, which are external to individual firms; and in turn, those persons caught up in such webs of conventions allow firms in situations of mutual interdependence (e.g., input–output or buyer–seller relations) to co-ordinate effectively with each other.

This explanation of geographical concentration and territorial differentiation is now quite far from that which relies on linkages, input–output systems, and even economies of scale and scope in factor markets. While not excluding any of the latter, it suggests that the content of linkages is shaped through convention and underlies the coordination of economic actors in production systems and gives rise to the level of economic efficiency they achieve and the specific qualities of products they are able to master.

In sum, the territorial element of the holy trinity needs refocusing, from the geography of input–output relations—industrial complexes and spatial divisions of labor—and the economics of proximity in traded linkages, to the geography of untraded interdependencies and the dialectics of proximity and distance in them. This, in turn, is necessarily bound up with the geography of conventions and relations, which have cognitive, informational, and psychological and cultural foundations. Throughout all of this, there must be simultaneous consideration of territory and region as derived outcomes of technology and organizations, and as the locales of differentiated conventions and relations.

From External Economies to Relational Assets

Regional economies are usually characterized theoretically as systems of external economies; the strong points of national economies are also usually understood via this concept. This notion has long figured in both economic and regionalist thought, but there remains great confusion about what it means. For some regionalists, external economies reduce simply to the effects of urbanization economies, simple scale economies that flow from indivisible infrastructures. In this conception, of course, the region does not enjoy the status of a fundamental level of economic life; it is a derived effect of technological indivisibilities. For other regionalists who consider the economics of proximity, localization economies have been analyzed as the source of the region's economic specializations. Until recently, localization economies were considered to be the spatial expressions of distance constraints on linkages. The integration of transaction-cost economics, and dynamic theories of the social division of labor, and the geography of transacting—or what we referred to above as the relations between technological, organizational, and geographical space—has reopened the linkage between externality theory and the theory of localization or agglomeration. A simple extension of transaction-costs theory to the geography of transaction costs, though analytically powerful, does not generate a different theoretical status for the region in economic thought, because agglomeration remains a mere result of individual maximization. But more complex extensions do change the status of the region:

once proximity becomes an input into the social division of labor—by allowing firms to make choices between what they do internally and what they buy externally—it in turn allows firms to experiment with different degrees of specialization than would otherwise be possible, and this in turn sets up dynamics of technological development that would not otherwise be possible. So the region is now a contributor to the dynamic of modern capitalism, not just an outcome. And the "economies" associated with proximity can no longer be brought back to individual maximization under stable conditions; they inherently involve spillover effects, blurred lines of efficiency, calculus with respect to a moving organizational target whose trajectory is linked to its geography. They very likely represent true positive externalities—in the sense identified by Young[53] and Kaldor[54]—and not merely Stiglerian–Smithian[55] division of labor effects (effects due to the mechanical relationship between greater scale and a deeper division of labor). There are many empirical forms this might take, ranging from high-technology specializations, to metropolitanization as a "flexibility pool."[56]

Even so, there are many ways in which the physical and managerial constraints on distance, for even very specialized input–output relations, are being progressively reduced over time. The distinct possibility exists, with the development of increasingly effective communications technologies and the diffusion of organizational metaroutines, that even very sophisticated transactional systems will enjoy greater and greater potential for avoiding agglomerations.

But the story does not end with these traded interdependencies. In many circumstances, constraints of proximity seem to remain extremely important to the communicative, interpretative, reflexive, and coordinative dimensions of transacting, where even e-mail does not substitute for proximity.

The existence of the conventions and relations that permit reflexivity are something like *assets* to the organizations or regions that have them, or even to the individual agents caught up in them. Regions and organizations who have them have advantages because these relations and conventions—much more so than stocks of physical capital, codified knowledge, or infrastructure—are difficult, slow, and costly to reproduce, and sometimes they are impossible to imitate. The status of the region is now not merely as a locus of true pecuniary externalities, but—for the lucky regions—as a site of important stocks of relational assets.

CONVENTIONS, COORDINATION, AND RATIONALITY: THE MICROFOUNDATIONS OF THE REFLEXIVE TURN

Economic behavior is not simply "embedded" in noneconomic forces, whether they be cultural, cognitive, political, or structural; the distinction between economic and noneconomic forces should be replaced with an analysis of the ways that diverse kinds of information underlie the coordination of economic actors. In this vein, the social science of conventions rejects the distinction, common to modern economics, between decision-making rationality—as the ways that individuals react to information—and action rooted in the pragmatic and cognitive acts of comprehension, understanding, or interpretation. It is not simply that different versions of comprehension, understanding or interpretation generate different "parameters" for decision making in the form of different preference schedules or different things to be maximized, but that action leading to coordination is often necessarily a process of mutual comprehension, understanding, and commonality of interpretation between actors under conditions of uncertainty.

The question naturally arises as to where the notion of reflexivity and the mechanism of convention are situated with respect to the decision-making rationality which is so central to all economic thought. Two brief aspects of this problem may be treated here: microfoundations and pragmatics.[57]

Conventions are much more than mere cognitive, cultural, or psychological skills that permit actors to survive in markets. When actors undertake an activity, they do so with the expectation that they have a framework of action in common with other actors engaged in that activity.[58] It follows for us that the expectations that underlie coordination with other actors are not, as is claimed by many other writers, principally psychological or cognitive, although they certainly have these dimensions. Nor are they mere anticipations, even though they contain anticipations. They are not so much "rational" as they are forms of practical reason. These expectations are fundamentally related to the *pragmatic* dimensions of action, which Herbert Simon[59] called their "effectivity." In all action, there is an ongoing tension due to the search for pragmatic coherence between ends and means. The intentions of actions are defined and clarified in the course of taking them, and are adjusted to changing circumstances. Action depends on and draws from the things and people involved in the pragmatic situation at hand. Such pursuit of pragmatic effectiveness has a practical coherence that may not resemble logical coherence; viewed from the standpoint of logical coherence, practical action may combine diverse logics.

It is for these reasons that conventions are best understood in terms of how they render accessible or deny access to different kinds of action. An environment of action is comprised of two major elements. First of all, there are other persons who act in a way that is coherent with our own actions, so that we both respond to uncertainty in mutually compatible ways: this is a *framework of action*. Second, it is a practical material and institutional environment, where the actors' actions are well-adapted to the practical problem at hand, that is, the tools, existing knowledge, materials, and external (e.g., institutional or competitive) conditions under which they are required to act. Different combinations of these are what we might call "possible worlds of action."

This way of looking at the problem opens up three questions relative to dynamic collective processes in the economy.

The first question is about the diversity of frameworks of action. Though in principle there are unlimited ways to coordinate economic action, there is in practice a limited number of practically coherent combinations of actions for each kind of material good or service produced in the economy. This diversity—leading to plurality of possible worlds—is in one sense much greater than that envisaged by orthodox theory, with its notion of a single production possibility frontier for each set of technologies and markets. We hold that in any given situation there is more than one *effective* economic solution. In another sense, it is more restrictive than orthodox theory, whose free and easy factor substitutions give us a world of unlimited, seamless, combinations—a circumstance that does not exist in real practical situations. In comparison to empirical business economics, it again leads us to admit of greater diversity, in the sense that it rejects the notion of convergence toward global best practices in given markets in favor of a considerable range of effective practical solutions to the problems of production.

The second question has to do with the role of rationality. Economic action is motivated neither uniquely by strict utilitarianism nor only by the satisfaction of individual desires, but by the will to make effective the action one undertakes. This motivation gives two fundamental characteristics to action. On the one hand is its particularity: a given situation of action is peopled with objects, circumstances, and persons, whose varied and heterogeneous nature makes for complex and particular synergies. It is impossible to reduce the situation to a series of preestablished, fixed routines. On the other hand is its collective character: because of this fundamental heterogeneity, mutually interdependent actions can succeed only if there is a truly collective character to them, in the sense of action within a common framework of action. Only if action were reducible to prefixed, fully anticipated situations, could its collective character be replaced by external rules involving no fundamental coordination by the persons involved. Fully fledged Taylorism is the exception, not the rule, and even Taylorism never entirely succeeded in replacing relations with rules. Heterogeneity also means a plurality of collective processes, a certain "fragmentation" of action; when put in the context of a "loose" competitive selection environment we arrive at the notion that there are many kinds of economically effective action, not a single hierarchy of action from best to worst.

The third question has to do with the nature of action itself. The social sciences were for a long time dominated by a utilitarian conception of action as the strategic manipulation of a datum, in the pursuit of satisfying a predefined interest within an external reality itself predefined before the action is undertaken . This conception led to a reductionist notion of intentionality: with ends given, the search for the optimal means to attain them. The economics and sociology of organizations have developed this notion of action. Even though they have stressed their differences with orthodox economic analysis in emphasizing the perverse and inefficient effects of rationality in organizational contexts, they have nonetheless remained well within the utilitarian-instrumentalist paradigm. To break with this paradigm, as we do, requires that we return to the sense of action as "to do," in which the fundamental uncertainty all actors find themselves in is not exclusively something they attempt strategically to insulate or protect themselves from via prediction or strategic maneuvering.[60] The uncertainty of situations of action is also a source of possibilities for realizing the intentions of action. In many situations, especially those of innovation and other dynamic processes in the economy, the actor may very well see the concrete situation as "incomplete," as one in which his or her action is designed to fill in coordination gaps and hence contribute toward the making of a new action framework. When this works, the actor's action framework has been pragmatically effective; when it doesn't work, coordination has failed (for example, in the economy, the product or firm fails some external test) and the actors have to try again, using a different action framework to resolve uncertainty.

The temporal dynamic of economic processes emerges because at any given moment there is a plurality of possibilities, but not an infinity. Action navigates incessantly between possible worlds and the present, and reality is defined in the course of the pragmatic unfolding of actions, both successful and failed. Therefore, theory cannot define, in any a priori way, the conventions actors will develop. But theory can do something that is second best: it can define general and probable groups of conventions that appear frequently in the resolution of certain kinds of practical economic dilemmas, and it can define how these seem often to go together. These are the "possible worlds" to which we refer above. These action frameworks are like clues to explorers, rather than generative grammar[61] or structures. Thus, not only does a social science rooted in the reflexive turn have different microfoundations from much existing social science, it also requires us to complement traditional methods of research and modeling with methods that are likely to be unfamiliar and uncomfortable to those trained within the dominant methodological paradigm.

THE WORLDS THAT MAKE REGIONS, AND REGIONS AS WORLDS

It remains now to begin reconstructing concrete areas of inquiry and explanation in the fields of territorial economic development, economic geography, and regional economics. Our fields can be reconstructed as a series of intentional, collective human projects—where pragmatic actions search for some kind of effectivity. The holy trinity—as reconceptualized—supplies some basic building blocks, in that technologies, organizations, and regions are pragmatic domains of intentional human activity. But they are not equal in power and importance. Territories and regions are no longer the principal pragmatic action spaces of capitalism. People do act to save regions and they act consciously to develop and promote them, in some countries more than others. Regional societies in some places have strong regionalist sentiments but are weak in others.[62] Regionalist pragmatics are nonetheless subservient to other pragmatic action networks today: this is because capitalism is increasingly based on geographically extensive product markets, firms, and factor markets. As a result, *markets*[63] have become the principal arbiters of what is *legitimate* collective action in contemporary capitalism; other groupings, such as regions, nations, families, and firms, must submit themselves to the test of the market, and they are more and more subject to political regimes that require proof that such groupings are not erected in opposition to markets.[64] Markets, in conjunction with contemporary technological capacities, make certain kinds of action spaces very important. To begin with, there is the *product,* the essential focus of markets. Product markets involve two principal elements of the holy trinity: technologies (of products and processes) and organizations (especially firms, but also the organizations that support firms, such as schools and states). Factor markets involve mostly organizations (firms, but also those of collective social reproduction, such as the state, schools, and the public R&D organizations). These two elements of the holy trinity are the principal vehicles of the primary intentional projects of economic action today. The deployment of these actions principally "makes" regional economies today,[65] when they are situated or subdivided into locations.

Through complex locational structures and patterns, however, such activities may come into close proximity in the restricted geographical spaces of regions, where they are constituted as *territorial economies.* In turn, these activities may develop various forms of regional coherence, spillovers, and feedbacks; when this occurs, it is because regional economic actors have developed conventions and relations that enable such regionally centered coevolutionary processes between organizations and technologies to unfold. Both the physical and the relational assets of production *become,* to some degree, regionally specific assets. In other words, *regional worlds of production* can emerge out of the *technological and organizational worlds that make regions.* But this occurs in only some cases; in many others, the regional economy remains, for the most part, a mere locational repository of organizational and technological worlds or artifacts, exogenously driven, exhibiting little regional coevolution, or what regionalists have traditionally labeled "disarticulated" or "peripheral."

The modern economy can therefore be conceived as a complex organizational puzzle, consisting of multiple and partially overlapping worlds in which reflexive collective action unfolds. For any given domain of economic analysis, the task is to understand the functional nature of the action spaces involved, and the substantive content of the conventions–relations—the world of action—by which actors coordinate and give shape to their concrete, functioning activities in that domain.[66] Figure 2.3 illustrates what this means.

In operational terms, these domains, which have strong influence on the evolution of regional economies when they become coordinated worlds of ac-

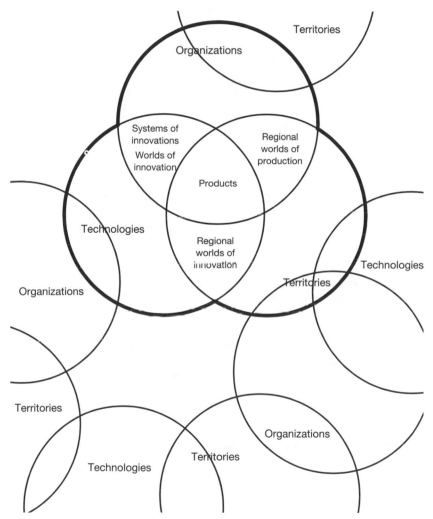

FIGURE 2.3. The economy as a set of intertwined, partially overlapping domains of action.

tion, are different "cuts" at regional analysis. Four such domains, which are complex interactions within the holy trinity, may be defined as priorities for theory and research, as follows.

Technologies and Organizations

Technologies and organizations are the principal generators of the "production possibilities" of capitalism. The first defines the envelope of physical and intellectual possibilities, and the second defines the institutional possibilities for deploying the first in an economically feasible manner. As we have noted, each of these elements of the holy trinity has been revolutionized in recent years, by the reflexive turn. In combination, they generate complex coordination possibilities and problems, two sorts of which are of greatest importance. The first is *products,* which are the results of coordinated reflexive action, against a background of technological and organizational constraints and possibilities; products are the results of different, conventionally–relationally founded action frameworks, or "worlds of production." The second is *systems of innovation,* which are based on action frameworks through which physical–intellectual capabilities are developed and evolved; these are "worlds of innovation." Products, worlds of production, systems of innovation, and their territoriality are analyzed in Chapters 3, 4, and 5.

Organizations and Territories

Organizations, especially firms, "make" regions through their locational behavior, but organizations such as firms are also products of the institutional environments of their locations. This is most obvious for single-location firms, but even the biggest multilocational firms are, in some ways, strongly influenced by the localities in which they situate certain of their activities.[67] For other sorts of organizations, such as schools, government institutions, and politically or culturally defined institutional "environments" (formal and informal rules for governance of the economy), the relationship to place is a great deal more direct. As we noted above, territorial economies may involve transversal effects between their different activities, through technologies (localized knowledge spillovers), through organizations (localized input–output linkages), or through aspects of the local action frameworks by which multiple sectors of the economy are coordinated and resources mobilized. These localized conventional–relational environments are *regional worlds of production.* In Chapter 4, we examine the nature of a single regional world—the cinema and television industry in Hollywood—and show how that regional world evolves in a region-specific way, opening up new branches on its evolutionary tree, but exhibiting fundamental continuities with its regional past as well. In Chapter 6, we analyze a variety of such regional worlds in the United States, France, and Italy.

Technologies and Territories

The development of knowledge and know-how is subject to a complex movement between codification/economic diffusion and innovation/tacitness. Whereas the first tends to lead to geographical diffusion, the second may, in some, but not all cases, emerge from restricted geographical contexts and impede, at least for a certain time, easy geographical diffusion. The role of localization in technological innovation and deployment is made all the more potent because certain forms of innovation emerge from interactivity knowledge and know-how spillovers, which themselves occur in restricted geographical spaces, as well as defined organizational spaces. One of the major issues for students of economic development in the reflexive learning economy of contemporary capitalism is, therefore, the geography of knowledge and know-how development, that is, the geography of innovation. Accompanying the geography of innovation is the question of how this exceedingly complex form of collective action emerges and is coordinated in particular contexts. Paralleling inquiries into worlds of innovation in general, then, we must examine how localization of knowledge and learning come about in the form of *regional worlds of innovation*. Following from the theoretical examination of this question in Chapters 3 and 5, in Chapters 7 and 8 we examine its consequences for the contemporary dialectic of globalization and regionalization.

Technologies, Organizations, and Territories

When all the elements of the holy trinity are considered equally and simultaneously, there is no theoretical "bracketing" for the purpose of simplification. As a result, only the most complex and concrete problems of economic development can be considered. But we can build up to them using insights gained through rigorous theorizing of the individual elements of the trinity, and the limited combinations identified above. One exercise in such complexity is found in Chapter 9, which examines the nature of the city in global society and economy.

CONCLUSION

The approach to territorial economic development that will be developed in this book has little to say about standard problems of spatial economics or location theory, staples of the literature on the geography of economic development, but it has much to say about the territorial differentiation of economic development, performance, and institutions. Its principal contribution to the spatial disciplines is to analyze the role of territorial proximity in the formation of conventions; the role of conventions in defining the "action capacities" of economic agents and, hence, the economic identities of territories and regions; the economic status of regional conventions of production as a type of regionally specific collective asset of the economy; the status of conventions as untraded interdependencies in economic systems; and why it is so difficult for some places to imitate or borrow conventions and institutions from other places. Its purpose is to enhance the explanatory power of regionalist social science, bringing it closer to the principal subjects of many other contemporary social sciences while making distinctive new contributions to those debates.

NOTES

1. The literature on technological change, in both economics and regional science, is vast. See the survey article by Dosi (1988), for the economics literature (although much has been added since then), and the several collections on the geography of technological change that have appeared in recent years: Angel (1994); Antonelli (1987); Aydalot and Keeble (1988); Bellandi (1989); DeBresson and Amesse (1991); Hakansson (1994); Lundvall (1990, 1993); Maillat et al. (1993); Malecki (1984); Maskell and Malmberg (1995); Nelson (1987); Rallet (1993); Todtling (1993).

2. Coase (1937); Williamson (1985).

3. On assets and appropriability, see the discussion in Seravalli (1992); on the firm, see the discussion of the Penrosian tradition in Best (1990).

4. Perroux (1950a,b, 1955); Leontief (1953); Richardson (1973).

5. Scott (1988a).

6. The term "localized" technological change means not only localized in the geographical sense, but also in the economic sense. It is used here solely in reference to the geographical sense. For a full examination, see Antonelli (1995).

7. Massey (1984); Bluestone and Harrison (1982); Vernon (1966, 1972); Norton and Rees (1978).

8. Giddens (1994); Beck (1992); Beck et al. (1994).

9. The states versus markets literature is enormous. For a good economic treatment of it, see North (1981).

10. This goes back to the debate over whether the market was an incentive to *le doux commerce* or simply to exploitation and accumulation for its own sake. Discussion of this can be found in Hirschman (1970).

11. This latter argument can be found in Arato and Cohen (1992).

12. Beck (1992).

13. See the critique of postindustrialism in Cohen and Zysman (1984). On the information economy, see Castells (1989); on flexible specialization, see Piore and Sabel (1984); and on post-Fordism, see Boyer (1992).

14. Lundvall and Johnson (1992); Arrow (1962); Rosenberg (1982).

15. The appellation "learning economy" has considerable and important differences—in both theoretical terms and policy orientations—with other concepts applied to the new economy of the post-1970 period (e.g., flexible specialization, post-Fordism, information economy, service economy, etc.). These differences are discussed in greater length in Chapter 10.

16. Rip (1991).

17. See, for the original focus on this issue, Asanuma (1989). My concept of relations will differ somewhat from his, but the inspiration is acknowledged.

18. Rosenberg (1982).

19. Mansfield (1972).

20. Norton and Rees (1979); Pred (1977); Rallet (1993).

21. But it should be remembered that certain economists in developing countries did not reduce the problem to one of diffusion. Celso Furtado (1963), for example, claims throughout his writings that the problem for developing areas was to master the creation of technology.

22. Nelson (1993); Griliches (1991); von Hippel (1987, 1988); Jaffe (1986, 1989); Jaffe et al. (1993); Antonelli (1995).

23. Lundvall (1990).

24. Hakansson (1987, 1989); Johansen and Mattson (1987); Cohendet and Llerena (1989); Callon (1992).

25. See the review of the resurgence of regional economies in Chapter 1, as well as the industrial district literature, which is now so vast as to make it difficult to cite with any justice.

26. I am grateful to several authors for sensitizing me to the question of cosmopolitan versus noncosmopolitan knowledge. The first is Rip (1991).

> In early design processes within unfamiliar domains, we may expect intuitive, "private" mental technical models to predominate. Although there is no doubt a link to exising cosmopolitan cognitive representations, this is seldom explicit; as a consequence, "meta-modelling" does not yet appear as a distinct activity. (p. 13)

The second is Haas-Lorenz (1994). See also the excellent papers on communication and knowledge in geographical context by Lecoq (1993).

27. Nelson and Winter (1982).

28. I am choosing to use the term "organizations" to refer to firms and production systems, rather than "institutions," which is the term favored by institutional (transactions-cost) economics. This is because I want to reserve the use of the term institution for routines, practices, and formal nonprivate organizations, such as governments, trade associations, and so on. It is also a way to link organizations to the subject of economic organization in general.

29. Coase (1937); Williamson (1985); Dosi and Salvatore (1992).

30. Perroux (1950a,b); Leontief (1953).

31. Richardson (1973).

32. As did Stiglerian development of the scale-division of labor analysis, and some neo-Sraffans (Stigler, 1951).

33. Scott (1988a).

34. Dunning (1979); see the critique of the "geography of enterprise" literature in Sayer and Walker (1992).

35. Camagni (1991); Malecki (1984); Maillat et al. (1990, 1993); Russo (1986); Bellandi (1986, 1989, 1995); Djellal and Gallouj (1995).

36. Romer (1986, 1987, 1990); Lucas (1988).

37. Krugman (1991b, 1992, 1995).

38. Sabel (1993); see also Bramanti and Maggioni (1994); Powell (1990).

39. Cooke and Morgan (1990, 1991), on *institutional* reflexivity in Baden–Wurtemburg, have inspired me in this reinterpretation of the networks and corporate organization literature.

40. This literature is discussed at length in Salais and Storper (1993).

41. Axelrod (1984).

42. See below for further discussion of these microfoundations.

43. Lecoq (1993); Haas-Lorenz (1994).

44. The "classical" definition of a convention is from Lewis (1969). The definition used here, however, differs from Lewis' formulation in that it does not lead to the notion of a coordination "equilibrium" but rather to a sort of "satisficing" form of coordination. For an extensive discussion of this, see Storper and Salais (1997, Chaps. 1 and 2).

45. See Chapter 5, or for a more extensive discussion, Storper and Salais (1997).

46. All of these issues are, of course, the subjects of investigations by institutionalists in many social science disciplines; the economics of conventions, however, goes beyond them in positing that they are elements of the coordination of actors, and that the reason they work is that they amount to a coherent coordination of the production systems involved.

47. There is much ambiguity about external economies in both the geographical and economic literatures. The basic question is whether agglomeration is simply an additive effect of individual, optimizing producers, where there are no truly collective goods with spillovers involved in the transacting system, in which case no real externalities exist. If, on the other hand, agglomeration is a site of such spillovers and feedbacks to the production system, i.e., where proximity opens up possibilities for production organization and development which would not otherwise exist, then true externalities exist. In the literature, two suggestions have been made along these lines: one is that there are intimate feedback effects between proximity and specialization within the division of labor (the work of Scott suggests this, as does Chapter 5 of this book). The other is that agglomerations are sites of transaction-dependent technological innovation. In both cases, agglomeration is not merely a static "Stiglerian–Smithian" effect, but a dynamic "Youngian" effect. Chapters 5 through 8 of this book explore different aspects of this latter view.

48. This idea comes from joint work with Allen Scott; see Storper and Scott (1995).

49. Lorenz (1992); Granovetter (1985); Hakansson and Johansen (1993); Powell (1990); Planque (1990); Axelrod (1984).

50. Salais and Storper (1993) discuss how market action, rather than being the universal form of homo economicus, is merely one way to coordinate with other actors in a market system, appropriate to certain products and ineffective for others.

51. This is the Williamsonian paradigm. Williamson (1985).

52. Evolution is taken up in greater detail in Chapter 3, so we will say little more about it in this chapter.

53. Young (1928). Notice that we are reviving a distinction between pecuniary and nonpecuniary externalities first pinpointed by Scitovsky (1952).

54. Kaldor (1972).

55. Stigler (1951).

56. Veltz (1995).

57. Much of what follows in this section comes out of work carried out in conjunction with Robert Salais and explained in part in our book *Les Mondes de Production* (1993, Paris). The focus on pragmatics is more developed in the English-language version of that book (Harvard University Press, 1997). I have also drawn from a recent unpublished text, "Conventions, mondes possible, et action économique." Any errors of interpretation are strictly my own.

58. But this in no way implies that all actors are equally satisfied, that they are equally enthusiastic, or that they are in relations of political or distributive equality. It is a description of the fact that they *do* according to the same rules of the game, not necessarily that they like to do this. An earlier and different way of dealing with this issue can be found in Crozier and Friedberg (1977).

59. Simon (1979).

60. Although it may certainly in part consist of these dimensions, under particular circumstances, this is not an accurate general description of the nature of action.

61. "Generative grammar" in linguistics: an analogy to explanatory theories in social science that are nondeterministic, but in which nonetheless a given "stock" of tools and a prefixed but still empirically fluid "structure" (the grammar) exist, which define the range of possible creativity of individual actions (speech acts). There has been much debate on whether generative grammar is restrictive or creative. Since we are not professional linguists, we certainly cannot comment on this. With respect to our purpose here, the claim is simply that the "generative grammar" of the economy should not be likened to a structure which prefixes the possible range of individual actions, and if there is an analogy to linguistic thought that claims the same, then we are in agreement with them. See Searle (1977).

62. On the subject of regionalism, see Markusen (1985).

63. This does not mean, necessarily, "perfect" markets, but rather markets as a general principle of the organization of legitimate interactions in contemporary capitalism. Within this general principle, there are innumerable variations.

64. We have said little about the links between pragmatic action and the "justification" and "legitimacy" of action undertaken. But suffice it to say that all pragmatic action—especially insofar as it targets reciprocity by other actors—rests on some notion of legitimacy, some form of justification, whether implicit or explicit, that must be shared by the actors caught up in the collective action. These issues have been extensively explored in Boltanski and Thévenot (1991). In the case of economic models of products, Salais and Storper (1993) discuss different principles of justification for different possible worlds of economic action.

65. Even admitting that there is much "drag" from the past and feedback from the present of existing regional economies.

66. It cannot be overemphasized, however, that the functional domains of action are not predefined, whether by a Parsonian functionalist logic of social organization or

even by any higher capitalist structure. The point of the theory of pragmatics outlined in this chapter is that structure and action unfold and redefine each other simultaneously. We can model the basic functional domains that appear to us now, but these are indicative, not in any way causal.

67. Patel and Pavitt (1991); Dunning (1979, 1988); Pianta (1996); Amendola et al. (1992).

PART II

EVOLUTION AND
TERRITORIAL DEVELOPMENT

CHAPTER 3

The Evolution of
Regional Specificities

REGIONAL CYCLES: THE FAILURE OF A PROJECT

Regionalists have long been fascinated with the prospect of being able to identify long-term regularities in the development of regions, just as macroeconomists have claimed that there are long- and medium-term patterns in the development of national economies. Cycles and patterns are attractive because, if they are accurate representations of repetitive regularities, they provide clues as to what we want policy to promote or avoid in the future. If we could not only find deep geographical patterns to economic development, but also trace their evolution over time, we might have a way to bring about more desirable outcomes. Barring this, for fatalists, they describe uneven patterns of growth and decline as normal and allow us to prepare ourselves for the inevitable.

There exists a considerable body of work on geographical patterns, such as the rank-size rule, central-place theory, or Löschian market geography. Whether the patterns they have discovered are valid is subject to considerable controversy. Beyond disputes over empirics are debates about whether the models underlying the patterns claimed to exist are appropriate or adequate.[1]

In regional economics, cycles are concerned more with time than space. They are derived by combining macroeconomic cyclical models with those of sectoral structure and growth patterns. In the medium run, this means regionalizing the forecast by correcting it for the sectoral composition of the regional economy; in the long run, the exercise involves sectoralizing the macroeconomic data by taking into account long-term developmental trends of the industries that comprise the region's economic base. I will concentrate on time in this chapter, for the view of time advanced here will make for skepticism about discovering deep universal geographical patterns.

The most important tool for analyzing long-run locational patterns is the product cycle. This theory proposes that products are born, mature, age, and die, and in so doing, generate changes in production technology, firm organization, labor demand, and locational patterns for each industry.[2] The basic cycle has four stages. A product is born, often times in many different locations. In the second stage, its technology begins to develop and stabilize; a few firms get ahead by perfecting technology and developing markets; they generate a "first mover" advantage for their locations, and one or a small number of geographical growth poles begins to form in the industry.[3] Agglomeration economies are powerful at this stage. In the third phase, the industry is mature. The technologies of products and production processes stabilize, allowing longer production runs. This also reduces the skill content of production jobs, slows down the innovation process, and makes interfirm or interestablishment transactions less costly. Hence, the industry can spread out to cheaper locations. Frequently, this involves the invasion of overseas markets.[4] Finally, the industry enters into decline, due to overcapacity, market saturation, or substitution by other products through technological innovation. Existing production capacity must be rationalized, made more efficient via plant closings, consolidation of operations, automation, and locational reorganization to achieve optimal national or international production system configurations. Employment-to-output ratios continue to decline.[5]

It is tempting to model a region's developmental pattern over time as a sum of different product cycles. The value of the model is to remind us that all sectors are moving targets, and no regional or national economy can be content merely because it has industries that are doing well. The problem is that the product cycle is actually not a very good predictive tool for the development of all industries. It is applicable principally to the consumer durables industries in the 20th century.[6] Thus, it helps explain why so many former industrial powerhouse regions underwent severe employment and output declines at the end of the postwar boom. It does not help with a variety of other phenomena, however. For one, it does not provide insight into how, why, and where the initial agglomerated core regions of sectors build themselves up. Then, it errs in implying that all industries grow toward mass production and locational decentralization: this does not occur for substantial portions of the capital goods industries, the fashion- and design-intensive portions of consumer goods industries, and for many business and retail services. The product cycle cannot account for the fact that certain technologically (and locationally) "mature" industries are "reinvented," with "younger" products and processes, and undergo other patterns of development as a result. It does not tell us why a given industry can display many different temporal, spatial, and organizational patterns of development: the Japanese versus American car industries, or the Italian versus German clothing industries, for example. While having a certain heuristic value, then, the product cycle theory dangerously ignores the diversity and complexity of sectoral development and location that result from it. The search for cycles and patterns as predictive devices in regional economics (as in macroeconomics) has largely failed.

Evolutionary economics, stemming from the seminal work of Nelson and Winter,[7] proposes a different way into dynamics from anything that came before it. As we noted in Chapter 1, for the case of resurgent regional economies, it provides microeconomic foundations for taking history seriously. Small events, rational choices or accidents, can have big and wide effects on the development of technologies (products and processes), because they are met by positive feedbacks. Many dimensions of sectors—technologies, organization of firms, and production networks—develop through positive feedbacks and set the industry on a cumulative developmental pathway.

What could such a theory offer the field of regional development? Many aspects of the process of sectoral or industry development are subject to path-dependent evolutionary dynamics. One dimension of such path-dependency is the coevolution of industry attributes and the regional environment, what we shall analyze in this chapter as the evolution of regional specificities in factors of production, forms of organization, rules, and conventions. These regional specificities, of course, do not exist in an isolated regional environment. Industries develop in many different territories and there is exchange between places, relocation from one place to another, and substitution of locations for each other, or their goods for those of other regions. This means that in-region evolution is always subject to tensions with what is occurring outside the region. Some of these aspects of industry evolution will be captured in this chapter as the tension between specific regional assets and practices and the forces that make such assets and practices more cosmopolitan and less place-specific. This leads us to a "cycle" of regional development very different from those of regional development theory to date: it concerns the region's role in opening up and closing down variety in technologies, techniques, and products over time. The region has a causal role in this process at the same time that regional economies express the effects of variety and convergence.

PATH DEPENDENCY IN TECHNOLOGICAL SPACE

Evolutionary economics was initially concerned with the problem of technological choice and change in capitalism, although it has since suggested that its new microeconomics could be applied to other phenomena such as the evolution of organizations or institutions. Technology is a good place to start, however. Technology is considered not to be a black box by evolutionary economics, but instead a "field of action," defined by certain basic physical (state of hardware, useful functions, materials) and cognitive (conceptual frameworks, knowledge) dimensions of the practical activity of production. The question is how, within these constraints, a technology is made to develop.

The starting point is to admit that many economic processes are amenable to increasing returns to scale. This point figures in much contemporary economic theorizing. Increasing returns may exist within the firm, of course, and such returns have largely been ignored by mainstream analysis because they render equilibrium analysis impossible, as was shown in Sraffa's 1926 article on the Laws of Returns.[8] More recently, evolutionary economics and the new growth economics have both concentrated on economy-wide increasing returns, which stem from overall increases in knowledge, spillovers of knowledge, or increases in specialization in the social division of labor (intermediate outputs, where a competitive though monopolistic equilibrium could be attained in spite of increasing returns based in external economies). Whereas the new growth theory is concerned with finding the sources of growth and reconciling them with competitive market structures, evolutionary economics has another purpose, more similar to that of Allyn Young in 1928 and, later on, Lord Kaldor, both of whom foresaw the evolutionists' stress on the economic *process*. For evolutionary economists, as for Young and Kaldor, what is important is that in the face of increasing returns, history produces its future and irrevocably alters what may come after it. In this way, it creates specific pathways of development and rules out others that might once have been possible. This could be true, as we shall see, at the level of a technology, a production system, or a *region*.

The most common definition of increasing returns is that they describe a condition wherein input costs per unit output decline with increases in the volume of output. This can mean several things, however. On one hand, there can be indivisibilities in production technology. Physical integration of operations will then enable unit costs to decline with increases in output; but returns to indivisibilities often become inoperative beyond a certain point. An economy could, therefore, have multiples of indivisible technologies.

Nonetheless, there are other kinds of increasing returns. This is because, in modern industrialism, there are steady improvements in the overall efficiency of the economy that are not exclusively due to improvements inside the firm; these include increases in knowledge, increases in interfirm specialization, and spillovers of knowledge.[9] Such improvements may generate new ways of doing things that upset existing relationships (such as input–output relationships) in the economy. Many of these improvements are themselves subject to indivisibilities. As they are inserted into the existing tissue of interfirm, interindustry, and producer–consumer relationships, they create vast ripple effects and can lead to indivisible effects much bigger than themselves. These are dynamic economies of scale, and much of the process of economic change in contemporary capitalism is defined by them, as Young had pointed out.

Evolutionary economics takes on the mechanism of such changes, showing that they come about in a stepwise and interdependent manner that does not conform to straightforward allocative efficiencies of the standard neoclassical model.[10] It applies to the rather restricted action of "technical choice" from a set of known blueprints, to the complex case of technological change through learning, and to cumulative changes in the interfirm division of labor and specialization in intermediate outputs. To illustrate it, we can straightforwardly reiterate the analysis advanced by Arthur.[11]

Usually, there are several ways to carry out any given purposeful economic action. These ways are called "technologies." For the moment, we are interested in technologies that fulfill the same purpose, and therefore compete for the market of potential adopters. Technologies may exist as pure method or pure information, or they may already be incorporated in physical plant or machinery, or they may be marketed as products. Here, we consider the case where two or more superior technologies (products or processes) compete with each other to replace an outmoded technology (thus, not the standard diffusion case where a single new superior technology competes with an older and inferior one). In the 1890s, for example, the steam engine, the electric motor, and the gasoline engine competed as power sources for the new automobile. In the early 1800s, the spinning mule competed with the ring frame in cotton manufacturing. Recently, different configurations of personal computers and video recorders have competed with each other.

A given technology combines a certain vector of economic inputs, or factors, for a given amount of desired output, so that monetary returns in use, or payoff to adoption to a particular agent, are simply the value of the output less factor cost, over an appropriate time horizon. Sometimes the number of choices can be very high, as in Paul David's case of the typewriter keyboard, where 1048 possible configurations competed with each other.[12] Rosenberg[13] shows that this fluidity is resolved through learning-by-using, at the end of which a standard, or convention-in-use, emerges.

Returns rise with the numbers who choose a technology, up to a certain point. In the standard textbook case of technical choice, all the technologies that compete for adoption show diminishing returns, and market sharing is the result. As demand increases, adoption follows a composite supply curve, which is obtained from the lateral addition of separate returns curves for each technology. The outcome is completely predictable—one can determine, in advance, the market shares after *n* choices, in this situation—and the configuration that emerges is efficient. The outcome is also flexible; adjustment of any returns curve can always shift the composite supply curve and hence change market shares.

Where objects with increasing returns compete, the market outcome is indeterminate, because nonconvexities[14] appear in the supply curve. Information on preferences, endowments, and on transformation possibilities enables one to locate possible long-run equilibria. But this says nothing about which technology will actually capture the market. Thus:

> From many initial positions of interest, the system—like a pencil perfectly balanced on its point—is equally attracted by several equilibrium outcomes. We cannot say which way it will fall; hence, we cannot predict

uniquely which path it will follow. Thus, we cannot pursue conventional analysis.[15]

Arthur illustrates this logic with the example of an island where cars are introduced, all of them at the same time. Drivers are free to choose between the left-hand and right-hand sides of the road and have no in-built bias toward either. Each side possesses increasing returns; as a higher proportion of drivers chooses one side, the returns to that side rise quickly. If one side gets sufficiently ahead, drivers will "fall in" on this side, so that eventually all cars will drive on that side of the road. The side that wins comes to dominate the market, but cannot be deduced in advance.

There are four aspects of these outcomes worthy of note. First, in contrast to the usual situation of diminishing returns, the outcome need possess no superior efficiency properties; the side that wins need not be the better of the two. Second, driving is now locked in to the chosen side. The outcome is structurally rigid, in that marginal inducements to drivers to change sides will prove ineffective. Third, even though we know drivers' preferences and possibilities, ex ante the outcome, is unpredictable. "Small events" outside the model—perhaps some drivers' reactions, perhaps a dog running into the road, perhaps the timing and positioning of traffic lights, may be crucial in deciding the outcome. Finally, ex post, exact causality is hard to assign and it would be a mistake to read into it some form of innate superiority.

Where the menu of technologies shows standard diminishing (or even constant) returns, and where choices follow a stochastic process, then the "random walk" of choosers has reflecting barriers. But if technologies have increasing returns, the same random walk has absorbing barriers. The four characteristics of this walk are as we have suggested above: (1) small events are not averaged out or forgotten, but may decide the path of future market shares; (2) there is a potential inefficiency of aggregate outcomes, even where individual choices are perfectly rational; (3) there is a potential inflexibility of outcomes, in that ultimate market shares cannot always be influenced on the margin, especially beyond a certain point of adoption; and (4) the process is unpredictable, in that knowledge of supply and demand functions and preferences does not lead to accurate forecasts of outcomes.

The evolutionary reasoning presented thus far is, of course, not about standard economies of scale inside the firm, but instead about increasing returns at the level of some system of economic interrelations (the users of a technologies, a production system, a region, a *filière* [commodity chain], etc), which are thus external economies. They are manifested as increasing efficiencies as a technology is adopted, and increasing efficiency gaps between it and other, once-competing technologies.

In this approach, an economy is theorized as an assemblage of heterogeneous, boundedly rational agents, with imperfect learning and information.

These agents generate variety through invention and innovation. These actions are interdependent: we cannot determine what others will do, yet our subsequent choices will be influenced by the choices they render feasible or infeasible for us. Interaction also reduces variety, once it is created, through specific selection processes. Thus, the theory bases itself on procedural rationality rather than comparative allocational optima. The emergent effects of such procedural rationalities are to generate evolutionary trajectories, where today's choices are constrained by history.

REGIONAL CONTRIBUTIONS TO TECHNOLOGICAL EVOLUTION

Evolutionary thinking can be applied to problems of regional development in two ways. On the one hand, do the interdependencies between actors in regional economies—under conditions of proximity—contribute to the evolutionary processes described above, i.e., the elaboration of technological trajectories? On the other hand, does evolutionary microeconomics help us to understand the evolution of a regional economy as an economic activity system? We take up the first question here, the second in following sections.

In order for a region to be fundamental to the evolution of a technological field or space, that region—a geographical space—must contain some of the key interdependent choices that make a technology evolve. The region must be a place where technological variety is created and then limited, where the pathway is traced out.

There are two basic senses of technological interdependency, both having to do with knowledge development and diffusion. The first concerns relations between different users and between users and producers of a technology.[16] Users and producers of complementary technologies define search behavior and influence each others' choices. As the number of users of a given technology rises, it tends to cut off the possibility of different patterns of use (and hence, of production) for other users. A region might play a role in this to the extent that particularly significant users or producers are localized there, whose choices can, in and of themselves, dominate all other users' and producers' choices or to the extent that a large number of users and producers are concentrated in the region. Such relations might affect, for example, the availability of key capital goods in an industry, or the state-of-the art product design.

Before going on, we need to make a clarification. Evolutionary economics represents technology—especially product technology—as a set of nonsubstitutable (in effect, semifixed output coefficient) packages of hardware or practices. But of course, that is not entirely the case in real economic life, especially with techniques of production. Changes in factor costs do not always force firms from one tecnology to another. There is a significant possibility of adjustment without moving from one technology to another, when a firm moves from one technique to another along a local reverse isoquant (pathway of techniques). Evolutionary tradeoffs occur between technique and technology—which have been most extensively explored to date in the pioneering work of Antonelli.[17] Localized pathways of technical change, without technological innovation per se, can accommodate certain kinds of changes in factor costs and competing technological efficiencies. This reasoning suggests, importantly, that there can be localized conditions in which change will move more or less in the direction of technological innovation, or more or less in the direction of adjustments of technique without innovation.

In regional terms, it can be shown[18] that the dynamics of interfirm diffusion of knowledge are region-specific. For a given level of R&D, for example, (1) caeteris paribus, geographical proximity increases the probability of diffusion of a given *technique;* (2) region-specific competences, after several rounds of imitation and diffusion of techniques, become endogenized, something like a stock of competences, routines, and conventions; (3) the probability of imitation at the regional level rises with the number of firms in the region; (4) regional concentration is favored when the degree of appropriability of knowledge is low, and vice versa. Importantly, it can be shown that an initially different distribution of competences within regions leads to significant in-region convergence, and to increasing interregional divergence, all as a result of evolutionary path-dependent consequences of imitation behavior, assuming procedural rationality.

The second kind of technological interdependency is that of knowledge spillover between similar technologies. Technologies may use similar knowledge base materials but be applied in different end uses. The pool of knowledge that enables manipulation of the base material is key to both. They might rely on similar kinds of basic theoretical knowledge or similar skills in manufacturing or marketing. A region would be important to spillovers if the vehicles of the spillovers—the knowledge base, the labor market that contains it, the institutions (e.g., research institutes or states), the relationships (business–business, public–private, etc.) that make it possible, or the rules (formal rules or informal conventions) which lead to creation of technology and spillovers, are highly regionalist and necessarily dependent on geographical proximity.[19]

In both cases, knowing how to do one thing is frequently consequent upon knowing how to do another, so the knowledge and skill development that occurs in one promotes the ability to do the other. These areas of the economy are technological fields or spaces, in the sense that they were intuitively defined by François Perroux in 1950. But these fields are not defined in Perroux's overly restricted sense as dense input–output relations between activities (as in the case of user–producer relations); they can also be defined by softer interdependencies, such as knowledge spillovers that do not involve input–output relations at all. Untraded interdependencies are just as important as market transactions in defining these spaces.

A regional economy, however, cannot be assumed to overlap significantly with these spaces of technological evolution. A region will only be a substantial contributor to an evolutionary dynamic in a technological space if it contains significant pieces of that space. Otherwise, the interdependent choice processes described by the evolutionary model cannot take place in the region or can be carried out without geographical proximity and hence with the influence of strongly nonregional factors. Is the geographical space of the region this type of technological/economic space? The answer is "no, yes, and maybe."

The negative case is that of a regional economy that is a collection of sectors having few technological complementarities or similarities and few important user–producer relations. This region will have no specifically regional technological dynamic from which evolutionary effects could emerge. This local collection of firms could have a regional pattern in the selection of techniques along a given isoquant. But it seems unlikely that such techniques could set a pattern for techniques used elsewhere in the industry. It is likely that technique adjustments made by local firms will be locally suitable, both in the sense of the geographical locality and in the sense of covering a limited range of situations, defined by costs and scales, in that industry. It is unlikely that they would simply stumble upon a globally superior technique, or innovate a new technology for the sector.

The answer could be "yes" when a region contains big segments of a technological space, as in the case of a core agglomeration of an industry, which serves to generate technology and knowledge for that sector, in a nation or at the global level. It would also be yes when such a core agglomeration is multisectoral, involving the key technologies that, because of similarity or complementarity of key technological inputs, serve several different final output sectors.

The mere fact of a core agglomeration makes it probable that contributions to the evolution of a technological space will occur there. But what is the status of the "region" in this technological dynamic? It depends on the status of geographical proximity in the production and research system. If the agglomeration exists because proximity is necessary to the industry's functioning, then there is probably something in the regional environment that is key to which technological choices get made. But sometimes regional core agglomerations exist because of locational inertia, following a previous period where proximity was necessary. Specifically regional factors may continue to play a role, but to the extent that the industry's technology is no longer specific to that region (what we shall call "cosmopolitan" technology in the following section) it is only a matter of time before the region's importance diminishes, as technologies are diffused within other regions.

The answer is "maybe" when a regional economy contains a significant quantity of production in a given industry, and where that industry is based on technologies that are subject to a path-dependent evolutionary dynamic. If the region is not a core agglomeration for that industry, in the sense that it has many locations among which its key technologies and functions are divided, or in the sense that many similar and therefore competitive agglomerations exist, then the question is whether there are dynamics at the regional level that can affect the pathway of the bigger sectoral–technological environment. Here, if regional firms have managerial discretion to adjust their techniques (and this is a big "if" in a world of global corporations, but could be consistent with some models of managerially decentralized "transregional" firms), then it is possible that technique adjustments could trace out a pathway in the region that could generate superior technologies for a wide range of the industry's firms. The degree to which such localized technological changes are then diffused would depend on their fit with heterogeneous conditions of factor costs, endowments, and adjustment costs on the part of other firms in that industry, in other regions.[20] This middle-ground situation, though most complex and ambiguous in analytical terms, may be empirically the most important case of regional contributions to technological evolution.

THE EVOLUTIONARY PROCESS INSIDE THE REGION: ASSETS BECOME SPECIFIC AND RELATIONAL

We turn now to our second, complementary, question: the in-region evolution of regional economies.

Evolution in Noncore Regions

In the first type of region—the collection of firms without significant concentration in an industry or in an integrated multisectoral technological space—there may be an evolutionary process at the regional level. The extent to which technique evolves in key firms will be related to whether decisions are taken at the regional level, or whether they are dictated from afar by corporate hierarchy and, in this light, whether there are tight or loose technological complementarities between what the region's firms are doing and what is accomplished elsewhere in the firm's production systems. If complementarities are tight, technological specifications may not be adjustable at the regional level and the evolutionary dynamic will be an imported one. On the other hand, if the regional firm uses local suppliers, local evolutionary dynamics could be locally important.

The evolutionary conception of technological innovation is most useful here as a way to analyze the developmental context for the regional economy in a dynamic way. Technological evolution is a key external constraint for the region's development. The region cannot rely simply on supply and demand forecasts and derive the region's share of them in the sector, when the industry's technology is evolving rapidly or significantly. Evolutionary economics calls for a different kind of regional forecasting, giving an evolutionary picture of the sector, with the multiple ways that possible branching points in technological trajectories of the industry at hand could affect the region's share, in qualitative and quantitative ways. The spatial division of labor in a multilocational industry now becomes the subject of this evolutionary reasoning. No cycles or developmental norms can be derived from this kind of reasoning, however; it calls for regional authorities to have a much more complex and dynamic intelligence about their regional economy and for regional economic modeling to undergo a complete conceptual overhaul.

Evolution in Core Regions

For core agglomeration regions, there are two evolutionary dynamics that could be important. First, the location of initial "breakthrough" innovations in an industry or technological space—such as the DC-3 for commercial aviation, or the first marketable silicon chip—often determine the durable locations of core agglomerations. Such initial innovations confer "first mover" advantages on the firms and regions in which they are situated. The early oligopolistic, or even monopolistic, structures of such innovations generate superprofits for the firms concerned, allowing them to draw into their orbit necessary suppliers of inputs and materials. Regional-scale economies thus come into being and set up a circular and cumulative dynamic of attraction of other specialized firms.[21] In this way, a small evolutionary event can have a durable effect on the location of core activities in the industry.

The second dimension of in-region evolution is the development of the industry's technologies, once it is established in its core regions; by considering this, we can extend the analysis of the previous section on how core regions contribute to evolution of a technological space. The traditional question of how regional cycles are produced is transformed into how regional production and R&D systems might drive industrial or sectoral dynamics through a regionalist process of technological innovation. In-region dynamics (technology) and organizational and technological dynamics are seen as key *coevolutionary processes:* the three elements of the holy trinity evolve together.

Technology must be thought of both as physical assets and as a *cognitive framework* that allows access to knowledge in the form of a practice or technique (discussed in greater detail in Chapter 5). Physical assets in technology are usually classified according to their degree of specificity or generality, which correspond roughly to the degree of their standardization. Specificity can mean idiosyncrasy or attachment to a particular firm, group of firms, or persons. But why would productive assets remain specific in a world where competition pushes for their imitation and diffusion? The answer is that assets remain specific when they cannot easily be imitated and standardized and made accessible to others, and this is the case largely when the knowledge or cognitive frameworks needed to produce or use them are not cosmopolitan. By cosmopolitan we mean accessible in a highly reproducible form; by non-cosmopolitan we mean embedded in particular concrete relations or cultures, which enable their members to get access to or to interpret knowledge and information or apply it in a useful way. For example, technologies that can be applied from blueprints are largely cosmopolitan, but those which have much uncodified knowledge or require much uncodifiable information to apply are substantially noncosmopolitan. Note that either could involve asset specificities in the way that term is used in transactions cost economics, so the cosmopolitan/noncosmopolitan distinction cannot be collapsed into generic versus specific assets. Much of the process of technological development and evolution of technologies, once invented, it can be argued, is the result of tension between cosmopolitan and noncosmopolitan cognitive frameworks, that is forces pushing to make technology more cosmopolitan and those pushing to make it more "localist," "specific," and "embedded."

A core regional agglomeration gets established as a core, that is, to the exclusion of other regions, precisely because it is the place where noncosmopolitan knowledge gets a productive foothold. Contrary to many popular impressions, a new industry is not, in its early days, characterized by industry-specific physical assets.[22] Precisely because a new industry does not yet exist, its inventors experiment with generic assets they borrow from existing sectors and try to combine them into new products and productive assets. Their labor forces, likewise, are people whose experiences come from other, established sectors; hence their cognitive frameworks are cosmopolitan, in the sense of ready to be applied outside the sector of origin. They develop a new, noncosmopolitan cognitive framework and type of knowledge, and this allows them to transform these generic assets into new assets that are specific to a new industry. Initially, this occurs with product and process technologies as hardwares are developed by combining generic developed technologies into new specific technologies, whether through practical experimentation or the application of formal scientific and engineering knowledge. As the industry initially grows, it develops an organizational structure, and this structure embodies noncosmopolitan industry- and region-specific assets, in the form of relations, rules and conventions.

The technological and organizational structure of the industry is constructed on the basis of this wide range of untraded interdependencies, the key to which is the fact that the technology is noncosmopolitan. Their increasing industry-specificity and untraded nature often accompanies the industry's rise in a particular and limited number of core agglomerations. It should be noted that this kind of system does not correspond strictly to one dominated by small- and medium-sized firms. Moreover, it accounts for certain kinds of agglomerations that cannot be derived from the geography of transactions costs associated with traded linkages between firms, in that a small number of large firms could be dependent on cognitively specialized knowledge, where the latter is strongly attached to a region.

Noncosmopolitan knowledge is not necessarily associated with proximity or localization. The two are theoretically distinct: noncosmopolitan knowledge can be "localized" in a restricted technological, organizational, or professional "space," that is, in certain interpretative networks that transcend local geographical space. The relationship between the two is one of the most fascinating questions in economics, psychology, and geography today and involves nothing less than the geography of economically useful cognition, knowledge, and interpretation. It is also analytically key to the geography of culture in today's media- and telecommunications-saturated world.

For the moment, it has not been shown that relations of proximity can be transcended for many important knowledge-developing and -using activities. Regular and sustained human contact within an interpretative, interpersonal community is necessary for many of these important dimensions of the economic process.[23] A pure case would be an industry totally dependent on noncosmopolitan knowledge. But in reality, most developing industries have portions of noncosmopolitan knowledge, some of which is strongly dependent on proximity for the reasons alluded to above.

This argument, it should be obvious, makes conventions a secondary effect of the information attributes of the input–output structure of production. Like many such agglomeration effects, conventions might be expected to disappear once the technical conditions requiring proximity give way to those permitting deagglomeration. But this is not always the case, for conventions once in existence have strong feedback effects on the production system itself and its geography. In some cases, the historical geographies and technological trajectories of sectors witness a causality quite the reverse of that presented immediately above: conventions drive the geography and technology of the production system. Just as proximity affects the formation of convention, so convention shapes what goes on in territorially proximate contexts.

Those conventions which have a geographically bounded character channel the development of their economic activity systems (cognitive and conventional communities, in effect) in territorially specific and different ways. The corollary of this is that in the process of economic development, production systems do not converge on any single, optimal best practice.

Much transactional activity is not merely guided by informal convention, of course: it may be incorporated in formal rules or institutions, such as administrative procedures, contracts, or laws. In these cases, previous rounds of interaction have resulted in that most visible form of convention, the institution, which once in existence channels the action situations and frameworks of actors who find themselves in circumstances similar to those of their forebears. This point is most obvious when there is an event, like the American Constitutional Convention, which sets down rules which, once established, don't have to be established again (but they do have to be continually communicated and reinterpreted and common understandings must be reestablished). Institutions thus may be regarded as a special form of convention; and most institutions, even those whose jurisdiction extends over wide spaces (e.g., national constitutions), have origins in territorially restricted processes of convention formation.

Here we leave the domain of evolutionary economics and rejoin the concerns of organizational studies and institutionalism. Technologies and techniques, it would appear, can evolve through the region-specific imitation processes described earlier. But it is not just technology and technique that are developing—so are wider frameworks of action and institutional contexts and their underlying conventions. These are frameworks through which the process of imitation and evolution of technologies and techniques are themselves structured. So a major question about the generation of these region-specific action contexts arises, and how such action contexts are embedded in the region's organizations (firms, governments, nongovernmental organizations, etc.).

The most plausible account of such construction of context is that of the institutional "field" found in the work of sociologists.[24] Organizations in a given network environment—in this case the sector and the region—work most frequently through mimetic behavior and analogy, leading to a kind of diffusion of ideas by "contagion." Numerous empirical studies have shown that even within a single sector affected by similar external competitive challenges, different methods of adjustment are chosen because firms tend to imitate those methods in their own territorial environment and to draw analogies from their "comparison" firms; they are suprisingly uncosmopolitan in so doing. This analogical reasoning allows them to create "equivalents" to their own situations and hence to imitate and adapt at the same time. They do so in part by the construction of a language that defines and describes, in a context-specific way, their "problem" and the solutions they consider possible.

These contexts are thus constructed "upstream" of particular choices of technologies and techniques. They are more temporally stable than the latter, acting somewhat like filters for technical choices and shaping evolutionary processes. This conventionally constructed and regionally specific pragmatics, a veritable construction of reality,[25] hence interacts with evolutionary trajectories.

Now we can flesh out this general conception of evolutionary processes in, and of, core regions, by making a number of specific analytical points. These are meant to be beginnings of the development of fully fledged evolutionary regional analysis, but they are only beginnings.

Regionally Specific Assets and Localization Patterns

An evolutionary perspective on localization goes beyond the recent theorization of agglomeration as a scale effect, where the bigger the region, the more it is possible for producers who draw on common pool resources, such as labor, or who depend on frequent external transactions with other producers, to do so efficiently. In that analysis, as we have noted in previous chapter, producers have the advantages of ready access to specialized resources, and they can externalize many costs without needing to hoard resources and thus use them suboptimally.

Evolutionary approaches do not deny the possible role of regional scale—essentially the regional pooling of resources—in pushing for agglomeration, but they do center on a very different mechanism, that of the *specificity*, hence interregional differentiation, of such things as factors, knowledge, skills, relationships, and conventions. Steve Bass has analyzed this difference of approach in some detail, and we will borrow liberally from his analysis to bring it out.[26]

Let us use the case of labor—a key factor and a key holder of the cognitive, knowledge, and skill resources critical to technological evolution—as an example of the difference in approaches. According to the regional scale-transactions approach that can be found in the recent work of Scott[27] if the quantities of labor used by different firms in a region are not perfectly correlated, and if this labor is externalized into a regional pool, its successive employment contracts would add up to high rates of overall employment for those in the pool.

Krugman[28] then develops this point into something like a developmental trajectory: labor pooling creates a tendency toward localization of an industry in one region. Consider two regions, *A* and *B*. Figure 3.1 shows the share of firms and labor in region *A*. According to Krugman, *F* equals firms' indifference curve with respect to region *A*'s share of firms and workers, and *W* equals workers' indifference curve with respect to the same two variables. Firms prefer their region to be labor rich, while workers prefer their region to be firm rich.

In the area above *W* and to the right of *F*, it is advantageous for firms and workers to migrate from *B* to *A* until *A* has 100% of firms and workers. In

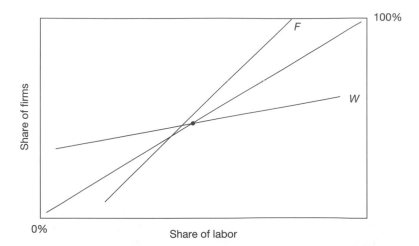

FIGURE 3.1. Localization as an unstable equilibrium. *Source:* Bass (1993), following Krugman (1991b).

the area below *W* and to the left of *F*, it is advantageous for them to migrate to *B* until *A* has 0% of these factors: both move toward the 45 degree line. The intersection of *F* and *W* represents equal shares of firms and labor for the two regions; it is an equilibrium. But it is unstable, since any small movement off it leads to the localization result described above. Thus, the existence of pooling economies creates a drive toward localization. But this explanation is not sufficiently robust. In Figure 3.2, we introduce relocation costs into the two-region model already at hand. If we include this cost, then the center point expands into a region of stability. From the region around the center point, there is no incentive to move towards further localization in one region. Labor pooling alone cannot induce further localization. This is likely to be the case in the early stages of an industry's development.

The explanation advanced here is different. It is not only the costs of labor use that are in question, but the evolution of labor qualities (this lesson could apply to any factor or relation). Labor pools can evolve in qualitatively different directions, even within the same broadly defined sector, according to the specificity of knowledge, skills, cognitive frameworks, or relations of that subsector. This creates a tendency toward localization that is stronger than in the Krugman–Scott explanation. *Thus, the economic and the geographical spaces evolve simultaneously, and cannot be separated.*

This definition of the problem sheds light on a wider range of the resurgent regional economies identified by recent scholarship than any of the preceding perspectives on regionalism. The elaboration of the technology over time, its differentiation into many different products and using more and more

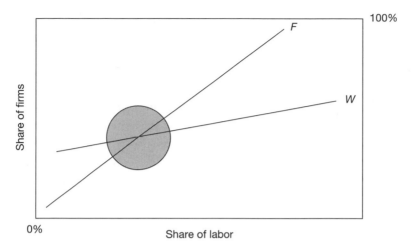

FIGURE 3.2. Localization becomes stable with region-specific assets. *Source:* Bass (1993).

differentiated inputs, makes the assets of the industry often highly specific to its firms and products. In the late 1940s and early 1950s, product and process technologies were quite specific for vacuum-tube based electronic products, in what was then an old technology that had little development left in it. But then miniaturization came along to replace the vacuum tube, first via the transistor, and then via the silicon-based semiconductor. When new, these technologies had few established inputs that were specific to them; they had to "invent" their own input chains, and the knowledge going into them, which had not yet become highly applications-specific. In other words, they began as generic assets that, over time, evolved into more specific assets. This is one reason why the semiconductor industry was not attached, geographically, to its parent industry—radio and television equipment—on the East Coast, and instead found its center in Silicon Valley.[29] It had to reinvent its own input chain, thus creating assets specific to the emerging technological space. It also had to convert generic electronic engineers into labor which had skills specific to semiconductors—labor which, by definition, could not have existed prior to the invention of the semiconductor. As a technology develops and both its inputs and applications become more differentiated, the technological spillovers we mentioned earlier come into existence, when technologically cognate fields of knowledge elaborate their parameters. In three ways—the labor market, the input–output system, and the knowledge system—there is a process of becoming specific.

This evolution in the region is not limited, of course, to discrete factors such as labor, but includes overall patterns of interaction in a given industrial system. Evolution is not just about physical or human asset specificity, but about conventions, rules, and other practices; in other words, regional evolution includes the development of regionally specific *worlds of production*, that is, regionally specific relational assets.

The Evolution of the Organization of an Industry, Inside the Regional Core

We have been taught, in the last few decades, that the overall organizational form of an industry is a function of the industry's scale, the costs associated with different scales of operation, and the transactions costs attached to them. As has been noted, the organizational question is generally seen as the question of the division of labor: the degree to which tasks and functions are subdivided and specialized, and the degree to which they are carried out inside the firm or externalized.

Intrinsic to the transaction-costs view of the division of labor is that the more specific a given type of equipment or asset may be, the more it will tend to be internalized within the firm, and the less specific it is, the more it will tend to be sought from external sources. Specific assets are generally available in small quantities, and firms would not want to depend exclusively on external suppliers for supplies of specific assets. The suppliers would then take advantage of them, and leave them recourse to no other suppliers: this is the problem of opportunism and moral hazard that is essential to that approach.

More generally, it is widely held that assets produced at large scales tend to be less specific (more generic) than assets produced in small quantities. This leads us back to the geography of production: to the extent that scale of production rises, it tends to reduce the specificity of assets required by an industry or a firm, and to make those assets available externally, without any risk posed by opportunistic behavior, because many sources of supply are available. And even though external supply—hence, interfirm trade—is the method for getting these assets, the large scale of procurement tends to reduce the need for proximity in transacting. So, we come back to a sort of product cycle: the industry evolves from small-scale to large-scale, from specific to general assets, from internal to external supply, and from localization to diffusion. Throughout, the analysis is essentially quantity driven; it is a kind of "Smithian" analysis, where growth drives the reduction in asset specificity.

Once again, however, the notion of coevolution of economic and geographical spaces upsets such neat logic. Two observations must be made here, for the case of a regional sectoral core. First, if, for a given growth process, the shape and slope of a production function itself—and the succession of such functions, which is the process of technological evolution—is determined in the context of a geographical space, with the asset specificities we have described above, then there is no determinate ubiquitous Smithian industry development pathway. It is simply not clear that the industry always will go from specific to general assets for a given increment of quantitative growth. A good recent example of this is the persistence of a nonmass-production format in the rapidly growing entertainment industry, a case which is examined in Chapter 4. Second, the growth process itself will be in part determined by geographical specificities in the regional core: how that complex grows will determine the price envelope of production, the qualities of the output, and hence not only the degree of change in demand, but the elasticity of the demand itself.

Evolution in the Region and Evolution Outside the Region

Of course, even regional cores are often highly tied to what occurs outside the region, through interfirm and intersectoral trading relations, as well as through the eventual transformation of the industry's cognitive framework from noncosmopolitan to cosmopolitan. More specifically, the industry's organizational form is influenced by organizational developments outside that industry and outside its core regions. This is because of the Smithian process referred to above: if certain inputs required by the industry are subject to growth in demand in a series of sectors, the increasing scale of the economic demand for them can lead them to be sectioned off into separate firms or sectors—this is the process of the ongoing development of the social division of labor in modern capitalism. As they are sectioned off, they have effects on sectors they can supply to, by altering those sectors' and firms' efficient economies of scope. An input that becomes externally available results in interfirm or interindustry trade, and hence results in another firm or industry reducing its scope of operations, in turn, we would assume, also changing its scale, its output prices, and so on.[30] General expansions of the economy, for example, create incentives for firms to increase their degrees of vertical disintegration, because, all other things being equal, they expand the variety of externally available inputs. A recent example is the hiving off of financial services activities from corporate headquarters activity: as the former became more and more developed in its own right in the years following the end of Bretton Woods, the advantage in seeking such services on the external market became greater and greater for big firms.

This ongoing process of endogenous organizational change in capitalism, then, which generates patterns of the internal organization of firms as well as patterns of interfirm and interindustry trade, may also be conceived as the ongoing alteration of region-specific production and generic production, outside of the core region. There is, however, *no determinate optimal solution to this problem*, precisely for the reasons outlined in the previous section, and more generally because of the fundamental indeterminacy, unforeseeable character, and unpredictability of evolutionary processes.

Some Possible Developmental Trajectories

With the above lessons in mind, we may ask how regional systems such as Silicon Valley, the Wall Street financial district, the Detroit or Tokyo automobile complexes evolve, once they are established as cores. The common notion is that there is a one-way street from noncosmopolitan to cosmopolitan knowledge, as in the product cycle. Products are standardized, leading to imitation, rival goods, more perfect competition, and locational decentralization away from the core region (due to substitution of less specific factor inputs and to the stretching out of transactions in geographical space). This tendency effectively breaks up the core agglomeration or cuts off its growth dynamic. In this case, resources may remain firm-specific (in the sense of sunk costs and dedicated equipment), but the evolutionary dynamic of the initial firms is to invent themselves and the core region out of their unique position. But other patterns of regional contribution to the evolution of a technological space are possible. The regional production economy, with its conventional–relational noncosmopolitan structure, could continue to generate noncosmopolitan processes that are competitively efficient, in a regionalist version of a "learning economy."[31] In this case, the core region could continue to master the technological frontier of its technological space.

There are two possible economic consequences of this mastery. In the first, the technology would not only be geographically localized, but localized in the economic sense of its applications, and hence only suitable to the region at hand. If it is globally superior, it would reinforce the absolute domination of the regional agglomeration that produces and uses it. In the second, the evolutionary pathway is paradoxical in that the core region uses its noncosmopolitan activity system to invent cosmopolitan processes and products, which are then diffused economically and geographically. The capacity to keep carrying out this inventing remains in the region, reinforcing its role as the "brains" of the sector. But diffusion of what it produces makes growth in the industry possible in other regions. Some of these possibilities are shown in Figure 3.3. At this time, we do not have the knowledge to predict particular pathways. That would involve knowledge of sectoral dynamics, regional dynamics, and technological dynamics in a way that is well beyond our current state of knowledge.

An Important Noncore Region

In the case of a region that contains an important productive base in an industry, or in a set of industries with complementary or similar technologies, but does not qualify as a core agglomeration, we observed that it is possible for the region to contribute to the technological evolution of the industry, but by no means sure. The typical case here would be a region that might once have

	Knowledge	
Organization	Noncosmopolitan	Cosmopolitan
Externalization	1 Relations–norms–specific knowledge . . . conventions	3 Markets
Internalization	2 Firm-dedicated cognitively specific knowledge	4 Firm-dedicated cognitively generic assets

Pathways:

3 → 4: The standard view of transactions–cost economics
1 → 4: From idiocyncratic to mass production
2 → 3: Rapid end of learning, growth in knowledge diffusion, eroding barriers
2 → 4: From technology-based oligopolies to classical oligopolies
1 → 3: From external network to markets (despecialization of product and knowledge inputs)

FIGURE 3.3. Possible evolutionary trajectories.

been a core agglomeration, but where the industry's technology has evolved in a cosmopolitan direction, much as described above. The technological frontier, in other words, is already cosmopolitan and this region's economy is a direct result of that cosmopolitan, reproducible character. The region contains important productive resources, but they must now compete with firms in other regions, using technologies that can easily be imitated. A good example of this is the part of the automobile industry in the Detroit region; a contemporary example is aerospace, which is now selectively decentralizing away from its core regions of Southern California and Puget Sound. Technological competition thus comes to concern standard price–cost efficiencies or movements along a price–quality curve.

It is probable that the major establishments in these regions have significant intraregional interactions with suppliers. If these major establishments are strongly controlled by central offices of their firms, they will have to enforce technical protocols on their suppliers and will take little local technological initiative. As noted, however, it is more than ever the trend today for large multiestablishment firms to devolve responsibility to divisions and establishments. In this case, where this permits local experimentation, then adjustments of technique according to local conditions and capacities could indeed result in new, locally superior techniques. This could come about simply as a result of local responsibility for cost management, where adjustments in factor mix along an isoquant could occur. Over time, however, a pathway of local technique adjustments could qualify as a true shift in technology in some sectors. These forms of learning-by-doing for incremental change could, in some cases, recreate noncosmopolitan sources of localized (in both the economic and geographical senses) technological advantage, if they involve techniques or products with great superiority over what exists elsewhere. In a sense, then, further "maturation" of an already mature, cosmopolitan technology can lead to selective "dematurity" under the right circumstances. One can probably also situate many examples of continuing competitive success through learning in mature industries in Germany. This kind of evolutionary dynamic—working within a fundamentally cosmopolitan and hence interregionally competitive environment to produce local advantage—is particularly delicate and requires much effort to sustain. But it may be one of the principal ways that appropriate local policy to promote coordination of actors within the industrial system has a real possibility of affecting the competitive and market structure of the industry and genuinely securing a future for the region in that industry. This is what much of the current debate about local industrial policy—networking, cooperation, coordination—is about, and which we analyze in detail in Chapter 10.

THE PURPOSES OF AN EVOLUTIONARY APPROACH

At the current state of the art, the evolutionary approach, whether dealing with technologies or, as in the present case, regions, is not capable of making predictions about such things as patterns and cycles of development.[32] If there is one cycle it might ultimately arrive at, it would concern the opening up and closing down of variety in the economy and the role of regions in this process. The region is one organizational level (among others) where processes of information spillover and development work to create technological and technical variety. The region is also a place where proximity facilitates the "contagion" of cognitive frameworks and knowledge, hence aiding region-specific imitation and evolution. It pushes toward region-specific selection among alternatives, hence the tendency to close down variety. At an interregional level, of course, competition between products and technologies also operates to open up and close down variety. There are, then, geographical contributions to this major evolutionary developmental dynamic of capitalism.

We are just now developing our conception of the microfoundations of endogenous technological and organizational change, through research on the nature of procedural rationality, the primitive routines of economic action. Much more needs to be done in this area, involving careful microstudies of untraded interdependencies—conventions and relations—and how they emerge and evolve. This would have to include understanding better how anticipations are formed and regularized, in a dialogue between economics and the cognitive sciences. These microstudies will have to be structured around the critical cognitive dimension of technology. Territorialization would be an integral element of this task.

From here, we would need to develop models of the emergence of economic patterns, but we do not yet know how to get from small processes of interaction and evolution to big regularities. In what has preceded, I have attempted to take a very preliminary step in the direction of stylizing some micropatterns, for noncore regions, core regions and big but noncore regions, seeking sources of possible evolution in them. This is a long way from rigorously attacking the relationship between micromodels and bigger regularities. Beyond that, we will still need to develop better conceptions of coevolution between technologies, organizations, and markets, which in this case would involve distinctive regional contributions to such broader dynamics.

The promise is great, however. Evolutionary approaches provide entry into important issues such as regional learning, different forms of regional economic adaptation, localized contributions to global dynamics, in both the economic and geographical senses, and geographical dimensions of the way that variety, in the form of technology and technique, is opened, closed, and reopened, in a never-ending process in modern capitalism. As a theoretical approach, the combination of the economics of evolution and the economics of conventions, appropriately territorialized, could someday have more utility to policy makers than any simple statistical patterning of development, for it provides a sense of possibilities opened up and foreclosed, strategic opening and closings, in real time and space.

NOTES

1. Krugman (1995).
2. Norton and Rees (1978).
3. Storper and Scott (1987).
4. Vernon (1966); Dollar (1986); Norton and Rees (1979).
5. Markusen (1985); Massey and Meegan (1982); Storper (1982); Bluestone and Harrison (1982).
6. Storper (1985).
7. Nelson and Winter (1982).
8. Marshall (1919); Sraffa (1960).
9. Kaldor (1972); Romer (1990).
10. There is much dispute about whether this movement tends toward suboptimal equilibrium within a multiple equilibria situation, or whether we should emphasize disequilibrium and change as did Young and Kaldor.
11. Arthur (1989, 1990).

12. David (1975).

13. Rosenberg (1982, 1972).

14. In the standard neoclassical model, a convex supply curve is key to unique efficient outcomes.

15. Arthur (1989).

16. Lundvall (1988, 1990, 1993); Andersen (1992).

17. Antonelli (1995).

18. This model was developed by Bouba-Olga (1993). For corroborating empirical studies, see Audretsch and Vivarelli (1994), and Antonelli (1987).

19. Rallet (1993).

20. Antonelli (1995).

21. Storper and Scott (1987); Krugman (1992, 1995).

22. Bass (1993, 1995).

23. Lundvall and Johnson (1992); Pavitt, and Patel (1991); Dosi et al. (1990).

24. Dimaggio (1986, 1991); Nicolas (1996); Zucker (1987, 1988). See also, in a different vein, Thevenot (1986); Spender (1989); Levinthal and March (1993); Callon (1986); Orlean (1994); Llerena (1993). For the economics behind this notion, see Hodgson (1988).

25. Berger and Luckmann (1966).

26. Bass (1993). I thank Steve for these ideas, but he should not be held responsible for my use or exposition of them here.

27. Scott (1988a).

28. Krugman (1991b).

29. Scott and Storper (1987).

30. For a formal treatment of this, see Pace (1995). The analysis echoes recent growth theories that center on the role of increasing specialization in the economy as a whole. See Romer (1987), and for the antecedent, Stigler (1951).

31. Haas-Lorenz (1994); Asanuma (1989).

32. This is a task that might be taken on later, when the paradigm has more fully developed its microfoundations and generated more empirical work. See Langlois (1993); Hodgson (1993).

CHAPTER 4

Crossing Industrial Divides in a Region

A REGION-SPECIFIC EVOLUTIONARY PROCESS

The case of a core agglomeration in a major industry—the film and television industry of Hollywood, the world capital of filmed entertainment—illustrates many of the processes to which we have alluded in previous chapters. These include: the persistence of agglomeration in spite of few cost-based transactional reasons for remaining in a region; the evolution of new organizational techniques as an unplanned response to external shocks, largely via intraregional imitation among firms; the emergent superiority of the new technique as increasing returns in the form of external economies drive the agglomeration down the new pathway of development; the way a big change comes about as a series of small events; the underpinning of the whole by region-specific conventions and practices that persist and reinforce their role as relational assets throughout.

THE RISE AND FALL OF MASS-PRODUCTION METHODS IN HOLLYWOOD

From Craft to mass production: The Golden Age of Hollywood

The history of the film industry is similar to that of many other industries as they developed in the United States after the turn of the century. It began as a craft but, with the creation of a a large, assured market, the product was standardized and the production process rationalized.

The film industry that developed in New York shortly after the turn of the century closely replicated the craft production techniques of the theater. Production was carried out by small crews in firms such as Lumière, where artisans worked together to produce an unstandardized product. Despite artisanal production techniques, however, pressure was applied on the industry to adopt mass-production methods by the then-existing entertainment industry—nickelodeons and vaudeville—who provided the speculative capital to produce films. They intended to develop the mass market of new immigrants who populated American cities. Movies were to be an entertainment product rather than strictly an art form.

By the time film making was established in California in the 1920s, it had become industrialized. While we now classify it as a "service" industry, one of the earliest studios was named the Universal Film *Manufacturing* Company. Its artificially lighted stage was dedicated by the mass-production capitalist of the age, Henry Ford. Within a year of its establishment in 1918, this one plant had produced 250 films, a figure equal to the annual feature film production of the entire American film industry today. The other early studios in California, such as D.W. Griffiths' Fine Arts Studio, were established as full-service film production facilities intended to produce a standardized film product. Films were sold by the foot rather than on the basis of content.[1]

Two other figures involved in building the film industry, Thomas Ince and Adolph Zukor, were also responsible for rationalizing its production process. Zukor, founder of Paramount Pictures, integrated production and distribution through the use of contracted exhibitors nationwide. From his office in Times Square in New York City, Zukor contracted with 6,000 theaters nationwide to provide three to four films per week. The U.S. public supported Zukor's marketing network by going to the movies three to four times weekly. Weekly attendance in the United States eventually reached 90 million. The downtown theaters typical of that period had seating capacities of 2,000, compared to today's average of 300–500 for a major theater and less than 100 for a minitheater.

Paralleling Zukor's innovations in corporate structure were the production innovations of Thomas Ince. With an assured and stable theatrical market, the entire range of filmmaking activities could be integrated within one large factory, the studio. Ince set up the studio to fabricate and assemble batches of a semistandardized product, the "formula" picture. Ince developed a management-oriented model that strictly separated conception from execution. The vehicle for this process was the "continuity script," which fragmented the story of a motion picture and reordered it so that each bloc of scenes in a set or location could be filmed at the same time or, alternatively so that a set of actors could film all the scenes in which they were to be involved in a continuous work session. The continuity script also impeded costly improvisation by giving the producer virtually complete control over film content. Scripts could be ordered from writers according to a desired formula, for a desired length, and producers could ensure that directors would be faithful to them. This production management process was honed in "Inceville" as it was known, under a schedule of two productions per week.

The production process established in this period consisted of: preproduction (selection and preparation of the script and shooting location); production (construction of sets, filming); and postproduction (film processing, editing, sound track). Each of the three labor processes was organized according to mass-production principles. For example, the major studios had permanent staffs of writers and production planners who were assigned to produce formula scripts in volume and push them through the production system. Production crews and stars were assembled in teams charged with making as many as thirty films per year. Studios had large departments to make sets, operate sound stages and film labs, and carry out marketing and distribution. A product would move from department to department in assembly line fashion. The studios endeavored to maximize capacity utilization and stabilize throughput. As a result, the internal organization, or technical division of labor, in each phase of the process became increasingly similar to that of true mass production. This factory-like organization and oligopolistic–corporate structure, popularly known as the "studio system," was well-established throughout Hollywood by the mid-1920s, and it prevailed until the late 1940s.

This period is viewed by many as the Golden Age of the industry because of the volume of production permitted by the establishment of something resembling a regional mass collective workforce in Hollywood. Workers had the expectation of stable work over a fairly long period of time. Apprenticeships within the patriarchal world of the studios represented admission to a restricted internal labor market. Entry barriers to someone not already "in the industry" were enormous.[2]

The studio system was a concentrated oligopoly: a small number of producers was responsible for the majority of the industry's output and they simultaneously controlled distribution and exhibition. In 1944, for example, the five major studios earned 73% of domestic cinema rentals and owned or had interests in 4424 theaters—24% of the U.S. total. The latter statistic, while impressive, understates the extent of the major studios' vertical interests, since their cinemas included 70% of the first-run cinemas in the 92 cities with populations greater than 100,000 and these same cinemas accounted for more than 50% of all U.S. box-office receipts. The extent of market concentration at smaller geographical scales is even more impressive: for example, RKO owned 100% of first-run capacity in Minneapolis and Cincinnati, and Warner Brothers owned 90% in Philadelphia. In 46% of U.S. markets, one distributor owned *all* cinemas.[3] It was the destruction of these assured market outlets that spelled the end of the studio system.

The studio system, moreover, functioned via a strong set of regional conventions, interpersonal relations, and processes of imitation, all within a fiercely competitive environment. Long before the advent of a strong union movement in Hollywood, the conventions that governed the interactions between studios and workers in the external labor market were widely remarked upon in the industry press, and intrastudio practices were likewise well known (if not widely admired). The business culture of Hollywood was distinctive from before the 1920s.

The Crisis of the Studio System

The studio sysem reached its zenith around World War II. The number of films released peaked in 1942 (Table 4.1). Direct studio employment in Los Angeles, by this time the center of the U.S. film industry, reached its high point in 1944, at 33,000. Attendance in U.S. cinemas peaked in 1946, with over 90 million admissions per week.

In the late 1940s and early 1950s, the absolute size of the market for films began to shrink and the remaining market was much less stable. There were two main shocks to the studio system. The first, antitrust action by the U.S. Supreme Court made the industry's market less certain. The "Paramount Decision" (*U.S. v. Paramount Pictures*, 334 US 131, 1948) forced the studios to divest their cinema chains. Since the assured market once enjoyed by the studios was now gone, average returns per picture declined and returns per film began to fluctuate wildly. The second shock to the studio system, the advent of television, altered the industry's market structure and overall growth prospects. Television's success was closely tied to demographic changes, such as the high rate of postwar family formation, and spatially to the process of suburbanization. With the diffusion of television ownership, what had been essentially a unified market for filmed entertainment, dominated by one medium, became a segmented market in which different products competed for the consumer's entertainment expenditures. The feature-film audience declined by 50% between 1946 and 1956. Box office receipts as a whole declined by almost 40% in real terms between 1945 and 1955 and in 1960 was only 39% of its real level at the end of the war (Table 4.2). The result, in combination with the Paramount decision, was that the gross revenues of the ten leading companies in the industry fell by 26% in this same period, from $968 million to $717 million. Profits of the leading eight studios declined by more than 50% in real terms (Table 4.3).

Early Flexibility Strategies: Vertical Disintegration and Product Innovation

The studios responded to the crisis with two strategies designed to increase their flexibility. They initially reduced the number of films produced; later, as we shall see, they turned to vertical disintegration as a way to cut overheads and increase the quantitative and qualitative flexibility of output. The number of U.S.-produced feature films declined by 28% in the 10 years after 1946 (Table 4.1). The average number of films made per year in the United States

TABLE 4.1. Films produced and reissued in the United States, 1930–1977

Year	New	Reissued	Total
1930	—	—	355
1935	388	3	391
1940	472	3	475
1941	497	7	504
1942	484	8	492
1943	426	6	432
1944	409	6	415
1945	367	8	375
1946	383	17	400
1947	371	55	426
1948	398	50	448
1949	406	85	491
1940–1949 Average	421	25	446
1950	425	48	473
1951	411	28	439
1952	353	33	386
1953	378	36	414
1954	294	75	369
1955	281	38	319
1956	311	35	346
1957	363	19	382
1958	327	25	352
1959	236	18	254
1950–1959 Average	338	36	374
1960	233	15	248
1961	225	15	240
1962	213	24	237
1963	203	20	223
1964	227	15	242
1965	257	22	279
1966	231	26	257
1967	229	35	264
1968	241	17	258
1969	241	10	251
1960–1969 Average	230	20	250
1970	267	39	306
1971	281	32	313
1972	279	39	318
1973	237	38	275
1974	229	45	274
1975	190	40	230
1976	187	30	217
1977	154	32	186
1970–1977 Average	228	37	265

Source: Motion Picture Association of America.

TABLE 4.2. U.S. box office receipts ($ million)

Year	Nominal $	1967 $
1945	1,450.0	2,690.0
1950	1,376.0	1,908.0
1955	1,326.0	1,653.0
1960	951.0	1,072.0
1965	927.0	980.9
1970	1,162.0	999.1
1975	2,115.0	1,312.0
1980	2,899.0	1,174.6
1982	3,450.0	1,193.0

Source: *International Motion Picture Almanac* (1983).

during the 1950s was only 80% of the 1940s level, and by the end of the 1950s stood at less than half the number produced in the peak production year of 1941 (Table 4.1).

The industry also began to increase qualitative flexibility to compensate for output reductions, by undertaking to differentiate their products through constant innovation. Initiallly, the most standardized categories of film making, short subjects and newsreels, were completely eliminated from the major studios' product range. In turn, studios drew people back into the cinemas with an innovative type of film known as the "spectacular," which recast the feature as a form of entertainment significantly different from television. Technical innovations were aimed at the "look" of the film in an effort to make the image in motion pictures superior to that of television. Cinerama, Technicolor, and 3D—all innovations of the 1950s—were aimed at constituting the film as an event rather than an everyday experience. The increased at-

TABLE 4.3. Profits in the U.S. film industry ($ million)

Year	Eight major studios[a]		Whole industry/posttax[b]	
	Nominal $	1967 $	Nominal $	1967 $
1945	57.2	106.1	99.0	183.6
1950	38.0	52.7	60.0	83.2
1955	37.4	46.6	61.0	76.0
1960	32.0	36.	1.0	1.1
1965	72.5	76.7	39.0	41.2
1970	−57.2	−49.8	8.0	6.8
1975	262.0	162.5	131.0	81.2

[a]Source: *The Economist,* as quoted in *Film Facts* (1980, pp. 85–87), Motion Picture Association of America.
[b]Source: U.S. Department of Commerce, Bureau of Economic Analysis, *Census of Service Industries* (1977).

tention to the individual film meant increased budgets for talent, marketing, and advertising. As Table 4.4 indicates, individual production budgets rose rapidly along with the decline in volume of total production in the immediate postwar period. The average cost per picture made by Metro Goldwyn/Mayer rose from $1.3 million in 1952–1953 to $1.8 million in 1954–1955. For Paramount the comparable figures are $1.7 million and $2.5 million.

This strategy of product differentiation increased the need for specialized inputs. The studios began to turn to independent producers to develop these differentiated film products. In the early 1950s, they established a putting-out system for preproduction work, in an effort to encourage innovative ideas. Warner Brothers made their first major advances to outside producers in 1951 to the tune of $6.4 million, and increased them rapidly to $25 million by 1956. As the decade progressed, additional aspects of the production process were split off from the studios' operations and moved to the external market. Eventually, this meant the end of the "term contract" under which writers, actors, and skilled production technicians worked exclusively for one studio full-time for a guaranteed period. This strategy of reducing labor overheads necessitated changes in employment contracts. In the late 1950s, writers, actors, producers, and directors were all put under project contracts, usually for just one film. The heavily unionized skilled craftworkers, on the other hand, were placed on seniority rosters, effectively shifting the old internal labor markets of the studios to an external, collectivized system. The unions came to serve as hiring halls.[4]

We have here a case of intraregional imitation: the strategy of externalization originated in a few studios, but was copied by the rest. Moreover, each

TABLE 4.4. U.S. production expenditures and production costs

	Total industry production expenditures[a]		Average production cost per feature[b]	
	$	1967 $	$	1967 $
1941	NA	NA	400,000	950,000
1949	2,881,600,000	4,035,854,300	1,000,000	1,400,000
1955	2,738,700,000	3,414,837,900	NA	
1960	2,966,000,000	3,343,855,000	NA	
1965	2,917,000,000	3,086,772,400	NA	
1972	NA	NA	1,890,000	1,508,370
1974	NA	NA	2,500,000	1,550,868
1978	NA	NA	5,000,000	2,558,850
1980	NA	NA	8,500,000	3,444,084
1982	2,500,000,000[c]	NA	11,300,000	3,908,682

[a]*Source:* Standard and Poor's *Industry Survey* (1961, p. A62; 1966, p. A72).
[b]*Source: International Motion Picture Almanac* (1983).
[c]*Daily Variety.*

round of overhead reduction in the face of a stagnant, less stable and more segmented market created unanticipated new pressures for further disintegration, which the studios could not control. For example, the studio system had functioned as a star creation machine, placing individuals under long-term contracts at favorable prices and then making them into very valuable commodities: stars. Under the "star system," as it was known, if an individual achieved star status, the studio reaped the benefits of having him/her under a long-term contract whose terms had been established prior to stardom. The studios thus obtained a monopoly over the actor's specific human capital by controlling access to training at the port of entry to the labor market for stars. Since the maturation of stardom necessitated long-term investments in specific human capital, the star system encouraged vertical integration.

With the end of long production runs came the end of long-term contracts. It not only became more difficult to control product markets long enough to produce stars, but in the short run stars became another form of the overheads the studios were attempting to shed. Thus, the need for asset specificity was overshadowed by scale, overheads, and other flexibility considerations in the studios' decision making. Successful stars, however, were no longer bound to long-term contracts and could now demand much higher salaries or very lucrative profit-sharing arrangements in return for appearing in a film. In exercising their newly found market power, stars shifted distribution of the rents to specific assets in their favor. According to industry sources, a significant proportion of the dramatic increase in production budgets in recent years is for steep increases in stars' salaries.[5] These increases have placed even greater pressure for cost reduction on other parts of the film budget which, in turn, encourages further vertical disintegration. Thus, the beginnings of vertical disintegration, intended to cut costs and achieve product differentiation and innovation, had, in turn, unforeseen consequences that promoted further vertical disintegration. The studios could not control the process they had started.

There is reason to believe, however, that the process was not entirely mechanical. It seems plausible that the big studio moguls could have chosen to arrest the process, had they attempted to develop another "model" for restructuring. What is most interesting is that they did not do so, but seemed instead to follow the emerging model of disintegration and externalization that increasingly surrounded them. Moreover, during the same period, the British and French film industries took different organizational pathways from each other and from their American counterpart,[6] suggesting that in each regional center of film production, firms copied from each other locally and dealt with their strategic problems via analogies derived from their counterpart firms and the information that circulated in their regional environments. As each of these regional restructuring processes moved forward, it became increasingly really rational in economic terms, due to the growth of its regionally specific external economies.

The 1960s: Failed Attempts at Building Stable Markets

The 1960s opened with the studios' attempt to restabilize markets at a tolerable minimum size by increasing distribution of American pictures abroad through international integration of exhibition. The market for privatized entertainment products such as television had developed much more slowly in Europe than in the United States during the 1950s, and so the market for cinema films continued to grow there. The major studios bought cinema chains in Europe and even in Africa, attempting to replace the loss of their domestic market. Foreign markets accounted for 50% of total revenues at this time, primarily through presales (Figure 4.1).

The most important strategy adopted by the major studios during this

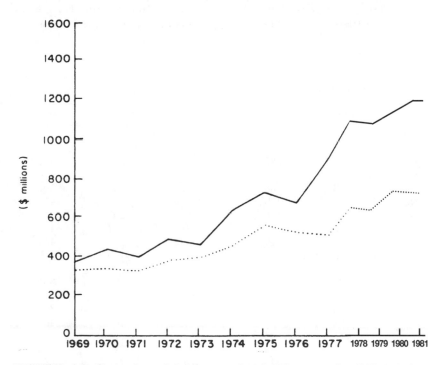

FIGURE 4.1. Domestic and foreign rentals of U.S. companies (Allied Artists, Columbia, Paramount, Twentieth Century Fox, United Artists, Universal, and Warner Brothers. ———— Domestic rentals; · · · · · foreign rentals. *Source:* Wertheimer Associates.

transition period was to attempt to dominate television markets. In 1965, television networks spent $115 million to commission made-for-television (MFT) films. The average budget per MFT increased from $169,000 in 1961 to $290,000 in 1966 because of the depletion of film libraries. The studios hoped that capturing the market for MFTs, combined with their growing European cinema market, would enlarge and restabilize their markets. The television networks, however (as oligopsonistic consumers of MFTs) began to contract with smaller studios (so-called "minimajors") in order to force the major studios into competitive bidding over the price of MFTs. Because the studios owned large physical plants ("back lots" and large sound stages), and because they were almost completely unionized, they were essentially forced out of these more cost-sensitive segments of the market, low-budget cinema films and MFTs, which were then taken over by the same independent production companies whose existence in the first place had been set into motion by subcontracting from the major studios. This blow was aggravated by the fact that European producers' presence in American markets grew dramatically in the early 1960s (Table 4.5). Thus, even though new sources of market growth arose in the 1960s, they could not be captured or controlled by the major studios.

TABLE 4.5. Film releases in the United States, 1943–1978

Year	Imported	Total	Year	Imported	Total
1943	30	427	1960	233	387
1944	41	442	1961	331	462
1945	27	377	1962	280	427
1946	89	467	1963	299	420
1947	118	486	1964	361	502
1948	93	459	1965	299	452
1949	123	470	1966	295	451
			1967	284	462
1950	239	622	1968	274	454
1951	263	654	1969	180	412
1952	139	463			
1953	190	534	1970	181	367
1954	174	427	1971	199	432
1955	138	392	1972	147	376
1956	207	479	1973	168	463
1957	233	533	1974	270	550
1958	266	507	1975	242	604
1959	252	439	1976	222	575
			1977	249	560
			1978	137	354

Source: Film Facts (1980), Motion Picture Association of America.

The failure to reassert mass markets was reflected in a return of the industry's profitability crisis in 1970, when the eight major studios all suffered large losses, and almost no profits were made in the industry as a whole (Table 4.3). The studios still held large quantities of property (in sound stages, back lots, and film libraries). With low profits but large assets, their stocks were undervalued and they became vulnerable to takeovers. Some studios, such as Paramount, responded by allowing friendly takeovers to occur, in their case by becoming a division of the conglomerate Gulf and Western. Most of the studios, however, began to trim their facilities and reduce overheads again. They redefined their production facilities as "profit centers," requiring them to support themselves through rentals to independent producers making films with studio financing. In a number of cases, the studios simply sold their back lots. Twentieth Century-Fox, for example, sold the land that is now Century City on Los Angeles' Westside, a large office, commercial, and residential development. Once again, this shifting from vertical integration to a market-led strategy—what we will term a shift from the Industrial World framework of action to the Market World framework of action in the following chapter—was region-specific: it did not occur in the British and French film industries at the same time, though they were under the same sorts of external pressures.[7]

Increased filming on location also promoted the reduction in physical scale of the major studios. Location shooting, contrary to the popular impression, was not a cause, but a consequence of vertical disintegration: it was a cost-cutting strategy for the studios during their period of crisis. There were endogenous technological innovations that facilitated it, such as the panaflex camera (hand-held, very quiet) and the Cinemobile (a mobile studio). Location shooting also permitted producers to avoid union work rules in Los Angeles and New York, which dramatically limit the length of the working day, causing extra days of shooting. By the 1970s, as a result, most of the studios had in effect ended their roles as physical movie factories. Even though disintegration had begun with the limited objectives of cost-cutting and product differentiation, in the end specialized firms and nonstudio locations came to benefit from external economies, not only for low-budget and MFTs, but for high-budget theatrical films as well. The studios could no longer compete against the independent production companies and specialized contractors they had helped to create, in the very market segments they had hoped to retain.

The New Structure of the Film Industry

After their initial experiment in contracting out writing in the 1950s, the studios developed a system of working jointly with independent production companies, also in order to encourage new ideas. Production costs per pic-

TABLE 4.6. Number and percentage of productions by organization type, selected years, 1960–1980

Year	1960	1965	1970	1975	1980
Independent	42 (28%)	40 (21%)	93 (44%)	138 (56%)	129 (58%)
Major	100 (66%)	130 (68%)	96 (46%)	81 (33%)	69 (31%)
Minimajor	9 (6%)	20 (11%)	18 (9%)	24 (10%)	24 (11%)
Totals	151	190	209	244	223

Source: Film Facts (1980), Motion Picture Association of America.

ture were already rising rapidly in the 1960s, so the studios also used the new system to share investment risks with the independents. In the event of success, profits are divided; but in the case of failure, the studio's investment exposure is minimized because the independent production company usually raises a substantial proportion of the initial investment using the major studio's capital as seed money. Table 4.6 reports the changes in the types of organizations carrying out film production between 1960 and 1980.[8] The trend toward production by independent companies and away from the studios is clear. In 1960, 28% of US films had independent participation, whereas 66% were made by the majors. By 1980, the earlier proportions were almost reversed.

The increase in independents, however, was only a small part of the organizational revolution in the industry. The external supply of various kinds of intermediate inputs grew steadily and diversified. Both the studios and the independent production companies turned to specialized, independent supplier firms and subcontractors to carry out thewhole range of preproduction functions. We examined the births and deaths of selected filmmaking services and facilities in Southern California, which all increased in absolute terms during the period (Tables 4.7 and 4.8). Given that film output was stable for the index years, the magnitude of these increases provides convincing evi-

TABLE 4.7. Number of Los Angeles area establishments: Production firms

	1966	1974	1982
Production companies	563	709	1473
Rental stages	13	24	76
Properties	66	33	184
Editing	4	31	113
Lighting	2	16	23

Source: Storper and Christopherson (1985).

TABLE 4.8. Number of Los Angeles area establishments:
Postproduction

	1966	1974	1982
Recording/sound	20	33	187
Film processing	43	76	55
Film effects	10	27	42

Source: Storper and Christopherson (1985).

dence of a trend toward vertical disintegration. The major increases occurred in the second half of the 1970s.

These statistics on proliferation of intermediate input providers are confirmed in Table 4.9, which shows the increases in total number of establishments in the industry. Significantly, SIC 7819 (services allied to motion picture production), which covers these new intermediate input providers, was only created as a separate reporting category in the mid-1970s in response to the increasing role of these firms. Moreover, this deepening of the interfirm division of labor was accompanied by increasing specialization of the firms: a film lab, for example, will no longer do all kinds of film processing, but will in turn have a greater variety of techniques it can apply within its specialized domain, and it constantly interacts with production companies and equipment makers to develop new ways of processing film. In other words, the predicted interactions of externalization, narrowing scope, and external economies are in evidence. And, it seems that region-specific, proximity-dependent processes of technique and technology development are occurring.

This changing division of labor, with narrowing scope due to specialization by intermediate input providers, should be reflected in declining firm size in an industry such as this, where total output is not growing. Table 4.10 shows that this was the case for this segment of the industry, that is, in SIC 7819. The steady decline in firm size contrasts with the cyclical fluctuations observable in other parts of the industry. Table 4.11 confirms this decline by

TABLE 4.9. U.S. establishments

	1968	1974	1981
SIC 7813: Motion pictures excluding TV	666	1,279	1,023
SIC 7814: Motion pictures and tape production for TV	490	978	1,420
SIC 7819: Services allied to motion picture production	NA	716	1,077
Total	1,156	2,973	3,520

Source: U.S. Department of Commerce, *County Business Patterns.*

TABLE 4.10. Employees per establishment

	1969	1974	Change[a] 1958–1974	1991	Change[a] 1974–1981
SIC 7813					
CA	38.98	15.89	40.76	45.42	285.94
NY	13.12	7.12	54.26	8.78	123.31
FL	16.08	4.75	29.53	7.78	163.78
TX	14.42	11.58	80.3	14.72	127.11
US	23.21	11.19	48.2	25.04	223.77
SIC 7814					
CA	26.25	36.28	138.20	31.48	86.7
NY	23.15	11.18	48.29	21.72	194.2
FL	13.33	NA	NA	12.08	NA
TX	18.3	NA	NA	NA	NA
US	21.2	20.82	98.2	24.10	115.75
SIC 7819					
CA	NA	34.02	NA	22.7	66.9
NY	NA	13.34	NA	10.8	81.3
FL	NA	14.7	NA	6.6	45.1
TX	NA	10.07	NA	15.60	154.9
US	NA	21.33	NA	16.87	79.09

Source: County Business Patterns.
[a]First year = 100.

showing that it is also manifested in a decrease in revenues per establishment over a 20-year period.

The Recomposition of the Film Industry into an Entertainment Industrial Complex

The process of crossing an industrial divide from mass production to specialized production does not end with vertical disintegration of the studios. Both the major studios and the specialized production firms have spread the risk that comes from unstable markets and highly differentiated products by diversifying into related markets. The studios, for example, form financial alliances with firms in other areas of entertainment provision, playing the role of institutional investor. They also finance multiple production packages and advance capital for distribution in return for some control over different marketing areas. The entertainment industries, including television, music, and video as well as films, are witnessing a wave of horizontal integration as new entertainment products are created, enjoying overlapping production processes and markets. A film, for example, has a profitable "after-life" in outlets other than cinemas, including television, videocassettes, sound tracks, and related

TABLE 4.11. Receipts per establishment

Year	Nominal $	1967 $
1963	533,869	582,190
1967	642,792	642,792
1972	607,313	484,687
1977	971,033	535,004
1982	1,279,827	442,693

Sources U.S. Department of Commerce, *Census of Service Industries Deflator;* U.S. Bureau of Labor Statistics, *Consumer Price Index.*

promotional devices. This is reflected very powerfully in the changing revenue mix for theatrical films (Table 4.12). Input-supplying firms respond to narrower scope by specializing in certain generic functions (props and scenery, film editing, sound mixing) but working on a broad variety of final outputs, which increases their scale, and constantly innovating, which maintains specialization and sometimes generates quasirents. Their success is very strongly dependent on their specific relations to other firms—for information that permits them to innovate—and via reputation effects and personal relations, which are the main vehicles of interfirm contacts. The principles of coordination of this sort of industrial complex—interpersonal relational networks and conventional reputations—in other words, are radically different from those of the big mass-production firm.

This recomposition and new type of order in the entertainment industrial complex appears to be more directly dependent on geographical proximity than even its forebear, which was already highly concentrated in Hollywood. This is suggested by the dramatic shift of the television industry from New York to Los Angeles in the period under examination. With the exception of network news, the vast majority of television production shifted to the West Coast in the 1970s.[9]

TABLE 4.12. Revenue mix for cinematic films, selected years, 1978–1984

	1978 (%)	1980 (%)	1983 (%)	1984 (%)
Rentals	80	74	48	54
Pay TV	2	5	12	12
Cassettes	NM	1	15	22
Networks and syndication	14	14	19	8
Other	4	6	6	4
Total	100	100	100	100

Source: Wertheimer Associates; Metro Goldwyn/Mayer.

Recent Developments

From the late 1980s to the mid-1990s, the organizational routines of the Hollywood entertainment industrial complex continued to evolve. The production model described above—consisting of a switch from integration to disintegration, from product differentiation to product variety through continuous learning—remains dominant. But the roles of studios and distributors have undergone further changes. The studios have become something like financial management houses—evaluating markets and providing capital to projects for individuals with promise and, in turn, committing the considerable capital needed for major distribution. For known artists, an intermediate level of stability is now offered: the multiyear "deal." Sometimes this takes on the telling physical form of the location of the independent producers' offices on the lot of a major studio while the multiyear contract is in effect (sometimes in an outbuilding or even a trailer!). Some measure of vertical control is effected in the industry via this access to capital for production and distribution.

At the same time, there has developed an enormous marketplace for venture and independent capital, which producers use as a way to leverage their positions with respect to the studios and even to compete with them if they are able to finance their productions in their entirety and separately negotiate their distribution contracts. There is also now a well-developed circuit of independent film market fairs and separate financial institutions for financing independent, highly risky films. In this way, there is considerable weight for the big firms, but by no means a standard oligopolistic equilibrium.

The studios are more than ever integrated into multinational conglomerates, without this involving them in production planning in the standard way. They are oligopolistic financial entrepreneurs in a sector that is organized via extremely complex and highly externalized networks based in convention and reputation. It is perhaps a unique form of big firm capitalism.

EXTERNAL ECONOMIES AND INDUSTRIAL DIVIDES

The history recounted above is puzzling in certain respects. Why did the studios not simply shed risk in the face of greater uncertainty or instability, and then arrest the process of vertical disintegration at that point by limiting the role of production subcontractors and independent producers? In other words, we have no explanation of why the breakdown of the mass-production system did not simply lead to industrial dualism rather than the networked system that came about. In what follows we try to explain this turn of events in evolutionary terms, exploring the notions of external economies and increasing returns to an organizational pathway in greater depth than was possible in the previous chapter, and combining evolutionary reasoning with the theory of the firm, or organization, which was introduced in Chapter 2 as one of the elements of our holy trinity.

The Division of Labor and the Firm

Ronald Coase's theory of the firm views the latter as a system of governance that serves as an alternative to the market when markets fail.[10] At the core of Coase's reasoning is the concept of organizational *scope:* internal economies of scope exist when the various tasks in a process, even when extensively fragmented into an elaborate technical division of labor, lend themselves to vertical integration under one roof. When such internal economies of scope are minor or negative, however, the different labor processes may be separated out into independent organizations linked by transactions on the market rather than inside the firm. The types of transactions that tend to be externalized are those subject to market failure[11]: when a given firm requires firm-specific assets, or when information is not equally shared between two firms, then one firm will tend to cheat on the other (a "moral hazard"). There are many other reasons for integration and disintegration as well, which extend this framework. Such insights allow us to see why real production systems are likely to be governed by a complex amalgam of organizational forms, running from the pure cases of firms and markets to a variety of intermediate forms such as contracts and strategic alliances.

In the case of the film and television industry of Hollywood, there was a clear decrease in asset specificity on the part of many input-providing firms. The origin of this phenomenon was in the demand of the studios themselves for product differentiation. Later, it became an endogenous product of the input-providing firms themselves, who began to develop their own internal flexibility so as to increase internal scale economies and diversify to spread risks. With disintegration, however, firm-specific assets were replaced by industry-specific assets in the form of new kinds of flexibly specialized human and physical capital and firm knowledge with a wide scope of applications.

The Pathway Chosen as a Consequence of Increasing Returns in the Network Model

We must comprehend some of the dynamic properties of the division of labor in production if we want to explain how an industry crosses a divide between such radically different models of production as occurred in Hollywood. We may begin with Adam Smith's notion that increases in the extent of the market afford opportunities to deepen the technical division of labor: the different tasks within the production process can be fragmented out into specialized activities. This conception of specialization as exclusively tied up with the development of the technical division of labor is too narrow, however, for a growing market is just as likely to trigger the deepening of the *social* division of labor. The development of both the technical and social divisions of labor is what Young (1928) referred to as the increasing "roundaboutness" of production.

Recently, it has been shown that this is a source of increasing returns in the development process.[12] Roundaboutness means that with increases in the total volume of production, the specialization of activities and firms and thus their internal efficiency can increase, while simultaneously reducing the costs of transactions between them. The existence and nature of increasing returns such as these is highly contested.[13] We cannot do justice to all the related issues here, so we will restrict our discussion to two issues: whether increasing returns really exist; and whether they take the form of external economies.

Much of the skepticism concerning increasing returns in general is an artifact of the theoretical distinction frequently made between changes in production techniques and increasing returns "without" changes in technique. Increasing returns are then said to attach only to an existing production function, while any other changes in returns are due to changes in technique. In other words, the analysis by definition becomes a static one, and increasing returns disappear by virtue of the decision to consider them exogenous. On the other hand, if an analysis of returns over time is undertaken and increasing returns do happen to appear empirically, they can be formally identified with the returns of particular firms by assuming that the technique changes that generate them are purely internal to firms; increasing roundaboutness is thus not a change in technique, it is simply ignored.

A more realistic view is that such increasing returns are rooted in the organizational dynamics of modern industry as a whole. Technical progress in the narrow sense of development of better machines and hardware generally depends on the development of the social and technical divisions of labor. Increasing returns of this sort cannot be said to be contained within machines, because both the latter develop in tandem historically. Allyn Young framed the issue this way:

> The mechanism of increasing returns is not to be discerned adequately by observing the effects of variation in the size of the individual firm or of a particular industry . . . what is required is that industrial operations be seen as an integrated whole.[14]

This is obvious in the pure Smithian case of a growing economy, where operations can be divided up into different tasks and then ultimately between different firms. In the first case, we normally think of increasing internal economies of scale. Yet even single operations on single machines within such a firm would not be able to realize their new efficiencies unless they were inserted within this technical division of labor: their efficiencies are a product of their interconnections with other phases of the process. These interconnections, what Marx labeled "cooperation," are external to the particular operations, above and beyond them, and they precede the particular operations in time. The same is basically true of the social, that is, interfirm, division of labor. The ability for any particular specialized corporation to realize internal economies is thus a historical outcome of the totality of its interconnections, intra- and intersectoral alike. In both cases, the distinction between internal and external is irrelevant.

The case for specifically external economies is more obvious when we consider an industry whose markets are not growing, as in the film industry in the postwar period. In the 1960s and 1970s, the studio system would have suffered lower returns than the new system, owing to what would have been a chronic condition of excess capacity or dramatically reduced production levels, while its opposite, an entirely artisanal production technique, would have had to forego returns to specialization. Each of the firms in the sector enjoys the benefits of the system that evolved, given the change in context.

The formation of a filmed-entertainment industrial complex, however, suggests even more clearly the existence of external economies of scale. In the face of stagnant and unstable markets, the process of competition in the film industry actually resulted in an interindustry recomposition of the division of labor, so as to increase the flexibility and throughput of the complex as a whole. The horizontal recombination of tasks of different final output sectors results in intersectoral scale economies of exactly the sort denied by much of the literature.[15]

The Endogenous Evolution of the Division of Labor and Geographical Agglomeration

It was argued in previous chapters that production systems, as nexuses of transactions, are organized by specific conventions and relations. The most obvious contemporary cases of this are the craft-based industrial districts in Italy (which we will analyze in detail in Chapter 6), where transactional relations are regulated by trust, reputation effects, and strong conventions of good behavior. As a result, the risks of opportunistic behavior, assumed by Coase and Williamson to be universal, are strongly reduced. In this sense, the conventions and relations of the community of actors make possible levels of vertical and horizontal disintegration that would not be possible in the presence of other sorts of action frameworks.

The same is true in the case of geographical concentration of an industrial system. We know that vertical disintegration tends to increase the transactions-intensiveness of production and tends to come from conditions that make contracting incomplete or infeasible. It therefore encourages geographical concentration, all other things being equal, as was discussed in the first two chapters. But once many different producers are concentrated in a region, bargaining alternatives are created for any given firm, and this would then tend to encourage even further vertical disintegration. The social division of labor is now both cause and effect of vertical disintegration: as a cause, it is an "input" into the kind of conventional or relational action framework that becomes possible in the locality, via the way it alters bargaining or relational alternatives through changes in the numbers of agents involved.

Branching Points and the Evolution of Technique

We may ask whether, under the changed institutional and technological circumstances of the 1950s, the flexible networked model of the film industry became more efficient than the hypothetical alternative, industrial dualism. We might imagine a point, probably somewhere in the early 1960s, when the studios could have found a level of production that would have supported the stable portion of demand and retained that production in-house, while contracting out the rest. The problem with this reasoning is that markets had already become strongly contested by that point, and one of the major means of contestation was product "design." Dualism lacks dynamic efficiency properties in contestable markets.

But it does not therefore follow that the precise pathway that is travelled is the first-best technique. As evolutionary economics suggests, given an initial technological–organizational "branching point," a variety of alternatives is possible, but the actual path taken is neither necessarily the best nor is it inevitable. It persists because of externally based increasing returns, both in pecuniary (price-capacity) terms, and through evolving conventions, relations, and action frameworks.

CONCLUSION

This case study of the Hollywood film and television industry evidences virtually all of the processes to which we have referred thus far in this book:

- How, in an early period, the Golden Age of Hollywood, an industry remains agglomerated even though in strictly input–output transactional terms its vertically integrated mode of operations would easily have permitted decentralization; such agglomeration was due to the common socialization of actors, their conventional and relational frameworks of action, in Hollywood.
- How this system breaks down, via a gradual change in technique, which evolves in an unplanned and unanticipated direction. The new technique—an organizationally decentralized network system—be-

comes solidified through a system of external economies that benefit all firms and simultaneously reinforces agglomeration.

• How firms in the region imitate each other via a common action framework and develop a new region-specific system.

• How, in the end, a major industrial divide, from something that resembles mass production to something that resembles "flexible specialization," comes about as a path-dependent process, this path-dependency being due as much to "hard" aspects of increasing returns (prices and quantities) as "soft" dimensions (conventions, relations, frameworks of action).

• How the cinema and television industries in Hollywood are organized to be highly adaptable learning systems, where the role of region-specific uncodified knowledge continues to play the essential role in their competitive advantage.

NOTES

1. Hampton (1970).
2. Christopherson and Storper (1986, 1989); Storper and Christopherson (1987).
3. Waterman (1982).
4. Christopherson and Storper (1989).
5. A recent argument to this effect has been made in Frank (1996).
6. Nicolas (1996).
7. Nicolas (1996).
8. Detailed information on sources and methodology for these data may be found in Storper (1989) and Storper and Christopherson (1985).
9. A detailed study of the geography of these industries may be found in Storper and Christopherson (1987).
10. Coase (1937).
11. Williamson (1985); Scott (1986).
12. Romer (1987).
13. Rowthorn (1975a,b); Thirlwall (1980); McCombie (1981); McCombie and de Ridder (1984); Douglas (1976).
14. Young (1928, p. 539).
15. Knight (1922) and Sraffa (1960) were among those who denied.

PART III

PRODUCTS, TECHNOLOGIES, AND TERRITORIES

CHAPTER 5

Innovation as Collective Action

CONVENTIONS, PRODUCTS, TECHNOLOGIES, AND TERRITORIES

TECHNOLOGICAL INNOVATION: FRAMING THE QUESTION AS THAT OF REFLEXIVE, COLLECTIVE ACTION

Learning and interaction are now widely accepted as central elements in the process of technological innovation: learning as that which allows agents to create dynamic advantages so that the force of imitation is outrun by the pace of innovation; interaction as the characteristic of complex systems, whether internal to firms or production units or between them and the environment, that articulates the economic phenomena of specialization and coordination. Learning, we now know, allows absolute advantage to be created in trade, such that exceptionally important economic benefits—notably, quasirents, employment intensity, and high wages —can be enjoyed by firms, production systems, regions, and nations that learn.[1] Interaction is a collective behavioral characteristic of such economic groupings, certain forms of which seem to create or appropriate asymmetric information better than others. Advantages seem often to be cumulative: they take lots of time to build up and quite some time to be given away or taken away.

This line of reasoning, now well established in the literature on innovation in evolutionary economics, largely rejects the traditional notion of "induced" innovation and focuses attention, whether implicitly or explicitly, on the supply side of economic life in general, and in particular on the institutions that deliver up resources crucial to learning and interaction.[2] Analysis is then needed to decipher the mysteries of innovative collective action: the forces that bind individuals into interactions that allow or stimulate them to create economically viable innovations. This is largely what a "system of innovation" is thought to be about.

Yet the "supply architecture"[3] for innovations is not likely to be the whole story. The extreme diversity of outputs of modern economies implies that different kinds of products will "demand" different kinds of innovation systems. Each economy requires a specific type of innovation system to stimulate the innovative behavior that is consistent with its actual or realistically desirable trade specializations and output compositions. Products (or product-based subsectors, the equivalent of five-digit SIC sectors)—not establishments, firms, commodity chains, branches of production, or territorial production complexes—are the basic units around which innovative action can be supplied.[4] Understanding and promoting innovation, it follows, requires that we understand both the demand and the supply sides.

A system of innovation refers to the interaction of demands, attached to products, and supplies, attached to these organizational structures of the economy, as dual sequential processes "out of equilibrium"[5] and involving reciprocal selection (a dynamic task beyond the scope of this chapter).[6] In place of such fashionable concepts as the "old" system of mass production or Fordism and a putative singular "new" system of innovation (whether it be "Toyotism," "networks," "flexibility," "coordinated capitalism," etc.), it is more appropriate to reason in terms of a diversity of possible (coherent, effective) innovative systems.

The demand architecture for systems of innovation defines a collective action problem for innovators, associated with each particular kind of product. By "collective action problem" is meant the rules and conventions that coordinate actors—give them a common and coherent action context—so that they can innovate in a particular kind of product area of the economy.

The first task in this analysis is therefore to build up an analytical picture of products as domains of collective and reflexive action. On the basis of this picture, we will draw out in greater detail the three main aspects of their collective action realms, those which comprise the holy trinity of regional development theory today: technologies, organizations, and territories. By going about the problem this way, we will be able to see how these multiple aspects of the productive economy are tied together, and how the ties that bind them into coherent wholes are largely conventional.

PRODUCTS, UNCERTAINTY, AND ACTION

We may identify four basic types of products, each associated with fundamentally different forms of markets and technology and hence defining different requirements for the coordination of actors in their development and production.[7] These are ideal types, in the sense that they represent basic product characteristics that can be decomposed no further, something like building blocks for the more complex outputs of the economy. In their ideal typical forms, their characteristics are internally consistent, as I will describe them in what follows. As will be seen further on, however, they can be combined into syncretic forms, and give rise to more complex action and innovation problems.

Two principal dimensions of the product can be identified: whether it is *standardized* or *specialized*, on the one hand, and whether it is *generic* or *dedicated* on the other. The first opposition refers to whether the supply of critical inputs to the producer, such as the technology, information, and skills necessary to carry out production, comes from a community of specialists, in which case such inputs are rare or costly and time-consuming to reproduce; or whether their supply is easy, and relatively cheap, to expand. It also refers to qualities of the product which are defined by the product's user. The second opposition is in terms of the structure of demand, specifically the degree of anonymity and uniformity of the client: generic products correspond to undifferentiated markets, while dedicated products are made for clients whose demands have precision and personality, that is, to whom the particular efforts of the producer must be targeted. The competitive process in capitalism is strongly marked by the identification of products according to this double opposition. For the producer, this is experienced as a type of market structure; for the user of the product, the way she or he approaches the satisfaction of wants. Each of the oppositions (standardized–specialized; generic–dedicated) thus means something different for action, depending on whether one is a user or a producer. These different needs have to be coordinated in a coherent way.

A standardized product is made with a known, widely diffused production technology in which quality is so widely attainable that competition comes to be inevitably centered on price. The specialized product, on the other hand, is made with technology and know-how that are restricted to a community of specialists. The quality of the product is always an important ingredient in the competitive strategy of these firms, where in the extreme case price becomes a secondary element in competition.

The generic product can be sold directly on the market, because its qualities are so well known (either through standardization of the product's qualities or through the opposite, as in the well-developed brand name that conveys the product's qualities in the name); the generic quality of the product, in other words, allows it to be sold via "anonymous" market mechanisms, the information being contained within the product itself (the pure case is a spot market). A generic product is thus typically associated with, and indispensable to, the construction of a *predictable* market, in the sense that its appeal to a large number of potential buyers at any given moment allows producers to estimate fluctuations of the market and thus *plan* their investments and allocation of resources (the law of large numbers).

A dedicated product, by contrast, is oriented toward a particular demand; its specifications or qualities are defined by the needs of a particular client or type of client. The limit case of dedication is customization, where the "market" as such reduces to interpersonal negotiations rather than normal supply and demand curves. Dedication assumes less radical forms as well, as in differentiation to particular groups of clients. Dedicated products face truly uncertain markets because the ratio of number of products to number of clients reduces the feasibility of probability estimations of demand; the law of large numbers no longer works.

Frank Knight[8] made the most penetrating observations about the differences between products, their markets, and their consequences for the organization of production. He clearly distinguished two forms of market fluctuation: that which is amenable to a probability estimate, which he called *risk* on the market; and those fluctuations that cannot be estimated and forecast, which he called true *uncertainty*. The market is really a temporal structure of expectations that guides investments and production planning. The time horizons of producers are a sort of continuum described by the extremes of certainty and uncertainty, but where certainty does not mean absence of fluctuations; it is simply a particularly marked form of demand predictability. The essential difference between risk and uncertainty is that in the latter the firm cannot construct a picture of the future in which it has confidence. Because it cannot perform ex ante risk calculations, it must attempt to hold open future options. Products have different kinds of fluctuations according to their mix or degree of generality or dedication. Thus, and in contrast to much of the recent literature on production "flexibility," we can say that not all fluctuations amount to uncertainty, and therefore each kind of economic fluctuation will have different consequences for the organization of production.

Knight distinguished two forms of dealing with fluctuations: one founded on reduction of risks by regrouping resources, the other founded on selection of individuals charged with reducing uncertainty. He labeled them, respectively, *consolidation* and *specialization*. In the first we find predictable markets and development of products intended for a mass of consumers who possess no individuality or "personality" for the producer; consolidation means aggregating these impersonal demands together so as to produce at high volume, which in turn (via the law of large numbers) offsets market fluctuations. In the second strategy, specialists are called in to reduce uncertainty via the quality of their judgement as to the needs of clients or the qualities of the output (whether these be aesthetic, functional, or scientific qualities); the specialist can do so better than the consolidator, whose judgement would not have the same degree of accuracy. These product qualities and the strategies that accompany them correspond rather closely to different types of markets and production technologies, as is seen in Figure 5.1.

Both uncertainty and predictability may be associated with either specialization or consolidation (standardization), according to two additional sets of constraints: those of the production technology at hand and of the costs and payoffs to using such technology. Every product and its associated pro-

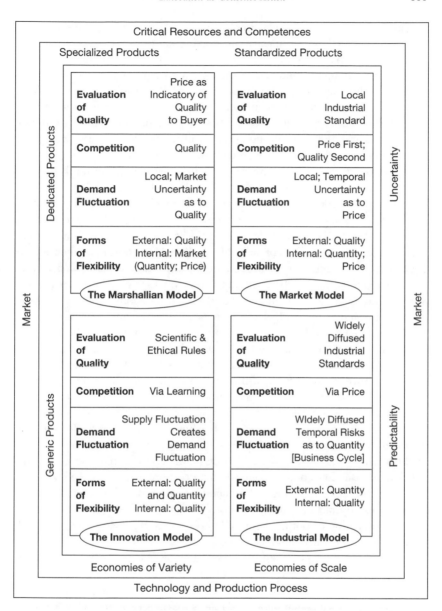

FIGURE 5.1. Worlds of production.

duction process have definite technological contours. Making a dashboard is different from making a transmission, making clothes shares few similarities with making airplanes. Yet the organizational (and, as we shall see, economic) effects of production technologies reduce fairly straightforwardly to a few major issues. The scale of production is a result of the possibility for consolidation or standardization. The scope–variety of production has to do in general with the benefits of specialization (whether in particular operations, or in particular products); this specialization is generally associated with rises in the variety of both, whether at firm or production system level.

Nontrivial uncertainties are resolved in constructing the market by selecting a product as generic or dedicated, and then by employing a consolidation–standardization strategy or one based on specialization. The problem is to resolve these uncertainties in a coherent way, given that there are many of them simultaneously at work. This resolution comes about, essentially, when actors generate conventions or rules-of-thumb, which coordinate their activities as producers and users. Each such set of conventions describes a *framework of action,* different for each basic kind of product, which we label a *world of production.* The theoretical notion of a world is meant to convey the interlinkage of people, organizations, objects, and ideas, with a certain indivisibility and wholeness. The central analytical content of this notion is that actions undertaken by various participants in the productive project are interdependent, and must be coordinated in order to arrive at useful and economically viable outputs. Conventions, as rules-of-thumb, constitute veritable guides to "what to do," which differ from one basic kind of product to another; hence, they are cognitive worlds in which actors exist. These action frameworks are collective because individual decisions can only generate their desired effects if they are taken with respect to expectations that are consistent with the expectations of those whose actions will have a bearing on the realization of our intentions. Efficient production comes about when uncertainties are resolved via economically coherent conventions; for each kind of product, some such conventions are appropriate and others are not.

For each kind of output described above, there is a corresponding world. Producers of dedicated products, faced with uncertainty, may thus in some cases be able to consolidate, and in other cases be obliged (or able) to specialize, their outputs. In the former case, uncertainty and consolidation (i.e., production of a high variety of dedicated products, generating economies of scale) generally means that they must follow markets extremely closely, which is why we may call their sphere of action the Market World. Note that this combination of standardized yet dedicated takes us beyond the usual simple opposition between mass production (standardization) and variety-based production. Examples of this world include, at one extreme, groups of small- and medium-sized firms that produce relatively short runs of products for highly fluctuating markets, as in central city garment or furniture complexes in the

United States,[9] and at another, the high-volume versions of flexible production networks centered on large firms, which are found in Japanese consumer durables industries.[10]

Producers of dedicated products who either cannot or do not want to consolidate, instead use specialization to increase the "personality" of their products, the interface between the know-how, specialized skill, or quality of judgment of producers and the particular demands to which the product is targeted. It is their ability to use such specialization to follow a series of changing demands, with specialization linking the capabilities of producers to the ongoing evolution of buyers' desires (themselves continuously redefined by what they understand to be the capabilities of the specialist producers), that constitutes the main offset to uncertainty. Critical here is the existence of a *community of specialists* who redesign the product, on very short time horizons, by deploying their tacit and customary knowledge of the product's qualities and possible dimensions. This is a highly interpersonal community of knowledge developers, based on traditional acquired skills, where constant communication between members of the community is necessary to carry out this kind of technology development. One major communicative process essential to innovation is interaction between the producers and the users of technologies: an example of this is the equipment maker who adapts to the needs of final product producers in order to accommodate the rapidly evolving final output. Typically, such communities are concentrated in particular geographical areas where informal processes of communication are central to their successful operation. This sphere of economic action based on true communities of producers and buyers may be labeled the Interpersonal World of economic coordination. The Interpersonal World applies not only to the famous cases of certain craft-oriented European industrial districts,[11] but also to the most specialized parts of the high-technology industries, as in nonmerchant semiconductor production in Silicon Valley,[12] the software industry in the Île-de-France,[13] biotechnology in San Diego,[14] or the medical and scientific instruments complex in Orange County south of Los Angeles.[15]

In the cases of generic products, the future is subject to a risk estimation: investment and capacity may be planned with greater confidence than in the other cases. Once again, both consolidation (standardization) or specialization may be options, depending on the availability and costs of technology. In the case of consolidation, large irreversible investments are called for, and products must be generated at high scale in order to offset them. Where economies of scale and long production runs dominate, as in many consumer durables industries, products are typically made by large oligopolistic firms. Such firms are capable of operating production systems at national and international scales, distributing parts and components and assembly plants across the landscape and coordinating the whole, as in the car industry. In their direct production activities in the high-wage market economies, there are downward employment trends, due to automation and relocation, and in many high-wage countries the wages paid in these industries have stagnated. These outcomes are, to a large degree, inscribed in the conventions associated with standardization of the product, which makes it economically and locationally substitutable. This is the sphere of action we call the Industrial World, that of mass production, as in the Chandlerian–Galbraithian firm of the postwar period and as still carried out for certain basic industrial inputs and relatively undifferentiated components for consumer durables.

There are some generic products for which demands cannot be consolidated and economies of scale are limited. Many high-technology outputs reflect, for the producer, precisely this dilemma: their nature is to be based on the application of codified scientific or engineering knowledge, and/or to find widespread application, either as final output or as component of more dedicated products. Because either the basic knowledge or its applied form is *not yet developed*, there is nothing to consolidate or standardize; yet the very possibility of developing such knowledge requires producers to proceed (usually via large-scale R&D investments) *as if* risk could be estimated in advance, by employing *specialists* in knowledge development. This is the sphere of large-scale science- and engineering-product development *par excellence*, or what we can designate the World of Intellectual Resources, developing products that are generic but dependent on extreme specialization of the key input. Basic industrial innovations are developed in this world of action and coordination.

This is a much more formal process than in the Interpersonal World referred to above. The formal processes of knowledge development rely on communication that can be stretched over large distances, because it is carried out at regular intervals in a planned fashion (through meetings, congresses, and private-sector projects with long planning horizons, where what is communicated involves highly codified and hence nonculture-dependent, cosmopolitan scientific, or professional languages). This occurs inside oligopolistic firms in high technology today. But often overlooked is that these oligopolists are tied, for some of their cutting-edge technology inputs, into precisely the kinds of interpersonal communities described above. Many of the core components of their large-scale research and development projects cannot be entirely planned; there is technological uncertainty. This uncertainty requires scientific and technical personnel to be able to interact informally, in unplanned and uncodifiable ways.

There are, of course, many complications to the development of these ideal–typical worlds. Products do not in any way automatically call forth an appropriate organizational structure; in many cases, organizations have to experiment in order to find the structure that meets the requirements of products they have chosen to produce, and sometimes they fail because they are not able to get into the appropriate world. They try to produce a product without developing the action framework needed to do so, leading to inefficiency or bad product qualities; they are beset by coordination failures in this case. By the same token, existing organizational structures have effects of orientation, which may propel them into certain worlds and make it unlikely that they enter others, at least without a difficult and risky process of managerial and organizational restructuring. Moreover, there is no strict identity between product and organization—in a world of highly differentiated products, a similar group of outputs may be produced in somewhat different organizational configurations, as in the differences between American, French, and British filmmaking referred to in Chapter 4. These differences of organizational configuration and hence of the action–coordination frameworks used by actors, will show up as differences in certain qualities of the products, and as differences in the economic performance of these organizations. Still, there is a point when differentiation of a product becomes a difference of product, and hence a change of world. That is, there are outer limits to the organizational variation that can be accommodated in a given world. In general, we can say that products and organizations have important effects of mutual orientation and coevolution.

A particularly complex issue is that of a production system that involves many different intermediate inputs coming from different worlds, sometimes also divided geographically and therefore inserted into very diverse local external environments. Several different action frameworks are thus "behind" a single final output. We will allude briefly to some dimensions of this in discussing coordination of worlds in multifaceted innovative production systems.

THE PROBLEM OF INNOVATION IN EACH WORLD OF PRODUCTION

Technological change does not concern some worlds rather than others, but all of them. In global markets where competition centers increasingly on innovation, the most competitive production systems, whatever the product may be, evidence the development, absorption, and deployment of asymmetric information, such that they construct absolute advantages and earn quasirents. We can identify the possible characteristics of the "innovation problem" for producers in each world, in two principal stages: first by pinpointing the the qualities of innovative products, and then by analyzing the economic pressures that follow from their combination of specialization/dedication or generality/standardization, in the form of the composition of profitability in each world.

Innovative Action and Product Qualities

By "qualities" of products, we refer to the particular kind of asymmetric information that constitutes an advantage over the average producer in the market at hand.

For the specialized–dedicated products of the Interpersonal World, for example, differentiated quality production that is specialized to particular uses or targeted niches of clients, innovation must consist of *inventing new dedicated qualities requiring specialized resources.* Continuous refinement and modification, and mastery of materials and designs in ways that are not entirely codifiable (through formal labor or scientific training off the job) and not highly amenable to being incorporated in or transferred via special-purpose equipment, are at the heart of product-based technological advantage in this world. An important role in this development of dedicated–specialized qualities is played by user–producer relations, where groups of "dedicated" demanders (users) and specialized producers engage in a communicative process that underlies knowledge evolution.

For the standardized–dedicated products of the Market World, differentiated (or "flexible") series production is the form of dedication of the product to a narrow band of tastes or uses. Innovation in this world consists of *inventing new dedicated qualities that are amenable to standardization.* Advantage is constructed by producing objects that are standardized (in the sense of drawing on codifiable combinations of products already widely available in standardized form), yet dedicated to particular uses (in the sense of combinations that are highly differentiated and targeted): the keys to such advantage are thus ability to respond to the market and to do so *rapidly.* Producers must either take new standardized–generic knowledge or product qualities and differentiate it rapidly and more than can other producers, thus following consumer tastes more closely, or they must do the opposite, by standardizing dedicated products through development of appropriate production techniques.

For the specialized–generic products of the World of Intellectual Resources, innovation consists of developing *new generic qualities via the exercise of specialized capabilities.* The creation of new scientific and technical know-how is based on the paradox of a community of specialists who function according to rules of method that are themselves known and reproducible; thus the knowledge they create is generic, but they can only create it by virtue of their specialization at the moment. The knowledge will be widely usable, hence generic; but it cannot be produced by standardized methods. Its product is thus a key input into innovations of the other worlds.

For the standardized–generic products of the Industrial World, competition is bounded by widely available products, widely diffused standards of quality and consumer expectations, and codifiable knowledge that can be incorporated in special-purpose capital equipment. Innovation consists of *inventing new generic product qualities amenable to standardization.* It involves *basic* technological innovations, in the sense of taking generic qualities and standardizing them, breaking them into constituent parts and tasks. New generic–specialized knowledge (coming from the World of Intellectual Resources, as noted above) is made codifiable and widely reproducible. The initial producers who do this will be able to drop their prices rapidly and will enjoy a (relatively short) period of quasirents before other producers imitate them or reverse-engineer their products, at which time they will need to repeat the process of taking new generic–specialized knowledge and standardizing it. Their advantage, like that of those in the Market World, is always fragile.

Economic Pressures and Constraints in Each World

Each of the four worlds has a different set of problems to solve in order to reach profitability, because there are different multiple and conflicting influences on profitability for each kind of product. The production process and market axes of the "model" presented in Figure 5.1 may be described by a series of variables that comprise profitability. These are presented in Table 5.1. The first formula describes action frameworks in which the search for profitability is guided by the market. The principal variables are: gross margin per unit sale, the rate of capacity utilization, and the ratio of net circulating capital to total sales (which reflect short-term commitments). Values of these variables describe the difference between predictable and uncertain markets. If the market is predictable, then the short-term management problem is to cope with fluctuations around a central and knowable trend line; as a result, stocks and short-term indebtedness (i.e., circulating capital) can be used to smooth out fluctuations. Management through stocking of inputs allows the firm to carry out long series production and thus to benefit from certain economies of scale. Market uncertainty, by contrast, requires factor mobility and reversibility, such that short-term capital commitments are pushed down. In contrast, if a generic product permits the firm to optimize the rate of capacity utilization, the corollary to long production runs is the acceptance of small margins. The situation is just the opposite for the dedicated product: the client who demands a service adapted to her needs accepts that the firm earns a higher margin, but the producer must accept lower average levels of capacity utilization.

The second formula in Table 5.1 describes frameworks of action in which the search for profitability relies on savings due to organizational and technological economies. It concerns the fixed resources of production, including both physical capital and some forms of labor. Standardized products and economies of scale imply that the producer gives priority to economizing on labor, resulting in a low share of labor costs in value added, considerable substitution of capital for labor, and high productivity of labor, to the detriment of the "efficiency" of capital (that is, the financial rate of return, or inverse of the capital–output ratio). Specialized products and economies of variety depend, by contrast, on a more important role for labor. The priority here is on reproduction and development of the know-how of the labor force

---

TABLE 5.1. The components of profitability

Defining capital as including both fixed and circulating capital, the profitability of a firm may be shown as follows:

$$r = \frac{EBE}{K + AC + PC}$$

where:

EBE = total surplus or gross profit
K = fixed capital
AC = active circulating capital (upstream, intermediate, and final stocks and short-term credit to clients)
PC = passive circulating captial (short-term credits from suppliers)

(1) One way to dissect profitability is in terms of the market, that is, the firm's choices of products and forms of organization are guided by market pressures.

$$r = \frac{EBE}{Q_v} \times \frac{\dfrac{Q_v}{Q_c}}{\dfrac{K}{Q_c} + \dfrac{AC - PC}{Q_v} \times \dfrac{Q_v}{Q_c}}$$

where:

Q_v = installed production capacity
Q_c = total sales

The ratios may be interpreted as follows:

$\dfrac{EBE}{Q_v}$ is the gross margin per unit sold;

$\dfrac{Q_v}{Q_c}$ is the rate of capacity utilization;

$\dfrac{K}{Q_c}$ is capital per unit of output;

$\dfrac{AC - PC}{Q_v}$ is the ratio of net circulating capital to sales.

The controlling variables are in this case gross margin per unit sold (EBE/Q_v); the rate of capacity utilization (Q_v/Q_c), as a measure of ability to adjust to short-term demand fluctuations; and the ratio of net circulating capital to sales $(AC - PC/Q_v)$. Optimization in the market thus give priority to flows, that is, to management of the short term.

(2) A second set of formulae emphasizes the production process; in other words, it looks at profitability in terms of the optimal management of technology. In the first case, the firm chooses the productivity of labor as its measure of efficiency; in the second, it focuses on the efficiency of captial. Note that both forms of optimization place priority on stocks—on resources immobilized in equipment and labor force, that is, on the management of the medium term.

(continued)

TABLE 5.1. *Continued*

The first formula is as follows:

(2a)

$$r = \frac{\left(1 - \dfrac{LC}{VA}\right)\dfrac{VA}{N}}{\dfrac{K}{N} + \dfrac{AC - PC}{K}}$$

where:

VA = value added
LC = labor costs (salaries and benefits)
N = number of workers

The firm using such a formulation will attempt to increase labor productivity (that is, value added per worker, VA/N) by substituting capital for labor (that is, increasing the K/N ratio) and by reducing labor costs per unit of output.

The second formula is as follows:

(2b)

$$r = \frac{\left(1 - \dfrac{LC}{VA}\right)\dfrac{VA}{K}}{1 + \dfrac{AC - PC}{K}}$$

Here, the firm's strategy is to maximize the efficiency of capital use, that is, to minimize the capital to output ratio. This implies production based on highly skilled labor—that is, investments in intangible resources destined to increase the quality and productivity of labor.

(specialized assets such as investments in labor skills, brand names, etc.). The role of labor costs is greater, but the efficiency of fixed capital is also higher, thus compensating for low direct labor productivity.

Figure 5.2 summarizes the composition of the different variables and their roles in each of the worlds of production. The constraints and possibilities for each world are quite different, as is the pattern of interaction of these factors. In the Interpersonal World, necessary economizing on short-term capital commitments makes increases in capacity quite difficult; producers must invest in specialized resources while maintaining a low capital–output ratio, and "cheap" increases in scope–variety are one way to do so. In the Industrial World, by contrast, the goal is to maximize capacity and its rate of utilization, but this raises the cost of circulating capital, which can weigh down the profit rate. Firms must therefore continually push down unit costs via standardization and scale, but this in turn is costly in terms of capital,

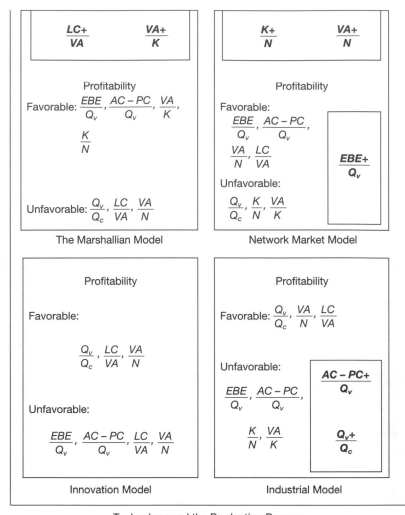

FIGURE 5.2. Production values that affect profitability in each world.

leading to a repetition of the effort to outrun both circulating and fixed capital costs. Recourse to low-cost capacity (price squeeze) subcontracting may also figure prominently, where quality controls can be effective and transactions costs can be managed.

In the Market World, rapid response to differentiated demands may carry with it a price premium, but to the extent that uncertainty prevents full process standardization, labor costs occupy an important role in price. Moreover, since the product is standardized, competition is stiff on the supply side (generally, supply exceeds demand for intermediate outputs), and there is severe downward pressure on prices.

In the World of Intellectual Resources, high value added and investment costs are likely to be reflected in high prices, but they also detract from unit margins. Labor and circulating capital costs are very high, as is the cost of specialized labor.

We may now summarize the effects of constraints on innovation in each of the four worlds. In all cases, they consist of product-based innovations that *deepen* the advantage related to the particular kind of product quality coveted in that world, while (in the best of all circumstances) coupling them to process innovations that *offset* the constraints and contradictions of profitability. In the Interpersonal World, for example, this would mean increasing the specialized and dedicated content of the product in order to raise producers' margins so as to offset high labor costs and low rates of value added, while increasing capacity and scale through efficient economies of variety.

In the Industrial World, product innovations should widen the generic content of the product in order to expand markets, thus raising scale and offsetting the nagging problem of capital costs; process innovations would also enhance scale, but once again by adding together different generic products through economies of variety.

In the Market World, product innovations should make the output *ever more differentiated*, or *more rapidly responsive* to emerging differentiated demands, so as to raise the producers' margins, while process innovations should, once again, confer greater scope–variety so as to raise the overall scale of production and capacity utilization in order to drive down unit costs.

In the World of Intellectual Resources, product innovation is concerned with expanding generically applicable new knowledge, in order to widen markets so as to amortize the very high labor and up front investment costs related to the mobilization of specialized intellectual resources. Process innovations (in the very broad sense of this term) should be concerned with making possible economies of scope–variety, that is, the production of more and more generic knowledge advances by the same groups of specialized producers, so as to enhance the "scale" of their output and thus drive down long-term average costs.

Thus, in each of these worlds actors carry out product innovation by deepening their mastery of the essential characteristics of their product, while at the same time trying to attain the golden fleece of all production, higher scale and lower unit costs. But—and this is crucial—in the worlds already standardized, more scale comes from greater scope–variety; and in the worlds that are specialized, more scale would *also* come from greater scope–variety, since standardized–scale is inimical to the product output.

INNOVATIVE PRODUCTIVE SYSTEMS:
ORGANIZATIONS AND TERRITORIES

Much has been written in recent years about the organizational form of innovative firms and production systems. There is much descriptive literature on the ways innovative networks or "network firms" are coming to replace old-style hierarchical "Chandlerian–Galbraithian" firms. There is a theoretical literature on new organizational "equilibria" in innovative situations, where the network is the way that the needs for resource reversibility (to avoid technological lock-in) and the advantages of specialization and scale (now both an external as well as an internal economy) are reconciled.[16] Valuable insights have come from these literatures. Yet we often seem to be saddled with caricatures, consisting of networks, districts, and cooperation, on one side, and old hierarchical oligopolies on the other. What is needed is a way to discriminate among organizational forms appropriate to the supply of different kinds of innovative capacities. Here we begin to move from the product's "demand" for innovative capacities to the organizations of actors required to supply them or, in the terms of the holy trinity, from technologies to the organizations of production and their territories.

Figure 5.3 presents the way this is done (in a very brief and preliminary way) for the different worlds of production. The right-hand vertical axis reproduces Knight's distinction between uncertain and predictable (though fluctuating) markets. Under conditions of true uncertainty, the capacity to plan and stabilize external transactions will be more limited than in those production systems where the probabilities and magnitudes of fluctuations can be reliably estimated. Thus, producers of dedicated products tend to have more variable external transactions than those of generic products. Note that this analysis differs considerably from the view of transactions-cost economics, where it is the nature of productive assets (specific vs. nonspecific, numbers, resulting hostage problems, etc.) that determines the volume and nature of external transactions. In their view, the distinction between standardized and specialized (which they would label "specific") would determine transactional patterns, with a tendency for standardized assets to have large numbers and hence, external-market transactions, and for specific ("specialized") assets to have small numbers, hostage problems, and hence to lead toward internalization. The explanation is different here, and predicted empirical outcomes are quite opposite. Note, also, that mere *quantity* of external transactions is not the sole issue, but the *nature* of those transactions, and in particular the degree of uncertainty or predictability associated with them: this latter should determine much about the unit cost of transacting as well as the qualities of the contractual or noncontractual relationship of the transaction.

The latter also requires a substantive view of what the transaction is all

	Specialized Products	Standardized Products	
Dedicated Products	**System Organization** Technology District Industrial District **Product Innovation:** Similar **Nature of Interdependencies:** Traded + Untraded Territorial Proximity **Production Transactions:** Nonsimilar + Complementary	**System Organization** Diffused Industrialization **Product Innovation:** Complementary (Recombination) **Nature of Interdependencies:** Traded + Untraded Territorial Proximity **Production Transactions:** Similar + Complementary (Capacity)	**Uncertainty**
Generic Products	**System Organization** Technology District; Strategic Alliances **Product Innovation:** Similar **Nature of Interdependencies:** Traded + Little Proximity **Production Transactions:** Nonsimilar + Complementary	**System Organization** Technological Core + Spatial Division of Labor **Product Innovation:** Complementary **Nature of Interdependencies:** Few; Traded **Production Transactions:** Similar + Complementary (Capacity)	**Predictability**
	Economies of Variety	Economies of Scale	

FIGURE 5.3. External relations in innovation in each world of production.

about. The horizontal axes of Figure 5.3 ask what principle is likely to shape the division of labor in production for each product, and hence what kind of coordination each production system requires, drawing from Richardson's[17] fourfold distinction between similar–nonsimilar and complementary–non-complementary phases of production. We need to divide the problem of external transactions into two, clear issues, which are often confused in the literature: transactions having to do with the management of "normal" production activities, and those having to do with asymmetric information development, which underlies product innovation, our subject here.

Specialized and standardized products have different divisions of labor in production and in innovation. For the day-to-day production of specialized products, the division of labor centers on securing of nonsimilar but complementary inputs, that is, a "vertical" division of labor. This principle is self-evident for certain products of the Interpersonal World, such as fashion- or design-intensive goods or certain outputs of the mechanical engineering industries. A word of clarification is needed for the World of Intellectual Resources, however. What constitutes the difference between "production" and "innovation" in this world? Production involves the application of specialized intellectual resources to the development of new, but generic knowledge; as such, producers in the Intellectual world seek out other producers with nonsimilar but complementary forms of knowledge, which are then recombined into a "whole" generic innovation, as when highly skilled research teams in the electronics industry, in differently specialized firms, teams, or units, come together to develop a new chip design, a material, or even a whole subassembly such as a peripheral or software package. But the dedicated–specialized elements of these whole, generic innovations constitute the "innovative" activity of this innovative world, as in those who experiment with software languages (which are then combined into generic forms). In effect, these latter actors, who are "deep" innovators upon whom the Intellectual World depends, are themselves in the Interpersonal World (e.g., much of that part of the electronics industry which is *in* Silicon Valley). Their external relations in innovation are with other specialists dedicated to *similar* problems. Thus, both of the worlds with specialized products have exernal relations in production that are nonsimilar and complementary, and external relations in innovation with other specialists, where knowledge frameworks are deepened within these small communities. The Intellectual World, however, takes those and then recombines them into new generic forms, often through formal traded interdependencies with firms having complementary and nonsimilar talents, as in technology partnerships and strategic alliances between big technological firms.[18] These transactions rely less on territorial proximity than do those of the Interpersonal World (which, remember, contains the most specialized–dedicated parts of the high-technology industries), where *uncertain* transactional relations *within communities of specialists* and between specialists and users, are the basis of transactions. Hence, there is a tendency for these relations to be untraded as well as traded, to rely on noncontractual as well as contractual forms of governance, and frequently to have high levels of territorial proximity as the basis of the common action frameworks of the cooperating specialists. This means, moreover, that the Intellectual World has a complex double pattern to its external transactions: in "production," over long distances in predictable, formal, contractual governance regimes; in "innovation" in the circumscribed "districts" of the Interpersonal World. Many big high-technology firms, for example, have relations "upward and outward" to other technology-based oligopolists, but continue to root their core technological capabilities in the Interpersonal Worlds of their home countries.[19]

For standardized products things are quite different. In the day-to-day production activities of the Market World, producers use external relations within the division of labor to secure similar and complementary inputs, that is, to smooth out market fluctuations with additional capacity, whether this be horizontal or vertical in nature. In the Market World, we find Marshall's famous supply-curve interdependencies (they may also exist in the Interpersonal World, but they are not the central reason for its territoriality). In the Industrial World, such capacity smoothing tends to be the object of long-term contracts and spread over large geographical distances, because market fluctuations are predictable; this gives us the typical multiregional or multinational production system. In the Market World, uncertainty is present, and immediate availability of vertical and horizontal suppliers is required, with little secure future promised to them. The specialized production region with a large collection of firms typifies this system.

The use of external transactions by actors in the two worlds of standardized products are in both cases designed to complement what they lack, not to deepen knowledge, as in the communities of specialists. In the Market World, product innovation is the continuous rapid differentiation of standardized outputs, the key to which is rapid and expanding recombination of differentiated standardized inputs. Territorial proximity can be of help here, and both traded and untraded contractual and hybrid interdependencies are likely to be found. In the Industrial World, producers of standardized–generic outputs innovate by finding new generic outputs that can be standardized. Firms may do this directly in their methods and engineering departments, through interconnections with third-party innovators, such as universities or government agencies, or, as is quite likely, via relationships with innovators of generic knowledge in the World of Intellectual Resources.

DEVELOPING CONVENTIONS AND ACTION CAPACITIES

Innovation is thus closely shaped by the kind of product at hand, with the set of constraints and opportunities it defines in terms of product qualities, construction of the market (as a temporal structure of expectations), technological contours of the production process, and its associated components of profitability. It is also a problem of action. It depends on the creation of particular kinds of persons, with particular capacities for action. These actors are not alone, however. The actors essential to innovation in a given world of production must have mutual expectations that coordinate their actions under the specific forms of uncertainty in that world. The action problem is collective in nature.

The regional development problem associated with building such different systems of innovation thus turns essentially on building the *capacities for reflexive, collective action* and the forms of coordination consistent with the kind of action required in each world. This resides in the construction of conventions that allow actors to act in a coherently coordinated fashion that generates economically viable innovations. For each kind of product (with its particular form of uncertainty), the coherence and coordination to be effected by these conventions is different. Having established this substantive nature of a system of innovation, we may inquire as to its visible form: what kinds of organizational, institutional, and territorial conditions are appropriate with the creation and exercise of such capacities?

In the Interpersonal World actors must have the capacities to increase the dedicated qualities of the product by deepening the application of their specialized knowledge. This is done by developing the communities of persons in which such knowledge is created, refined, and transferred. Though there are other strategies for redressing the latent problems of profitability in this world (for example, attempting to standardize and increase the scale of production), such strategies are inconsistent with the continued existence of the world and its particular way of earning quasirents when it innovates. As we have seen, innovation in the Interpersonal World is inherently based on close relations between specialist producers and close user–producer relations. The economic dilemmas that come from low scale and high variety, the need to offset high overhead costs, and the ongoing "theft" of its products by the Industrial or Market Worlds, as they are standardized and subjected to production methods with greater direct productivity, however, cannot be met by imitating those worlds. Why? Because standardized products are no longer Interpersonal World products—they lose the essential *qualities* that underlie their economic performance: their loss of "personality" condemns them to price competition. Thus, while individual producers might solve their problems in the short run by standardizing such products, the world itself will ultimately be undermined as such, losing its identity and becoming something else, and then having to face the competitive struggle that exists in those other worlds. The system of innovation for this world is inherently defined by the problem of knowledge deepening, and policies for the Interpersonal World must devote themselves to promoting the capabilities of specialist communities to deepen knowledge in concert with its dedication to the needs of users. Mission-oriented policies are unlikely to be very helpful for developing such products; diffusion-oriented policies, structured to encourage horizontal relations between government and firms will be most appropriate. Moreover, such policies should provide collective goods (services, especially) for clusters of products and producers, at a focused territorial level (e.g., the region). Finally, because of the tendency toward organizational decentralization but territorial focus of the production system, such policies often need to address the tendency toward the formation of regressive coalitions, the downside of interpersonal relations, where solidarity turns into protectionism, exclusionism, and closure.[20]

This is just part of the issue of capacity formation, however; the rest concerns capacities in production technology. The economic contradictions of the Interpersonal World have one great solution: major increases in scope–variety of production, which offset the costs of production and the problem of capacity utilization. The problem here has to do both with finding technologies appropriate to such increased scope–variety, and with finding management techniques capable of realizing its benefits without destroying the community of specialists and its interpersonal character. Greater scope–variety and larger production units would imply greater internal hierarchy and increasingly formal external relations of production units that tend to *depersonalize* the production system, substituting bureaucratic knowledge for personal knowledge. If this destroys the ongoing deepening of practical knowledge and conceptual frameworks that are key to action in this world, it merely returns us to the problem noted above: instead of making the Interpersonal World more viable, it substitutes a world based on standardization, and a new set of economic constraints replaces the old one. Mission- and diffusion-oriented policies may both be appropriate here, as production technologies often require sustained economic and research resources and cover many different particular, but cognate, final output sectors. Mission-oriented components, however, need close and ongoing contact with final-output users, both in terms of defining needs and in terms of determining economic feasibility. Rather than the pure form of a centralized (both organizationally and territorially) mission-oriented program, then, we may think here of a new, sectorally and territorially focused, hybrid mission structure.

Innovation in the Market World centers on the degree and pace of product dedication. Innovation may also involve new conceptual frameworks for dedication, such as closer ties to clients, faster changeovers, and greater scope–variety to offset costs. Examples of the Market World include the central-city garment or furniture complexes in the United States. Here, competition leads to something approaching spot-market pricing, with low levels of formal contracting and hierarchy. These complexes can respond rapidly to the market and subcontractors survive or die on this response capability. Innovation lies largely outside of the production system, in the Interpersonal World communities of designers, who themselves are subject to extreme levels of uncertainty. The economic constraints we pointed out earlier—the fact that downstream order-giving firms can place their suppliers into competition with each other because the inputs are based on standardized components or skills—make life extremely difficult for all concerned. The result is a tendency for severe downward pressure on subcontractor and supplier prices (i.e., wages); and, in general, product innovators must either find ways to increase the generic quality of their products in order to survive (the compromise found by Benetton) or become more specialized (moving toward the Interpersonal World). The pure "liberal" version of the Market World is a hard life for all concerned.

Apparently more stable and highly innovative versions of the Market World — or we might call them compromises between the Market World and the Industrial World—have been organized, via creation of institutions that reshape economic coordination in these sectors. The Japanese car industry, for example, replaced Fordism with Ohno-ism (or Toyotism), thereby taking the essentially generic products of the American car industry and making them more dedicated. It did so via a managerial and organizational revolution whose details are now so well known as not to require repetition here. Its innovative labor is located both in direct production activity—the famous quality and adaptability of Japanese line workers, and the close interties between different tiers of subcontractors and final assembly, through *kan ban* and just-in-time—but also in the conception that Japanese managers have of what competition is all about. Specifically, they rejected the idea of competition strictly via the long production run and its cost advantage, and complemented it with an idea of extremely frequent model changeovers, and they set up participation in the production system, and the expectations of participants, to conform to this rapid pace of redifferentiation of products.

They also mobilized financial and productive resources to make high volume compatible with such differentiation. For example, "upstream" institutional frameworks were made consistent with this form of innovation, notably the banking system, on one hand (i.e., patient capital with low financial rates of return, permitting frequent intensive recapitalization of the production system without dragging down profit rates), while the "horizontal" organization in the form of the *keiretsu*, as resource-pooling and loyalty-inducing devices, permitted high levels of flexibility-without-exit or opportunism. The mechanical engineering industries of southern Germany have also used institutions to reshape expectations, blending attentiveness to the market with the capability to mobilize long-term, expensive labor and capital resources otherwise not available under the conditions of uncertainty characteristic of this world. Note that in both the German and Japanese cases, the social "cement" that allows this to happen seems to have an interpersonal character: communities of persons in which *voice* is exercised over time, binding them to each other.[21] We may say, then, that collective action leading to innovation in capital-intensive products in the Market World rests on a paradox: the need to underpin the market with forms of social commitment. Thus, in development of high-volume flexible production in the Market World, both mission-oriented and diffusion-oriented policies can be found: the former for certain kinds of basic capital goods, the latter for sector-wide assistance; but *neither* is fully hier-archical. Critical to this world are organizational forms that underpin progressive coalitions. This includes both firm and group organization (as in Japanese *keiretsu*) and contracting procedures, so that volume, flexibility and learning are reconciled.

The problem of innovation in the Industrial World is clear and classical: formal corporate R&D to invent new generic product qualities compatible with standardization. Product innovation is a great deal more mysterious than process innovation in this world. In effect, such innovation has little to do with the rationalization of production processes. It is a form of intellectual work, applying standardization to new generic knowledge, crystallized in the product. It is now understood that this form of innovation is not contained within this world or its firms, but involves a host of extremely complex external relations, to other worlds and to the public and private R&D infrastructure. Moreover, the breaking-in stage for truly new standardized–generic products—the first few years when massive quasirents are earned, markets are shaped, brand names created, and technological trajectories for the product set into motion—often requires high levels of territorial proximity, between producers, Intellectual World innovators, production engineers, customers, and service-support agents.[22] After that, increasing codification of all these processes permits greater and greater territorial distance between them.

We know from hard experience over the past two decades that the Industrial World—once heralded by Chandler, Galbraith, and others as the leading light of innovative activity, because the big corporation could *plan* its technology development programs—no longer allows high-wage, high-cost countries to get ahead. It is to the failure of the Industrial World to earn innovative quasirents to which the voluminous literature on post-Fordism, flexibility, and so on, is addressed. It might be more insightful to recast the "post-Fordist" claim by noting that the advantages once possessed by the Industrial World's firms have been chipped away on two sides: the Japanese and German versions of the Market World combine standardization and dedication with more rapid changeovers of products, while consumers turn toward products of the Inter-personal World. Moreover, Industrial World firms in the developed countries are imitated by, or move to, cheap Third World production zones.

The ground for economically viable innovation in the Industrial World is thus very narrow. Policy for innovative Industrial Worlds must truly identify new generic–standardizable products as its target. This means discovering such generic qualities that are not likely to be subject to rapid dedication and thus to easy imitation by firms in the Market World, and which are durable enough to not be subject to cheap Third World competition before investments are amortized. It is extremely difficult to protect such investments via legal means (patents and copyrights) today. Innovation in the Industrial World must also not be analytically confused with mere imitation of state-of-the-art products or production technologies; here, the constraint of very high capital costs and price competition will impede innovative quasirents, and subject high-cost, developed-country producers to Third World competition or, worse, competition from more flexible Market World producers. The travails of General Motors, attempting to imitate every Japanese product and process invention a few years after, comes to mind here; clearly, for at least a decade, they failed to understand that the Japanese were operating in the Market World and not in the Industrial World. Though General Motors' performance is satisfactory in the mid-1990s, it must be remembered that it suffered a large and probably permanent loss of market share in the 1980s.

This suggests that the main hope for the Industrial World on the production side is in the Market World and on the product side in the Intellectual World. In the latter, innovation means invention of new generic qualities through the deployment of specialized resources. This is very costly and producers must operate via a paradox: in the face of high levels of uncertainty, they must proceed "as if" the latter did not exist, that is, by going forth with methodologically coherent programs of R&D.

R&D in the Intellectual World involves three main groups of actors and their interdependencies. First are the "internal" agents of a given firm—its scientific, engineering, and conceptual workers. The firm must invest in them and give them appropriate incentives. Society must create them and give them an appropriate identity. If these workers belong to large companies whose main activity is in the Industrial World, how are they to be given the culture they need to perform in the World of Intellectual Resources, whose principles of identity and collective action are so different from those of the Industrial World?[23]

For any given firm, such workers are specialists, coming from specialized milieux in some cases, dependent on interactions with specialists external to the firm in all cases. This is the second group: such communities of specialists are always, to some degree, based on interpersonal ties. They are frequently highly territorialized. This is why we find even the big-firm technological partners to multinational strategic alliances often "sourcing" their inputs to those alliances from well-known technology districts in their own countries.[24] .

Such workers, in turn, are inserted into alliances with their partners in other Intellectual World firms or units: this is the third group. The specialized workers in such firms must relate to each other through formal, traded interdependencies. The thorny question of the "terms of trade" now arises: how to execute contracts and other agreements with the correct ex ante incentives and ex post payoffs. Here, it appears that there is a standoff between transactions costs and property rights (appropriation by agents): if we minimize transactions costs ex ante, then ex post rewards are not always correct; and vice versa.[25] There is no way around the need to create appropriate conventions by which rewards are shared out, and it is doubtful that either contract law or formal management practice can resolve the question. How could policy intervene to create such "virtuous" social conventions about the rewards to innovators? Inducing firms to participate in formal and virtuous interfirm relations might rest on the provision of certain kinds of collective research resources (mission-oriented research policies), but such provision would have to be carefully balanced with mechanisms to prevent closing ranks for protectionism and it would have to be carefully balanced in order to resist technological closure. Such policies would, in any case, have to be complemented by the standard fare of a highly performing private and public R&D structure: the university system, patents and property rights, internal R&D organization of firms, and so on.

This question might apply not only to the formal traded innovative relationships of the Intellectual World, but also to the frequently informal and territorialized technology-development relationships of the Interpersonal World. What sorts of conventions should policy attempt to develop for communities of specialists, if contracts and property rights alone cannot do the job efficiently? I venture a preliminary suggestion: society's distribution of income to these communities of people is critical. It has to provide them incentive to survive as communities, for their members to avoid exit.[26] Beyond such economic incentive, such communities—as the producers of key innovative inputs to the Intellectual and Industrial Worlds—must have their place in other mission- and diffusion-oriented policies. They must have their place *as communities*, and not simply as representatives of firms, whose interests are frequently too narrowly identified with particular product lines, not with whole technological spillover fields. We have barely begun to think about the "community" quality of these groups of actors and the particular mechanisms by which they could be incorporated in systems of innovation and policies, as such.

CONCLUSION: THE DIFFERENT TERRITORIALITIES OF INNOVATION

There is a diversity of possible systems of innovation, involving both the collective-action problem of a world of production and the supply architecture appropriate to resolving that collective-action problem by enabling the development and exercise of correct action capacities. Regional examples of some of these systems are examined in Chapter 6. These systems move through time, with the demand and supply architectures modifying each other through collective action, as we described in Chapter 3.

In addition, each demand architecture has a distinctive locational logic; there are many such logics in today's complex economy, ranging from highly localized components to far-flung, organizationally internalized networks; there is no single emergent formula that fits all products and all worlds of production. Corresponding to such locational logics, the ideal supply architectures of systems of innovation are many, with different degrees of territorialization and mixes of qualitatively different territorial components, as suggested in Figure 5.3. If we were to view things from the starting point of supply, or from the standpoint of particular territories, we would need to take these relationships into consideration. Most importantly, worlds of action at a territorial level are not self-contained but inserted into these functional worlds of products. Only in some cases are territories coextensive with whole worlds of production; in most cases they are but parts of a more complex spatiality of collective, reflexive economic action; we have opened up this issue in Chapter 3, and more will be said about it in Chapter 7.

In any case, the subject of systems of innovation involves no simple choice between different all-purpose "models of innovation," but rather a recognition of the fundamental diversity of modern economies as a starting point. Policy, in coming to grips with this diversity of coherent combinations of the basic elements—products, collective-action problems, actors' capacities, and supply architectures—must be oriented toward the substantive content of innovation in each world of production; their organizational and territorial architectures must enable actors to realize this substantive content, and to keep doing so over time.

NOTES

1. Dosi et al. (1990); Arrow (1962).

2. See, *inter alia,* the country studies in Nelson (1993); and Lundvall and Johnson (1992); Porter (1990); McKelvey (1991); Powell (1990); Haas-Lorenz (1994); Feldman and Florida (1994); Feldman (1993); Andersen (1992).

3. The term is from Borrus in Tyson et al. (1989), although it is employed somewhat differently here.

4. For definitions of these terms, see Storper and Harrison (1990).

5. Amendola and Gaffard (1990).

6. But we do make an attempt in Storper and Salais (1997).

7. Greater detail can be found in Storper and Salais (1997, Chap. 3).

8. Knight (1921).

9. See, *inter alia,* Scott (1988a).

10. The literature on this subject is so vast as to not need citation here. There are many contending characterizations of the ideal-type "Japanese production system." My choice of "high-volume, flexible production" is deliberate.

11. See, especially, Bagnasco (1977); Becattini (1987); Cappecchi (1990a,b); Piore and Sabel (1984).

12. Scott (1988b); Saxenian (1994).

13. Storper and Salais (1997).

14. Enany (1991).

15. de Vet (1990, 1993).

16. Again, these issues are dealt with in detail in Storper and Salais (1997).

17. Richardson (1972).

18. Mytelka (1990).

19. Dunning (1988).

20. Recently debated for the case of Italy. See Forlai and Bertini (1989).

21. For Japan, a central point in Aoki (1989, 1990), as well as that of Dore (1987); for Germany, see Herrigel (1995).

22. There are no historical examples of an industry *not* having a close territorial core in their early years. See, on a theoretical level, Scott and Storper (1987); Arthur (1990b). For the story of the semiconductor industry, see Angel (1994).

23. As suggested by the voluminous literature on different management styles, as in Intel versus IBM. See Saxenian's (1994) study of different firm practices in Route 128 and Silicon Valley.

24. See, *inter alia*, Mytelka (1990); Dunning (1988); Storper (1992); Chapter 8 of this book.

25. Seravalli (1992).

26. Exit as suggested in Storper and Salais (1997) or Florida and Kenney (1990).

CHAPTER 6

Regional Worlds of Production

CONVENTIONS OF LEARNING AND INNOVATION IN THE TECHNOLOGY DISTRICTS OF FRANCE, ITALY, AND THE UNITED STATES

TRANSACTIONS, AGGLOMERATION, AND TECHNOLOGICAL DYNAMISM

A given transactional relationship in the presence of learning tends to be qualitatively more dense than in the case of simple market fluctuations, for it involves knowledge that is not only not yet standardized, but which is often not yet developed.[1] User–producer interactions thus involve the difficult and not easily objectifiable process of interpretation. In addition, the whole transactional structure may be subject to redefinition as new types of products and new firms enter the structure, and as whole new subnodes, channels, and codes of transaction are defined.[2] In other words, where rapid learning is taking place, the transactional structure is likely to involve constant negotiation, renegotiation, and dependence on achieved understandings as the basis of achieving common reinterpretations of new evidence and opportunities. This hypothesis applies not only to incremental innovations, but to radical innovations as well:

> . . . the codes developed to communicate a constant, or a gradually changing technology will become inadequate. Established producers, following a given technological trajectory, will have difficulties in evaluating the potentials of the new paradigm. Users will have difficulties in decoding the communication coming from producers, developing new products, built according to the new paradigm. In this case, geographical and cultural distance

might play an even more important role than in the case of incremental innovation. The lack of standard criteria for sorting out what is the best paradigm, implies that "subjective" elements in user–producer relationships . . . will become important.[3]

In technologically dynamic production complexes, then, there is particularly strong reason for the existence of regional clusters or agglomerations. But in and of itself, as we have seen in preceding chapters, agglomeration does not ensure learning or determine its content. The use and development of information in such a way that technological learning takes place has to do with the qualitative behaviors of agents in a network.

There is significant evidence that all agents are not alike when it comes to transactional activity, whether geographically concentrated or not. Economists such as Williamson assume that all actors have universal behavioral principles, such as short-run maximizing and opportunism. In contrast to the Williamsonian paradigm, much of the recent case study literature on dynamic production networks suggests that they are differentiated by the mixes of competition, cooperation, trust, and opportunism of the transactors, and that agents (firms, individuals) have different values about what is good and bad, or just and unjust. These localized expectations motivate them and structure their short-term choices (time horizons, payoff points, etc.).[4] In one well-known recent critique of standard transactional theory, these features of transactional behavior were aptly described as the social "embeddedness" of economic activity, in contrast to the "undersocialized" nature of *homo economicus*.[5]

If the behaviors of producers and users—their expectations, preference structures, and so on—differ considerably from place to place, it stands to reason that some types of behavioral routines, and the rules and institutions that underlie them, are more effective at promoting interactions that sustain technological learning than others. This suggests, in other words, that the potential positive externalities of production networks, in the form of technological learning, are only realized—or are differentially realized—according to the concrete qualities of the transacting that is carried out. It directs our attention toward the theoretical and empirical problem of the *qualitative basis and differentiation of external economies*.

Although some of these differences in outcome could, in principle, reflect different behavioral preferences of the people who constitute the production network, the question would still arise as to why some preferences are shared or why, in any case, the preferences of some people become the norms of the network.[6] Stated another way, only some preferences take the form of mutual engagements and thus become enforceable social habits of the transactional activity that underlies technological learning. It is therefore necessary to identify the key principles of mutual engagement of the critical agents in the production system, what we have termed the conventions of that production network and its agglomeration. Conventions reduce the uncertainty that is felt by economic agents as they confront a bewildering variety of factors; they create specific possibilities by mobilizing qualitatively distinct forms of physical and intangible resources that go into particular products (such as the mobilization of a qualitatively distinct kind of labor or entrepreneurial activity); and they define the relative economic values of qualitatively distinct products and factors of production (and thus define principles of the distribution of income). The conventions that support technological dynamism were identified in the previous chapter, among the most important of which are (1) patterns of resource mobilization; (2) forms of collective order in labor markets and interfirm relations; (3) the conventions that define product quality; (4) the relations between key innovating groups and other groups in the production system; (5) the roles of regional and local third parties in harmonizing preference structures; and (6) the ideologies and cultures of local economic actors. A set of conventions defines a local world of production. Such a world consists of practices, institutions, and material objects/tools, but it is also a universe of action that incorporates specific forms of cognition, theories, doctrines, institutions, and rules.[7]

If we assume that systems of production characterized by technological learning have different evolutionary properties from those systems that are not oriented toward such learning, then it is by looking at the worlds of production and their underlying conventions of different systems that we may be able to discover the sources of learning and the different forms it may take.[8] This, then, is the field of inquiry into the sources of technologically dynamic or learning-rich production systems, and the differences between these systems and others. It involves a structured conceptualization of a broad set of features of a regional political–economic culture, its institutions, and the behavioral routines of its collective agents.

IDENTIFYING LEARNING-BASED PRODUCTION SYSTEMS

In this chapter, we visit cases of technologically dynamic, geographically agglomerated, flexible production regions in France, Italy, and the United States.[9] Each region contains an industrial complex in a sector that represents a significant international trade specialization for its country. It was noted previously, in Chapter 2, that investigations by evolutionary economists have shown trade specialization among advanced economies to be increasing, and that the reason for such specialization is the advent of absolute advantage based on superior localized technological learning. We will show systematically, in Chapter 8, that such learning-specialized sectors also have a distinct geography of agglomeration in a restricted number of subnational core regions in their respective countries. In this chapter, we look at the conventions of learning in three such "technology districts": high-technology systems construction and fashion industries in the Paris region, craft-based consumer articles in Northeast Central Italy, and microelectronics in California. Much has been written about each of them and no pretense to replicating the depth of such literature can be made here; instead, a reinterpretation in terms of the notion of conventionally-based and regionalized frameworks of action—*regional worlds of production*—is offered. The existence and persistence of these region-specific relational assets permits a compelling account of their ongoing agglomerative character, as well as of their organizational specificities and absolute technological advantages.

NORTHEAST CENTRAL ITALY: HIGH ENTRY, CLOSE COORDINATION, REGIONAL CLOSURE

The story of industrial growth in Northeast Central Italy (NEC Italy), or what is now known as the "Third" Italy of Emilia–Romagna, Tuscany, the Veneto, and the Marches, has now been told so many times that little can be added to the factual account here.[10] In these regions, especially over the 1960s and 1970s, there was a remarkable growth of employment and output in the design-intensive or craft-based industries, producing mostly fashion goods— clothing, leather, fabrics, furniture, and personal accessories—but also frequently extending to the machinery sectors associated with these final outputs, and occasionally including other metalworking or mechanical industries (such as food processing or packaging machinery). In a number of sectors, these regions produce very high proportions of Italian exported outputs, and in a few, they are absolutely dominant in world markets (e.g., woolen fabrics in Prato).[11]

These areas are distinguished by their dense clusters of very small firms (those whose size averages 10 employees or less). It is important to note that other local industrial areas in Italy share these characteristics of small size, large numbers, and dense local concentration in narrow sectoral specializations, but that only in NEC Italy has rapid growth in per-capita income relative to these other areas occurred in tandem with the growth process in general. Numerous quantitative and qualitative analyses have shown that NEC Italy is different from the other areas in that the firms partake of a local, vertical division of labor, whereas in other areas there tend to be clusters of firms that carry out similar tasks. Also, in NEC Italy, the local production system is richly endowed with commercial agents who organize the production activities and market the local products as final outputs, with a local, independent brand name, whereas in other areas, firms are frequently either subcontractors to larger, external firms (especially to Piemontese or Milanese firms), or they sell intermediate inputs on open markets.[12]

Southern European Latin–Catholic Capitalism

There exists a long line of thought on the specificities of capitalist development in the Latin countries of Southern Europe. These places have developed along fundamentally different lines from the Protestant, Anglo-Saxon capitalism of the Rhenish–Lotharingian system (with Lombardy, however, included in the latter). Barrington Moore's well-known thesis of a "conservative modernization" that preserves political stability at the price of more rapid growth and technological change is the key point of reference.[13] Southern Europe is distinguished by: the importance of its petite bourgeoisie (20–30% of the total workforce as compared to 8–12% in Northern Europe); by political institutions rooted in clientelism (frequently church-, class- and family-based, sometimes Mafia-based), whose exchanges of favors secure political stability but slow down economic adjustments by impeding factor mobility; and by a conflictual and group-based form of democracy wherein rights are secured through hard, active social conflicts, as opposed to the individualistic forms of citizenship and the administered quality of Northern European democracies.[14]

This background to NEC Italian development, however, does not account for why the economic experience of these regions has been so different from most areas in Italy, Spain, and France: on the one hand, why the systems of NEC Italy have not stagnated as in Southern Italy; on the other, why the decentralized model of production has so much more force here than in France. In NEC Italy, for example, the traditional petite bourgeoisie has transformed itself into a rich and privileged entrepreneurial middle class, extremely rapid economic growth has now been joined to high levels of political stability, and clientelism seems to have assumed highly modern forms that do not, at least to the degree envisioned by Moore's theory, impede economic adjustments, but instead channel them in qualitatively specific ways.

Many accounts of the development of the Third Italy identify the traditional roots of the contemporary situation. The elites of the region (the Tuscan moderates [*moderati Toscani*] and their more urban Emilian counterparts) were essentially antiindustrial in outlook, preferring production of strictly artisanal, very high quality items via the labor of "court artisans" (essentially urban designers) and their rural artisan–laborers, especially in the time of the Renaissance.[15] These were rural, but not socially backward, societies. It is said that the unusual postwar communism of some parts of the Third Italy was built on these cultural foundations, which also underlie the strong modernistic commitments of its local governments.[16]

While all this is important, it does not, in and of itself, explain what happened in the postwar period to form the existing production systems. In the postwar period, the first two groups (designers and rural artisans) have somehow managed to construct production systems with the latter two groups (new entrepreneur/artisans and new skilled workers), in a way that suits them both. It seems that in the first phase, the 1950s, the new entrepreneur/artisans were leaving agriculture, but taking with them their esteem for independence, craft, and their rejection of paternalism—their traditional ideologies.[17] They did not enter industry and compete with the existing designer elites and artisans, however; instead, they defined another market niche, that of relatively standardized goods, and began to produce for Italy's then rapidly expanding consumer markets. In this respect, the early configuration of Third Italian industry is typical of any developing country: vertical disintegration adjusts the production structure to a demand that is in continuous formation.[18] What is notable here is that this job of industrialization could be carried out in this manner because of the simultaneous existence of these entrepreneurs and the fact that no superior organizational structure (for example, large companies as in the United States or Britain, or the state and rigid local elites as in France) existed to block them.

As the burst of postwar market growth slowed down, however, the industries entered a critical stage, which might very well have resulted in consolidation of industrial structures around mass production of standardized goods. The "first" crisis of the Third Italy played itself out in the late 1950s and early 1960s in the form of massive surplus capacity in the production of standardized goods. The crisis was solved by moving up-market into higher quality goods, and by moving from national to international markets.[19] Here, cooperation between the existing highly skilled groups and the new entrepreneurs was critical in turning a potentially catastrophic situation into a great success. How did this happen?

The point of departure of virtually all the detailed studies of the NEC Italian production systems by both admirers and detractors—is that they should not be regarded as collections of small firms, but rather something akin to multiproduct organizations, and that the internal institutional arrangements of the systems are deeply inscribed in broader social arrangements (or what economists might call the "institutional environment"). The original contribution of the present analysis is to systematize the understanding of how these arrangements constitute conventions that underlie the economic performance of these production systems.

Conventions of Participation and Identity, and Action Frameworks in NEC Italy

Figure 6.1 offers a schematic view of the conventions of participation and identity in the Emilian and Tuscan real worlds of export-specialized produc-

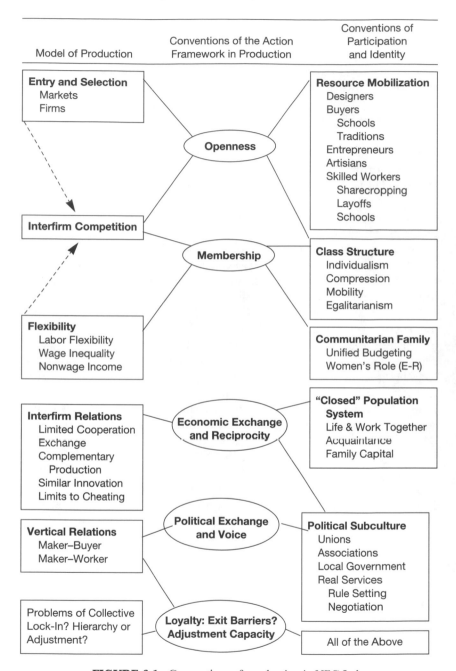

FIGURE 6.1. Conventions of production in NEC Italy.

tion systems. On the left are components of the model of production (markets, firms, the division of labor, innovation, economic efficiency): these are *domains of economic action* and its results. On the right are the conventions of participation and identity mobilized by different groups, as well as the form they take. The middle column indicates the *conventions* of the action framework in production.

Selection and Entry: Resource Mobilization and the Identities of Groups

Five basic communities have been mobilized to construct the production systems of NEC Italy: (1) buyers, designers, and innovators; (2) middle-class entrepreneurs; (3) new entrepreneur/artisans; (4) homeworkers; and (5) skilled workers. The conventions of identity of these groups are quite diverse, and the borders between some of them are quite fluid.

For example, in the Tuscan fashion industries, there are special agents who almost always take care of buying products from producing firms, intermediating between the production system and the market; and there are designers who possess brand names or skills recognized directly on national and international markets. The ranks of these key agents are difficult to penetrate—there are skill and reputation barriers—but surprisingly, there is considerable turnover. Thus although designers are the modern heirs of aristocratic tastes (in Tuscany), their ranks were never fully closed as in the case of French *corporations*.[20] And in Emilia, product innovators rather frequently are former skilled workers who have attended technical schools, or have teamed up with scientists and technicians encountered through those schools. These production systems are thus strongly shaped by conventions of participation that allow entry into key technology-mastering groups.

Entrepreneurial activity in Emilia and Tuscany is mobilized by a series of push and pull factors that favor innovation. Middle-class entrepreneurs are usually first-generation inheritors of enterprises started by their parents; the stratified class barriers typical of the industrial north do not exist in the industrial economies of these regions. More recent firms are frequently of the smaller, artisanal (less than 10 worker) type. Here, entrepreneurs in the twentieth century have had three principal avenues of access to industrial activity: many were released from agriculture, specifically from *mezzadria* (sharecropping), the dominant form of agricultural organization in both regions. Indeed, sharecropping was dominant in NEC Italy only; historically it was fully dominant in *no* other European region.[21] This provided unusually strong experience in organizing independent, small-scale, family-based economic activity, and an extremely strong ideology of economic independence, or at least an unwillingness to work directly as a wage laborer. As late as 1950, 40% of the population of these regions was employed in agriculture; that figure had dropped to below 10% by the end of the 1970s.

A second source of entrepreneurs, principally in the metalworking sector of Emilia, is technical schools, which have a long history in the region. These schools combine theoretical and practical training, thus enabling innovative, but applied, activity. And as they were founded and operated in a region noted for its socialist orientation, they have been accessible to people from all classes.[22] Third, in the postwar period, both Emilia and Tuscany suffered massive layoffs of workers from large industrial plants, but those workers typically did not emigrate from the region, turning instead to entrepreneurial activity. Many were highly skilled workers provided with machines by former employers to start their own firms. One further asset: many families that remained in agriculture, and some who turned to urban work, had at least one member available for industrial homework, including many women with skills in earlier specialties of these regions, such as weaving straw hats (*paglia*) in Emilia, a predecessor of the knitwear industry. Women homeworkers in Emilia have been politically organized for many decades, able to formalize their work and institutionalize their position in the regional economy. In both these regions, but especially in Emilia–Romagna, the class structure is compressed: the structural differentiation typical of large-scale industrial centers has not been heavily in evidence in the 20th century; rather, the region has manifested such qualities as a spirit of egalitarianism and there have been high levels of upward mobility from working to entrepreneurial class, and quantitatively a low level of income inequality when compared to the North or the South.[23]

These conventions of participation have had a clear functional effect: the rate of entry into entrepreneurial activity has been extraordinarily high. And that, in turn, has had distinct economic outcomes as it tends to favor regional production activity directed at markets for products whose qualities are most amenable to a structure with low barriers to entry and resulting high levels of productive decentralization.

Flexibility: Resources, Membership, and the Family[24]

NEC Italy is characterized by a family structure—the "communitarian family"—almost unique in Europe: extended family households, in which parental (usually paternal) authority is secure, hierarchical, and multigenerational, coupled with a tradition of fully equal inheritance among siblings. The economic logic in this kind of situation very clearly calls for unified family budgeting, that is, families share income with a goal of maximizing the income of the whole rather than the individual parts. This is enforced by the authority wielded by the *capofamiglia*. The logic of individual labor is not predominant,[25] nor is the logic of individual survival, which makes economic fluctuations less traumatic for individuals.[26] Most students of NEC Italy insist that work, entrepreneurship, and participation in the region cannot be understood by looking at the individual in the labor market, but must be analyzed in terms of the individual within the family unit. This membership has many effects on the structure of the production system; for instance, as noted above, smaller firms generally are characterized by lower productivity and hourly wages than larger firms, but in this region, income redistribution within the communitarian family compensates for lower individual earnings as a rule in the short run, and in the long run by accumulation of productive and real capital, which is then used to generate rents.

For both entrepreneurs and workers, profit is a source of income in boom times. Quasirents earned on some products made in the region come directly to entrepreneurs, who, in some cases, share them out with higher wages for loyal, skilled employees. This mechanism, combined with family income pooling, has allowed the extraordinary levels of capital accumulation and firm formation in the region. The principal way of raising incomes, over the 1960s and 1970s, was not, in any case, through productivity-led price reductions, but by moving up the price–performance curve to "better" goods, and by enlarging markets geographically (that is, by further internationalization).[27]

For entrepreneurs, then, the advantages are clear. But why are workers willing to tolerate wage inequalities vis-à-vis larger firms? To be sure, many have few formal skills and could not secure positions in larger "industrial" operations; this is certainly true of a significant number of workers in the smaller firms, and of homeworkers, who are frequently overworked and underpaid. On the other hand, interviews with workers in the small firms suggest that many hope to become entrepreneurs themselves, and prefer smaller firms because of family and friendship connections, and they can use their experience in these firms to learn about entrepreneurship.[28] Where extended family relations are involved, these workers will often be partially financed by their "employers" later on.[29] This is not an unusual trajectory: one recent survey found 56% of workers had moved from firm to firm voluntarily at least three times, and 10% more than three times.[30] As a representative of the *Confederazione Generale Italiana del Lavoro* (Italian General Confederation of Labor) put it recently:

> The features of work in industrial districts are at the root of the difference between district workers and workers in traditional businesses. In districts, for example, work may be paid for by a combination of earnings and a share in company ownership. Those workers who possess the greatest professional skills are in a position to use this as a lever on the labour market and hence to move from one firm to the next until they are offered a real stake in the ownership of the firm for which they work.[31]

In short, membership has a redistributive, income-smoothing effect that provides firms extraordinary labor flexibility while providing nonwage income for a large number of entrepreneurs, and training for a certain number of workers. The one group that is largely left out is the homeworkers.

These circumstances call attention to a critical dimension of the role of labor in the production system: the motivations of those who work—the ways they interpret their own circumstances—have to do with their wider network of social relations. Their interpretation of overall income and life-chance structures is as important in mobilizing them as a collective resource as their immediate hourly pay conditions and their formal status as wage labor.[32]

Interfirm Competition: Openness and Membership[23]

In NEC Italy, ease and continuity of entry virtually guarantee high levels of interfirm competition. Ideologies of economic independence, combined with a compressed class structure, make entrepreneurs equals among equals; there is little of the paternalism and local hierarchy—both of which limit the possibility of interfirm competition—found in many systems for producing design-intensive products elsewhere in Europe. Interfirm competition is assured, moreover, by the system of commercialization: buyers, designers, or final-output manufacturers are all keenly aware of the prices and qualities that the area's best producers can offer, and enforce these standards on all firms to which they give orders.[34] Fierce, though bounded, local competition is the order of the day.

Interfirm Relations: Reciprocity and Social Closure[35]

At the same time, local populations of NEC Italy are characterized by high levels of closure, that is, high percentages of those living and working in the area were born there.[36] In strictly economic terms, this is reflected in the very low levels of internationalization of ownership and control of firms, and in very high levels of ownership and control by natives of the regions.[37] This does not imply the absence of capital and resources from outside the regions, or outside Italy—indeed, the levels of strategic alliances and external capital participation have tended to rise in recent years—but overall extraregional and international participation remain strikingly low.

Here, economic reciprocity depends essentially on dense interpersonal ties between individuals and families who know each other for life. The most common form of cooperation between firms is work sharing: a firm with too much work may share it out with other firms, expecting a return when the shoe is on the other foot. At times, firms will even permit workers from another firm to use their equipment on their premises. There are also limits to cheating, which takes two principal forms in these contexts. In a fiercely competitive environment, when work loads are low, producers might bid below their average costs rather than have no work at all, in an effort to buttress their connections to the buyers. For their part, buyers might force down prices to untenable levels when their power is great. Both of these behaviors do occur, but they have been surprisingly rare, even in the very difficult 1980s. One can only assume that the circulation of information is such that the negative reputation effects outweigh, in most cases, the temptation to cheat.

Finally, as we noted earlier, dense connections between people promote complementary technological developments in both the fashion and mechanical engineering sectors. In the latter, there are numerous documented instances of firms aiding skilled workers to set up their own firms, but in complementary or cognate, rather than directly competitive product lines. User–producer relations for complementary technological improvements and market widening are thus the basis for economic reciprocity.[38]

Vertical Relations: Voice and the Definition of the Common Good[39]

The regions of NEC Italy are characterized by distinctive political subcultures: both the communist ("red") areas of Emilia and Tuscany, and the Christian Democratic ("white") areas of the Veneto or Friuli–Venezia–Giulia, have distinctive, uncontested local political majorities. These unified political subcultures tend to aggregate fragmented demands and free the local political system from pressures of divided loyalties[40] (this did not change in the 1993 elections, where the PDS is well installed in Emilia, for example). Political stability also provides the opportunity to construct mechanisms for voice between the principal parties in the local economy, and so to negotiate solutions to problems. Neither the "red" nor the "white" regimes are heavily associated with the ideologically motivated programs those labels normally suggest: both are fundamentally neolocalist, devoted to a local definition of the common good, although the organizations through which voice is exercised do have different ideological colors: in the red areas, through unions and cooperatives, as well as artisanal associations and local government agencies; in the white areas through linkage to the local church, rural savings banks, charities, and agricultural organizations.

In Emilia, unions have been considerably more favorable to the system of decentralized production than in Tuscany, where they have opposed small firms as backward and contrary to the interests of the working class.[41] In both, only about one-third of the workers in the artisanal firms are organized, while more than 70% in firms employing more than 100 workers in Emilia are in unions. In both regions, however, unions have been critical in securing district-wide agreements that protect wages even in the smallest, artisanal firms, even where—as in Tuscany—they refuse to participate actively and ideologically in political projects to "build" the decentralized production structure. Other critical organizational bases of voice include the local branches of the *Confederazione Nazionale d'Artigianato* (CNA), which negotiate for the smallest firms, as well as industry associations of the kind found elsewhere. Thus, the local system is highly negotiated and inclusive, but in the form of a four-party local corporatism: artisans, unions, political party locals, and local–regional governments. The leadership of these groups is strongly interlocking in Emilia–Romagna and Tuscany; an unusually strong case of "tight" social networks is in evidence. In combination with the relatively low level of entry–exit in the regional population and the communitarian family system, the effect is a strong push for mutual acceptance of collective actors.

These conventions of participation have a strong influence on the nature of products made in these regions: their collective capacity to innovate is rooted in the very high motivation for problem solving at the regional level and for avoiding deep distributional conflicts; both are consistent with gradual innovation rather than radical departures that could cause upheavals in roles and divisions of labor.

Labor Conventions

One outcome of such problem solving is "flexible rigidities."[42] Unions secure district-wide agreements on wages and working conditions. In the Prato woolen textiles district, for example, unions have negotiated an agreement on the production calendar covering hundreds of mills that share the same production cycles, agreeing to reduce the work week but allowing overtime (without wage premiums) when demand is high, with overtime hours banked against slack periods of the year. The agreement's preamble states that "both unions and industry recognize the need to find solutions to plant restructuring, above all regarding personnel redundancy."[43] This type of agreement is important for the mutual obligations it creates: unions support the modernization of firms, and do not take advantage of boom times to press for conditions that are untenable across the entire production cycle or across the booms and busts inherent to the fashion industries. Employers commit themselves to paying wages in the slack parts of the production cycle, and to avoid redundancy when there are cyclical downturns. How important are these mechanisms? Perulli surveyed a large number of firms in Modena (Emilia–Romagna) and found that 20% of artisanal firms bargained with unions for flexible working arrangements, 50% of all firms had temporary contracts for young workers, 50% incorporated internal mobility and flexible work organization in their contracts, and fully 60% had agreements for working-time flexibility over the year.[44]

There are certain differences between red and white areas in the ways these flexible rigidities are maintained—the former tend to have more, but less severe, labor conflicts than the latter—but in both cases, there are almost never strong, prolonged attempts by employers to deunionize or severely reduce worker protections in the district-wide agreements.[45]

There are two weak points in employer–worker relations. First, homeworkers are rarely unionized, although they have secured legal protections through regional government actions in recent years (indeed, homework is highly regulated in Emilia and Tuscany); this gives homeworkers certain legal minima, but little collective bargaining power.[46] Second, a critical group of "employers," the buyers, operate largely outside the system of flexible rigidities. They remain extremely flexible with respect even to the established middle-sized firms in the fashion industries, and everybody else must absorb the effects of such flexibility. Buyers transmit the force of the market to the production system directly, and can create significant stress on firms and workers who are party to the kinds of flexibly rigid agreements described here.

A Local Definition of the Common Good

Local political solidarity in NEC Italy also takes the more traditional form of "sectionalism," that is, lobbying in the local interest with respect to the national government. This sectionalism can even involve strong vertical solidarities. Artisanal firms, for example, have been steadily institutionalized in the form of a series of national laws on financial assistance for machinery acquisition, R&D support, supporting cooperatives,[17] and the basic artisanal statute, which deregulates labor markets for firms with fewer than 10 employees. The CNA, which has powerful branches throughout Italy, has been instrumental in securing such protections for small firms. Local governments in the red areas have helped passage of these laws by contributing to the national majorities, despite the fact that the national government was dominated by the Christian Democrats for most of the postwar period. This is another example of how solid local structures can exercise voice on behalf of particular strata in local production systems. While sectionalism on behalf of local *firms* is not unknown in other countries, vertical solidarity works to considerable effect in the presence of local voice systems such as those described here: national protections for homeworkers (largely unenforced elsewhere) were supported by the entire political spectrum in Emilia, including employers of all types.

SPLENDOR, CADRE, AND CORPORATION IN THE ÎLE-DE-FRANCE

France has not been a favored subject of either the literature on technological innovation (where the subjects are almost always Japan and the United States) or on production flexibility (where the subjects are almost always Italy and

Germany). In large part, this is because France is a weak specializer at this moment in history; it has few dramatic strong points in international trade, in the sense of whole clusters of related industries such as the broad American position in high technology or the Italian position in craft-based industries, although it has many moderately good positions.[48] This is curious in light of the fact that France is a wealthy, technologically advanced nation. In part, it is a legacy of French economic planning, which for quite some time stressed self-sufficiency rather than specialization. But this is not an adequate response to the question of why France is generally technologically *competent* but not very *specialized* or *dynamic*.

France has also been ignored because there is no single, most visible model of technological dynamism underlying its international successes. There are *many Frances,* an observation that may carry some irony in that European nation with longest-lasting highly centralizing state economic policy apparatus.[49] The *Francilien* model is that of high technology and, to a lesser extent, design-intensive crafts industries in the Paris region: the Île-de-France. The *Rhôdanien* model concerns design-intensive and craft-based industries, and metalworking-mechanical sectors in the Rhône–Alpes region. The *Occitanien–Provençal* model (in which I include Grenoble and the Val d'Isère) refers to the growth of high-technology manufacturing and services in selected areas of southern France. A fourth model, that of the "nouvelle ouest" (Vendée, parts of Bretagne), refers to a form of low-wage, highly flexible rural industrialization which is not technologically dynamic. Length limitations permit us to analyze only the Francilien model here.

The Pieces of the Puzzle: Foundations of the Conventions of Production

There are common features to the way that conventions of economic activity are structured in France, whatever the region. All of the systems have three basic building groups, each of which is highly internally ("horizontally") organized: (1) employers or the *patronat*; (2) the state (including both the central state and local political brokers or *notables*); (3) workers, and their communities and cultures of *métier* (craft). The different regions are distinguished by the qualities of these groups and their modes of insertion into their respective regional political economies. All of the systems are also *vertically conflictual,* in a way that the Third Italy is not. In each of the cases of a successful regional specialization, one of the groups has the ability and incentive to define the advanced products. A set of detailed practices for mobilizing innovative knowledge, creating markets, and regulating labor market transactions either resolves, in a very specific way, the underlying vertical conflict which is typical of French economic life or allows the group with innovative capacity to impose its will on the others. It is these conventions of the identity of innovating groups and their participation with respect to other groups in the hierarchy that are described below for the specializations of the Île-de-France.

The Francilien Model: High Technology and High Fashion

Different as they are, both the high-fashion and the high-technology industries of the Île-de-France derive their dynamism from the existence of steep organizational hierarchies and the power of parallel elites in creating, defining, and organizing their markets. In the Francilien model, we observe a stop-and-go system of innovation in the high technologies that is dependent on decisions of the state technocracy; in the *haute couture* industries of the same region, the couturiers are the equivalent of the state; they make and impose decisions about fashion innovation.

Fashion Clothing in the Île-de-France

The high-fashion industries of the Paris region include two basic segments: true *haute couture*, where the product is made in batches of less than 10 and the production process is truly artisanal (St. Laurent has less than 50 in-house couturiers), and the much larger brand name ready-to-wear market (moderately expensive clothes produced in small-to-medium-sized batches on a strictly seasonal basis). Notwithstanding the decentralization of significant amounts of production in the latter segment to other regions of France or even abroad (for example, to former French colonies in the Mediterranean), the production complex has not only held its own in the central Paris neighborhood known as the *sentier*, but has grown somewhat in recent years.[50]

What are now known as the *maisons de haute couture*, of course, date back to the early part of the 20th century when Paris, as one of the cultural capitals of the western world, took the lead in developing clothes for the woman liberated from bourgeois dress of the 19th century.[51] But the Chanels of the world are really just the latest phase in Paris' role as capital of fashion and luxury goods production. It was under Louis XIV that Colbert established the various royal manufactures, such as the one at Sèvres for porcelain and crystal, and at the Gobelins for tapestries and rugs.[52] The centralization of royal commands and the enforcement and centralization of standards of quality for a production process that continued to be artisanal, mobilized resources and made possible shifts in commands according to the whims of royal fashion. It was a means to quality control: the establishment of a *convention of quality*, deeply rooted in the use of clothing to eroticize and play on identities among the elites of the court.

Paris was already a center of clothing fashion in the 17th century because it was the political capital of Europe, locus of Europe's most centralized court: men and women from England to the west and Poland and Russia to the east looked to Paris to know how to dress. Clothes were made to order by individual artisans, of which the Paris region counted a considerable number. There were, however, already two elements of consolidation of the production system: on one hand, a system of fashion magazines that channeled commands; on the other, a system of input manufactures—silk in Lyon, lace and *bonnetterie* in the North—which were well-organized to produce in volume. What motivated the whole system was the fashion authority of the court. Because of its commitment to luxury and refinement, many refer to this type of production as based on the French commitment to *splendeur* (splendor). Throughout the 18th century, this system grew ever more splendid.[53] In the bourgeois society that succeeded the Revolution, the fetish of fashion lived on, and clothing design was considered to be one of the *beaux arts*. Bourgeois men engaged in dandyism in the 19th century[54]; for women, the situation is summed up in the slogan of the *Magasin des Modes:* "l'ennui nâquit un jour de l'uniformité."[55]

The modern *haute couture* system is, in many ways, a natural reincarnation of the old royal system, where the designers occupy a key position in dictating the norms of fashion. Like their royal counterparts, they are the authority behind the convention of quality for the fashion good: they give it empirical substance and organizational continuity. As long as their ranks are stable, there are no shake-ups in the structure of the production system because they control the brand name.[56] Splendor, as a convention of product quality, has been carried forth to the present day.

With the rise of new social groups, especially the urban professional classes, new forms of social distinction in fashion have also come about: strict high fashion has been replaced by more widely marketed but nonetheless not mass-produced garments. The *prêt-à-porter* (ready-to-wear) system is a kind of half-way house between high fashion and the competitive sweatshop system found in the United States. The principal resource is the design of the garment—the trademark that carries the signification of quality—and this is still well guarded by the fashion houses, whose ranks are fairly closed, and the upper levels of the distribution network.[58] These garments cannot be produced in-house if costs are to be controlled. A classic system of subcontracted cutting and sewing is used, where ethnic solidarity characterizes each level of the system: the design houses and distribution network of boutiques (French), the cutters (Middle Eastern or Jewish), and the sewers (Turkish, North African). The labor market for this industry, while relying on ethnic selection, is essentially a *liberal* one, lacking unions and any strong role for familiies. Only the more highly skilled workers, such as cutters, have a strong craft identity: their work rules are their own, and their labor processes are not rationalized or codified by any outside force, including their employers. Jewish-owned sewing houses, I was told in an interview, have an informal cartel that has maintained constant real prices over the last 20 years and this explains why manufacturers (design houses) have not eliminated them through the price squeeze tactics used in many other garment districts of the world. Vertical conflict between highly skilled workers and small subcontracting firms, or between the latter and design houses, is very strong in this kind of industry. Price squeezing is not unknown, as is illegal labor, although these types of activity are reserved for "knock-off" fashion, the next lowest level in the system (that is, fashionable but cheaper). The key way that vertical conflict is dampened is that the whole industry depends on considerable quasirents, owing to the brand names of the garments and the relatively closed ranks of the Paris boutique trade. As a result, there is still a great deal of cost pass-through in the fashionable ready-to-wear market.[59]

A third level of the fashion system is "young look" or knock-off apparel, which are copies of better ready-to-wear at much lower quality, and aimed at younger buyers via low prices. Fashions have a short life span, so proximity to the design community is essential. This is the sweatshop segment of the industry, yet it does not threaten ready-to-wear because of the strong vertical control noted above, and its dependence on those same designers. Spatial proximity and organizationally distinct roles are the rule.

The dynamism of the system is thus the design apparatus and it is able to maintain its position through its control of conventions of product quality and the distribution network. This dynamism is also the source of what might be dubbed the "technological conservatism" of the system, since it prevents major new groups from entering the ranks of designers; the system remains "royal," in the sense of hierarchical and closed. The conservatism of the system, due to the oligopoly that controls it, prevents the liberal labor market from becoming a sweatshop market, by enabling the designers to pass through quasirents for these relatively expensive garments; it also avoids (at least in part) the temptation to move much of the subcontracting outside of Paris altogether. Yet, this is not, in the end, an inclusive system as in the Third Italy. In overseas markets, the fashionable prêt-à-porter industries of other countries, including Italy and Germany, have grown more rapidly than the French, for both cost and design reasons.[60]

High Technology in the Île-de-France

The high-technology industries of the Île-de-France are also organized by an elite and they are conservatively innovative. In aerospace and electronics, there are only a few important systems integrators and components producers in France, such as Thomson, Matra, Dassault, Aérospatiale, and SNECMA. The products in which French high technology has been internationally successful are overwhelmingly those in which the state's purchases are important and include: nuclear reactors, digital processors, off-line data processing equipment, radar equipment, telecommunications switching gear, and large aircraft. It must also be remembered that since the 1950s, French industrial planning has been based on a technological concept—that of the *filière* (commodity chain)—and not on final markets: the idea is that industrial competence includes the entire commodity chain.[61] The convention of quality is a *technological* one and the tradition of splendor continues here, where French industrial planners are noted for undertaking ambitious high-technology projects. Thus, when a command for an existing or developing high-technology product is received by a prime contractor in France, it may also be accompanied by an analysis of the filière, and an offer on the part of the state (in the form of a plan or a set of coordinated incentives), to support further development of that filière. The most recent example of this is the *plan calcul* (computer industry development plan).[62] This differs from the American defense contracting system, where the development of the filière (through subcontracting or in-house divisions) is left up to the prime contractors themselves.

The definition of the convention of quality comes out of a restricted milieu of agents. As is well known, France has an extremely able and highly prestigious state technocracy, graduates of the institutes of specialized higher education, which constitute a system of superuniversities known as the *grandes écoles*.[63] These engineers and administrators not only occupy the upper ranks of various ministries and state-owned consumers of high-technology systems (such as France Télécom), but also most of the private or semiprivate high-technology firms.[64] The first tier of the production system, the large contractors and the state bureaucracies, are run by a closed elite. The purchasing power of the state is very important. There is, as a result, very little "user–producer" feedback in the way this is normally understood: markets are concentrated, and the key producers are also members of the key user (state) group.

Resources are mobilized in a very different way in the second tier, that is, the network of input suppliers. The first thing to note is that, in spite of the centralizing traditions of both state and employers in France, the Paris region is an extremely large and diversified economy; the opportunity grid is enormous and the rate of new firm start-ups in high-technology industries has been very high over the past decade.[65] But there are few examples, in France, of a start-up company becoming a major high-technology enterprise, as did Apple in the United States in the 1970s or Hewlett-Packard in the 1950s. This is because the system of commands, of access to markets, is highly organized by the state and the large companies.

The counterpart, however, is that networks are more faithful: a subcontractor firm that curries the right relationships can enjoy a high degree of loyalty, although access is still determined in large measure by the type of connections the principal of the firm possesses: if an engineer is from a *grande école*, he has a much greater probability of receiving state or large-firm contracts than someone who doesn't. In sum: the rate of spin-off is lower than in the United States, but the interfirm relations between these two levels of the production network are likely to be more faithful, due to smaller numbers and social solidarity at both levels.

Labor relations play an important role in technological dynamism and its limits. The Paris region is often taken to be *the* model of French labor relations, but in fact its labor markets are constructed on a cultural base and political history that is relatively specific to the region.[66] The old guild-like organizations (*corporations*) of artisans (*compagnons*) were destroyed in the Revolution, but their spirit, paradoxically, lives on in another form—in French working habits, where the rules of the *métier* are guides for conduct.[67] As a result, one can find a kind of disrespect for organizational–bureaucratic rules and weak organizational capacity among the French working class of the Paris region; its famous "anarcho-syndicalist" mix. The French employer class has historically reacted with great resistance to the demands of workers, whether this be the strictly private-owner class or their equivalents in state-owned companies. Large French companies have a well-documented mix of Taylorist work processes and a tendency toward patriarchal and personalistic treatment of workers, including frequent violations by employers of their own Tayloristic rules.[68] The result is that French industry has, for much of the 20th century, been characterized by strong vertical conflict, in the form of occasional violent labor–capital conflicts; but these are not translated into sustained struggles on the part of workers. Anarcho-syndicalists are unionists with passionate convictions but low organizational capacity.[69]

It is the state that has intermediated between these two groups, usually through the system of branch agreements (*conventions collectives*), that is, sector-level contracts that set the minimum standards of work and pay for each branch of industrial activity. These agreements have a mixed record; while they serve to standardize conditions for each branch, thus encouraging horizontal solidarity for both workers and employers, they also tend to rigidify work and pay conditions, and they do nothing to offset the fundamental vertical conflict between employers and workers. The system of values related to *métier* counteracts, to some extent, the branch agreements by precluding strong organizational loyalty for the worker, while the employer's essential hostility to workers and general unwillingness to engage in on-the-job training also remains in place.[70] This is as much the case in high-technology industries as anywhere else, and it has led to a rather persistent inability of French high-technology industries to reach the manufacturing quality standards of its major competitors. Labor markets are orderly, but at the price of inability to meet best-practice standards.

The state and its closely associated (or owned) companies, then, remains the key to the specializations of the Île-de-France's high-technology industries: in defense, telecommunications, and certain civilian aerospace industries, state technocrats and their equivalents in private industry pursue a market that mobilizes their technological talents, and reproduces the commercial weaknesses of French high technology.[71] With enough resolve and isolation from civilian markets, the blockages of the labor process, too, can be overcome. The result is that when the decisions of the technocratic managers are good ones, when the markets are sufficiently noncompetitive, and when the *corporations* can be made to go along, the Francilien (essentially "royal") system succeeds, often splendidly.

These systems—with their hierarchies, categorical rights and privileges, vertical conflicts, and notions of what the work of each categorical group should be—are constituted by conventions that, together, amount to a distinctive framework of action and coordination for all concerned. Out of the framework emerge products with specific qualities, adapted to particular markets by dint of these qualities. Negative selection is also at work: these systems do not do well at certain other kinds of products, in spite of massive formal efforts to promote innovation in those areas. This confirms that policy for learning is unlikely to succeed unless it acts favorably on the action frameworks of those concerned, not simply on traditional factors of production or through standard institutional channels.

INNOVATION, STANDARDIZATION, AND SUCCESSION IN CALIFORNIA

High technology and advanced services are just the latest in a series of innovative American products in the 20th century. The logic of American industrial development over this period has been to invent or—where the United States is not the first mover in purely scientific or inventive terms—to commercialize production and create mass markets for new types of goods, based on the utilization of new *basic* technologies.

Much has been written about the relationship between technological dynamism and American economic growth, with the debate centering on the relative influence of demand conditions and factor supplies. The notion that the United States has presented a special, perhaps unique, set of demand conditions for new technologies has been central to the analyses of Fishlow,[72] Rosenberg,[73] and others. In the 19th century, the occupation of a largely empty continent generated a demand for goods that were "light, fast, and cheap," rather than durable, steady, precise, or heavily ornamented. In virtually all the intermediate or producer goods sectors (guns, locomotives, industrial machinery, bicycles, agricultural equipment), American industry came up with versions that shared these three characteristics and were available to much larger markets than their European counterparts. The advent of the consumer society came early on in the United States, and it was based on a technological configuration of daily life that included capital-intensiveness (household consumer durables), large personal spaces (the need for a lot of personal goods), and a high degree of spatial separation (cars, airplanes, telephones). For much of this century the American economy has been the global leader in one after another of the different industries producing the package.

This demand-side explanation, while important, is insufficient to account for the sources of American specializations. I shall argue that the mobilization of factor supplies in innovative American production complexes stems from a set of conventions that underlie the developmental trajectory of these complexes. This trajectory may be schematized as follows:

1. The United States is the pioneer of the basic product group.
2. Industrial complexes develop rapidly through proliferation of independent firms—spin-off by new groups of entrepreneurs, involving collective identity creation and participation at the local level.
3. These industrial complexes are typically highly agglomerated, in spite of the geographical mobility and interconnectness of the American national territory.
4. Entrepreneurs typically sell out at a certain point to larger companies, who then concentrate the market. These companies mostly locate their core activities in product-pioneering industrial agglomerations.
5. Taylorization and high average productivity are attained through product standardization.
6. The United States loses its position as producer of state-of-the-art products in that sector, but its role in the U.S. economy is "succeeded" by another product-pioneering industry.

This sequence of events, and the particular way that the system operates at each of its stages, has deep and coherent causes, in the set of conventions and rationalities we shall now investigate with respect to California high-technology districts in electronics and aerospace.

In France we observed a clear vertical structure with respect to the important collective actors in the industrial system, with well-defined groups and a tendency toward conflict, and we showed that French specializations tend to be those cases where one group is capable of simultaneously overcoming the conflict and in addition has a strong technological talent. In Italy we observed high levels of horizontal inflow and a tendency for the system to adjust the relations between different groups in order to attain new cooperative "equilibria" at the level of the regional production system as a whole; new markets are actively searched out to accommodate the new actors. In the United States, we shall observe high levels of horizontal inflow into new activities and new markets, but we shall see that the principal solution to long-term problems of adjustment is *exit* of capital and labor resources rather than the search for new markets within those sectors. We can thus call this the model "Innovation, Standardization, and Succession."

The Mobilization of Resources: Innovations and Startups

Key resource mobilizing and innovating groups in the American economy have, of course, varied according to the period and the industry at hand; if, in the early 19th century it was the frontier settler, and from the mid-19th to the mid-20th it was the industrial capitalist, it is certainly now the entrepreneur/professional or scientist, especially the engineer-turned-entrepreneur. Each of these groups, while sharing the basic American faith in individual achievement, has been constituted by a distinctive set of conventions of work and identity, and each has ultimately come to be identified with a particular region of the United States.

In the 1930s, 1940s, and 1950s, the initial resource-mobilizers in what were to become the American high-technology industries were entrepreneurs whose identities were defined by their membership in a scientific–professional culture.[74] The interaction of economic process and scientific–professional culture in the United States and in the Francilien system is considerable. Formal knowledge and training are the key elements that underly admission in both cases; but unlike the engineers and scientists who graduate from the prestigious *grandes écoles* such as the École des Mines or the École Polytechnique, the American scientist–engineer receives his/her greatest social approval when formal knowledge is applied to entrepreneurial activity. Whereas in the one case, professionalism means insertion into a prestigious established hierarchy, in another it is a means to break away. The professional–scientific culture of the United States is not like craft in France or artisanship in Italy, either, for in both these cases the mastery of the skill involves solidarity and creativity within the rules, not innovation in the American sense of technological experimentation whose purpose is to break away from the existing, normal path of technological adaptation.[75] The American system is extraordinarily effective at motivating and mobilizing talent to do new things.[76]

It should be remembered that the initial entrepreneurs in the high technology sectors did have particular prior industrial or institutional experience. In the microelectronics industry, the scientists and engineers who were eventually to become the scions of Silicon Valley were originally associated either with university research programs or with defense-oriented research laboratories. The founders of what were to become the important firms in the aircraft industry were initially associated with one or another kind of machine-building industries in the eastern United States. In aerospace as well, many of today's important companies were started by individuals who had prior experience in a related sector. In some cases, these formative experiences occurred in the locality that would ultimately come to dominate the new industry (Silicon Valley); just as often, they did not (Los Angeles aerospace). The other conditions that facilitate entrepreneurial activity in the United States, despite the overwhelming importance of the large-firm sector, are well known, and include the well-developed and highly fluid capital market, and relatively low social wage and overhead costs.[77] But there are other routes as well, which depart from this purely entrepreneurial model. A number of the most important high-technology specializations of the United States today have, for considerable periods of their history, been supported by military procurement or by regulated oligopolistic markets (as in the civilian aircraft industry in the 1950s and 1960s, where the big airlines supported much of Boeing's research and development and product planning). Our purpose here is not to resolve the debate over the sources of all technological innovation in American high technology, but to note that all the high-technology industries had their origins in the technological experimentation alluded to above, even if they later developed under highly subsidized or regulated conditions. The record is clear on this for both aircraft and microelectronics, and it is currently the case for the biotechnology and medical instruments industries.[78]

The convention of quality that underlies the innovative small firm in contemporary Californian high technology is clearly the (difficult to attain) combination of adherence to a scientific rule, while coming up with a novelty (the World of Intellectual Resources as defined in Chapter 5). This may involve the new application of existing scientific knowledge, or it may involve research and development "prospecting," which is equivalent to *planning* research and development to serve a market that is yet to come into existence.[79] One can find this same phenomenon in the early history of the aircraft industry (the Loughhead [Lockheed] Brothers and Donald Douglas in the 1920s and 1930s), the microelectronics industry in Silicon Valley (Fred Terman, Steve Jobs, and others), and in the defense-related equipment sector (Simon Ramo and Howard Hughes).

Interfirm Relations: Spinoff and Agglomeration

In the California industrial districts of the 20th century, once a new domain of products becomes identified in technological terms,—that is, once we know that the industry is the "semiconductor industry" or the "aircraft industry"— the process of new firm formation takes on a much more regular pattern, that of spinoff.[80] Spinoff essentially consists of a process where *key personnel* separate themselves from existing companies in the now-established industry and set up their own firms. Two dimensions of spinoff may be noted here. On one hand, the fact that key personnel have such a strong impulse to separate themselves from existing companies and to start up their own is evidence of the deep, underlying rationality of entrepreneurialism in the United States; this career is rare for similarly competent engineers in France, where loyalty to prestigious large companies is the rule. On the other hand, these key personnel are no longer precisely the same genre of entrepreneurs who start up the industry: they are formed within an industry that is already institutionalized:

not only is the basic technological scope of the industry now defined, but its professional culture is now considerably more specific.

Spinoff begins to create a more dense transactional tissue in the industry: the proliferation of new product pioneering companies, as well as of specialized input suppliers, deepens the vertical and horizontal divisions of labor and is manifest in the growth of the local industrial complex and a tendency for average firm size to decline in early years; this has been the history of the semiconductor and aerospace industries in Silicon Valley and Los Angeles, respectively, and the process is currently unfolding in the medical instruments industry of Orange County, just south of Los Angeles.[81]

The existence of industry-specific "human capital," that is, a professional culture that is now rather precisely delimited, is an important basis of the proliferation and regulation of interfirm relations, and their geographical configuration. New firm founders are linked by their strong professional culture, which defines the rules of the game and is reinforced by relatively small numbers and personal-reputation effects. Interviews with the founders of the military equipment industry and the semiconductor industry confirm that these two mechanisms give a powerful order and coordination to transactional relations, while allowing them remarkable fluidity.[82] At the same time, since such relations are so fluid and are not governed by formal contracts, producers tend to group themselves together in geographical space so as to minimize the costs of contracting and recontracting and to maximize the probability of successful market search. This helps to explain the "paradox" of agglomeration in the United States, where the extraordinary geographical mobility of resources and the highly developed system of transport and absence of customs barriers might otherwise be thought to encourage an even more dispersed set of spatial production relations than exists.

As the industry develops, several different production complexes may come into existence (as in the cases of Dallas, Boston, Minneapolis, and Southern California in the microelectronics and computer industries, in addition to Silicon Valley). Certain highly specialized inputs may only be available from outside the locality. It is nonetheless striking that most specialized production continues to occur in a small number of highly concentrated local production complexes; it does not take on a generally dispersed pattern. The key personnel who spin off new firms have strong roots in the professional culture, which is now both industry- and agglomeration-specific, and they are highly dependent on their existing networks of contacts for information crucial to the development and marketing of technologically advanced products.[83]

Industrial "Maturity"

Industrial maturity in innovative American industries is neither strictly an outcome of product standardization nor evidence of the failure of the American

system of innovation, as is nowadays frequently claimed. It is a logical outcome of a system of conventions that privileges product-pioneering innovations but discourages certain forms of incremental innovation.

From Spinoff to Sellout

In the highly regulated military-oriented industries, the problem of interfirm
coordination is resolved by the establishment of a hierarchical system directed
by the prime contractors. But this is a special case. In other sectors, many observers have noted the relative absence of strong associational ties at the industry level, and a resistance to government regulation.[84] Market relations
and "arms-length" contracting appear to dominate.

Once a product-pioneering industry grows to the point where reputation
effects weaken, that is, where entrepreneurs are linked by their technical–professional culture but not by personal knowledge of each other, a qualitative
change in interfirm relations appears to take place. Most of the surveys of
start-up firms reveal that small entrepreneurs feel that they have no time to
coordinate among each other. They appear to feel enormous pressures from
their lenders (whether private lenders or capital markets, especially in the case
of "impatient" venture capital), the existence of legal barriers to collaboration, and the sense that there is a race to the market because others are doing
what they are doing. Under these conditions, the temptations to engage in opportunistic behavior grow, and with them the possibilities of business failure.
Opportunism includes both the "large" final-output firm that cannot secure
sufficient loyalty on the part of its input suppliers and large firms who use
their superior legal and market power to unload risk on their smaller suppliers.

The high rate of "sellout" of even successful small- and medium-sized
firms is a rational response to this system of interfirm relations; that is, a high
percentage of those firms that do not fairly rapidly go beyond a certain
threshhold of size and product diversity, and do not die in their first few years,
are sold to larger companies by their founders. The motivations cited by these
entrepreneurs are very clear: they are successful at innovation, and—faced
with the hazardous transactional environment of American industry and the
vastly superior financial resources of the large firms—they decide to capitalize
a portion of their possible stream of innovative quasirents by selling out to the
large firm.[85] They avoid a risk that is largely created by the transactional environment itself. That environment, however, is a product of the ideology of
creating and taking risks, which is deeply ingrained in the key actors' culture;
those who sell out often claim that they prefer to move on to something else
rather than struggle to survive in a morally hazardous environment.[86] The result is not simply a process of development characterized by high rates of
spinoff, but, via sellout, a generally high rate of *turbulence*.[87]

Much of this is well predicted by transactions-cost theory, for what we observe is, indeed, a series of market failures followed by a tendency toward vertical integration. Our point here is that this market "failure" is caused by the conventional nature of the market itself in American high-technology agglomerations. The markets are ordered by conventions in such a way that they fail. The sellout process is a consequence of powerful positive motivations, deeply rooted in the rationalities that lead entrepreneurs to create markets in the first place.

Selecting Innovation

The idea of *craft*—in the sense of long-term commitment to incremental improvement—is largely absent from the notion of *innovation* in the context described above. It has been closely documented that American industries lead either in very new, "breakthrough" technologies, or in applying breakthroughs that come from elsewhere directly to very standardized production processes. Japanese, German, and Italian industries, by contrast, appear to be much better at implementing continuous innovations through either factory-level or production-level learning-by-doing, *where the key to both is close transactional coordination.*[87]

From Breakthrough to Maturity

Innovation, followed by transactional "failure," ultimately encourages vertical integration. Moreover, managerial practices in large American firms are consistently more oriented toward imposing very rigid and hierarchical role distinctions and limited information feedbacks as compared to large Japanese or German firms.[89] Under these circumstances, it is perfectly logical that large American firms will do better in the manufacture of standardized products than those that require either incremental improvement or coordination of many components than competitors who are better at coordinating transactional systems, whether external or internal. It helps to explain why American product-pioneering industries enjoy a period of very high productivity, hence "maturity," after they cease to be product-pioneering.

The American System in Perspective: The Importance of Exit

The California industrial districts have a number of characteristics often seen as deviations from "normal" logics of industrial development. Yet, when viewed in light of American conventions of identity and participation in general, it can be seen that these features are deeply inscribed in a specific conventional logic of industrialization and innovation.

Product-pioneering industries in the United States are not only typically agglomerated, but these agglomerations are located outside of zones of traditional industrialization. In the case of high technology, most of the important agglomerations (Silicon Valley, Orange County, Dallas) are outside of the northeastern and midwestern industrial regions; they are also located outside of the cores of large metropolitan regions. In the new industrial spaces of the United States, there is initially no well-defined local elite that organizes the new system of social relations and mediates between interests; new industrial elites (consisting of successful entrepreneur/professionals) are formed, and they are integrated into the structure of landowning elites already in place, who profit from the rapid rise in land prices that results from the local industrialization process.[90]

In such places in California, professional culture consists of adherence to a set of conventions about work quality, one of which is the mastery of scientific or technical knowledge, the other of which is individual achievement via the use of that knowledge. The deeply rooted themes of American rationality are strongly present: equal chances via professionality or training; unequal fates via differences in level of intelligence, hard work, or luck.[91] The new industrial space is one whose politics often unfold on the basis of this rationality: the locality makes it possible for this individual effort to unfold in propitious conditions, it is not a milieu that should encourage equality and solidarity. Indeed, the latter set of conditions are held to be inimical to the product pioneering that brings the industrial complex into being in the first place.

Thus, to use Hirschman's[92] terminology, we find in contemporary California high-technology communities the paradox of a social order based on agreement about the rationality and disciplining force of exit, and this includes the phenomenon of spinoff, which is a key form that exit takes. In contrast, in the industrial communities of NEC Italy, entry is followed by loyalty and voice; and in the Francilien system, the barriers to entry are extremely high, and hierarchy combined with loyalty govern the transactional system.

Another supposed anomaly of the American innovation and manufacturing system is that it excels at basic technological innovations ("breakthroughs"), but does less well at follow-through, that is, at commercializing innovations and maintaining market shares.[93] Some have even recently claimed that the American system of breakthroughs is breaking down. [94]

On the basis of the account given here, it may be seen that follow-through is not absent in the American system; in the form of product standardization, Taylorization, and introduction of mass-production methods, American industry does follow through on its basic innovations. With the dramatic evidence of loss of American share in many high-technology markets (such as semiconductors, consumer electronics, capital goods in the electronics sector), the correct question to pose is: why do American follow-up methods not succeed in keeping their market shares? The provisional answer that follows from our account is that this follow-up privileges standardization and the efficiencies of mass production to the detriment of mixing in adaptive capacity with production, that is, incremental innovation, as seems to be so strongly in evidence in the Japanese and German manufacturing systems.[95] While much of the now extensive literature on American production methods has centered on the commitment to mass production methods as the source of this problem,[96] there may be other reasons for this systematic bias of the American productive apparatus. The conventions of the system that so effectively encourage invention and initial innovation also encourage exit on the part of innovators and do little to encourage them to turn their talents to incremental improvements that do not have immediate high payoffs. Two sectors of the economy—the highly innovative and the highly productive—have less long-term interaction than in other countries. Moreover, at a larger scale, the American economy functions via a developmental path in which sectoral succession compensates for maturity and decline; the consequences of the latter are seen as tolerable because resource mobility is such as to, so the theory goes, secure the former. When we observe advanced, high-wage economies such as the German, where the level of manufacturing employment is high and stable, we can see that the pattern of succession is not at all automatic, but governed by conventions, both informal and institutionalized. In short, the "failures" of the American system that are so often discussed today must be seen as deeply related to a set of broader, underlying conventions, as are its many strengths.

CONCLUSION

In all of the cases examined in preceding sections, there are strong points of resemblance: technologically dynamic production systems consist of clusters of firms in which the presence of an intricate social division of labor—both horizontal and vertical in nature—is in evidence at the regional level. All display high levels of external economies of scale (a large number of firms in the regional complex) and external economies of scope (a large variety of phases in the division of labor accounted for by different firms in the regional complex).

Yet the mere existence of this form of production organization—although perhaps necessary to the attainment of a high level of technological dynamism and product quality in the face of dynamism—does not constitute an explanation of the origins, developmental tendencies, or deep logics of such systems. These production systems, which are leaders in international trade, are themselves defining the best practices for their respective markets, and in some cases even creating those markets as they go along. The analytical paradox, then, is that even though all such systems do seem to share certain basic organizational characteristics, the actions that underpin them vary considerably. The conventional content of transactions is what makes them work as they do. Much of the way a given production complex functions relies on the untraded interdependencies of the actors in that complex. In the three cases examined here, we can see three very different frameworks of action and coordination, and positive selection effects of the resulting product qualities. In effect, the different regional worlds of production that are found in each of these cases also correspond to different product-based worlds, such as those analyzed in Chapter 5; more precisely, they correspond to different regional–sectoral combinations of elements from those four basic possible worlds. In all of the cases examined, the conventions are heavily inscribed in concrete relations between the participants, even in big-firm systems, where depersonalized bureaucratic rules, cosmopolitan knowledge, and far-flung exchanges of goods, personnel, and information are also in evidence. Each of these systems is therefore a regional economy of relational assets.

NOTES

1. Lundvall (1990); Hakansson (1989); Lorenz (1988).

2. Russo (1986); von Hippel (1987).

3. Lundvall (1990, p. 19).

4. For a case study of trust relations in French subcontracting networks, for example, see Lorenz (1988).

5. Granovetter (1985).

6. See Elster (1984).

7. See, inter alia, Eymard-Duvernay (1987); Thevenot (1986); Salais (1989); Centre d'Études de l'Emploi (1987); Choffel et al. (1988).

8. Nelson and Winter (1982).

9. Much more detailed versions of these case studies may be found (in French) in Salais and Storper (1993), and in abridged but still more detailed versions, in Storper and Salais (1997).

10. Bagnasco (1977); Balestri (1982); Becattini (1978); Brusco (1982); Russo (1986); Piore and Sabel (1984).

11. Sforzi (1990); Becattini (1987); Nuti (1990); Balestri (1982).

12. Sforzi (1990); Nuti (1990).

13. Moore (1966).

14. Berger (1981); Carboni (1991).

15. Becattini (1978).

16. Becattini (1978); Tinacci Mosello (1983).

17. Giovannini (1987). See also Coleman (1987) for a theoretical discussion of the link between social capital and economic capital.

18. Nuti (1990).

19. Berardi and Romagnoli (1984); Becattini (1987).

20. Becattini (1987).

21. Todd (1990).

22. Salvestrini (1965); Tinacci-Mosello (1983); Cappecchi (1990b).
23. Cappecchi (1990b).
24. Beccatini (1975, 1978); Brusco (1982); Fua and Zacchia (1983); Fua (1985).
25. Paci (1973).
26. Becattini's (1987) interpretation is thus at odds with that of Barca (1989).
27. Rey (1989).
28. Solinas (1982).
29. Dei Ottati (1987); Cappecchi (1990a,b).
30. Trigilia (1990).
31. Brutti (1990, p. 3).
32. This failure to analyze labor from both "external" and "internal" perspectives marks much non-Italian writing about labor in NEC Italy. British critics of the system, for example, stress what they see as the exploitative nature of wage-labor conditions and picture the family as inherently regressive and oppressive (Amin and Robbins, 1990). On the first point, they ignore the workers' own interpretative framework; on the second, they assume that the family is the nuclear family, saddled with obligations but containing no opportunities. Often, they make empirically untenable claims by confusing Emilia–Romagna and Tuscany with other areas of Italy, where different conditions obtain (Paci, 1973; Pesce, 1990), and virtually all tend to assume, in contrast to the views of Italian feminist scholars, that the family in the Third Italy oppresses women.
33. Le Play (1879); Becattini (1975); Ardigo and Donati (1976); Berger (1980); Paci (1980); Kertzer (1984); Giovannini (1987); Pesce (1990); Ritaine (1989); Todd (1990); Paloscia (1991).
34. Brusco (1982); Bursi (1982, 1989).
35. Becattini (1984); Bagnasco and Trigilia (1985); Trigilia (1985).
36. Bellandi (1992, personal communication).
37. Mutinelli, et al. (1991).
38. Russo (1986); Bursi (1982).
39. Becattini (1978); Bagnasco (1985); Trigilia (1985); Bordogna (1987); Perulli (1987); Scarpitti and Trigilia (1987); Becattini (1989); Ritaine (1989).
40. Trigilia (1990).
41. Trigilia (1986a,b, 1990).
42. The term is used by Trigilia (1990), who borrows it from Dore's (1987) characterization of the negotiated character of Japanese production systems.
43. The Bridge (1988).
44. Perulli (1988).
45. Trigilia (1986a,b).
46. Lazerson (1989).
47. The Sabatini Laws: 364/76, 675/77, 46/82; and the "Marcora Law."
48. Lafay and Herzog (1990).
49. Le Bras and Todd (1981).
50. Brunet (1986).
51. Lipovetsky (1987).
52. Boissonade (1931).
53. See, *inter alia,* Goncourt (1982).
54. Prevost (1957).

55. "Boredom was born one day out of uniformity."
56. Simon (1931).
57. Bourdieu and Delsaut (1975).
58. Latour (1961).
59. Montagne-Villette (1987).
60. Montagne-Villette (1987).
61. Bauchet (1986).
62. Storper and Walker (1989).
63. Suleiman (1979).
64. Bourdieu (1989).
65. Carroué (1984).
66. Le Bras and Todd (1981).
67. d'Iribarne (1989).
68. d'Iribarne (1990).
69. d'Iribarne (1990).
70. Segrestin (1985).
71. Stoffaes (1983).
72. Fishlow (1965).
73. Rosenberg (1972).
74. Ramo (1988).
75. Nelson (1988).
76. Kenney and Florida (1990).
77. Bucaille and Beauregard (1987).
78. de Vet (1990).
79. Salais and Storper (1992).
80. Scott (1988a,b).
81. Scott (1988a); de Vet (1990); Saxenian (1994).
82. Ramo (1988).
83. de Vet, (1990).
84. Saxenian (1991).
85. Bass (1993).
86. Ramo (1988).
87. Hickmann (1989).
88. For an excellent case study of Californian failure in this regard, see Stowsky (1987).
89. Aoki (1990); Coriat (1991); Hyman and Streeck (1988); Sabel et al. (1989).
90. Molotch (1975); Di Lellio (1987).
91. Bellah et al. (1985); Bloch (1991); Hartz (1955).
92. Hirschman (1970).
93. Cohen and Zysman (1986); Reich (1991).
94. Kenney and Florida (1990).
95. Best (1990); Cusumano (1985); Coriat (1991); Aoki (1990).
96. For example, Jaikumar (1986); Piore (1989).

PART IV

GLOBALIZATION AND TERRITORIAL SPECIFICITY

CHAPTER 7

Territories, Flows, and Hierarchies in the Global Economy

GLOBALIZATION AND THE INSTITUTIONS OF ECONOMIC DEVELOPMENT

In recent years, the flows of goods, services, information, capital, and people across national and regional lines have increased greatly, giving rise to the notion that modern economic activity is somehow becoming "globalized." Do these phenomena mean that contemporary economies are becoming placeless, mere flows of resources via corporate hierarchies, which are themselves not rooted in national or regional territories and therefore not subject to territorially based state institutions? This view is the underlying message of many contemporary analyses.[1] Though many commentators assign territorially based institutions, especially nation-states, a continuing role in the global economy, the balance of power is thought to be tipping in favor of globalized organizations, networks, practices, and flows. They imply that the locus of control over important dimensions of the economic development process— both in the narrow sense of formal decision making and resource deployment and in the larger sense of influences to which we must respond—is passing from territorialized institutions such as states to deterritorialized institutions such as intrafirm, international corporate hierarchies or international markets that know no bounds.[2] The perfection of hierarchies and markets, as management systems and transactional structures, is said to be gaining on territorial barriers, specificities, and frictions.[3]

There is another view, of course, and it comes from the rich literature on different ways that organizations and markets are shaped by political and business institutions. The "Japanese model" and J-firm, the "German model," the American model, and such, are different ways that advanced capitalist activity can be organized.[4] There is a competition between such territorially based, institutionally organized production systems for world market share in many sectors.

These two views correspond, in many ways, to the two main disciplinary discourses that deal with globalization—economics and political science. Much of the former implies that economic development is becoming deterritorialized, whereas there is a strong body of research in the latter that indicates continued territorial specificity in development patterns owing to the institutions alluded to above. Political economists and political scientists have begun to consider the effects of global capitalism on the margin of maneuver left to nation-states,[5] but curiously have devoted less attention to scrutinizing how globalized capitalism really is. As a result, the theoretical meaning and practical impact of economic globalization remain obscure.

In this chapter I propose to sketch out what a confrontation between the territorialization of economic development and the emergence of global hierarchies and flows would look like. The reason for this confrontation is the hypothesis that the ability of territorially bounded states and other institutions to bargain with hierarchical global business organizations, and to shape the development process in general, should rise with the territorialization of economic activity. Territorialization thus becomes the analytical key to the debate about the politics and economics of globalization.

An Economic Definition of Territorialization

Territorialized economic development may be defined as something quite different from mere location or localization of economic activity. It consists, for our purposes, in economic activity that is dependent on territorially specific resources. These "resources" can range from asset specificities available only from a certain place or, more importantly, assets that are available only in the context of certain interorganizational or firm–market relationships that necessarily involve geographical proximity, or where relations of proximity are markedly more efficient than other ways of generating these asset specificities. Geographically proximate relations constitute valuable asset specificities if they are necessary to the generation of spillover effects (positive externalities) in an economic activity system. Proximity would also be a basis of valuable specific assets, insofar as these latter are necessary to the efficient functioning of the firm under normal circumstances, and where the firm cannot replace them (either by internalizing functions or by carrying out its external relations in a way that does not involve proximity in them). The assets to which we refer can be hard (labor, technology) or soft (information, conventions of interaction, relation-specific skills).[6]

An activity is fully territorialized when its economic viability is rooted in assets (including practices and relations) that are not available in many other places and cannot easily or rapidly be created or imitated in places that lack them. Locational substitutability is not possible, and feasible locations are small in number, making locational "markets" highly imperfect. This definition of territorialization thus does not cover all cases of agglomeration, localization, or urbanization, but a distinctive subset of those cases.

MAINSTREAM ARGUMENTS ABOUT GLOBALIZATION AND WHAT THEY OMIT

As noted, huge research efforts have been devoted to the behavior of firms in a global economy, to consequences for markets, and to the ways that institutions shape markets and firms. There are major lacunae in these efforts because they do not pose the question of territorialization clearly.

Who Is Us? Markets versus Hierarchies

In the United States, the recent debate over the national economy in a global economy, made famous because it was carried out by two scholars who became high-ranking members of the Clinton Administration, illustrates this conceptual lacuna well. On one side, it was argued that development-inducing investment will flow to those areas that possess appropriate factors of production, which, in the global economy, means high-quality labor ("symbolic analysts"), high-technology infrastructure, and the like.[7] The argument stressed the importance and mobility of foreign investment capital, and how ownership of assets—the nationality of firms—is unimportant. The role of regions and nations is to develop appropriate factor supplies so as to attract this highly mobile investment. But the argument said nothing about whether those factors are territorialized or not, in the sense that we have defined it. As such, it can be interpreted either as an endorsement of globalization as placelessness or globalization as the attraction of capital to territorialized economic formations. There is simply nothing in the argument that gets at the issue.

On the other side of the debate, it was claimed that ownership—the nationality of firms—is important.[8] It is necessary to have firms that produce all technologies essential to national security, for political reasons, because even major multinational firms concentrate their core technology producing activities in their home territories. Even without security concerns, the existence of technological spillovers means that for an economy to master fully certain innovation and development processes, it must possess a complement of other capacities.

Both these claims are probably quite sound, in and of themselves, but they do not say much of anything about globalization. The argument does not show why even major multinationals continue to concentrate their principal technology based activities at home and therefore why the factor–market–attraction argument is not valid.[9] As a result, it could still be claimed that investment is becoming increasingly mobile and that the observed rootedness of major multinationals in their home economies is a transitory, not necessary, condition. Moreover, while it correctly suggests interdependence-through-spillover as key to many of the most important forms of innovation, it does not say why such spillovers should be localized within a national economy, except for security reasons. In other words, there is no economic reasoning about the territorialization of such spillovers. So the debate over "who is us?" tells us little about who we really are in a global economy.

Commodity Trade

The growth of commodity trade figures prominently in claims that the economy is globalizing. Rising intraindustry trade is said to be evidence of globalization, as firms create a global functional division of labor.[10] One possibility is that intraindustry trade is accompanied by the advent of global oligopolistic supply structures for many commodities and for knowledge inputs.[11] The big firms who dominate these supply chains benefit from entry barriers due to scale and the firm-specific assets they deploy on a global level. This argument, however, says nothing about the problem of territorialization per se. Global supply structures, even highly oligopolistic ones, could reflect (1) an internalized supply structure of assets, in which case they could be considered deterritorialized[12]; or (2) an attempt by firms to optimize access to factors of production in order to produce the inputs to their global supply structures in the sense described by Robert Reich, another form of deterritorialization, in the sense that regions and nations must simply make themselves attractive to mobile investments; or (3) also an attempt by firms to optimize access to territorialized factors of production (which meet the criteria of our definition). Without a conceptual apparatus specific to the problem, the existing evidence can be made to reveal little about it. The oft-cited rise in foreign direct investment, which is the vehicle of rising intraindustry and intrafirm trade, suffers from the same conceptual void.[13] It suggests a rise in activity by major world firms, and the development of a somewhat deeper world division of labor, but little about the meaning of globalization-as-deterritorialization.

The Global Business Hierarchy

As noted, much attention has been devoted to the apparent rise of global business hierarchies, the organizations that manage global supply structures. From theorizing about the "multinational," "transnational," or even "multidomestic" firm in the 1960s and 1970s, concern has shifted to organizations that manage global production and investment systems in "real time," involving simultaneous manipulation and optimization of manufactured inputs, capital, information, and marketing.[14]

There was considerable optimism about the possibility of such organizations in the late 1970s and early 1980s. Ford Motor Company announced its intention to build a "world car"; General Motors invested tens of billions of dollars in telecommunications and other infrastructure intended to permit not only worldwide supply and market coordination, but also worldwide concurrent engineering (that is, innovation and knowledge production). Some analysts label the outcome of development of such systems the global "hypermobility" of capital, as firms search for ever better deals from presumably substitutable locations.

The importance of such an approach is the notion of a production system, spread across the world, involving intrafirm trade in inputs, between locations lacking specificities.[15] Were such a model to become dominant, we would expect intermediate products to account for a very high share of world trade; but this is not the case, as can be seen in Table 7.1. We would also expect international sourcing to be very important, and it is in some industries; the problem is that we cannot know whether such sourcing emanates from substitutable locations or territorialized locations. And we would expect that finished-product trade, which is high in some industries, would be the result of such locationally substitutable sourcing in intermediates, and not the result of territorialized sourcing, knowledge production, and assets. The statistics shed no light on these issues.

Anecdotally, the results of attempts to build worldwide locationally substitutable sourcing systems have been mixed. The coordination of such an organization has proved to be much more problematic than was initially envisioned. Ford and GM have substantially cut back their earlier ambitions in favor of highly regionalized operations.[16] The management literature describes it as the ultimate goal of many firms in both manufacturing and advanced services.[17] It would seem that the possibility of a fully deterritorialized firm is limited to a set of special cases, however: certain kinds of assembly and fabrication activities carried out at high scale, involving low levels of firm- or industry-specific human and physical capital. But these operations certainly do not add up to hypermobility-as-deterritorialization of contemporary capitalism as a whole. Indeed, they likely constitute a relatively modest share of the economic process today.[18]

The same is true for discussions of global business hierarchies in the generation of knowledge and technological innovation. It appears that many forms of innovation require investments so great that even the biggest firms, to earn a decent return, attempt to monopolize returns on global markets.[19] Once such knowledge is developed, it often becomes a global state-of-the-art in product or process. It rests on temporarily nonrival and excludable firm-specific assets that firms use as the basis for earning temporary superprofits.[20] The character of these assets encourages firms to internalize them. But does this mean deterritorialization? Not necessarily. The production of firm-specific assets might occur only via use of complementary territorialized resources, that is, the mobilization of territory-specific resources in the firm's core location that permit it to invade world markets by virtue of technological superiority. It could then be made firm-specific via intellectual property rights, and serve as the basis of a global, monopolistic supply structure, deterritorialized from the areas that receive it.[21] This interpretation is consistent with the fact that intrafirm trade accounts for a high proportion of foreign direct investment in high-technology industries (Table 7.1).

Things are not unambiguous even in these cases, however, for the very same set of risks pushes firms to enter into risk- and cost-sharing strategic alliances with other major firms; and some such alliances come about because firms want to tap into other firms' expertise in order to avoid the concomitant risk of technological lock-in (avoid making wrong, very expensive firm-specific asset choices).[22] Where does such expertise come from? Perhaps from those firms' deterritorialized, fully internalized capabilities; but just as likely from the territorial contexts in which they are inserted. Clearly, the deployment of advanced technology and knowledge, especially if it is firm-specific and where access is subject to significant legal or economic barriers to entry, means major developmental power in today's world, and the global business organization seeks such power of deployment. There are strong effects on receiving economies. But the search for this power, again, says little about territorialization or deterritorialization of technology and knowledge generation in the world economy, and much more about corporate supply of such knowledge and technology once developed.

Indeed, in place of the model of the international firm as vertically integrated worldwide business hierarchy, much recent reflection about the organization of global business advances the idea of the firm as the central node in a variety of global linkages, ranging from ownership to alliance, and including cross-investment, technology and production partnerships, and R&D collaborations.[23] This may well be a new kind of network business organization, whose impacts on economic development processes we have barely begun to grasp; but such a model of the global firm does not so much imply deterritorialization of the economic process as a recasting of the role of territories in complex, intraorganizationally and interorganizationally linked global business flows.

Foreign Direct Investment

The most obvious category of globalization has been left for consideration until now because it is a chaotic conception. Foreign direct investment (FDI) is a catch-all category that refers to the volume of international investment in subsidiary operations of firms. It leads to intraindustry, interindustry and intrafirm trade; but then again, it may reduce commodity trade when it leads to

TABLE 7.1. Pattern of globalization by industry

Industries included in the survey	Trade						Direct investment			Cooperative agreements		
	Finished products (% sales)	Intermediate products (% sales)	Intl. sourcing (% total sourcing)	Intrafirm (% trade)	Flows (% gfcf)	AFFs sales (% sales)	M&As (% ops)	Equity parts. (% ops)	Devel. purpose (% agrs)	Prod. purpose (% agrs)	Market purpose (% agrs)
Pharmaceuticals	10	8	10–30	70	50–70	40–50	52	48	38–68	13–29	19–41
Computers	26	14	20–60	50–80	30–40	50–60	43	57	50–70	15–28	17–32
Semiconductors	20	n.a.	10–40	70	15–25	20–25	39	61	n.a.	n.a.	n.a.
Motor vehicles	21	13	25–35	50–80	15–25	10–20	33	67	24–48	39–66	9–20
Consumer electronics	55	30	10–40	30–50	20–35	20–30	39	61	24–40	36–62	12–33
Nonferrous metals	21	21[a]	30–50	30	20–35	15–25	45	55	n.a.	n.a.	n.a.
Steel	27	35–45[b]	15–25	5–10	5–10	15–25	72	28	n.a.	n.a.	n.a.
Clothing	25–30	25–30[c]	10–40	5–10	15–20	5–15	n.a.	n.a.	(limited)		

Source: OECD, Industry Division compilation (1993).
[a]Unwrought aluminium.
[b]Iron ore, coking coal, scrap.
[c]Textiles.

installation of locally serving final-output capacity in major markets, so-called "regional" or "triad" locational patterns. So FDI may be a vehicle for or substitute for trade. It may reflect firm strategies to control foreign markets via intrafirm trade, but then again, it may reflect the need to tap into intermediate inputs produced by firms, through alliances and local trade. It may reflect global supply oligopolies in goods, intellectual property, or technology, but then again, it may reflect needs to be in contact with territorially rooted foreign contexts of goods or technology development. There is little in the statistics that reveals much about the territoriality of economic dynamics.

Another argument, which underlies much of the claim that the global economy is deterritorializing in favor of global business organizations, has to do with corporate power. It has been correctly observed that the biggest global firms are getting bigger: there is ongoing concentration of capital. There has been a certain centralization of capital, in that the shares of the largest 100 or 500 corporations in global output are greater than they were 20 years ago.[24] These large organizations, it is said, are increasingly powerful across territorial boundaries. Their deployment of investments can shape markets, determine which technologies get developed, and, above all, exercise influence on national and regional governments.[25]

Power, in this sense, probably does have impacts on territorialization as we have defined it. But we need to examine precisely how. One of the paradoxes of globalization, in the sense of interpenetration of markets by companies from different nations, is that market structures in many industries have actually become less concentrated over the past 30 years; there are more competitors in them than when such markets were composed of national or regional firms, though at a world level the first ten or twenty companies control high proportions of output in many industries, especially technology-intensive ones.[26] Global firms, while constituting a small club, especially in industries with very high barriers to entry, are therefore locked into competitive battle; they do not rule their world markets in any straightforward sense, as any major automobile, computer, clothing, or chemical company will readily admit.

Still, their power to shift vast quantities of capital, technology, or human capital across territorial borders, into different product markets and R&D programs, is considerable. These firms can obviously influence the development of markets by shaping supply structures through their decisions. And they can bargain with territorially rooted states in so doing. But the image of nations and regions as Davids facing the global Goliaths cannot be deduced from the mere existence of global firms, for the latter are subject to all the complexities of territorialization we have described in preceding paragraphs. Merely being bigger does not give them command and control and pricing power in the sense that Berle and Means[27] thought of it, nor does it confer locational substitutability.

The Poverty of Existing Categories

The traditional categories in which the globalization debate has been framed—foreign direct investment, commodity trade, the global business hierarchy, the global supply structure of commodities, knowledge, and technology—seem instinctively to indicate the steady deterritorialization of economic power. But upon closer observation, they are conceptual categories that are inadequate to the job of shedding light on the question of territorialization and deterritorialization. It is, indeed, quite curious that a fundamentally geographical process labeled with a geographical term—"globalization"—is analyzed as a set of resource flows largely without considering their interactions with the territoriality of economic development.

REFRAMING THE QUESTION: TERRITORIES AND FLOWS

In order to see what the terms territorialized and deterritorialized might mean with respect to the global economy, we can imagine two polar opposite cases, a fully deterritorialized "economy of flows and substitutions," and a fully territorialized "economy of interdependencies and specificities." In constructing these images, we will combine reasoning about organizations (firms), assets, markets, and places.

A Pure Flow-Substitution Economy

Imagine the extreme case of a fully realized global supply oligopoly. Resources would flow between parts of a firm, between places, without having any particular dependence on any particular place. Such assets—whether goods or information—would be producible in so many different places as to constitute a true (almost) perfect "market" in locations for their production. It matters little whether they are actually produced at many locations; one could imagine the extreme case of global supply from a single place (due to scale economies, for example), but where that place has no specificities that render it immune to substitution by another place.

This sort of economy could be the result of two possible developmental processes. On one hand, activities that are well developed in a wide variety of places make necessary productive resources available in near ubiquity, but have historically been separated by transport barriers or differentiated tastes. Improvements in transportation, standardization of tastes, or increases in the possible scale of production open up this wide variety of locations to global business organizations, who then enjoy huge potential locational choice and ubiquitous markets, but they are bound by no locational specificities or local interdependencies. On the other hand, such organizations perfect production processes that eliminate the need for locationally scarce specific assets: techno-logical change via product standardization and routinization of production processes does the job.

In both cases, a pure flow form of globalization becomes possible. It matters little whether the flows are via markets or hierarchies: global firms could purchase locally and sell through global commodity trade, for example. It matters little whether the flows concern intermediate or finished products. Those considerations, well analyzed through industrial organization theory, are simply different forms that the global flows of resources and optimization of factor use and capacity may take. The essential condition for a pure flow economy is that *a location offer only those factors of production that could potentially be substituted by a large number of other locations*. One can even imagine the extreme case where the only international flows of resources are financial and intellec-tual, but where, in the presence of few scale economies, a global firm adminis-ters many local production systems as opposed to a few that serve broad terri-tories; but in this case, the possibility of switching from local to centralized systems would be critical to enforce the condition of substitutability, in con-cert with the absence of locally specific assets.

This case of nonspecific, locationally substitutable and perfectly elastic factor supplies is probably not found in pure form anywhere. But in some sec-tors, notably certain manufacturing industries and consumer services, these conditions are increasingly close to reality. Low-wage, low-skill, low-sunk-cost manufacturing processes, certain highly standardized consumer durable man-ufacturing (where sunk costs are higher, but modular and widely available equipment is used), and certain consumer services where centralized produc-tion can be combined with local delivery, come to mind.

One could imagine a pure market version of this globalization process, where numerous local economies, characterized by relatively small firms, competed with each other in global markets. Purchasers, armed with perfect information and highly developed and very flexible marketing networks, could switch from one locality's product to another almost instantaneously. Hierarchy is not necessary, then, to the flow economy's definition, in contrast to the image of oligopoly = globalization often implied in the literature. In re-ality, however, this ability to switch tends to be associated with scale in market-ing and an ability to coordinate supplies from different, substitutable sources.

The potential political consequences of flow economies are what bother many of the critics of globalization.[28] Instead of seeing such flows as the means to resource optimization at a world scale, their point of departure is that economic progress has always depended on political economics, where everything ranging from the distribution of income between labor and capital to the correction of a wide variety of market failures is carried out by territo-rially rooted institutions such as states. The advent of deterritorialized flow economies would seem to reduce the margin of maneuver of such states dramatically, in favor of that of the private sector and thereby to open up a number of unfavorable consequences in both distributional and efficiency terms.[29]

A Pure Territorial Economy

A fully territorialized economic activity would satisfy conditions quite opposite to those described above. The essential condition of territorialization is that the activity be dependent on resources with specificities that are strongly territorialized and where the supply of these resources is subject to important inelasticities. The traditional case of scarce natural resources is a pure example but little relevant to most productive activity, where "resources" are mostly produced inputs such as labor and technology. We know that for many labor and technology inputs, there are no functional substitutes at any price; but even though such labor and technology may be highly product-specific, in many cases they are nonetheless available in different locations or easily produced, at rather different prices. So, territorialization is not in evidence. Where they are not widely available at any price, however, that is, where scarcities or inelasticities are in evidence, then not only localization but territorialization exist due to the geographically limited conditions of their production.

It is really with respect to special meanings of the terms "labor" and "technology" that territorialization becomes most relevant in today's economy. Certain kinds of labor qualities are different from mere skills. There are many contexts in which nonroutine judgments are made and where the success of the judgment depends on how a condition of uncertainty that involves other people is interpreted, or where noncodified traditions and ways of doing things are essential to the job. The former corresponds to demands for creativity or convention, the latter to learned custom. In all these cases, labor qualities are produced in what may be called a relation-specific fashion: they are produced and are exercised via insertion into a system of relations, whether it be interpersonal or bounded by specific, not fully codifiable rules of the game.[30] These skills are not only specific in nature but subject to important supply inelasticities in the medium run.[31]

Analogous observations may be made about technology, if what we mean by this is not merely hardware, but know-how, especially know-how that involves an outwardly moving and unknown scientific frontier (as in high technology) or an uncertain movement around such dynamics as product differentiation (for many low-tech or fashion-dependent industries and services). It is likely to involve asset specificities and supply inelasticities.[32]

This probably understates the extent of relation- and place-specific assets in production. Many production systems, as has been amply demonstrated in recent years, turn on an intricate web of external interfirm transactions or internal intrafirm transactions. And in some cases there are—at one moment or another—various sorts of standard economizing reasons for such transactions to be carried out across limited geographical distances: in these cases, territorialization is the result of necessary *relations of proximity* in the production system, which limit the number of sites at which production can be carried out. Over time, however, such cost barriers tend to be eroded due to transport improvements or changes in the nature of the transactions themselves that lead to higher scale, greater certainty, and lower costs of covering distance.

But cost barriers are not the only reasons for the existence of relations of proximity in production systems. Many such relationships, such as buyer–supplier interfirm relations, R&D–producer relations, or firm–labor market relations, come to be structured in ways that are highly specific to a given, initially geographically bounded, transactional context (usually regions or nations). Over time, they become more and more specific as unwritten rules of the game (conventions), formal institutions, and customary forms of knowledge are built up and become indispensable to admission to the producers' community and to efficient interpretation of how to reciprocate via transactions with other agents under conditions of uncertainty. In other words, regional or national production systems become nexuses of interdependencies between organizations and persons that involve relational asset specificities.[33] These interdependencies must, of course, be efficient in some sense (e.g., a factor in cost minimization or innovation–improvement).

Territorialization is thus not equivalent to geographical proximity or agglomeration, although such agglomeration may be at some times the cause and at others the effect of territorialization: it is an effect when scarcities and specificities of key resources such as labor and technology draw producers to a place, and when nonsubstitutabilities keep them there; it is a cause when the transactional structure of production draws producers into an agglomeration, and then key dimensions of the production system become relation-specific and key to its ongoing efficiencies.

There are very few industries in which pure territorialization, in the sense of a uniquely efficient location for the totality of the industry's output, exists; in this case, there would be a localized global supply monopoly. But the condition of territorialization, in the sense of a few possible locations for significant parts of the industry's output, can be found quite frequently. Certain very high quality goods, those that involve technological innovation, ongoing rapid differentiation, or highly specialized services, come to mind as examples. There are two very different versions of this territorialization. One concerns activities that serve tastes so localized that the localized supply structure corresponds to a unique localized demand structure. The more interesting case, of course, is one in which the localized supply structure satisfies a national or global demand, and in which there is therefore the possibility of entry by competitors in other places. This is likely to show up as a case of commodity trade exports, whether intra- or interindustry. It is analytically indifferent to ownership (that is, the definition says nothing about whether ownership of territorialized assets must be local). In practice, most such cases of multinationals who have core activities in their home country and in a specific region of that country, also have national ownership[34]; but counterexamples, such as Sony's ownership of Columbia Pictures, are reasonably abundant. Territorialization, therefore, cuts across the standard terms of the globalization debate, such as "who is us?" and local versus export-oriented production.

THE DYNAMICS OF GLOBALIZATION

What should be clear from the above is that *global capitalism is being constructed through interactions between flow economies and territorial economies.* Internationalization of capitalism has long been measured simply as a function of the increasing intensities of flows, but little was said about territories. Globalization is said to refer to something qualitatively different, in the sense of an economy or its subsystems that operate globally. That is, globalization should involve not merely international flows of resources, but economic systems that operate as international flow economies, as they have been defined here. And if globalization is truly gaining on territorial economic organization, then we should find evidence not merely of increasing international flows of resources, but also of decreasing territorialization.

Some of the possible interactions are represented schematically in Figure 7.1. On the horizontal axis is the degree of territorialization of economic activities, and on the vertical axis the level of international flows associated with these activities. The first case (cell 1) describes those activities that are both highly territorialized and highly internationalized: territorially specific, nonsubstitutable assets are involved, but there are relationships that are not bound by such territorialization. Examples include the high-technology production system in which the firm has certain important territorialized activities, but engages in intrafirm trade in intermediate inputs and intrafirm trade for its world-wide marketing network. Intermediate inputs might be sourced for cost reasons alone (in which case this part of the system is effectively deterritorialized) or because the firm is tapping into territorial contexts of expertise elsewhere. Other examples are the now-famous industrial districts, such as the NEC Italian cases that were examined in the previous chapter, where localized production systems dominate world markets. Both interfirm and interindustry trade, within complex social divisions of labor, can involve highly territorialized production for international commodity chains. Foreign direct investment is a means to carry out some of these processes as well.

Cell 2 describes cases of low levels of territorialization and high levels of international flow, and includes territorially dispersed commodity chains in

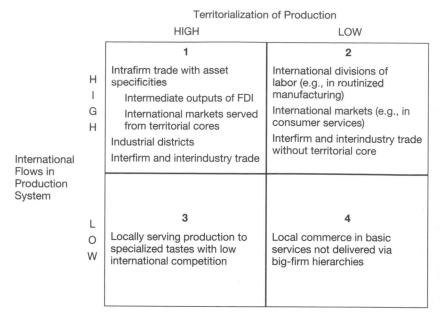

FIGURE 7.1. Flows and territories.

which no nonsubstitutable locations are involved (in which technological standardization has reached a high level of development, generally).[35] It also includes dispersed production systems oriented to international markets, as in many consumer services. Note that this category would lead to interfirm, intrafirm, and interindustry trade, as well as foreign direct investment.

Cell 3 consists of systems with both low levels of territorialization and international flow, such things as local commerce in basic services that are not provided by far-flung, big-firm hierarchies. In this cell we would find the industries of yore, which were localized due to transportation barriers but not truly territorialized; today we might find them there because of very low economies of scale, but less so due to transport barriers.

Finally, there are highly territorialized systems with few international connections (cell 4). These are not simply localized due to insurmountable cost barriers to serving other areas from the local production system; they are territorialized because of nonsubstitutable local assets, as in the case of industries producing for specialized regional tastes.[36]

The caricatural version of globalization is based on the notion that advanced capitalism has substituted type 2 production systems for type 3 production systems; and some of this has indeed come about with the progressive reduction of transport barriers, increase in scale of delivery of commodities and services, and changes in trading regimes. Many manufactured goods, including both durables and nondurables, which were formerly produced in isolated regional economies, were first converted to national production systems in the postwar period (especially in Europe), and then to commodity chains, which are now internationalized.[37]

An even more extreme set of cases is that of type 4 becoming type 2, that is, formerly territorialized and mostly closed production systems now becoming international commodity chains. This is in evidence because as more internationalized middle-class ways of life and tastes sweep their way across many places, old place-specific tastes disappear and with them the economic reasons for local asset-specificity. When needs are redefined, so is demand, which can then be served via other kinds of products, furnished by production systems with assets available at many different locations, and without territorial cores. Crucial to this set of events is *not* changes in transportation, or even scale, but actual product substitutions—the culture of demand is the key causal mechanism.

Many sophisticated analyses also call attention to a transformation of production systems from type 1 to type 2: this is the movement from "internationalization" of production to its true "globalization." Now it can be seen that the real claim here is not simply that there are high levels of international flow, of whatever sort, involved in the operation of these systems; in and of themselves, they do not transform these production systems into deterritorialized flow economies. The claim is rather that substitutability of locations increases; and territorially specific assets decrease dramatically in their importance to competitive production.[38] There is almost no way to distinguish the two cases or a movement between them using common statistical measures such as foreign investment or the various forms of trade. In manufacturing, such cases might be production systems for goods for which little technological change is occurring, and where scale, capital-intensity, and standardization of tastes are very high; this probably corresponds to large parts of the commodity chains of certain consumer durables.

Two other important cases, however, seem to characterize the current era. The first is transformation of type 3 and 4 production systems not to type 2, but to type 1 systems. Formerly highly territorialized but not internationalized systems can become internationalized, as they gain the ability to market their products around the world, but without losing their locationally specific assets. This requires, as we have noted, development of demand for their products beyond local or regional borders. And this is precisely what appears to have happened in the cases of many European industrial districts in the postwar period: the product qualities once prized locally have become desired elsewhere, and the relationally specific assets that exist in producer regions now permit those regions to meet broader demands through downstream internationalization, but not through internationalization of production itself.[39]

Perhaps even more important is the transformation of type 2 production systems into type 1 systems: from highly internationalized but not especially territorialized systems to increasingly territorialized and internationalized. The mass-production industries of the postwar period, for example, seemed at one point to be on the road to ever greater standardization, and with it, locational substitutability, but forces such as increased product differentiation and newly revived product-based technological learning have given a new lease on life to locationally specific relational assets in production.

Indeed, the *principal* trend to which we can call attention today is that in many sectors, there is *simultaneous and ongoing development of the characteristics of both type 1 and type 2 systems:* the latter as ongoing standardization of tastes and techniques occurs, the former as technological learning, product differentiation, and the hiving off of new branches of production, materials and processes occur, all of which are causes of locational specificity, but also precisely outcomes of the interactive processes permitted by the locationally specific relational assets that underlie territorialization. This form of territorialization is qualitatively quite different from that which is found in cell 3 of Figure 7.1, in that it is not developed as the result of "tradition via isolation," but via what might be called the ongoing reinvention of relational assets in the context of high levels of geographical openness in trade and communications.

The formation of this *global context* of trade, investment, and communications and organized networks of human relations in production is perhaps the clearest dimension of globalization. The global economy is being constructed as an increasingly widely spread and accepted "grid" of these sorts of transactions, akin to a new global lingua franca of commerce, investment, and organization, based on historical and secular advances in transportation and communication technologies, and the development and diffusion of modern organizational "science," both of these in the context of the increasingly global political order of trade.[40] But the paradox is that it is precisely this global grid or language that leads both to type 2 and type 1 outcomes. In the former case, it breaks down barriers of taste, transport, and scale; in the latter case, it opens up markets to products based on superior forms of "local knowledge"; it consolidates markets and leads to such fantastic product differentiation possibilities that markets refragment and with them, new specialized and localized divisions of labor reemerge; and it in some ways heats up the competitive process (albeit among giants), creating new premia on technological learning that require the same firms that become new global supply oligopolists to root themselves in locationally specific relational assets. The point is that globalization and territorialization are not just about the geography of flows and its technological or organizational determinants, but are in some cases dependent on the ways production systems and their products are changed by new patterns of competition unleashed by territorial integration.

To summarize, four principal territorial–organizational dynamics can be isolated from these complex, intersecting forces. In some cases, the opening up of interterritorial relations places previously existing locationally specific assets into a new position of global dominance. In a second set of cases, those assets are devalued via substitution by other products, which now penetrate local markets; this is not a straightforward economic process, however; it is culturally intermediated. In a third set of cases, territorial integration permits the fabled attainment of massive economies of scale and organization, devalues locationally specific assets and leads to deterritorialization and widespread market penetration. In a fourth set of cases, territorial integration is met by differentiation and destandardization of at least some crucial elements of the commodity chain, necessitating the reinvention of territory-specific relational assets.

HIERARCHY, REGULATION, AND COMPETITION: INSTITUTIONAL DILEMMAS

State institutions exercise their authority over limited territories, but they do so in fields of forces—whether political or economic—that extend well beyond these borders. At least in matters of economic affairs, for much of the postwar period the economic authority of nation-states and the substantive power to back it up was considerable within the national territory. Globalization of economic processes seems to have weakened that substantive power, if not the formal authority. The global business organizations that control certain important international resource flows seem, in many cases, to be deterritorialized, and thus not directly dependent on processes that states, whether regional or national, can effectively regulate.

Yet, as we have seen, the mere existence of large-scale international flows does not lead directly to a conclusion that a productive activity is deterritorialized. Likewise, we can now see that the mere existence of territorialization does not mean that local or national states can exercise strong regulatory control over the economic development process.[41] Territorialization is a necessary but not sufficient condition for a strong state role, because it may involve hierarchies that are in turn inserted into larger contexts. We now want to sketch out some of the complex interactions between territorial economies and flow economies, and the ways they may mix hierarchical, market, and network forms of governance of production systems. Territorially based state institutions are now forced to confront these sorts of interactions in undertaking economic development strategies.

Figure 7.2 shows different ways of governing production systems, in the context of patterns of territorialization and flow. It makes a primary division between those processes that are internalized within large business organizations, labeled "hierarchies," and those carried out via high levels of external relations of large numbers of agents, where no single or small number of

International Flows of Production System		TERRITORIALIZATION OF PRODUCTION SYSTEM			
		HIGH		LOW	
		GOVERNANCE OF PRODUCTION SYSTEM'S DYNAMIC			
		Hierarchies	Networks/ Markets	Hierarchies	Networks/ Markets
HIGH Governance	Hierarchies	**1** Intrafirm trade where firm has a territorial core	Territorial core systems, especially in high-tech industries	**2** Global supply oligopolists with world division of labor manufacturing and services	Isolated captive suppliers to global oligopolists
	Networks/Markets	Global supply oligopolists Strategic alliances	Industrial Districts	Global supply oligopolists with few intermediates	Isolated specialist suppliers and contractors
LOW Governance	Hierarchies	**3** Local champion firms with little internationalization	Locally serving production, especially for specialized tastes	**4** Global supply oligopolists with franchising and brand-name strategies	
	Networks/Markets				Local commerce in basic services

FIGURE 7.2. Hierarchies, territories, and flows.

186

agents is dominant, labeled "networks and markets." These represent two fundamentally different nexuses of decision-making power, centralized and decentralized, whose existence is widely recognized in the literature. The point is not that power only exists in the presence of hierarchy, but that the nature of possible interactions between state institutions and the private sector will depend both on the degree of territorialization of the latter, and on its mix of hierarchies, networks, and markets. What follows is just a suggestion of some of these configurations.

It can be seen from the top half of the figure that for productive activities with high levels of international flow, there is evidence of both territorialization and deterritorialization. Thus, high levels of flow do not necessarily imply deterritorialization. Moreover, there is a great diversity of institutional arrangements that govern both the primary dynamic of the prooduction systems—investment, technical choice and change, and knowledge development—and their international flows. For example, many global high-technology firms manage extensive intrafirm supply chains, but at the same time are inserted into one or multiple territorialized production systems in which network or market relations are dominant. Their power is more absolute with respect to their international flows than it is with respect to their territorial core. In certain other industries, global supply oligopolists are highly territorialized and interact locally via hierarchical relations, but then must compete in international markets with other such oligopolists, or they may enter into strategic alliances for marketing or for certain input supplies. The paradox is that while such oligopolists may exercise considerable power over local suppliers and partners, to the extent that they depend on locationally specific relational assets, the state may have considerable potential bargaining power with them.

Industrial districts are frequently characterized by strongly territorialized network relations in the core region, and by networked markets internationally: the institutional construction of international market networks is critical to them. We know from experience that states can play strong roles in supporting the competitiveness of such districts.[42]

The classical image of globalization is, of course, the global supply oligopolist that has a low level of territorialization, and a high degree of hierarchical control over its inputs and markets on a world-wide basis.[43] This can be found as a tendency in certain manufacturing industries and certain consumer service sectors. Isolated captive suppliers to these global oligopolists also have little territorialization and are subject to the strong hierarchy of these firms in their sales relations (semiconductor assemblers in Asia or clothing firms in developing countries are examples). Global supply oligopolists with few intermediate inputs and little territorialization are likely to have little intrafirm trade and foreign direct investment, and instead internationalize through global sales via markets.[44] Isolated specialized suppliers or contractors, on the other hand, will interact internationally via networks or markets, as they do with any local suppliers, the terms of their interactions being set by the degree and nature of substitutability of their products by the purchasing firm.

In the bottom half of the figure may be found cases of low levels of international flow, and various combinations of territorialization and governance. Local champion firms, for instance, who dominate a market, will tend to govern their territorialized production systems in a hierarchical way and have little internationalization, whereas other forms of localized production, for localized and specialized tastes, will probably correspond to the nonhierarchical system of traditional local firms. They may export some of their excess output but this will likely be a small proportion of the total. Global supply oligopolists may not always have high levels of international flow—oligopoly can be attained through control of intellectual and intangible assets such as knowledge and brand names, but carried out through franchising. Hence, there will be low flows that are governed hierarchically.

These are just a few of the many possible examples of complex configurations of institutions with respect to territoriality and flows in production systems. Small firms can enjoy relatively great market, network, or even hierarchical power, sometimes territorially and other times globally, while big firms can be subject to the forces of other big firms or markets they do not control, whether in their territorialized or global interactions.

Policy Problems

Many dilemmas of aligning the governance of production systems with efficient and desirable patterns of territorialization and flow present themselves in the contemporary world economy, and these are problems faced not only by territorially bound state institutions but also by the private sector.

The most obvious set of problems concerns the cases on the right-hand side of the Figure 7.2. Where territorialization is low or declining, that is, where locational substitution becomes more and more possible, there is often a "race to the bottom" for territorially defined states, a competitive bidding war for economic activity, which transfers increasing amounts of benefit from the public to the private sector. In the United States, this has been the history of postwar routinized manufacturing, encouraged not only by federalism but by the passage of the Taft-Hartley Act in the late 1940s, which enabled states to make a big institutional concession to employers by making unionization locally more difficult (through "right-to-work" laws). More recently, such bidding has become a frenetic activity of states and localities. There is evidence that similar trends are developing within the European Union, and we can certainly see them on broader international scales within North America and Southeast Asia. Moreover, this dynamic is no longer limited to manufacturing. Corporate headquarters learned that they could demand concessions for remaining in New York, for example, in the 1970s, and since then have generalized these demands. Hollywood film productions now expect to be wooed to locations in order to shoot films there. Corporations involved in relatively routine administration, such as in the consumer service or retailing sectors, now also regularly demand concessions or threaten to move.[45]

The demands of firms are usually less naked when territorialization of activity is strongly in evidence precisely because they have less locational substitutability, at least in the short run. Nonetheless, the fact that certain kinds of productive activity are territorialized does not mean that they are wedded permanently to one single territory. Global companies do not just scan the globe for single locations; some interact with multiple territorial economies. To some extent, these territorial economies cannot be substituted by these firms, since the latter are inserted into them in order to tap into the technological or knowledge specificities of such territorial systems. The firm thus has a division of labor that involves multiple territories, which are functionally specialized. For the moment, global technology firms remain mostly attached to territorialized resources in their nations of origin.[46] But one could imagine that for inputs that are not on the cutting edge of technological knowledge, such firms could over time develop parallel territories, in the same way that mass-production firms in the 1970s developed parallel assembly or fabrication plants. Developing states in Southeast Asia, for example, have had some successes in helping their firms to build up territory-specific relational assets, and these assets are now enjoyed by firms from elsewhere. The paradox here is that states participate in a kind of *competitive* endogenous development, which creates new forms of capital mobility even in the territorialized parts of the contemporary economy.

A second concern is that when major hierarchical global business organizations interact with different territorial economies, there may be little harmony between the rules by which such firms intend to relate to these environments and the relational assets already built up in those places. Problems of this nature, however, only become apparent over time, and when they do, multinational firms may not have the commitment required to work them out. And they are problems that are not generally technical, but relational in nature and thus slow to resolve. We might think here of subcontracting policies established by such firms, which are designed to economize for them, but at the medium-term price of the region's subcontracting tissue as a whole.[47]

A third concern has to do with territorialized developmental spillovers. Territorial economies exist as such in part because there are knowledge or technology spillovers between activities, and the overall developmental trajectory of a territorial economy is strongly influenced by such spillovers. But firms whose primary loyalties lie outside a particular territorial economy— firms with a highly elaborate interterritorial division of labor—may inadvertently make decisions that undercut development of such spillovers, precisely by territorially dividing what might better (from the territory's and technology's standpoint) be kept in proximity.[48] This is not a problem unique to "foreign" firms, but to all multilocational, multiterritorial firms.

A corollary is that when territorialized technological spillovers exist, there is an efficiency rationale for targeted technology policies, even from the standpoint of global output. Where such spillovers do not exist or are not territorialized, however, technology policies tend merely to transfer technological performance from one place to another, usually at a high overall cost.[49] The problem is to construct such policies so that the community of subjects of the policy is not only local but global; many firms operate in many different institutional and conventional contexts. Such policies therefore have to be "translated" for them, and these global business organizations must find ways to reconcile operations in very different contexts.

The management literature has raised many issues with respect to the operation of global supply and marketing systems. They have not conceptualized some of these problems, however, as the need for global business organizations to operate in multiple territorial economies, that is, to interact with specific relational assets in different places. This is clearly a major challenge to firms that require such assets, whether for innovation or for sales, but whose mission is precisely to rationalize the allocation of resources on a global basis.

GLOBALIZATION AND LOCALIZATION:
A PERMANENT TENSION

It has been a commonplace in development economics for several decades that technologically advanced activities are concentrated in advanced economies due to the superior scientific and knowledge infrastructures of those countries.[50] Yet some of the classical conditions cited by the development analysts of the 1950s have changed, notably the more rapid worldwide diffusion of technologies and certain kinds of knowledge. Major firms have gone global, and one would think this would promote a more even distribution of production in major technology- and knowledge-intensive goods and services. Yet this is not the case empirically: the core technology- and knowledge-intensive outputs of the world economy continue to be produced in relatively few places on the globe, and they are traded. The wealthy countries manifest increasing specializations despite their similar income levels.[51] Specialization manifests itself in terms of final outputs and as intraindustry trade.

It was noted earlier that in many industries there are noncosmopolitan cognitive representations of what is being done, that is, no easily reproducible metamodels of the activity, and that under these circumstances, conventional–relational (C-R) transactions are particularly important to the firms and production systems concerned. Some of these relations may be embedded in large organizations and carried out at great distances. But many, in fact, are highly localized, including those that are internal to large firms. Even in the case of semicosmopolitan cognitive representations (e.g., use of metamodels to solve particular problems), actual coordination of actors may be rooted in highly localized and specific conventions.

There appears to be a paradoxical aspect of today's global economy: C-R transactions are by definition highly endogenous forms of economic coordination. They are generated through rounds of action and interaction among economic agents, leading to taken-for-granted regularities in what they expect from each other and what they do. Much social science tends to view such phenomena as mere residue from the past, destined to disappear in the face of modern, universal best practices or logics of development. Yet the leading edges of contemporary economic development are in many ways highly dependent on these historically evolved and geographically differentiated phenomena.

Nexuses of indirect traded linkages and these C-R transactions are not territorially concentrated in all industries or at all times. We may imagine a complex set of territorialities—at different geographical scales, from local to national to regional to global—for different types of such traded and untraded interdependencies. Some will be highly localized, as in the case of extremely uncodified information or interpretative dimensions of skills. Others will be national in scope, as in the cases of industrial coordination conventions that are established in a national territory through successive rounds of national economic integration and diffusion of behavioral precedents and rules-of-thumb, embodied usually in nontechnical, culturally specific national linguistic tropes. Some may be established through formal national institutions, such as professional associations or standardized national curricula (the subject of the recent national systems of innovation literature).[52] Still others will be international in scale, often embodied in internationally recognized multinational corporate practice and professional behavior.

In evolutionary terms, there are always two active forces tugging in different directions on the geography of interdependencies. One is the bureaucratization of capitalist enterprise, with its tendency to diffuse an internationally recognized matrix of rules, especially for managers and professionals. For specific technologies, there is the tendency to evolve cosmopolitan—abstract and codified and reproducible—knowledge and substitutable or imitatable components in hardware. The other is the ongoing development—unplanned and unforeseeable at the outset—of new forms of knowledge and the means to interpret and communicate it, as well as new nexuses of highly context-specific human relations. The former is related directly to the technological and organizational evolution of variety in the economy; the latter, more difficult to

grasp, occurs because local (in both the organizational and geographical senses of local) groups of people are constantly redifferentiating their practices
and relations at the same time that rounds of bureaucratic standardization
sweep over them from the management schools and control centers of the
world. Thus, major global corporations are places where management increasingly speaks an interindustry, global language of management (a cosmopolitan metamodel), easily reproduced from one firm to another and
across the continents; but paradoxically, each multinational also has its own
company culture, including international but firm-specific human relations,
many times achieved by relocating managers from the country or region of
origin, so important is this form of asset specificity to the workings of the
corporate bureaucracy. Thus, certain highly complex, relational interdependencies are imbricated in large corporate networks and even in scientific–
professional associations, through intensive human contact and sustained investments in networks of human relations. These evolutionary tendencies are
in constant combat with each other, making geographical outcomes a two-
way street between localization and diffusion, not a one-way highway to dispersion.[53]

NOTES

1. Castells (1989).
2. Ohmae (1990); Reich (1990); Gilpin (1975).
3. Julius (1990); Ostry (1990); Veltz (1993).
4. Albert (1992); Hill (1989).
5. Carnoy (1993).
6. Asanuma (1989).
7. Reich (1990).
8. Tyson (1991).
9. See also Carnoy (1993); Patel and Pavitt (1991); Amendola et al. (1992);
OECD (1991).
10. There are measurement problems having to do with the level of statistical ag-
gregation. If it is not fine enough, the firm mixes together products that are so different as to belong to different commodity chains.
11. Ernst (1990); OECD (1991, pp. 361 ff). This is not a new idea, either. The
earliest use of global supply oligopolies apparently comes from Vernon (1974). Some
of the most recent work on this topic has been carried out by C. Sauviat in Paris, at the
Institut de Recherches Economiques et Sociales (IRES). See also, most recently, Lafay
and Herzog (1989); Mathis et al. (1988).
12. Dicken (1988).
13. Cf. Julius (1990); Ostry (1990).
14. Dicken (1988); Ohmae (1990); Ballance (1987); Glickman and Woodward
(1989); OECD (1991); Dupuy and Gilly (1995a).

15. Frobel et al. (1980); Hymer (1976).
16. Morales (1994).
17. Caves (1982); Dicken (1988); Ohmae (1990).
18. Carnoy (1993); Dupuy and Gilly (1995b).
19. Dunning and Norman (1985); Krugman (1992).
20. Grossman and Helpman (1992).
21. Patel and Pavitt (1991); Dosi et al. (1990).
22. OECD (1991); Mytelka (1990).
23. Mowery (1988); Mytelka (1990).
24. OECD (1991).
25. Harrison (1994).
26. OECD (1991).
27. Berle and Means (1932).
28. See, for example, Harrison (1994).
29. Glickman and Woodward (1989); Hymer (1976); Frobel et al. (1980); Harrison (1994).
30. Asanuma (1989).
31. Amin and Thrift (1993); Lecoq (1993).
32. Dosi et al. (1991); Rallet (1993).
33. Saxenian (1994); Amin and Thrift (1993); Salais and Storper (1993); de Vet (1993).
34. Patel and Pavitt (1991); Tyson (1991).
35. Frobel et al. (1980); Hymer (1976).
36. The forerunners of many successful world market-serving industrial districts in Italy today were locally serving industrial complexes, with specific assets related to particular local tastes. This comes out in the historical work on Tuscany carried out by Becattini's group (the Prato histories) and on Emilia–Romagna by Cappecchi. An overall review of European cases is found in Sabel and Zeitlin (1985). Some of the Italian literature is reviewed in Salais and Storper (1993).
37. Vernon and Spar (1989).
38. Dunning (1992).
39. Colombo et al. (1991); Bianchi (1992); Becattini (1987).
40. Cf. Naponen et al. (1993); Lung and Mair (1993).
41. Dunning (1992); Carnoy (1993).
42. Bianchi (1992).
43. Hymer (1976).
44. Dunning and Norman (1985).
45. Mytelka (1996).
46. Dosi et al. (1990).
47. Dunning (1992).
48. Markusen (1994).
49. Grossman and Helpman (1992).
50. See Leontief (1953).
51. Amendola et al. (1992); Tyson (1991). See also Chapter 8 in this book.
52. We are making an economic equivalent of Benedict Anderson's general point in his *Imagined Communities* (1982).

53. Even dispersion has many different routes. Antonelli (1995) distinguishes at least seven possible routes to dispersion of knowledge: the polya urn; snow shoveling; percolation; replication; interdependent diffusion; localized technical change; and pecuniary scale economies. Each has a different rhythm and pattern. So even when dispersion is a possibility due to the presence of a cosmopolitan model, the pattern it will take is not automatic, nor is it necessarily like other dispersion patterns.

CHAPTER 8

The Limits to Globalization
TECHNOLOGY DISTRICTS AND INTERNATIONAL TRADE

INTERNATIONAL SPECIALIZATION AND THE
ECONOMIC IDENTITIES OF NATIONS AND REGIONS

Two images dominate our thinking about the changes sweeping across the economy over the last two decades. An extensive case study literature calls attention to the geographical reconcentration of production, the resurgence of regional economies examined in Chapter 1. At the same time, our minds are flooded by impressions of global firms and production systems no longer identifiable with any particular region or nation and of a world economy governed by a few globe-girdling firms. Couched in these terms, moreover, such images encourage different, sometimes incompatible, priorities for economic and regional policy.

These images may be refined to capture two interdependent aspects of contemporary industrial reality alluded to in the previous chapter. In this chapter, we will see that the leading edges of economic activity are highly identified with production systems that are organized to carry out continuous product innovation. Production systems engaged in such "product-based technological learning" (henceforth PBTL) account for important and increasing proportions of world exports; they are an essential element in the globalization of economic relations. Yet important parts of such PBTL systems are highly concentrated in distinctive subnational regions, in agglomerations we can label "technology districts," the most important form of territorial economy that exists today.

EXPORT SPECIALIZATION AND
TECHNOLOGICAL DYNAMISM

There are two statistically striking changes in the advanced economies over the last two decades. On the one hand, the sectors rooted in the "second industrial revolution," (the metalworking and mechanical sectors) have declined in relative importance and have been replaced as motors of growth by commodity chains centered on the "third revolution" in electronics and certain services. On the other hand, many markets have become much more internationalized, in manufacturing and finance, and increasingly in services. Between 1955 and 1989, the world GDP index grew from 100 to 350, while the world export index increased to almost 1,100. The share of trade in output thus increased from 6% to 22%. This rise in trade can be seen in an extraordinary variety of sectors. Trade in goods (excluding energy) increased from about 8% to 12% of total world output, and trade in services from about 1.5% to 2.5%.[1] Within the goods-producing sectors, the increase is surprisingly widespread; *filières* (commodity chains) with a stable or increasing share of world trade include metalworking, machinery, motor vehicles, electronics, chemicals, textiles, woodworking, and paper. The dramatic rise in trade is also associated with increases in the overall specialization of the world's advanced industrial economies. A high level of commodity disaggregation is necessary to appreciate this specialization: when statistics are highly aggregated, one sees instead a trend toward convergence in broad sectoral patterns of production of different countries, in part because more similar consumption patterns among advanced economies require similar local market-serving activities, and in part because intraindustry exchanges account for an increasing share of their traded activities (up to 70% in the case of some European countries). Running counter to this, however, is an increase in intraindustry product specialization, that is, differentiation of production within the same broad sectors.[2] Thus, when one examines trade at the level of five-digit SITC (Standard International Trade Classification) products, one sees that export vectors of the main industrial countries have become steadily less similar since 1978.[3] This should not be surprising: industrial production is organized around the making of particular *products;* it is in specific product markets that competition takes place. Moreover, this specialization is not a function of differential access to major production process technologies[4]: major firms in advanced countries have access to a wide and similar range of *production technologies* but stick to a much narrower range of *products.*[5]

The Increase in Export Specialization: What Theory Has to Say

Three explanations can be offered for the growth of trade among countries of similar overall levels of development: factor cost differentials, economies of scale, and technological mastery. A large, and growing, share of world trade consists of exchanges that cannot be explained by the first of these, which is the traditional theory of comparative advantage. In the standard Ricardian understanding, comparative advantage is the result of either the range of natural resources available in a given place, or of reductions in relative costs of production that flow from choosing activities best adapted to the local factor mix. In today's world, however, there is ample reason to expect that when a product is subject to the conditions of perfect competition, upon which the standard theory rests, it would cease to be an object of international trade. Ricardian trade theory was once criticized for ignoring differences in technology or capital endowments between countries, but we now live in a very different world, where factors of production for technologically stable products are not *endowed*, but *produced* (as intermediate inputs). Almost any developed country can become as efficient as the next country in a technologically stable manufacturing sector. As Vernon[6] intimated, the time required for diffusion of standardized technologies has progressively diminished. This is due in part to global corporations whose networks have spread and deepened over the past few decades, and in part to interfirm and intercountry technological imitation. This is confirmed by Amendola, Guerrieri, and Padoan[7] who examined technologies by looking at patents, and found that aggregate technologically based efficiency differences among major countries tended to diminish rapidly and steadily following major technological revolutions. Basic technologies thus become a sort of common knowledge of the developed (and a number of developing) economies, and this leads to rapidly converging costs of production for standardized or generic products. This runs quite opposite to the predictions of Ricardian theory.

A second current explanation, the "new trade theory," argues that trade patterns are largely consequences of economies of scale in production, and therefore that many markets are imperfectly competitive.[8] The global economy as a whole is characterized by much greater product variety than formerly, and the increasing complexity, specialization, and differentiation of many products mean that economies of scale in both final outputs and intermediate outputs overwhelm even the biggest national markets. As a result, according to new trade theory, many broad industrial markets have become contested through international invasion since the end of the 1960s, even though factor prices are similar and technological improvements rapidly diffused. Indeed, worldwide market concentration has tended to fall in many industries, despite the fact that in many sectors and countries domestic production is concentrated in fewer hands than ever before.

This explanation is powerful, and there is little reason to doubt that it applies to certain standardized products differentiated by segmented demands, as well as to trade between highly interdependent neighboring economies (as in Europe). It is nonetheless incomplete in certain respects. First, it is widely thought that minimal optimal scale economies in the production of many goods are either stable or falling, owing to the increasing flexibility (programmability in particular) of capital equipment[9]; this offsets some of the need for scale in intermediate outputs referred to above. Yet trade is rising in a number of markets affected by this phenomenon, such as automobile parts. Second, trade appears to be rising even in product markets where economies of scale have traditionally been quite low (most evidently in traditional industries such as clothing and textiles). Third, there is a critical ambiguity with respect to the significance of economies of scale in the case of small, open economies. Consider, for instance, the situation in which a nation's citizens demand high quantities and very specific qualities of a certain good, and where that nation's economy is small and open—for example, Belgium, where the degree of openness is 45% (in comparison, that of the United States is about 12%). Belgium might produce a certain kind of beer for the specialized tastes of Belgians; but if minimal optimal scale economies are greater than domestic demand, she might then export some of her production. If Belgium's exports are a very small share of world trade in that sector, then her trade specialization in beer has to do with economies of scale. But if that same quantity of exports amounted to a relatively high share of the world's production of certain kinds of beer, her trade specialization cannot be attributed exclusively to economies of scale; scale reasons might have "pushed" the Belgians into external markets in the first place, but world market demand for their output now "pulls" production along, because of the qualities of the Belgian product. Thus, in some circumstances, the mere existence of scale economies explains little about why trade specialization appears and persists. In markets without high barriers to entry, or in markets where barriers are present but trade specialization is stable or increasing, a product must have qualities that provide some kind of advantage in the face of rapid imitation by potential competitors.

This advantage is technological mastery, due to locally superior process or product technology. Product technology appears to be particularly important, as noted earlier, because of the increasing speed of diffusion of process technologies and their increasing flexibility with respect to output mix over time. Thus technological mastery is more and more reflected in the range and speed of product innovation, so that at any given moment certain centers of scarce outputs exist, giving rise to trade. These "economies of variety over time" depend on the ability of a specialized production system to generate a changing array of outputs in its product field, so it can outrun the catch-up effect from ever more rapid imitation and convergent productivity levels. This can be accomplished with or without the usual economies of variety (i.e., making many products at the same time). The process, simultaneously "intellectual" and "material," that continually generates such products, which are not fully standardized or directed to generic markets, is the process of *technological and organizational learning*.[10] This means the ability to reinvent, differentiate, improve, and reconfigure products continuously through a dynamic redeployment of specialized production skills and equipment.

A Historical Divide?

The existing literature on technological innovation and evolutionary economics is overwhelmingly oriented toward the engineering and science-intensive industries and their principal oligopolistic firms, but product-based technological and organizational learning is important across the economy. If learning-based dynamic economies of variety were truly so limited, it would be easy to claim that the contemporary surge in trade and specialization are ephemeral phenomena related to the electronics revolution and its application to other sectors. In this view, microelectronics, by destandardizing knowledge and production processes for a short time, permits a few countries that master state-of-the-art base technologies and applications to gain world market shares. But this "infant industry" perspective also predicts that the transition from the postwar mass production economy to a new system will be achieved when standardization, imitation, and convergence return. In other words, learning would only be a one-time advantage for the first movers in the microelectronics age. This view converges nicely with standard comparative advantage theory, of course, since such advantage, in the form of imperfect competition, would be just a temporary deviation from the "normal" course of economic history.

We argue instead that the contemporary microelectronics revolution (among other forces, including the increasing openness of world markets, shifting consumption patterns related to sociological and demographic changes, and so on), has brought to certain sectors the technological possibility of *beginning* a long-run process of ongoing *respecialization and redefinition* of outputs. World trade is rising even in traditional industries where microelectronics does not revolutionize production; trade is declining as a share of world output only in the nonenergy resource and agricultural sectors, and certain materials processing sectors such as steel.

Leontief[11] prefigured contemporary developments by identifying the paradox of "contrary factor intensities," such that rich countries were specialized in labor-intensive products and poor countries in capital-intensive outputs. He concluded that skill- and knowledge-intensity was a principal determinant of output and trade patterns. Vernon[12] followed with the product-cycle concept, attempting to show why, in organizational terms, the technological and skill cores of an economy were reinvigorated through product pioneering. Vernon[6] later updated the product cycle model in an international context, pointing to ever more rapid international catch-up effects—both between rich and poor countries and among rich nations—through technological imitation and diffusion. He suggested that multinational enterprises could continue to dominate world markets through international location and technology licensing, or what we now recognize as "triad" locational strategies in the world's three major markets. Many supposedly skill- and knowledge-intensive products are now very widely diffused through this process.

Neither Leontief nor Vernon, however, could fully anticipate today's central dynamic: the changing definition of skill and knowledge intensity and its effects on the organizational and locational dynamics of industry. Skill and knowledge intensity is no longer as securely tied, in a given sector, to the internal resources of one or a few major firms as it was when Leontief and Vernon wrote, when technological advantage, once achieved, was effectively embedded in internal economies of scale and stabilized for a certain period of time. Skill- and knowledge-based competition is now more dependent than ever before on resources that lie outside of major firms (and hence are not fully appropriable by them). Partly as a result of the latter, such competition now takes a different temporal form than it did 30 years ago; instead of being intermittent and leaving intact medium-term advantages, it has become more continuous, with much briefer advantages. The reduction of temporal advantages is not now due only to rapid imitation, in other words, but to real skill- and knowledge-based competition.

It appears that we have entered a period in the development of capitalism in which trade and specialization are driven by the supply side learning behavior of specializers. Such behavior has become a broad characteristic of the logic of "best practice" in advanced capitalist economies. This ongoing differentiation of products has the effect of continually unsettling the division of labor through dynamic economies of variety, leading to what Freeman[13] suspects may be a "permanent shift in industrial structure and behavior." Trade must still be seen as a handmaiden rather than as an autonomous engine of growth. Supply side learning behaviors underlie dynamic specialization and emerging patterns of trade. The question is why certain places build up advantages that permit them, over and over, to turn out products that cannot be easily and rapidly imitated.

CONTRASTING SPECIALIZATIONS IN THREE COUNTRIES

There are two basic ways to approach specialization in operational terms. The Commercial Trade Balance index (CTB) developed by French researchers identifies those sectors whose contribution to the overall balance is higher (or lower) than their percentage share of the nation's total trade.[14] The Balassa Specialization Index, on the other hand, relies on exports only, and it shows specialization when a country's exports account for a greater share of world exports than the country's overall share in world exports.[15] The CTB in effect measures traded sectors against other traded sectors of the economy, whereas the Balassa index is more directly oriented toward describing the strengths of the country's exports relative to the world as a whole, in the sense of the desirability of its products per se. Both are useful, but the latter is more appropriate to our theoretical concern, because it is possible (though not likely) that a country could have a weak or negative trade balance and still enjoy strong or increasing export performance. Take, for example, U.S. trade in "analog hybrid data processing machines," in which exports are slightly greater than imports. This means that other countries also specialize in exporting such machines, and such exchanges probably reflect product differentiation at greater than five-digit level.

We can thus say that a country is successfully specialized in today's world economy when its *share of world exports of a specific product is greater than its share of world trade as a whole* (i.e., its imports and exports as a share of total imports and exports in the world). The country is producing something that the world wants in greater proportion than its overall participation in world trade. This criterion is more restrictive than a comparative advantage perspective in that it tends to reveal fewer but more intense areas of strength. Dosi, Pavitt, and Soete (Chap. 6)[16] show, in an international and intersectoral test, that precisely the sectors with high absolute export share are highly innovative and are relatively unaffected by comparative advantage locational dynamics. Research by Porter,[17] using a similar definition, reveals that the specializations of Italy, Germany, the United States, Sweden, Switzerland, and Japan are suprisingly different from one another, even though the sectoral distribution of activities in these economies would look relatively similar and increasingly convergent if viewed side by side and in terms of more aggregated sectoral definitions, such as three-digit SIC sectors.

It should be possible to separate the three potential sources of export specialization alluded to above: cost, scale, and PBTL. By separating export specialization sectors into these three causes, we could assess the overall importance of PBTL. Unfortunately, no tried and true method of assigning such causes exists.

To sharpen this analysis and provide a basis for comparing the specializations of France to those of the United States and Italy, we defined three groups of products in which competition is highly likely to be based on elements other than price, that is, on technological mastery or product quality. The first group consists of a subset of the supplier-dominated industries, the design- intensive or craft-based (DIC) outputs, products based on fashion or luxury (such as clothing or personal accessories); here competition is centered on creative skills or, for manufacturing, on artisanal methods. The production problems correspond closely to the Interpersonal World (though some, as we shall see, are found in the Market World). The second group is a subset of the science-based industries, the high-technology products (HTI). These correspond mainly to the Intellectual World, although more standardized outputs are tied into the Market World and more dedicated products into the Interpersonal World. The third group, precision metalworking and machining products (PMM), consists of specialized and dedicated mechanical items, found across the economy. Their producers correspond strongly to the Interpersonal and Market Worlds and are commonly categorized as "specialized supplier" industries.

Our method initially distinguished PBTI, industries from others using a variety of criteria applied to U.S. four-digit census sectors. HTI industries were defined as those sectors with greater than 25% scientists and engineers in their workforces. The DIC industries were defined on the basis of the diversity of their products. We used an index developed for the U.S. Census Bureau[18] to rank manufacturing establishments on the basis of their level of product diversification for the years 1963, 1967, 1972, 1977, and 1982. We defined DIC industries as those having a product diversification greater than the U.S. all-industry average in 1982, or those with a rapidly increasing index of diversification.[19]

Table 8.1 presents figures on trade composition and trade ratios for a set of industrialized countries, using the OECD's classification of industry groups. These categories overlap with possible worlds of production to some extent: scale-intensive industry with the Industrial World; supplier-dominated

TABLE 8.1. Trade composition and trade ratios for main industrialized countries by typology of industrial sectors

Industrial sectors	Italy	France	West Germany	United Kingdom	United States	Japan
Exports (E) %						
Supplier-dominated	41.57	19.96	18.63	21.88	13.70	12.10
Scale-intensive	26.90	42.85	44.27	29.85	27.17	57.18
Specialized supplier	21.99	21.15	25.36	25.86	28.29	23.25
Science-based	8.54	16.04	11.74	22.40	30.29	7.47
Total	100.00	100.00	100.00	100.00	100.00	100.00
Imports (I) %						
Supplier-dominated	18.78	25.48	29.94	26.78	28.18	26.40
Scale-intensive	46.95	43.53	38.74	39.19	44.98	36.62
Specialized supplier	18.15	21.26	16.00	18.97	16.22	15.02
Science-based	16.12	9.73	15.31	15.05	10.61	21.96
Total	100.00	100.00	100.00	100.00	100.00	100.00
Trade ratios (E/I, $ value)						
Supplier-dominated	57.57	−6.23	3.56	−12.21	−39.82	33.91
Scale-intensive	−0.15	5.18	32.71	−15.64	−29.43	74.69
Specialized supplier	33.78	5.72	46.46	13.26	21.38	74.50
Science-based	−5.91	13.11	13.91	1.55	43.28	20.11

Source: OECD.

industry with the Interpersonal World; some specialized supplier industries with the Market World, others in the Interpersonal World; and a part of the Intellectual World with science-based industry. Note the extraordinary presence of the supplier-dominated industries in Italian exports, along with the near absence of science-based products and very high imports from scale-intensive sectors. In contrast, France is very strong in scale-related exports, and the United States very weak in exports from supplier-dominated industries, with the rest spread among the other three categories.

Table 8.2 shows the direction of change in export specializations over the 1970s and 1980s, albeit at a rather aggregated *filière* level, for four European countries. Note that while Italy has strongly reinforced her position in the supplier-dominated and specialized supplier industries, France has had neither dramatic successes nor dramatic reversals, holding steady in scale-related production, slipping somewhat in supplier-dominated and science-based products, and improving modestly in specialized supplier sectors (due, almost exclusively, to the growth of the Airbus Industrie consortium, as reflected in the "transportation" category).

France: A Weakly Specialized Economy, Poorly Adapted to International Demand

Table 8.3 provides a compact summary picture of the situation for the different countries in 1985. France is specialized in the first (design-intensive, craft-based) group, with 6.7% of world exports in 1985 (as compared to her total share of world trade, 5.2%). Her strongest positions are in products for the home, textiles, and personal accessories, which together account for 10% of French exports. This position remains strong and deep, but the country's share for several products declined in the 1980s. In the second group, high-technology outputs, France has 6.4% of world exports, and the group accounts for 16% of the country's exports. This reflects French dominance in a number of areas, including radioactive elements, aircraft, reactors, and computer peripherals. France is not specialized in the third group as a whole, but does have certain strengths, in mechanical engineering, cutlery, instruments, and some types of industrial machinery. Taken together, the three groups examined here account for only about 30% of French exports. France performs moderately well in all, but spectacularly in none. As Table 8.4A illustrates, the 50 leading French exports in 1985 accounted for only 22.5% of French exports; corresponding figures are 33.8% for the United States and 27.2% for Italy.

Note that very few products on the list seem to be based on dynamic economies of variety and collective technological learning. A relatively large number are very likely listed because of favorable cost structures or simple scale economies, as shown in Table 8.5A. For example, except for wines

TABLE 8.2. Export specialization by type of industry and country

	1970–1973					1984–1987					Change				
	Germany	France	U.K.	Italy	Total	Germany	France	U.K.	Italy	Total	Germany	France	U.K.	Italy	Total
Scale-intensive industries (industrial)															
Chemicals	124.70	120.40	112.00	98.30	113.90	122.50	150.00	140.80	90.60	126.00	-2.20	29.60	28.80	-7.70	12.10
Oil	50.70	54.60	66.30	145.40	79.30	40.40	50.30	86.20	72.80	62.40	-10.30	-4.30	19.90	-72.60	-16.90
Electrical machinery	145.20	114.90	109.70	140.50	127.60	123.40	110.50	99.40	104.60	109.50	-21.80	-4.40	-10.30	-35.90	-18.10
Motor vehicles	145.50	123.20	114.40	96.70	120.00	146.90	105.50	62.20	61.10	93.90	1.40	-17.70	-52.20	-35.60	-26.10
Total	116.50	103.30	100.60	120.20	110.20	108.30	104.10	97.15	82.30	97.90	-8.20	0.80	3.45	-37.90	-12.30
Supplier-dominated (interpersonal/market)															
Textiles	70.80	114.70	80.60	209.10	118.80	60.90	74.10	58.70	219.10	103.20	-9.90	-40.60	-21.90	10.00	-15.60
Nonmetallic minerals	115.50	132.90	105.30	210.50	141.10	107.60	138.50	91.50	244.40	145.50	-7.90	5.60	-13.80	33.90	4.45
Metal products	136.50	106.80	128.60	128.80	125.20	133.30	112.30	100.70	164.80	127.80	-3.20	5.50	-27.90	36.00	2.60
Total	107.60	118.10	104.80	182.80	128.40	100.60	108.30	83.63	209.40	125.50	-7.00	-9.80	-21.17	26.60	-2.90

Specialized suppliers (market/interpersonal)

Mechanical engineering	188.10	84.70	143.80	136.60	138.50	168.20	76.20	118.00	168.20	132.70	-19.90	-8.50	-25.80	31.60	-5.60
Mechanical and thermo-mechanical equipment	149.40	105.40	117.90	134.80	126.50	147.80	108.60	127.90	155.40	134.90	-1.60	3.20	10.00	20.60	8.00
Other transportation	48.50	85.50	105.80	41.90	70.40	66.10	119.50	162.20	53.90	100.40	17.60	34.00	56.40	12.00	30.00
Total	128.70	91.87	122.50	104.40	111.90	127.40	101.40	136.00	125.80	122.70	-1.30	9.53	13.50	21.40	10.80

Science-based industries (intellectual)

Office	111.30	101.40	129.80	109.80	113.10	67.40	80.30	150.40	62.30	90.10	-43.90	-21.10	20.60	-47.50	-23.00
Electronics	90.30	60.10	75.90	69.50	73.90	60.50	57.30	75.60	37.50	57.70	-29.80	-2.80	-0.30	-32.00	-16.20
Instruments	128.70	88.30	108.10	59.90	96.25	111.70	87.00	140.50	54.60	98.40	-17.00	-1.30	32.40	-5.30	2.15
Total	110.10	83.27	104.60	79.73	94.42	79.87	74.87	122.20	51.47	82.07	-30.23	-8.42	17.60	-28.30	-12.35
Scale	116.50	103.30	100.60	120.20	110.20	108.30	104.10	97.15	82.30	97.90	-8.20	0.80	-3.45	-37.90	-12.30
Rest	115.50	97.76	110.60	122.30	111.50	102.60	94.87	113.90	128.90	110.10	-12.80	-2.89	3.30	6.59	-1.47

Source: OECD.
Note. Figures represent ratio of exports to imports. Totals are for all industries measured.

TABLE 8.3. The degree of country specialization in HTI, DIC, and PMM industries

Clusters	Countries		
	U.S.	France	Italy
High-technology industries			
Value of exports ($ billion)	60.13	15.76	7.85
Value of imports ($ billion)	57.17	13.61	9.83
Country's share of total world exports in cluster (%)	24.72%	6.48%	3.23%
Cluster's share of country's total exports	28.21%	16.13%	9.94%
Design-intensive products industries			
Value of exports ($ billion)	6.42	10.07	22.04
Value of imports ($ billion)	41.66	10.50	6.00
Country's share of total world exports in cluster (%)	4.27%	6.69%	14.64%
Cluster's share of country's total exports	3.01%	10.31%	27.92%
Precision machinery and metalworking industries			
Value of exports ($ billion)	1.38	0.56	1.15
Value of imports ($ billion)	3.31	0.69	0.40
Country's share of total world exports in cluster (%)	10.01%	4.02%	8.30%
Cluster's share of country's total exports	0.65%	0.57%	1.46%

Source: UNIDO (United Nations Industrial Development Organization); our calculation.
Note. Cluster's definition based on SITC's. High technologies' SITC's = 524, 541, 713, 714, 718, 751, 752, 759, 761, 762, 763, 764, 772, 776, 792, 871, 872, 874. Design-intensive/craft-based industry items = 551, 553, 61, 65, 665, 666, 724, 82, 85, 883, 88, 897, 898. Precision machinery and metalworking = 696, 73.

(where France is absolutely dominant in world markets, more by reason of her savoir faire than climate or cost advantages), most of the food and beverage group are large-scale food processing firms. In the transportation category, only aircraft engines and reaction engines, electrical traction vehicles (locomotives, etc.), and radar apparatus are obvious cases of specialization based on learning or economies of variety. By contrast, numerous specializations in the clothing–textile sector are probably linked to savoir faire: fabrics, lace, women's dresses and clothing, woolen yarns, furs, weaving machinery. In energy production, a number of products have benefited from scale economies due to the State's modernization of the national electric system, including rapid nuclearization, and the corresponding scale effects on related capital-goods sectors (although some energy products are knowledge-intensive). State direction has also affected the electronics and telecommunications sectors, which require technological mastery for competition. Finally, in the "health care" group, some firms—although they are beneficiaries of purchases by the public health care system—export certain drugs developed on the basis of superior scientific knowledge.

TABLE 8.4A. Top 50 French industries ranked in terms of world export share, 1985

Industry	Share of total world exports (%)	Export value ($ millions)	Import value ($ millions)	Share of total French exports
Distilled wine from grapes	86.99	659,838	0	0.68
Xylenes, chemically pure	66.24	1,507,452	14,807	1.54
Wine of fresh grapes	49.33	1,916,520	237,807	1.96
Radioactive elements	46.36	1,457,550	926,161	1.49
Malt, including flour	37.03	204,319	4,668	0.21
Perfumery and cosmetics	36.77	1,245,578	172,522	1.28
Glass, household, hotel	34.69	484,445	67,841	0.50
Polymides, pure	31.48	359,402	83,301	0.37
Aircraft over 15,000 kg	31.37	1,953,012	147,789	2.00
Other wheat, unmilled	30.61	2,285,921	24,042	2.34
Wheat flour	29.06	287,539	4,976	0.29
Chemical elements	26.02	504,654	29,846	0.52
Poultry	25.74	325,463	3,978	0.33
Barley, unmilled	24.25	611,368	19,643	0.63
Copper scrap	23.17	282,649	38,522	0.29
Reduced sugar	21.44	514,820	4,655	0.53
Fresh apples	20.60	230,479	44,782	0.24
Nonalcoholic drinks	19.22	145,297	—	0.15
Anti-knock preparations	19.06	380,365	86,068	0.39
Essences, oils	18.71	108,426	94,462	0.11
Glass bottles	18.70	153,595	122,176	0.16
Reaction engines	18.53	384,132	248,977	0.39
New tires for cars	18.38	460,581	187,865	0.47
Wool, hair, yarn, including tops	18.16	400,350	90,594	0.41
Railway vehicles and parts	18.14	359,216	29,039	0.37
Combustible products	17.52	117,586	43,602	0.12
Residual of 0224	17.47	64,477	11,658	0.07
Refractory bricks	17.15	133,421	54,097	0.14
Tires for buses	16.61	365,302	92,567	0.37
Residual of 8211	16.48	68,482	(neg)	0.07
Residual of women's outerwear (nonknitted)	16.17	302,932	71,810	0.31
Central heating equipment	15.84	121,377	92,775	0.12
Off-line data processing equipment	15.65	89,314	111,895	0.09
Yachts, sports vessels	15.21	192,508	66,367	0.20
Industrial furnaces, nonelectric	15.19	111,440	24,453	0.11
Dry milk	14.73	354,221	34,611	0.36
Electric vehicles, light	14.65	148,104	80,163	0.15
Electric accumulators	14.55	159,497	76,850	0.16
Polystyrene, primary	14.51	311,133	245,216	0.32
Polyvinyl chloride in primary form	14.35	187,046	113,378	0.19
Pile, etc., cotton fabric	14.30	62,607	38,060	0.06
Spectacle frames	14.24	105,117	28,867	0.11
Mixed perfumes	13.95	157,588	65,198	0.16
Stainless steel plates	13.89	177,129	49,482	0.18
Lace, ribbons, tulle	13.70	143,821	—	0.15
Tinned plates, sheets	13.67	220,889	54,539	0.23
Shovels and excavators	13.58	340,857	88,453	0.35
Bovine meat with bone	13.49	407,506	630,896	0.42
Butter	13.24	278,111	91,397	0.28
Blended yarn	13.04	119,674	—	0.12
Total				22.49

Source: UNIDO International Commodity Trade Statistics (1985).

In sum, only 17 of the top 50 specializations shown in Table 8.4A seem to be attributable to economies of variety or collective technological learning. Not only are French exports as a whole not very specialized, but when divided into the three principal causes of export positions—costs, economies of scale, economies of variety/learning—costs and scale, least appealing in terms of developmental effects, carry the day. The answer has already been suggested, in Chapter 6: the industrial modernization activities of the State in the post-war period systematically deemphasized local productive activity in favor of large-scale mass production. But a few cases, in which the State or the private sector jointly assure the conventions of learning, did survive.

The United States: The Importance of the Intellectual World

The picture in the United States contrasts significantly with that seen in France. The United States is quite specialized in high-technology exports, with more than 25% of the world's total. Its share of PMMs does not qualify as a specialization, as it is just below the "cutoff," but it is respectably close, while the share of design-intensive products is less than half the country's overall share, thus falling far short of specialization. ("Cutoff" refers to the country's overall share of all world exports and imports, which was about 12% for the United States in 1985, 5.2% for France, and 4.6% for Italy.)

Among U.S. specializations in high-technology industries are a number of extremely strong positions: aircraft and aircraft parts, gas turbines, measuring and drawing equipment, electromedical equipment, ADP peripherals, and digital computers all account for at least three times the cutoff level. Among the top fifty American exports, as ranked by world market shares (Tables 8.4B and 8.5B), are semiconductors, instruments, computers, and aircraft; in terms of both dollar volume and share in total U.S. exports, the most important specializations are commercial aircraft and helicopters, computers, firearms and ammunition, aircraft parts, piezoelectric crystals, aircraft engines, and office machine and computer parts. U.S. performance is strong in other high-technology areas, especially in technologies related to health care, ranging from equipment to pharmaceuticals and related chemical products. While the U.S. position in PMM industries has fallen in recent years, it remains strong in steelmaking equipment, metalworking machinery, and certain equipment sectors linked to high technology, such as semiconductor manufacturing machinery. The United States had very few strong positions in the design-intensive industries, however. What is it that makes intellectual action so strong in the United States and why is interpersonal action apparently so weak? Our answer in Chapter 6 was the particular American model of innovation, exit, and sectoral succession, itself underpinned by uniquely American conventions of participation in the production system.

TABLE 8.4B. Top 50 U.S. industries ranked in terms of world export share, 1985

Industry	Share of total world exports (%)	Export value ($ millions)	Import value ($ millions)	Share of total U.S. exports
Cottonseed oil	84.4	124,770	3,047	0.06
Unexposed, undeveloped photo film	81.9	885,712	630,695	0.42
Petroleum coke	80.3	760,981	19,522	0.36
Commercial aircraft and helicopters[a]	79.4	8,823,833	1,806,783	4.14
Rough sawn veneer logs	75.8	1,170,516	17,408	0.55
Other manufactured fertilizers	69.6	1,272,439	92	0.06
Beet pulp bagasse	69.5	5,335,039	20,558	2.50
Unmilled maize	69.5	5,335,039	20,558	2.50
Aircraft internal combustion piston engines and parts	67.4	383,483	9,766	0.18
Soya beans	67.1	3,749,941	976	1.76
Unmilled sorghum	65.8	769,266	13	0.36
Coal, lignite, and peat	64.4	4,399,776	135,986	2.06
Analog hybrid data processing machines, storage units	64.3	4,323,864	4,116,526	2.03
Fresh fish	63.5	664,102	631,303	0.31
Aircraft gas turbine engines	62.8	1,229,403	1,254,813	0.58
War firearms, ammunition	62.7	2,888,887	203,863	1.36
Fats of bovine, sheep	60.3	554,747	—	0.26
Measuring, drawing, instrument parts	60.0	104,473	23,586	0.05
Nitrogen phosphate fertilizer	57.3	649,698	30,129	0.30
Radioactive materials	57.1	980,118	1,399,330	0.46
Aircraft parts	56.6	5,674,001	1,793,513	2.66
Whey	54.2	199,938	—	0.09
Warships and boats	53.1	278,283	—	0.13
Clay	52.4	310,053	3,246	0.15
Green groundnuts	51.3	209,987	461	0.10
Piesoelectric crystals	50.7	3,019,250	1,100,923	1.42
Measuring, drawing, etc., instruments	48.4	600,200	177,534	0.28
Regenerated fiber to spin	48.0	226,088	2,018	0.11
Typewriters, checkwriters	47.8	167,562	375,209	0.08
Wholly or partly stripped tobacco	47.7	129,913	177,163	0.06
Iron pyrites	47.2	240,557	556,954	0.11
Electromedical equipment	46.6	865,609	524,326	0.41
Dissolving chemical wood pulp	45.3	299,445	62,012	0.14
Raw bovine equine hides	45.3	1,021,116	30,670	0.48
Cyclic alcohols	44.5	154,502	22,238	0.07
Glycosides, glands, sera	44.5	505,183	201,777	0.24
Footware with soles of cork wood	44.4	80,675	173,548	0.04
Edible offal	43.1	298,557	7,063	0.14
Rolling mills	42.5	77,911	11,642	0.04
Roadrollers, civil engineering equipment, etc.	42.2	4,091,920	1,937,088	1.91
Pharmaceuticals other than medicaments	41.8	806,956	52,058	0.38
Aircraft engines and motor parts	41.6	2,451,731	1,202,089	1.15
Track laying tractors	40.5	230,718	116,851	0.37
Kraft liner	40.3	481,920	—	0.23
Polyethylene in rods	39.9	647,607	151,409	0.30
Polyvinyl choride in rods	39.1	262,736	98,344	0.12
Artificial fur products	38.9	8,697	—	0.00
Motor vehicle chassis	37.7	386,818	968,789	0.18
Office ADP machine parts, accessories	37.1	7,816,542	5,326,652	3.70
Total				33.80

Source: UNIDO International Commodity Trade Statistics (1985).
Note. No import data are reported if import value is less than 0.3% of total trade for 1985.
[a]Commercial aircraft is estimated to account for $5.5 billion of exports in this category.

Italy: The Predominance of the Interpersonal World

Italy looks something like the inverse of the U.S. case, with an overwhelmingly strong position in design-intensive products (almost 15% of the world total, or three times the Italian cutoff level), and PMMs (with a share almost double the cutoff), but an unimpressive 3.2% of world high-technology exports. Table 8.3 shows how important high technology is to U.S. exports, and the analogous role played by DICs for Italy, with France having a certain balance between the two and a small role for PMMs.

What is so striking about Italy's design-intensive exports is the sheer number of sectors in which she is dominant, and the very high shares of world exports Italian firms hold in those product markets (in a dozen sectors Italy's shares exceed 25%, six times the cutoff) (Tables 8.4C and 8.5C). Italian presence is particularly strong in textiles and apparel; household products such as furniture, lamps, glass, and ceramic tiles; personal products such as jewelry, and miscellaneous fashion items such as eyeglasses, and toiletries; other specializations include paper making, film and film processing, and automobile design. The Italian economy also stands out frequently for specializing in intermediate products or equipment associated with her final output specializations. Thus, the list includes textile machinery, marble cutting tools, kilns for tile making, and some metalworking and woodworking machinery.

TECHNOLOGY DISTRICTS AS REGIONAL WORLDS OF PRODUCTION

The export specialization industries of the United States, France, and Italy are not distributed evenly across their national territories. Indeed, the geography of these industries conforms rather well to popular impressions about these nations' "dynamic" regions. Thus the U.S. high-technology industries, centered on microelectronics (semiconductors and computers), are highly concentrated in Silicon Valley in northern California, Orange County–San Diego in southern California, and the Boston area, with lesser concentrations in Minneapolis–St. Paul (Minnesota), Dallas–Fort Worth, and the southern Atlantic coast of Florida. Aerospace has its primary concentration in the Los Angeles region, with other significant concentrations in Texas, New York, Connecticut–Massachusetts, and Washington state. (In technical terms, the sectors mentioned have location quotients in these places that are greater than 1.2, suggesting genuine [statistically significant] localizations; see Table 8.6.)

In Italy, the export-oriented DICs and PMMs are highly concentrated in the northeastern regions of Lombardy (outside of Milan, for the most part),

TABLE 8.4C. Top 50 Italian industries ranked in terms of world export share, 1985

Industry	Share of total world exports (%)	Export value ($ millions)	Import value ($ millions)	Share of total Italian exports
Groats, meal, and pellets of wheat	69.5	159,765	3,631	0.20
Worked building stone	62.2	701,208	5,319	0.89
Other wine of fresh grapes (aperitifs)	58.1	75,754	513	0.10
Glazed ceramic sets	56.6	866,879	16,437	1.10
Precious metal jewelry	49.6	2,288,256	19,978	2.90
Fresh stone fruit	45.5	247,385	10,159	0.31
Rubber and plastic footwear	41.9	452,469	20,402	0.57
Fabrics of combed wool	41.8	278,003	34,861	0.35
Domestic washing machines	38.2	396,595	32,123	0.50
Steel high pressure conduit	35.9	319,193	11,271	0.40
Sweaters of synthetic fibers	34.0	631,213	5,419	0.80
Handbags	33.7	343,408	3,978	0.41
Woolen sweaters	33.1	499,221	55,460	0.61
Leather footwear	32.8	3,285,427	178,156	4.16
Other woven textile fabric	32.3	510,145	48,634	0.65
Woven silk fabrics	31.7	215,629	53,632	0.27
Cement, artificial stone products	31.2	124,617	4,224	0.36
Chairs and other seats	30.6	685,124	29,894	0.87
Textiles, clothing, accessories	27.8	251,618	24,303	0.32
Fresh grapes	27.8	235,494	7,105	0.30
Domestic deep freezers	26.8	80,738	3,379	0.10
Women's outerwear	26.2	491,478	50,159	0.62
Domestic refrigerators	26.1	314,900	16,353	0.40
Wood furniture	25.5	1,026,911	40,390	1.30
Machine tools for wood, ceramics	24.7	485,500	35,141	0.61
Leather	24.6	452,233	266,542	0.57
Other sweaters, pullovers	24.5	641,799	16,830	0.81
Coke and semi-coke of lignite	24.2	323	1,159	0.00
Unbleached sulphite woodpulp	23.3	20,576	36,907	0.03
Footwear components	23.0	198,785	11,270	0.25
Olive oil	22.4	131,742	283,534	0.17
Furniture and parts	22.3	186,395	14,522	0.24
Men's suits	22.2	145,837	17,341	0.18
Spectacle frames	22.2	164,124	30,899	0.21
Knitted clothing accessories	22.2	186,366	25,954	0.24
Metal furniture	21.5	174,076	11,804	0.22
Wine of fresh grapes	20.7	803,915	75,121	1.02
Bulk antibiotics	20.5	321,442	228,622	0.41
Ceramic ornaments	20.3	114,451	23,432	0.14
Nontextured yarn containing polyamide	20.3	97,411	64,949	0.12
Packaging, bottling machines	19.8	464,507	55,063	0.59
Men's overcoats	19.8	435,710	99,379	0.55
Sinks, washbasins, bidets	19.5	77,117	3,781	0.10
Domestic heating, cooking apparatus	19.5	199,544	27,309	0.25
Foliage, branches, and other parts of plants	19.3	26,045	2,750	0.01
Lamps, fittings of base metal	19.1	275,239	26,915	0.35
Other textile specialized leather machinery	18.6	425,736	100,203	0.54
Solid sodium hydroxide	18.3	35,690	1,711	0.05
Woven syntheic fiber fabric	18.1	753,426	189,393	0.95
Plastic coated textiles	18.0	157,913	30,376	0.20
Total				27.16

Source: UNIDO International Commodity Trade Statistics (1985).
Note. No import data reported if import value is less than 0.3% of the total trade for 1985.

TABLE 8.5A. Learning industries versus the rest, France

Scale or process-based technological advantages in scale or costs	Product-based technological learning: economies of variety
Xylenes, chemically pure	Distilled wine from grapes
Malt, including flour	Wine of fresh grapes
Polyamides	Radioactive elements
Other wheat, unmilled	Household, hotel glass
Wheat flour	Aircraft over 15,000 kg
Chemical elements	Essences, oils
Poultry	Reaction engines
Copper scrap	Off-line data processing equipment
Refined sugar	Yachts, sports vessels
Fresh apples	Light electric vehicles
Dry milk > 1.5% fat	Pile, cotton fabrics
Anti-knock preparations	Spectacle frames
Glass bottles	Mixed perfumes
New tires for cars	Medicaments nonantibody
Combustible products	Perfumery and cosmetics
Residual of 224	Residual of women's outerwear
Refractory bricks	(nonknitted)
Tires for buses	Lace, ribbons, tulle
Chair components	
Central heating equipment	
Industrial furnaces, nonelectric	
Parts for refrigerator equipment	
Electric accumulators	
Polystyrene, primary	
Polyvinyl chloride feedstock	
Stainless steel plates	
Tinned plates, sheets	
Shovels, excavators	
Bovine meat with bone	
Insecticides, retail	
Iron and steel wire	
Railway vehicles and parts	
Butter	
$N = 33$	$N = 17$
Export Value: $12.1 billion	Export Value: $9.86 billion
Value: 55.1%	Value: 44.9%

Total: $21.96 billion

Source: UNIDO (United Nations Industrial Development Organization), World Trade Statistics.

TABLE 8.5B. Learning industries versus the rest, United States

Scale or process-based technological advantages in scale or costs	Product-based technological learning: economies of variety
Cottonseed oil	Commercial aircraft/helicopters
Photo film	Aircraft engines and parts
Petroleum coke	Analog hybrid data processing machines
Rough-sawn, veneer logs	Aircraft gas turbine engines
Fertilizers	War firearms, ammunition
Beet bulp, bagasse	Measuring, drawing instruments (parts)
Unmilled maize	Warships, boats
Soya beans	Measuring, drawing instruments (complete)
Unmilled sorghum	Piezoelectric crystals
Coal, lignite, and peat	Electromedical equipment
Fresh fish	Glycosides, glands, sera
Fats of bovine, sheep	Footwear with soles of cork
Nitrogen, phosphate fertilizer	Rolling mills
Whey	Civil engineering equipment
Clay	Pharmaceuticals
Green groundnuts	Aircraft engine and motor parts
Typewriters, checkwriters	Office, ADP machine parts,
Stripped tobacco	accessories
Iron pyrites	Radioactive materials
Dissolving chemical wood pulp	Aircraft parts
Raw bovine, equine hides	
Cyclic alcohols	
Edible offal	
Track-laying tractors	
Fungicides, disinfectants	
Kraft liner	
Polyethylene in rods	
Polyvinyl chloride in rods	
Artificial fur products	
Motor vehicles chassis	
$N = 30$	$N = 19$
Export Value: $26.9 billion	Export Value: $45.0 billion
Value: 37.46%	Value: 62.54%
Total: $71.9 billion	

Source: UNIDO (United Nations Industrial Development Organization), World Trade Statistics.

the Veneto, Trentino–Alto Adige, Friuli–Venezia–Giuilia (FVG), Emilia–Romagna, and Tuscany, with some extensions into the Marches and Umbria. Sforzi documented the existence of about one hundred "industrial districts" in the DIC and PMM industries.[20] And within these regions, particular provinces and communes are highly specialized: Udine (FVG) in chairs, Como (Lombardy) in silk fabrics, Sassuolo (Emilia–Romagna) in ceramic tiles

TABLE 8.5C. Learning industries versus the rest, Italy

Scale or process-based technological advantages in scale or costs	Product-based technological learning: economies of variety
Groats, meal, pellets	Aperitifs
Worked building stone	Glazed ceramic sets
Fresh stone fruit	Precious metal jewelry
Rubber and plastic footware	Fabrics of combed wool
Domestic washing machines	Sweaters of synthetic fibers
Steel high-pressure conduit	Handbags
Fresh grapes	Woolen sweaters
Domestic deep freezers	Leather footwear
Domestic refrigerators	Other woven textile fabric
Coke/semi-coke of lignite	Woven silk fabric
Unbleached sulfited woodpulp	Cement, artificial stone products
Olive oil	Chairs and other seats
Bulk antibodies	Textile clothing accessories
Domestic heating, cooking apparatus	Women's outerwear
Foliage, branches, plants	Wood furniture
Solid sodium hydroxide	Machine tools for wood, ceramics
Plastic coated textiles	Leather
	Other sweaters, pullovers
	Footwear components
	Furniture and parts
	Men's suits
	Spectacle frames
	Knitted clothing accessories
	Metal furniture
	Wine of fresh grapes
	Ceramic ornaments
	Nontextured yarn containing polyamide
	Packaging and bottling machines
	Men's overcoats
	Sinks, washbasins, bidets
	Lamps, fittings of base metal
	Other textile, special leather machines
	Woven synthetic fiber fabric
$N = 17$	$N = 33$
Export Value: $3.8 billion	Export Value: $17.7 billion
Value: 17.71%	Value: 82.29%

Total: $21.5 billion

Source: UNIDO (United Nations Industrial Development Organization), World Trade Statistics.

TABLE 8.5D. Learning industries versus the rest, total

Scale or process-based technological advantages in scale or costs	Product-based technological learning: economies of variety
$N = 80$	$N = 69$
Export Value: $42.9 billion	Export Value: $72.56 billion
Value: 37.15%	Value: 62.84%
Total for 149 sectors: $115.46 billion	

Source: UNIDO (United Nations Industrial Development Organization), World Trade Statistics.

and tile equipment, Poggibonsi (Tuscany) in wooden furniture, mechanical engineering (Bologna and Modena in Emilia–Romagna), Santa Croce (Tuscany) in leather shoes, and so on. Thus, Italy shows not only extremely strong economic specializations, but a dramatically focused geography. The action frameworks of these districts were studied in Chapter 6. The Interpersonal Worlds of production in these places can be seen as the principal influence on Italy's presence in the international economy.

In trying to locate real worlds of production in France, it is helpful to note that several of the country's trade specializations are based on natural resources; others appear to be rooted in the economies of scale adroitly constructed in mass-production sectors by the State's economic planning agency; and, finally, one group of industries qualifying as a trade specialization, very probably rooted in the existence of economies of variety or skill, the key corollaries of technological learning as defined here.

The geography of French specializations is quite complex and less well-known than the other two countries'. French high-technology specializations in aerospace and defense are concentrated in the Paris region, as examined in Chapter 6, in the Midi–Pyrénées (Toulouse), in Acquitaine (Bordeaux), and in the Loire (Nantes); in telecommunications and electronic components, in the Paris region and Rhône–Alpes. In design-intensive or craft-based industries, the French specialties in shoes are concentrated in the Rhône–Alpes region (Roanne, Romans, the Monts du Lyonnais), and fashion clothing (studied in Chapter 6) in the Paris region and the Vendée (Chôlet). Certain other isolated specialties, such as porcelain (Limoges) and perfumes (Cannes), also make their appearance. In advanced services, the only important region for export (of engineering and financial services) is that of Paris. The Rhône–Alpes, France's second industrial region, is highly specialized in metalworking and machinery industries (the Vallée de l'Arve in the Upper Savoy); other concentrations may be found in the northern part of the French Jura.

TABLE 8.6. Technology Districts in the United States

Industry	Employment	Location quotients[a]
California		
Aerospace	229,124	3.02
Biologicals	5,255	2.08
Electronics and components	509,692	2.05
Precision instruments	40,913	1.59
Medical equipment	25,627	1.48
Massachusetts and Connecticut		
Aircraft and engines	17,918	7.78
Financial services	21,849	6.39
Aerospace and armaments	77,911	4.14
Precision instruments	36,042	2.81
Electronics and components	101,150	2.73
Radio, TV, and telecommunications	67,545	1.82
Research and development labs	12,272	1.80
Medical equipment	8,119	1.65
New York and New Jersey		
Pharmaceuticals and biologicals	47,599	2.41
Medical equipment	21,950	1.86
Banking and finance	319,952	1.51
Advanced services	504,500	1.50
Electronics and components	54,150	1.26
Texas		
Construction and engineering	677,463	1.73
Aircraft	29,374	1.57
Electronics	76,597	1.47
Ohio, Michigan, and Pennsylvania		
Instruments	31,816	1.40
Washington		
Aircraft	54,523	7.85
Electronics and components	3,809	2.62

[a]Location quotient is the ratio of the percentage of output of industry x in economy y (the locality in question), to the percentage of output of industry x in the nation's economy as a whole.

The Technology District as a Particular Form of the Industrial District

Marshall remarked, in 1919,[21] that in the major English industrial regions, the intangible elements of the industrial system seemed quite important, as evidenced in his famous comment about the "secrets of industry" being "in the air." Though Marshall made reference to the technological dynamism of English industrial districts, he did not clearly distinguish between localization as a means of reducing production costs under conditions of uncertainty and localization as an underpinning of the technological trajectory of an industry.

We have distinguished agglomerations at the center of PBTL industries from other kinds of industrial localizations in three ways: in the economic sense that they have dynamic externally based increasing returns owing to the nature of technological change; in the organizational sense that their production networks are characterized frequently by more than markets and hierarchies, by conventions and relations that organize interfirm relationships and labor market exchanges; and in the sociological sense that these conventions mobilize resources and provide durable collective identities to major participants in these systems.

In this light, the concept of Marshallian industrial district, while significant in its own right, needs additional specification to distinguish those agglomerations that lie at the heart of advanced economic development from other territorial collections of economic activities. Industrial districts based on PBTL should be defined as "technology districts."

THE LIMITS TO GLOBALIZATION

PBTL is not the only form technological change can assume; rapidly changing average production or product technologies may come through imitating others, as well as by the kind of innovation discussed here, and the two processes may complement each other. But it is one thing to buy equipment or even knowledge and another to learn how to use it and apply it to real problems. The market share advantages due to imitation are likely to be shorter-lived than those due to learning, because by definition imitators are subject to rapid competition from elsewhere, that is, to the spread of a catch-up process that is already in motion. (Learning can concern processes other than those based in product innovation; but these forms of learning have the most economic interest for our purposes.)

Moreover, the developmental consequences of imitation, while important to maintaining shares of trade and employment by raising average productivity to world standards, are quite different from the developmental potentials afforded by PBTL. In the case of imitation without significant scale effects, competition must necessarily be cost–price based, such that the pace of capital accumulation will be limited. Where this is achieved through technology intensiveness, capital requirements will be high and employment effects limited; where it is achieved through the use of cheap factors of production, especially labor, wages will be limited. In the case of imitation with significant scale effects, capital requirements are also necessarily high, and employment creation effects must be limited; technological catch-up makes it probable that advantages will be short-lived unless large quantities of capital are pumped into the production system to outrun imitators.

The PBTL system's products, by contrast, tend to earn supernormal returns (quasirents). Quasirents can be distributed not only in the form of high returns to capital and high rates of reinvestment, but also in the form of high-wage jobs. The aggregate developmental outcomes of such export specializations are therefore likely to be greater than what their narrow quantitative importance in jobs or proportion of national output would tend to suggest.[22]

Defining technology districts in this way goes to the heart of the argument that localized production systems are central to contemporary global economic development.[23] The growth in trade and foreign investment is mainly among the advanced economies and not, as is often maintained, principally the result of decentralization of production from advanced countries to Third World nations. While the flows of capital, jobs, and values associated with export-oriented production may be important in Third World countries themselves, they constitute a small proportion of world trade and an even smaller share of the trade of any given advanced economy: their share in world trade has dropped considerably over the past two decades. At the present time, the United States imports about one-tenth the number of automobiles from low-wage Mexico as it does from high-wage Japan. Whereas trade in manufactured goods between the wealthy economies and the Third World is heavily based on price, trade among the wealthy economies is principally based on scale or quality.

It is in this sense that the global economy may be thought of as consisting, in important measure, of a mosaic of specialized technology districts. Certain key regions are at the heart of generating important kinds of economic rents in contemporary capitalism. While these key regions may be relatively few in number, their economic impacts on their respective national economies and on the world trading system as a whole, are likely to be relatively large. Though the presence of technology districts is not the only source of trade or economic growth for a country, it is probably necessary for any country that pursues prosperity today. As a corollary, the image of the global economy as a sort of delocalized "space of flows" of human, physical and financial capital controlled from major corporate headquarters manifestly fails to grasp the nature of the new competition. It fails to grasp the complex ties among these global agents (especially the technology-based oligopolists) and the territorialized relations and conventions upon which they draw and which they often help to construct, and without which they cannot function.

NOTES

1. Lafay and Herzog (1989).
2. Greenaway and Milner (1986); Gerstenberger (1990).
3. Amendola et al. (1991).
4. Amendola et al. (1991).
5. Pavitt and Patel (1990).
6. Vernon (1979).
7. Amendola et al. (1992).
8. Krugman (1990).
9. Coriat (1991); Dertouzos et al. (1990).
10. Lundvall and Johnson (1992); Dosi et al. (1990); Gibbons and Metcalfe (1986); see also references to discussion of technological learning, in Chapters 2 and 5.
11. Leontief (1953).
12. Vernon (1966).
13. Freeman (1991).
14. Lafay and Herzog (1989).
15. Balassa (1965).
16. Dosi et al. (1991).
17. Porter (1990).
18. Gollop and Monahan (1982).
19. In another research project, we included a group of sectors not examined here, which we labeled the "intellectual capital" industries, essentially overlapping with advanced services and management functions. (Pollard and Storper, 1996).
20. Sforzi (1990).
21. Marshall (1979); Becattini (1987); Sabel (1989); Scott (1988a).
22. The standard approach in economics is to view these forces   factor costs, organizational capabilities, etc.—in relation to a single continuum of best practices: those that maximize or impede maximization of productivity, minimize or impede minimization of costs. Yet, despite a very large volume of research, the relationship between productivity, income, and growth is inconclusive (Dollar and Woolf, 1988; see also Robinson, 1956; Hodgson, 1988; Mokyr, 1990). Naturally, there is a rough correlation between high levels of aggregate productivity and high levels of income on the globe, but research has never been able to separate result from cause. For example, in both Adam Smith (1776) and Stigler (1951) the relationship is reversed as it is in Romer (1986, 1990), although orthodoxy continues to repeat that productivity maximization is the root cause of income growth. As we have noted, technology gaps are often responsible for the highest rates of income per unit of investment, since absolute advantages are rewarded through quasirents. Indeed, those activities in capitalism with the highest price–cost ratios (and hence highest potential for capital accumulation and presumably for further supply-creating investment and demand-generating income) are often the activities without the highest standard factor productivities, precisely because they operate according to different pricing rules from those governing perfect competition (Robinson, 1956; Kaldor, 1972; Harris, 1978). In other words, short-term income growth of any specific firm, region, or nation, is often maximized under conditions where productivity—in the standard sense of money output per unit of input—is not maximized; it is the secondary consequences of these same, nonmaximizing tech-

nological innovations that generate the possibility of "long-term" average productivity improvements through diffusion. (On innovation, see David, 1975; Nelson and Winter, 1982; Dosi, 1988; Amendola and Gaffard, 1991. See also Perroux, 1950, on diffusion channels and the discussion in Sheppard, Webber, and Rigby, 1991, on average productivity improvements.) A paradox exists: some people have to "break the rules." for the system to progress, some actors must violate equilibrium (Young, 1928; Kaldor, 1972).

Overall levels of output growth, in turn, may be exogenous, in the case of tradable products—they may be dependent on income levels and elasticities in buying areas (where, again, technology gaps are critical in producing income-maximizing outputs), but highly endogenous and not directly dependent on productivity in the case of domestic demand. This is because demand is related not strictly to aggregate income levels, but to long-run trends in income distribution (in concert with returns to foreign trade, in part determined by absolute advantages); these, in combination with income elasticities, will determine output levels (Robinson, 1956; Harris, 1978; Dosi et al., 1990).

The strong possibility exists that maximizing standard, Ricardian, allocative efficiencies in an economy (through standard factor productivity maximization and determination of output) could work counter to maximizing income growth: in part because they would detract from development of more income-maximizing absolute advantage activities, in part because they might counteract long-term income distribution strategies that would maximize elasticity of growth for the "right" (income maximizing) products. In other words, Ricardian efficiencies may not be compatible with dynamic Schumpeterian efficiencies or growth efficiencies (Schumpeter, 1934). And it is dynamic income growth, in turn, that generates the scale effects that have been demonstrated to be the single greatest key to average productivity growth (Romer, 1986). There is thus no single criterion that allows us to judge that best practice, even in limited comparative advantage terms, consists of the maximization of standard factor productivity. In technical terms, economics attempts to deal with this problem under the "reevaluation of prices" problem, that is, weighting output values so as to reflect quality changes (Gordon, 1986). This is an interesting measurement technique, and it shows that productivity is not always what it seems, but it does not get at the problem from the standpoint of what economic actors do or should be doing, which is not always to maximize money output per unit of currently valued money input, but often to defy that "rule" in favor of allocational inefficiencies.

23. Zysman (1995) has made this point about nations from an institutionalist point of view. We are modifying it, both in terms of its geographical level and the substance of what makes that level function (from formal institutions to the wider problem of conventions, relations, and untraded interdependencies). See also Scott (1996).

CHAPTER 9

The World of the City
LOCAL RELATIONS IN A
GLOBAL ECONOMY

THE NATURE OF THE CITY IN THE
GLOBALIZING CAPITALIST ECONOMY

Those who are interested in cities have found themselves in a curious position in recent years. The encompassing theories that once guided our understanding of the city—neoclassical welfare economics, Marxism, or urban ecology—have given way to a wide array of theoretically unorthodox attempts to come to grips with evolutions in Western cities that seem no longer to be illuminated by those grander perspectives, at least in their pure forms. The urban economy is now seen, variously, as an agglomeration of internationally oriented business and financial services[1]; a flexibility pool for "post-Fordist capitalism"[2]; or an informational economy.[3] Most of these new theories, however, cannot account convincingly for why cities should continue to be the geographical foci of capitalist economic activity in a period where the constraints of proximity seem to be disappearing. The story of urbanization they tell does not resemble the living result of the urban economies that are before us.

At the same time, those concerned with urban society have been overwhelmingly preoccupied with the city as a site of social disaster: oppression, poverty, dualism, and crime are the themes, a dark view which has certainly always been present in urban sociology, but which traditionally took its place alongside visions of the city as the bearer of modernity, progress, liberty, and creative experimentation or, more neutrally, as a cauldron of change *tout court*. Both of these fields of reflection about the city are shot through with a concern about "globalization." Globalization has come to refer to a set of theories about urban growth, some of which link the notion of a contemporary urban social disaster to the advent of a global economy. These notions, too, seem to fall short in accounting for urban social processes today.

In addition to frequent problems of empirical generalization, which can be found in some major contemporary theories of urbanization, all such theories share a fundamental theoretical lacuna. They all conceive of the city as a *machine*, by which is meant a geographically dense socioeconomic system that functions according to the laws of a kind of urban-economic physics. The changes with which urbanists are concerned—in economy and society—are then viewed as the result of a change in the motive power of the machine, from national capitalism to global capitalism, and from manufacturing to service industries. Via the intermediation of particular factors, these forms of motive power "produce" cities, which are seen as subassemblies in the overall mechanical structure of the forces and flows of global capitalist society.

This is a misleading metaphor of the economics and social dynamics of cities in high-income countries (and some middle-income countries) in today's global economy. The economic role of these cities is not as a mechanical node in a bigger machine; the society of cities, likewise, while altered by urban economic forces beyond the control of urban citizens, is not a simple outcome of economic change. Two main arguments will be developed in this chapter.

First, the nature of the contemporary city is as a local or regional "socioeconomy," whose very usefulness to the forces of global capitalism is precisely as an ensemble of specific, differentiated, and localized relations.[4] These relations consist of concrete relations between persons and organizations that are central to the economic functioning of those entities. Cities are sites where such relations are conventional, and they are different from one city to another. Economic activities that cluster together in cities—both manufacturing and services—are frequently characterized by interdependencies that are indirect or untraded and take the form of these conventions and relations. This conception of the urban economy is different from that of standard urban economics, which focuses on direct, locally traded linkages.

Conventions and relations have always been central elements in the distinctiveness of the economies of big and middle-sized cities. In many ways, however, their importance is increasing because of the enormous leap in economic reflexivity to which we have referred throughout this book.[5] *Important and distinctive dimensions of this reflexivity, in both production and consumption, in manufacturing as well as in services, take place in cities; they are dependent on the concrete relations between persons and organizations that are formed in cities; and they are coordinated by conventions that have specifically urban dimensions and in addition are often different from one city to another.* Specifically, cities are the privileged sites for the parts of manufacturing and service activity where reflexivity is carried out. The localization of these activities occurs in virtually all large- and medium-sized cities in the developed countries, not just in the very largest. Cities also continue to specialize within this general tendency, in different reflexive manufacturing and service activities.

The second and closely related major point we shall argue in this chapter is that the city in a global economy is not a mere basing point for globalized, placeless economic forces, that is, a mere subassembly in the global machine.

Instead, when global firms locate in big cities, they do so in part to tap into their distinctiveness, for two reasons. They attempt, on the one hand, to gain access to the local, conventionally and relationally distinctive society in order to service it and earn profits there. They try, on the other hand, to gain access to the specific forms of reflexivity that reside there, so as to use them as inputs into their global systems of production and marketing. The causality is therefore two-way in nature.

The focus of contemporary urban theory should be very different, according to the analysis proposed here, from what it is when the city is conceived of as a machine. In the latter, the city machine is broken down into traditional subassemblies such as industries, occupational groups, income groups, and such, and the discrete interactions between the parts examined. No matter how well done, this procedure, as we shall see in the following section, leads to empirical dead ends, phenomena whose specifically urban character cannot be accounted for, as well as whole dimensions of urban life about which it has little to say. What is distinctive about cities is the ways in which groups of actors—tied together by their relations and conventions—engage in specific processes of economic and social reflexivity. The city is then the locus of spheres of action whose components do not correspond neatly to traditional categories of urban theory or statistical measurement. These "worlds" of urban action must become the focus of urban theory, analysis, and policy.

THE STATE OF URBAN THEORY TODAY: GLOBAL CITY, DUAL CITY, WORLD CITY, INFORMATIONAL CITY, POST-FORDIST CITY

The major new theories of urban development have generated significant insights, but each creates limits to its explanatory power when it treats the city as a machine. Four such machines are examined here as a way of assessing the state of the art in recent urban research: the city as the machine of global financial capital, or the "global–dual city"; the city as the machine of multinational enterprises, or the "world city"; the city as the machine of information processing, the "informational city"; and the city as the machine of flexible input–output structures, or the "post-Fordist city."

The Global–Dual City

The notions of "global"[6] and "dual"[7] city result from ambitious attempts to link big theoretical categories—industry, location, labor markets, population demographics—to large-scale empirical outcomes. The purest version of the story is told in Sassen's work on New York, Tokyo, and London.[6] Certain industries are held to be global industries by virtue of the high degree of internationalization of their inputs and outputs: the financial services industries are the key examples. These industries, in turn, have an occupational structure characterized by large numbers of very highly paid workers, who have decisive effects on the private and collective consumption patterns in the cities where they are clustered. They have high incomes but little time, leading them to demand high levels of personal consumer services, which are furnished by low-waged, mostly immigrant populations. Thus, the global city is a dual city.

There are core elements of truth in this story, but it it has some serious problems of measurement, evidence, and conceptualization. It invents general categories of city—global and dual—on the basis of a small number of particular cases, even though many of the phenomena to which it refers can be found in cities lacking the causal structures said to exist in these three big cities. Four principal criticisms can be levied at the notion of global–dual city.

First, it cannot stand in as a theory of urban growth, even for these three very big cities. The tendencies toward growth of financial and advanced services industries, as well as their urban agglomeration, can be found much further down the urban hierarchy than merely in these three global cities. For the American case, it is true that the location quotients for financial services are considerably higher in New York than in any other city; but it is also the case that other advanced services industries have high and growing location quotients in a surprisingly large number of cities.[8] Moreover, a wider sample of industries share the essential characteristics of the financial services ensemble— high-wage composition and export orientation—notably, a broad group of what we may call the "intellectual capital" industries.[9] These industries have a much more complex localization pattern than as implied by global city theory. In a sample of twelve major U.S. metropolitan areas, we discovered that the growth rates of intellectual capital industries tend to reflect overall growth rates for the metropolitan areas, holding location quotients stable. There is an overall shift toward these activities in the American economy, and this shift is occurring even in regional economies where no particular signs of specialization in such industries is apparent. It may be that such industries have a decreasing propensity to agglomerate, or that there are incipient agglomerations whose presence is not strong enough to detect at the moment. This pattern differed significantly from another group of industries with high wage and high skill composition, the "innovation-based sectors," in which locational differentiation is much more pronounced from one metropolitan area to another. Table 9.1 shows these findings. Similar findings apply to the French urban system[10]: advanced tertiarization applies to all cities of a certain size, not just to Paris.

Second, there are ambiguities in the definition of "globalness." Defined as the dependence on international transactions in the inputs and outputs of a city's economic base, globalness is more pronounced in the financial– advanced services sector in New York, London, and Tokyo than in other big and middle-sized cities in the advanced economies, and this is consistent with global city theory. However, such globalness is also more pronounced in financial services in Paris than in the rest of France, Frankfurt with respect to Germany, or even Los Angeles and San Francisco with respect to the United States. Hence, globalness, defined in this way, is not specific to the Big Three. Beyond this, if internationalization of exchanges as a whole is considered—in all manufacturing and service sectors—then it appears that New York, for example, is not more dependent on international exchanges than are Chicago, San Francisco, Atlanta, or Minneapolis.[11]

In the globalized tertiary sectors, in any case, no more than about 15% of the employment of even the Big Three can be accounted for, while for the wider set of internationally or trade-dependent sectors in big cities, this figure

TABLE 9.1A. Employment change in American cities: intellectual capital industries

	Employment, %			Index (LQs)		
	1977	1982	1987	1977	1982	1987
U.S.	11.95	13.58	13.87	100	129.98	152.75
Dallas Fort Worth CMSA	8.80	9.88	11.28	100 (0.74)	145.91 (0.73)	202.11 (0.81)
San Diego MSA	11.46	14.36	14.04	100 (0.96)	173.62 (1.06)	225.76 (1.01)
Phoenix MSA	9.85	10.69	11.29	100 (0.82)	151.30 (0.79)	277.15 (0.81)
Los Angeles PMSA	12.19	14.09	14.01	100 (1.02)	136.71 (1.04)	154 (1.01)
San Francisco–Oakland CMSA	12.91	14.30	14.73	100 (1.08)	138.3 (1.05)	167.46 (1.06)
Boston CMSA	17.51	19.62	19.78	100 (1.47)	136.48 (1.44)	164.5 (1.43)
Atlanta MSA	9.10	10.18	11.05	100 (0.76)	138.92 (0.75)	211.86 (0.8)
Minneapolis–St. Paul MSA	11.87	13.46	13.18	100 (0.99)	125.61 (0.99)	148.19 (0.95)
New York–New Jersey CMSA	16.92	19.71	21.17	100 (1.42)	125.61 (1.45)	157.48 (1.53)
Pittsburgh CMSA	12.37	15.89	18.45	100 (1.04)	133.54 (1.17)	154.06 (1.33)
Chicago–Gary CMSA	13.07	15.81	15.22	100 (1.09)	133.54 (1.16)	126.77 (1.10)
Detroit–Ann Arbor CMSA	10.15	12.80	13.61	100 (0.85)	116.84 (0.93)	154.77 (0.98)

Source: Pollard and Storper (1996).

TABLE 9.1B. Employment change in American cities: innovation-based industries

	Employment, %			Index (LQs)		
	1977	1982	1987	1977	1982	1987
U.S.	2.87	3.35	3.05	100	133.72	140.07
Dallas–Fort Worth CMSA	5.19	6.29	6.00	100	157.53	182.49
					(1.81)	(1.87)	(1.97)
San Diego MSA	5.96	8.50	6.29	100	197.57	194.35
					(2.08)	(2.53)	(2.06)
Phoenix MSA	7.39	9.07	7.64	100	171	204.63
					(0.82)	(2.7)	(2.5)
Los Angeles PMSA	7.34	7.87	7.16	100	126.82	130.83
					(2.56)	(2.34)	(2.35)
San Francisco–Oakland CMSA	6.23	9.22	7.85	100	184.88	185.09
					(2.17)	(2.75)	(2.57)
Boston CMSA	4.14	5.05	4.36	100	148.6	153.37
					(1.44)	(1.5)	(1.43)
Atlanta MSA	0.94	1.69	1.66	100	222.98	307.99
					(0.33)	(0.5)	(0.54)
Minneapolis–St. Paul MSA	3.30	3.49	3.12	100	127.54	134
					(1.15)	(1.04)	(1.02)
New York–New Jersey CMSA	0.61	0.70	0.63	100	123.15	123.24
					(0.21)	(0.21)	(0.21)
Pittsburgh CMSA	0.85	0.73	0.55	100	89.59	67.14
					(0.29)	(0.22)	(0.18)
Chicago–Gary CMSA	2.53	2.43	1.88	100	96.42	80.93
					(0.88)	(0.72)	(0.62)
Detroit–Ann Arbor CMSA	0.92	0.99	0.68	100	101.09	85.46
					(0.32)	(0.3)	(0.22)

Source: Pollard and Storper (1996).

can rise to about 30%, but not beyond it.[12] So there is no reason to base a theory of the globalization of the urban economy narrowly on the financial services sectors, and no reason to limit its geography to the Big Three. The sectoral basis and territorial diffusion of the effects of globalization is greater than announced by the theory.

Third, while the Big Three are centers of financial capitalism, and capitalism is definitely becoming more financialized,[13] it is not clear that this is the way into the problem of dualness, inequality or social polarization in these cities or in big cities in general. In the United States, for example, the "global city" of New York and the very big city of Los Angeles do not manifest occupational structures radically different from those of the American economy as a whole, as shown in Figures 9.1A, B, and C, from the work of Edmond Prete-

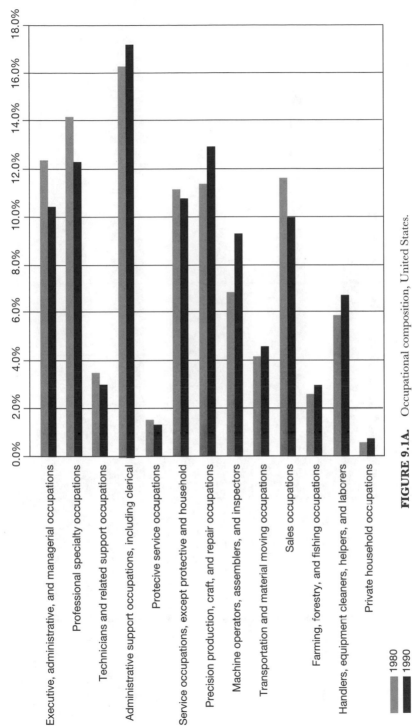

FIGURE 9.1A. Occupational composition, United States.

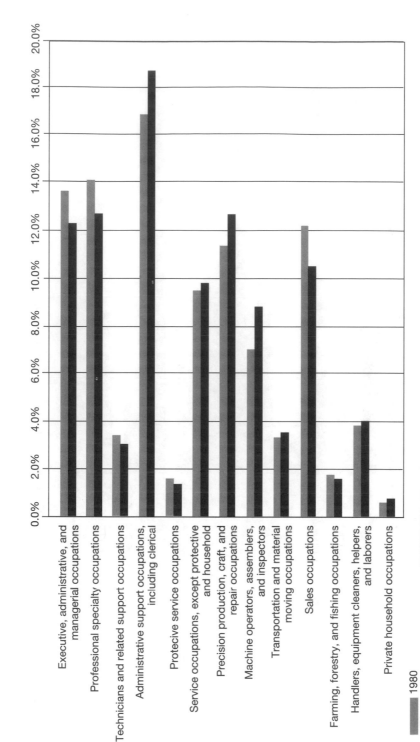

FIGURE 9.1B. Occupational composition, Los Angeles CMSA.

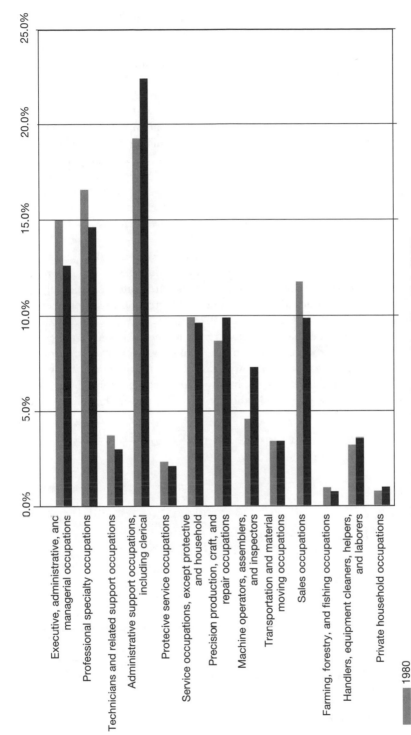

FIGURE 9.1C. Occupational composition, New York CMSA.

ceille.[14] New York and Los Angeles have slightly higher percentages of executive and managerial workers (United States: 12.4%, New York: 15%, Los Angeles: 13.5%), and professional specialties (United States: 14.2%, Los Angeles: 14%, New York: 17%); on the lower end, the proportion of domestic workers is virtually identical at all levels, as is the case for manual workers.

When we examine household income distribution data, the results do not conform to the theory. Figure 9.2A shows a shifting of the entire distribution to the right-hand side during the 1980s, not at all equivalent to polarization. Complementing this picture, research on occupational wage structures in the United States has revealed a wage split in all industries, not just financial services, advanced services, or even services generally; it affects industries in all sizes of cities and nonmetropolitan areas, so it is not a uniquely urban phenomenon.[15] The occupational–wage split is the result of technological change across the board, rendering certain skills and the populations who have them vulnerable to wage reductions.[16] The difference between the results has to do with household income strategies, especially increasing workforce participation of women and increasing work hours across the board. Indeed, as shown in Figures 9.2B and C and Table 9.2, with respect to household-income inequality trends in the two biggest American cities—frequently cited in the literature on dualism as exemplary cases of urban economic polarization—the lower tail of the distribution actually declined more in these big cities than in the American economy in general, while the upper tail grew more in those cities. This appearance of polariza-

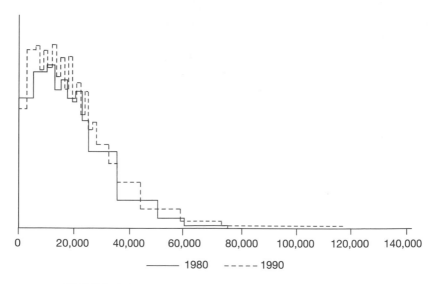

FIGURE 9.2A. Household income distribution, United States.

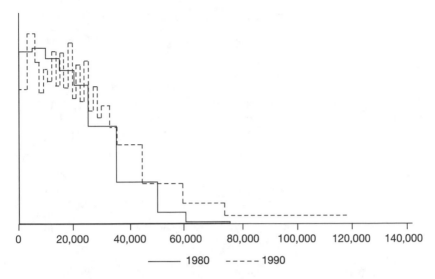

FIGURE 9.2B. Household income distribution, New York CMSA.

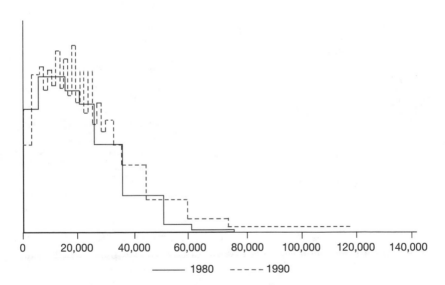

FIGURE 9.2C. Household income distribution, Los Angeles CMSA.

TABLE 9.2. Income distributions. United States/Los Angeles/New York

	United States	Los Angeles CMSA	New York CMSA
1980			
Less than $10,000	23,435,850	1,076,092	1,667,192
$10,000 to $24,000	33,725,531	1,644,742	2,196,010
$25,000 to $49,999	19,613,981	1,139,840	1,556,606
$50,000 or more	3,692,065	286,672	415,678
Total	80,467,427	4,147,346	5,835,486
1990			
Less than $10,000	25,926,475	1,061,024	1,499,850
$10,000 to $24,000	36,824,996	1,780,364	2,156,266
$25,000 to $49,999	22,477,423	1,453,767	1,979,943
$50,000 or more	6,764,688	614,063	981,015
Total	91,993,582	4,909,218	6,617,074
Δ (1980–1990)			
Less than $10,000	2,490,625	−15,068	−167,342
$10,000 to $24,000	3,099,465	135,622	−39,744
$25,000 to $49,999	2,863,442	313,927	423,337
$50,000 or more	3,072,623	327,391	565,337
Total	11,526,155	761,872	781,588
Δ rel (1980–1990)			
Less than $10,000	10.6%	−1.4%	−10.0%
$10,000 to $24,000	9.2%	8.2%	−1.8%
$25,000 to $49,999	14.6%	27.5%	27.2%
$50,000 or more	83.2%	114.2%	136.0%
Total	14.3%	18.4%	13.4%
Median income			
1980	16,841	18,498	17,948
1990	17,576	21,468	22,482
1990/1980	104.4%	116.1%	125.3%

Note. All data in dollars of 1980.

tion is false: the whole distribution followed a more generally upward direction than in the economy as a whole, hardly the catastrophic picture painted by the global–dual city theory. Given the occupational and sectoral structures of these cities' economies, these data also imply that for those interested in inequality, the distinction—both occupational and locational—between manufacturing and services, is largely unhelpful. The "yuppie plus servant classes" analysis of inequality does not work; and some detailed research on the low-wage immigrant worker populations—such as that of

Waldinger on New York—actually suggests that those populations do not universally do so poorly.[17]

Fourth, the spatial distributions of immigrants and poor people do not attach uniquely to the advanced services industries in particular nor to the biggest cities in general. Immigrant population densities in the United States are now just as high in medium-sized cities as in the big metropolitan areas, even though the economic bases of these places are often not strongly attached to advanced or financial services. [18]

Thus, a theory of the urbanization of New York, London, and Tokyo would certainly have to be based in part on analysis of their statuses as financial capitals, but rather little can be said about the urbanization process in general—the influence of internationalization, the process of agglomeration, and the degree and nature of socioeconomic polarization—from this particular story. In addition, the growth of not only financial services, but also other intellectual functions in the economy, is very widespread among big and medium-sized cities, as was shown in Table 9.1. The growth of such intellectual activities—involving both manufacturing and services, and all kinds of service industries—*is the single most general element of the growth of the economic bases of big and medium-sized cities.* This fact is central to an effective understanding of the urban economic process today. But it does not help us much with an explanation of the apparent social tensions in big and medium-sized cities, including the perception of polarization or inequality.

In sum, there are certainly connections between what is happening in the capitalist economy at large and what is hapening in cities: technological change, occupational and sectoral shifts, changes in wage and labor-force participation patterns, and a general tendency to deregulate these areas of economic life appear to be creating tendencies toward greater inequality in many nations. But these changes, while very important, are not limited to cities, and simultaneously, what is happening in cities seems more dramatic than what can be accounted for by them alone. Ironically, these theories of global and dual cities seem to exclude what is specifically urban about the process of social polarization—the way that specific practices in the urban milieu not only transmit, but transform these global forces into concrete social patterns and relations.

The World City: Multinational Capitalism's Bureaucratic Hierarchy

The "world city hypothesis" was initially outlined by John Friedmann and Goetz Wolff[19] as an extension and reworking of urban hierarchy theory. The theory is rich in its observations about the social and demographic character of the biggest cities in the world, but we shall concentrate here on the core elements it adduces to explain patterns of world urbanization. The theory maps out a rather conventional hierarchy of cities—first tier, second tier, third tier, and so on—but instead of remaining at national level, it argues that a unified global hierarchy of cities has now come into existence. National urban hierarchies are subjacent components of this system, in the sense that the primary motors of growth transmission have shifted from national to global scale, and therefore the cities at the top of each nation's urban system are something like first-line receivers of such growth impulses, which they then divide and distribute down their respective national urban systems.

What is it that influences patterns of urban growth in this world city system? The primary force is held to be the administrative order of transnational enterprises: such firms have planetary spatial logics of production and marketing in which cities become functional nodes, arranged hierarchically. Thus, the top cities in the world urban system—the "world cities"—are the places preferred by transnationals as basing points for their top administrative and decision-making activities; the second tier cities are those that account for secondary regions and/or functions in the corporate hierarchy; and so on down the pyramid. Implicit is the notion that these supranational actors determine the shape and form of urban growth today.

From this point on, much of what world city theory has to say about the character of world cities resembles that of global–dual city theory, although world city theory said it much earlier. The surfeit of highly paid transnational corporation (TNC) workers, the armies of the poor, the hyperurbanization of world city regions, and so on, are attributed to the exigencies of transnationals to use such regions to their ends. Special attention is paid to the ways that local development and land use policies—urban renewal, emphasis on downtown headquarters complexes, and so on—are tailored to the needs and demands of transnational corporations, and under current circumstances, the ways they exacerbate the social and spatial polarization of world cities.

The world city hypothesis certainly called our attention to a growing reality: the growth of transnational enterprise and its implantation in the world's great cities, at a time when those cities seemed to be undergoing widespread transformations in their economic bases, social character, and spatial structures. The central empirical claim of the hypothesis—the locational behavior of the world's largest and most transnational firms—has been largely upheld.[20]

Yet it is not clear that the world city hypothesis can stand in as an explanation of contemporary growth and change in the cities comprising the first and second tiers of its global urban hierarchy. While foreign transnationals are certainly visible in New York, Paris, São Paulo, London, Los Angeles, and Sydney, no research has ever shown that they constitute either the lion's share of growth or the structural "motor force" of metropolitan growth in any of them or that TNC locational behavior has altered existing national urban hierarchies. Even in cases of extreme internationalization—the most extreme is probably the City of London, whose firms' inputs and outputs are extraordinarily mobile, a high percentage of the firms are British, and their employees are U.K. citizens.[21] The fact that Los Angeles firms are now more sensitive to international markets has big impacts on employment and location in Los Angeles, and certainly alters the ground rules for economic growth there. But most Los Angeles transnationals grew up in Los Angeles and their success in international markets was due to an expansion of their core, locally acquired, expertise; the latter permitted them access to world markets. Paris is certainly the basing point for transnationals wishing access to the French or European markets, as will attest a look around La Défense. But to claim that the primary force in the growth of Paris has shifted from national to transnational, from city–hinterland relationships to city–international relationships, would be unsustainable. Paris became the primate city in the French urban system because of the structure of the French State, and later continued this as its agglomeration economies became unbeatable—inducing massive migration from the provinces—and complemented the concentration of administrative, social, and political power.[22] Were things the other way around, one would expect Germany—as Europe's economic superpower—to have cities on the scale of London and Paris, and to have more financial influence than London. Likewise, the United States has proportionally much "less" of a world city in New York than its corporate economic power would suggest, and this has much more to do with the particularities of the American political and urban systems than with the behavior of transnational enterprises.[23] Tokyo certainly fits the definition of a world city, but in an economy as fundamentally closed (on the input side) as the Japanese, this is because Tokyo (like Paris) is the primate city in a powerful national economy.[24]

With respect to the international manufacturing and marketing activities of multinational enterprises, there is a large body of theory and evidence, showing that such firms have complex motivations for going where they go. Dunning's "eclectic paradigm"[25] sums up the major motivations as those of ownership (the structure of production involves assets that the firm needs to own instead of buy from others), internalization (the structure of transactions inside the production or marketing system makes it difficult to use contractors or external suppliers), and location-specific advantages (the array of what is present in a place, whether markets for products or a particular and rare kind of labor or knowledge).[26] In none of the principal theories of multinational location or investment—whether in the orthodox or heterodox economic literature—can one find the suggestion that the causality for the locational patterns of transnationals is principally an idealized internal administrative logic, as expressed in a neat spatial geometry.

The problem, then, is not in world city theory's descriptive veracity, although the theory does exaggerate the role of global as opposed to national forces. All the big cities are more penetrated by foreign investments—in both administrative activities of transnationals and in production and service activities—than they were 20 years ago, in step with the growth in world trade as a proportion of world output and with the financialization of capitalism.[27] It is, rather, that the world city hypothesis sheds little light on the process of urban growth today; it simply asserts that these big cities are subassemblies in the world urban machine for the optimal flows of capital, labor, and goods. In fact, the world city hierarchy it maps out corresponds quite neatly to already existing national urban hierarchies; all that is necessary is to draw international lines linking the national pyramids into a superpyramid. In this sense it adds little to urban growth theory as a whole.[28]

The role of transnationals in contemporary urbanization undoubtedly involves a subtle dialectic in which local and national forces are at least as important in determining what transnationals do as transnationals are in shaping, from some abstracted supranational logic, a putative world urban system. As noted, the theory of multinational location suggests that such firms' locational behavior is as much shaped by the geographical structure of existing cities and their economies as the other way around. To appreciate this dialectic fully, we would need to step back and ask questions that are upstream of the world city hypothesis: to what extent transnationals succeed in imposing an ideal spatial administrative logic; the extent to which international or intrafirm growth transmission now dominates other forms of growth transmission; or, on the contrary, to what extent such firms are followers of the spatial patterns of existing economic, political, or administrative structures.[29] For the time being, the great cities of the world cannot be viewed primarily as cogs designed to fit into the bigger administrative machine of transnational enterprises.

The Informational City: The Machine of Cyberflows

For Manuel Castells,[30] the Informational City is merely the manifestation of a broader phenomenon, the Informational Society. Though many others have attempted to come to grips with the effects of high-technology revolution on the city, Castells' theory is the most ambitious, because he analyzes not just the high-technology industries, but more importantly, their effects on economic and social practices across the board. His argument is especially pertinent to those interested in the city as an advanced service economy because he argues that the principal effect of the technological revolution is the service transformation. He uses little of the conventional language of the service economy literature, eschewing sectoral analysis in favor of a more panoramic approach. For Castells, there is

> the new social structure that characterizes our world: the informational society. By such a concept, I understand the social structure where the sources of economic productivity, cultural hegemony, and political–military power

depend, fundamentally, on the capacity to retrieve, store, process and generate information and knowledge. Although information and knowledge have been critical for economic accumulation and power throughout history, it is only under current technological, social, and cultural parameters that they become directly productive forces. . . . Information becomes the critical raw material of what all social processes and social organization are made.[31]

Castells sees information as the raw material of the economic process, itself quite indifferent to space, because the technologies of information transmission are now supposedly approaching the point where the friction of distance is nil. Thus, his economy is a service economy in the sense that information is something like a service. It has transformed the world economy from a space of places to a "space of flows."[32] Still, there is a structure to the flows of the informational economy: a structure of networks. Most of these are the networks constructed by multinational corporations, whether internal to the enterprise or restricted to their selected interlocutors. In this sense, Castells' map of the urban hierarchy depends on factors similar to those identified by the world city hypothesis. What anchors these networks, gives them shape and makes them urban? The social class that runs these networks—the new information elite—has to be socialized, and this is done in the world's great cities, where the masters of the global space of flows congregate, and between which they circulate comfortably in a sociological space that is largely similar, from Cologne to Chicago to Caracas. The service *industry* analysis of the global city is transformed into an information *class* and *social networks* argument here.

This description hardly does justice to Castells' analysis of the geography and urbanism of the informational society, which is rich in observations, many of them critical and relevant. In what follows, I will address the positive analytics of Castells' theory, rather than its social critique. Three major criticisms can be levied at the notion of an Informational City as a node in a territory-less global "space of flows" of global firms, weakly anchored into such nodes principally by information elite socialization and association.

First, every epoch of capitalist development has had some set of scarce factors or processes which, because of their scarcity, constitute the focal point of competition and the motor of change. These have always, in some way, reduced to *knowledge*, in the broad sense of the capacity of the dominant firms or nations to do things the others could not do: late 18th-century England possessed hardware and methods of production organization that were scarce and gave her producers fantastic advantages over others and hence defined the relations of domination–subordination within the capitalist world economy of that time.[33] The "American system" of production came along much later and did the same thing for American firms.[34] Such advantages permit great wealth accumulation in the form of higher-than-normal profits, but also often translate into military superiority.[35] These examples could be multiplied many times over and in many ways could be applied to precapitalist European economies. In this sense, a focus on knowledge as the center of what makes a wide variety of social processes tick is correct but not new.

"Information" as the core concept of a metatheory of contemporary capitalism is, however, seriously imprecise. Information, by contrast with knowledge, is *not* a scarce commodity today.[36] It has become totally banalized, mass produced, and distributed. The fact that lots of it is distributed by huge global firms is, in many ways, not very significant, because in terms of capitalist competition, the markets in which they operate are often highly open and highly contested, even by Third World firms and countries.

Knowledge, defined as know-how or skill, however, is another matter. It has been radically redefined, away from principally manual forms to intellectual or abstract forms, and away from direct goods production. Knowledge and know-how are not routinized, standardized, and perfectly codified. They take many forms. The first type is formal but nonstandardized knowledge, as in the activities of conception, production planning, and into the constant pushing outward of the technological frontiers of many industries. The second and quantitatively most important form is the quasicustomization of professional services and the linking of goods and services to customers,[37] in which the human relation and its dialectical relationship to knowledge and interpretation is critical. Knowledge-based labor is the rare, scarce, not easily imitatable heart of the competitive process in contemporary capitalism, the source of superprofits and the key to relations of domination and subordination. Knowledge and know-how are specific, not general-purpose assets.[38] Castells' focus on information technologies and the material networks of information transmission and exchange errs fundamentally in stressing the nonscarce, banal element of the economic process today, not its rare, competitive, driving edge.

This leads directly to the second problem with the informational city theory. The organization and spatiality of knowledge is very different from that of information. The same forces that are currently pushing for a globalization of the knowledge-based economy also encourage a certain reterritorialization of key economic and social processes. Ironically, Castells' space of flows resembles nothing more closely than the vision of neoclassical economics with respect to territory: a grid of homogeneous, interchangeable, frictionless, perfectly substitutable inputs. Certain contemporary developments do push in this direction. They include increased economies of scale that cheapen transmission, telecommunications and travel technologies, and the internationalized lingua franca of business and bureaucracy, as well as Castells' elite solidarity.

But this is only part of the story. It misses the most important aspects of contemporary economic organization: knowledge is highly embedded in organizations, dependent on specific communication channels and structures, which make it possible not only to get access to it in raw form, but more critically, to interpret it and apply it successfully to concrete uses. Some of these push very strongly against the seamless abstract space of flows and reembed knowledge in territorially specific actors and assets. These include (1) uncertainty as to the meanings of information and as to unstandardized or unknown future applications, which require noncodified, culturally embedded, and trustful communication among knowledge holders, whether inside big firms or in external economic relations; examples include technological frontiers, but also customized or semi-customized service delivery[39]; (2) ongoing change in information and its transformation into knowledge, or evolution of knowledge, leading to the same emphasis on interpretation and the same need for embedded human relations to make interpretation and communication possible; examples include markets characterized by uncertainty, fashion, or demographic shifts[40]; (3) spillover effects, that is, relations of interdependency between one type of knowledge and another, whose frontiers change, again requiring interpretation and communication; examples include the manufacturing–manufacturing link (upstream–downstream or cognate technological fields), or the manufacturing–conception–services link (engineering–manufacturing).[41] All of these processes require relations and routines that are specific to the product, the sector, or the operant cultural context, not standardized anonymous interactions. Such relations and routines frequently involve dense human relations, many of which in turn involve locational specificities and proximity between individuals, firms, and institutions.

Statistically, this relational and territorial embeddedness of knowledge has been found to have significant effects: abstract and codifiable technological information moves in Castells' space of flows, but technological and practical mastery—knowledge—is *not* globalized. Patel and Pavitt's careful statistical work has shown that the technological excellence of global companies is highly national and not very globalized.[42] Of the world's 500 biggest firms, only a handful have less than two-thirds of their employment and three-quarters of their value added in their home countries. And the increase in world trade has been accompanied by increased national specialization, not convergence.[43] A global economy is emerging, then, but it is not about a homogeneous space of flows. It is instead a complex meeting of new kinds of globalized flows and new kinds of territorial economies. Castells' theory takes one side of this complex process and elevates it into a highly misleading metaphor for the whole.

Third, and closely related, it can be argued that all three of the theories of contemporary urban development we have examined thus far—global/dual city, world city, informational city—assume too much novelty in the existence of globalization and then read off almost everything they see in big cities from this assumption, placing it in theoretical opposition to a mythical past in which localness existed. The claim that long-distance networks are privileged over local, territorialized networks, for example,[44] or that private business organizations have replaced states as controllers of developmental forces, seems rather unspectacular when we think of the hierarchies and nodes in Europe and her colonies in the 16th century. The notion that financial internationalization is fundamentally new pales when we think of Europe's single price system in the 16th century and the waves of generalized international inflation it transmitted. And international elites have not made their first appearance only recently: the Church, the European ruling houses, and the money merchants of the 17th and 18th centuries are all parallel phenomena. The notion that powerful forms of internationalization are necessarily opposed to territorialization does not follow from a wider historical perspective, just as it does not follow from analytical models or statistical evidence.

Fourth, while we can recognize that big cities today are places where global economic flows are managed by global corporations—something we find in both the world city and the informational city hypotheses—much of the rest of what Castells attributes to the advent of the information society is not explainable by that theory and hence mischaracterizes much of what is going on in big cities.

Castells claims that very high percentages of workers in our economies are "information workers." But this is a clearly hyperbolic claim. Jean Gottman long ago identified big cities as major transactional nodes due to the need for face-to-face interaction[45] in corporate administration, R&D, trade, media, and so on. High percentages of urban workers are still involved in making goods and delivering routine services directly to consumers. Even using a very liberal definition of information workers, our research suggests that this percentage, for the United States as a whole, is about 74%, and for our sample of twelve big cities, it is not less than 65% (see Table 9.1). Routine information services are now increasingly decentralized to the suburbs, small cities, or even offshore, as manifested in the front-office/back-office split locational pattern. The knowledge part of the economy goes well beyond the financial services sector of the global–dual city theory, but it is much more restricted than what is identified by Castells. It includes many intellectual functions in the economy that are characterized by uncertainty, interpretative interdependence, and hence the need for confidence and specificity in relations. These are the functions likely to have strong needs for proximity to other activities and to be embedded in specific territorial contexts as a result of the development of the relational frameworks in which knowledge is developed and deployed.

There is an important practical consequence of this difference between the categories of "financial services," "information" activities, and "knowledge" activities. Whereas the first two suggest development strategies of transforming cities into all-purpose basing points for global business organizations, the latter suggests very careful targeting to specific knowledge activities, clearly demarcated from what is done in competing cities, based on the notion of competitive specialization, local specificity, and differentiation from other places. In the information economy, there is a huge potential oversupply of information transmission cities—essentially every big and middle-sized city in the developed world. Only specialized knowledge-based activities are truly localized in the spaces of big cities, as their economic bases.[46]

The Post-Fordist, or Flexible, City and the Revival of Urbanization Economies

The redefinition of the theory of localization has been more than ten years in the making, part of a widespread inquiry into the "resurgence of regional economies."[47] Localization economies, of course, have long figured prominently in theories of urban growth. Beginning in the early 1980s, however, social scientists began to try and understand an apparent reregionalization of certain forms of production, and as a subset of this phenomenon, the general reprise of urban growth at the expense of more peripheral or less urbanized regions. In the United States, for example, nonmetropolitan growth was much greater in the 1970s than the growth of metropolitan areas, leading many to predict that the final turning point away from cities had been reached as a result of the perfection of technologies permitting the reduction of the frictions of distance. This all fell apart in the 1980s, as metropolitan areas again grew faster than nonmetropolitan areas.

The various recent attempts to revive and refashion localization and agglomeration theory have attempted to respond to two particular historical realities: one is the breakdown of the postwar economic order and the apparent transition away from the organizational model of mass production; the other is change in the sectoral composition of employment and output, away from manufacturing and toward services, and within manufacturing toward high-technology products. We can signal three versions of agglomeration theory.

The first was formulated by Allen Scott as an extension of transaction-cost economics,[48] and has been referred to extensively in Chapters 1 and 2. Empirically, the vision is of a "post-Fordist city." The economic bases of some cities are made up of industries that need flexibility and get it through agglomeration. These are not typical postwar mass-production sectors but are based on a different organizational model from that of postwar mass production. Hence, there is a "post-Fordist urban economy."

A second version of agglomeration theory distances it from sectoral analysis. It argues that macroeconomic instability affects a wide range of sectors, not just cutting-edge services and high technology. This, combined with the liberalization of labor markets, permits and obliges firms in many industries to seek greater and greater flexibility. From this point onward, the story's detailed analytics are similar to those described above. The important difference is that the city is no longer theorized as a set of overlapping sectoral agglomerations, but rather as a single, gigantic "flexibility and risk aversion pool."[49]

Third, Paul Krugman's new geographical economics revives urbanization economies, and would explain the existence of big cities today as a consequences of multiple, territorially overlapping market areas. These areas are carved out by scale effects in production combined with high levels of product differentiation, and cities dominate other areas through spatial oligopoly effects.

The first two theories lead to fruitful observations about transactions-rich urban economies and they allow us to understand the *dynamics* of agglomeration and deagglomeration. Post-Fordist city research shows that the agglomeration effect attached to such externalization is particularly powerful for parts of the advanced business and financial services industries (including , but not often studied, media and advertising), certain parts of the high-technology industries, and to a lesser extent (at least in the United States), certain design-intensive manufacturing processes. Contemporary capitalism is an enormous machine for generating change and variety: this constantly recreates the basis of agglomeration, through new products and services and the forms of transacting they require. But modern capitalism also pushes in the direction of routinization and standardization of knowledge, products, and hence, transactions, leading to a tendency to peel activities away from high-cost areas such as cities. This is just as true of services as it is of manufacturing. The ratio between the two generates a rate of urban growth in a particular place, and a rate of urban versus nonurban or periurban growth in general.

But there are also some apparent anomalies. One has to do with the locational behavior of very big firms. Many of the activities that have been localized in big cities are branches of big firms. Why, if such firms internalize certain functions, do they keep them in big cities, or in cities at all? If they do so because they continue to rely on outside suppliers, why do they not routinize their supply relations and decentralize them? Or, why do they not use their enormous monopsony power to attract those services to themselves, wherever they locate? The partial answer to both these questions is that they do. High-technology aerospace firms in the United States are doing both of these increasingly (e.g., Lockheed's moves to Georgia). But many cases remain where such firms do not do so, and they remain in big cities.

What is missing? Two things, in the view advanced here. First, the nature of the risk which gives rise to the compensating strategy of "flexibility through externalization plus agglomeration," can no longer be accommodated within standard analyses. Risk has become an increasingly endogenous property of the economic system itself, a product of reflexivity: one firm's or person's reflexivity is the other's uncertainty, and vice-versa. Firms and individuals have to use flexibility to hedge, not against current conditions, but against this overall, increasingly unknown, and increasingly general condition of the economy, its markets, technologies, and organizational arrangements. There is a kind of "superrisk" at work, well beyond what the post-Fordist city hypothesis analyzes through its model of the division of labor.[50]

Second, the post-Fordist city hypothesis is overwhelmingly concerned with "hard" transactions, essentially input–output relations between firms (buying and selling goods, services, and information), and between firms and workers (hiring and firing). The city is depicted as a risk- and proximity-based input–output machine, designed to reduce firms' transacting costs. But certainly firms have vastly increasing capabilities to reduce those costs, through telecommunications, organizational streamlining, and transportation improvements. More importantly, firms and individuals are interdependent in ways that do not get expressed through trade with each other: signals and cues from the environment that hone the sensibilities of key actors, for example, and integrate them into the relational context necessary for them to maintain their competitiveness. Input-output relations are only the tip of the iceberg, which concerns the overall context, defined by conventions and relations, that permit actors to understand how to negotiate complex input–output relations. These conventions and relations are true externalities, in the sense that they are assets that cannot be fully privatized. We are now far away from the transactional analysis of post-Fordist agglomeration theory and into a domain where we are concerned with agglomerations as the urban contexts for action frameworks.

The problem with the explanation offered by the Krugman school is that it cannot explain why a fully dispersed pattern of markets and overlapping spatial scale economies does not dominate the landscape. There is nothing in it that explains urban concentration per se, only separate firm-based scale effects. Only in the case of localization through intraindustry trade should urban concentration as we know it arise. Without an analysis of proximity and specificity, however, the latter is not possible, and urbanization economies cannot emerge.

The locational behavior of the world's biggest and most powerful firms still follows big cities because they need to base themselves in these contexts for a variety of noncost-based reasons: to gain access to local production capacities, which are often rooted in subtle local action frameworks and competences; to gain access to the contexts in which they can learn how to tailor their international products to local or national markets; to benefit from spillovers in both cases, which may permit them forms of access and development that they cannot otherwise anticipate, opening up forms of action and channels of interaction unknown to them. This is true of international firms that spread out, of national firms that move "downward" from the capital into regional capitals, and of regional firms that, as they grow, move into the economic capital(s) of their country.

This story applies to higher order service conception and delivery, market tailoring for market spread, advanced financial services, higher order government activity and research, media–entertainment, telecommunications, advertising, and certain kinds of customized manufacturing: firms in all of these areas are highly dependent on successful reflexivity for their survival. This pattern is much more sectorally broad and geographically extensive than the New York, Tokyo, and London economies; they are just particular cases of the general nature of city economies in late modern capitalism.

The theory of agglomeration as transactions *costs* and the theory of spatial scale economies need complements that go beyond the notion of a cost-driven input–output machine to something more qualitatively rich and complex. [51]

A THEORY OF THE URBAN ECONOMY: THE SOCIAL ORGANIZATION OF ECONOMIC REFLEXIVITY

Many of the central aspects of contemporary urbanization receive attention in the theories reviewed above and must figure prominently in any effective theory of the city today: the service industries, and especially financial services and advanced business services; flows of information, and the development of technologies that make them possible; the location of big, multinational firms; the flows of capital, information, knowledge, and goods administered by those firms; and the financialization of capitalism. But none of the theories reviewed seems to put these phenomena together in a way that effectively accounts for what it is about them that might drive the degree or nature of urbanization today. This would require that we separate their effects on urbanization from their effects on advanced capitalist economies and societies more generally.

If we put this in a more critical way, it can be seen that most of the categories used to theorize and to measure the urban economy are no longer adequate to the task. This is especially true of economic categories. Such units as "industries," or "occupations"—the categories used by global dual city theory—are much too aggregated, in many cases, for it is distinctive subsets of industries or occupational groups that we find in cities. But they are also too small, in the sense that urban economic agglomerations often contain parts of many different industries. Even the concept of "commodity chain" (*filière*)—at the heart of post-Fordist city theory—subtle as it is, misses the mark, for it is often just selected parts of such chains and combinations of the parts of different chains that can be found in cities. "The firm," which is the theoretical and accounting unit of world city theory, is certainly well wide of the mark, for it is only certain parts of firms, especially the world's biggest firms, that are to be found in the world cities. The use of a critical input unique to cities might work, as in the attempt of informational city theory, except that it is precisely this input whose management and distribution is not unique to or even particularly concentrated in, cities, with the advent of spatially dispersed data processing, technology, and back offices.

To construct an effective theory, then, we need more targeted theoretical and statistical categories. The distinction between export-oriented and locally serving activities is still relevant to the understanding of urban economies, in the sense that this is the fundamental source of their economic specialization, differentiation, and much of interurban growth transmission, through trade. *What is principally common to the export-oriented economic specialization activities of cities is that they are concerned with the social organization of economic reflexivity.* We defined this earlier as a characteristic of contemporary modernity in which organizations—both private and public—and individuals devote themselves to the deliberate and strategic shaping of their environments, in part by taking a critical perspective on them.[52]

The organization of reflexivity is importantly, though not exclusively, urban. This is because reflexivity involves complex and uncertain relationships between organizations, between the parts of complex organizations, between individuals, and between individuals and organizations, in which proximity is important because of the substantive complexity and uncertainty of these relationships. These two characteristics of relationships frequently require that they be embedded either in direct, concrete relations between individuals or that they be carried out according to locally evolved routines or conventions that permit actors caught up in these complex relations to go forward under conditions of great uncertainty or substantive complexity. In other words, the transactional tissue of these urban activities is of a conventional/relational nature, and it is urban because certain conventions and relations only work in the context of proximity.

This permits us to redefine the "what" of the export-oriented urban economy as the parts of firms, production systems, industries, and the overlapping parts of different industries or firms articulated into urban economies, and which carry out reflexive activity. Redefining the urban economy as worlds of purposive reflexive action, however, gives us an object of analysis that cuts across the categories used by all the theories reviewed in the previous section, targeting the theoretical specificity of what is the urban export base. *The economies of big cities, in other words, should be analyzed as sets of partially overlapping spheres of reflexive economic action,* and the structures of those activities, in addition to traditional economic descriptors, must include *their conventional and relational structures of coordination and coherence.*

Now we need to turn to the "how" of the urban economy. The image of the urban economy as a mere input–output machine is insufficient. Conventions and relations, once established, function much like *productive assets* for the organizations, individuals, and places—cities, in this case—that possess them, because these relations and conventions are both *localized* and *specific*. Reflexivity is given shape and order through the development of proximity-dependent relations and conventions, ensembles of which define cognitive and pragmatic contexts common to a group of actors and permit them to carry out a particular kind of purposeful collective economic action. Rather than try to define the urban economy by the traditional categories, which are both too big and too small, we must redefine it as specific worlds of action sculpted by these conventions and relations. The empirical task is to identify for each city, the "what"—the particular spheres of purposeful reflexive economic action that are localized there—and the "how"—the way these activities are coordinated by conventions and relations. Examples of such urban worlds of reflexive action might include the following:

- The New York financial services complex, viewed in terms of its specific pragmatics—the "securitization" of capital in this case—and in terms of the principal ways firms and individuals are coordinated in this world, the specific rules, routines, and principles of evaluation they use. A contrast between New York, London, Tokyo and other financial markets, would reveal very important differences.
- The Hollywood entertainment/media complex—how its economic, technical, and artistic actors are built into a system for producing mass-entertainment products and how this differs radically from its English, French, or Italian counterparts.
- Silicon Valley as a core-technology agglomeration, viewed in terms of the specific relations and conventions that give rise to its technological prowess, in comparison with other places such as the the southwestern part of the Paris region, Cambridge, Boston, or Taipei.
- Intersecting pragmatic contexts—such as the worlds of art, fashion, and media in Paris—which are tied together by complex networks, routines, unwritten rules, and formal institutions.
- The evolution of Lyon as a reflexivity capital, but no longer absolute productive center, of the Rhône-Alpes region, in terms of the overlapping political and business services provided to the region's good-producing economy, as a key space of representation for regional political and business elites.

In all these cases, it is not just the geometry of these systems that is of interest, but the constructed mentalities and frameworks by which the actors involved evaluate and interpret their contexts in an ongoing way, and on that basis adjust their participation in the context.

The urban parts of productive activity, of course, are often inserted into bigger, nonurban networks, such as firms, industries, *filières*, and so on, in which other sets of geographically extensive rules and relations give order to the overall system, whether these be the bureaucratic structures of big multinational firms, the laws of a nation, or the structure of a market.

Reflexivity is by no means limited to the export-specialization activities of cities. It may be found in many and sundry domains of urban and nonurban economic tissues. Indeed, different forms of reflexivity are coming to mark the locally serving economies of different cities with distinctive characters. But the effect of these locally serving reflexive activities, while perhaps a critical force in driving the overall level of urbanization continually higher, is not critical in determining the structures of systems of cities, that is, the particular geographical division of growth. The importance of reflexivity in these activities for the nature of work and consumption (discussed below) should not be underestimated.

This gives us some insight into the statistical complexities of contemporary urban growth and change, referred to earlier. On the one hand, all medium- and large-sized cities are becoming centers of what we might call the reflexive or "intellectually" oriented parts of manufacturing and services, and these parts are growing as shares of output and employment in contemporary capitalism as a whole. So there is convergence between all big and medium-sized cities in this respect. On the other hand, there is differentiation according to the export-oriented and heavily traded subsets of these parts of sectors, giving rise to a reinforced urban-size hierarchy and generating some urban economies that are generally more important in national and international exchanges than others.

The Reflexivity Class in the City, the Nation, and the World

The city is indeed a place where social processes, figures, and objects are represented[53] and socialized, a key place where collective identities are formed and solidified. Sociologists have long attempted to understand the contemporary city by calling attention to the professional–managerial–technical occupational stratum (global–dual city) or the information elite (informational city) that carries out this key process of representation.[54] At the same time, however, it is claimed that new technologies make possible new patterns of "time sharing" and of segmentation and recombination of actors, all of this without direct proximity. It is difficult to reconcile these views, for the city cannot be the center of representation of key social processes without people who interact to carry out this activity.

As with the production categories of industry, firm or *filière*, our analysis suggests that the categories of "representation" and the occupational strata that go with it are both too broad and too narrow to capture the specificity of the contemporary urban economy. They cover workers in nonreflexive as well as reflexive activities. The theoretical object should be redefined as the population that generates and manages reflexivity.

The problem then becomes how this population is formed and how it functions, and the role of the city in both these processes. Cities appear to contain specific groups of such actors, tied together by complex combinations of their formal professional credentials, cultures, and the conventional–relational tissues in which they evolve their skills through local on-the-job experience. For example, certain kinds of professional–scientific–technical skills are more and more internationalized, through the convergence of business school training and scientific education among the advanced countries, as well as through experience in globe-girdling corporations. All of these forces promote interfirm and international mobility through routinization and codification of skills. Yet such skills are often honed, added to, and specialized when they are deployed in a specific sectoral/geographical context, in two senses. First, specific career experience progressively distances an individual from skills learned in school. Second, relations are built up (networks) and routines or conventions are learned, which become part of each worker's "human capital," well beyond the stock that is created via formal schooling.[55] Cities thus contain communities of reflexivity workers who insert geographically generic skills into geographically (and otherwise) specific conventional and relational contexts, such that they are made effective under conditions of uncertainty. These groups of actors engage in a kind of cognitive "translation" between geographical levels: national–regional, national–international, and city–regional hinterland.[56] By way of metaphor, there is something like a relationship between a lingua franca and local dialects and specific customs of speech at work. This relationship takes a hierarchical pattern in the case of ubiquitous activities like financial transactions; it takes a more nodal and disorganized pattern in the case of manufacturing and in the delivery of services by transnational corporations in which extensive market adaptation, customization, and after-sales follow-up is needed.[57] Each kind of activity will have a different spatial pattern of translation, reflecting the spatial arrangement of its reflexivity workers and the conventional–relational tissues by which they are bound into effective worlds of economic action. In other words, we need a completely new way of conceiving the geography of the key urban actors of contemporary capitalism and a new analytical problematic, which is the nature and functioning of worlds of action of the reflexive classes, at different, partially overlapping geographical scales.

Globalization and Territorialization of Urban Economies

There is a dialectical dynamic of globalization and territorialization at work in the construction of city economies today, with many apparently paradoxical dimensions. The organization of reflexivity by local, regional, national, and global firms pushes all of them toward cities. Globalization is both the top-down force of organizing markets and production systems according to supranational competitive criteria and resource flows, and the bottom-up pull of territorialization of both market penetration (a process requiring global firms to insert themselves in conventional–relational contexts of their markets, not a simple technocratic operation) and the effort to tap into geographically differentiated producers' capabilities (the specialization of technological knowledge and sensibilities and its ongoing redifferentiation through reflexivity in the advanced industrial world). Both globalization and territorialization are made possible by the new global lingua franca used by reflexive workers to communicate, combined with the ongoing fragmentation and redifferentiation of specific groups of reflexive producers into specific productive communities, defined by their particular technical skills and the deployment of those skills through specific conventions and relations. City economies are pulled simultaneously in both these directions by these forces and it is the interrelationship between the two that has to be appreciated in the study of any particular city's economy.

REFLEXIVE URBAN CONSUMERS AND CITIZENS AND URBAN COLLECTIVE CONSUMPTION

Cities are not just sites of production, they are also important sites of consumption. Reflexivity is not a characteristic only of producers in capitalism; individuals in their roles as consumers, workers, and citizens are now critically reflexive,[58] generating an enormous variety of new consumer tastes, worker capacities and creativities, and citizen demands and reactions. Not long ago, both orthodox urban theory, in the guise of central place theory, and Marxist urban theory, in the form of the theory of collective consumption, placed consumption at the heart of the urbanization process. *Reflexive consumption* has become an important constituent of the contemporary city economy, and there are important organizational and geographical linkages between reflexive production and consumption that are highly urbanized today, most notably in the form of certain kinds of services. One of the key linkages is that of the city as a space of social representation, to which we have alluded above.

For what we might call certain kinds of "elite" services—forms of consumer variety that, only a generation ago, were found exclusively in the downtown commercial districts of the major cities—there has been a clear decline in central-place functions. Consumer variety has increased and has been decentralized, such that (in the American case) regional malls within metropolitan areas and in smaller city regions now offer astonishing arrays of fine goods. Similarly, such goods are now available in the downtowns of many provincial European cities, whereas they were once available only in major capitals. The same is true of many consumer-oriented services, through the development of better service-delivery organizations. At the same time, other new specialized consumption habits have developed, and they do appear to have strong hierarchical central-place characteristics: these are what Sassen and others refer to as the "yuppie" economy of the global cities.[59] In all this, however, certain important geographically localized forms of specialization seem to exist. In part, long-lasting, distinctive aesthetic cultures of production and consumption are in evidence, and have little to do with the yuppie phenomenon: we can find this in the production of theater, music, art and to some extent, food. At the same time, new versions of local-elite consumption are highly internationalized, with the same products and services making their appearance in standardized forms in many places (rue du Fbg. St. Honoré, Rodeo Drive, Fifth Avenue, or malls like the South Coast Plaza or those in Bergen County and Chevy Chase); but there are also many instances of particular services and products appearing to serve distinctive urban populations, and generating supply as a result of such demand. Elite consumer reflexivity is thus a curious mixture of the very cosmopolitan and the local, and its feedbacks to production of goods and delivery of services is most complex. This includes, very importantly, *collective consumption*. This is a special case, since collective consumption is by definition highly rooted in long-lasting institutions (social and urban services) and in the built environment (housing, streets, parks, etc.); as such, it has a tendency to be highly differentiated from place to place. But it is differentiated not only as a result of inertia from the past; the collective reflexivity of urban consuming classes appears to lead them in widely different directions from city to city and nation to nation.

Middle-class or "mass" city consumption presents its own set of complex dynamics. Big urban conglomerations appear, more and more, as repeating patterns: the same movies (multiplex chains in the 13th, 9th, or 6th arrondissements of Paris show the same films as they do from Universal City to Hollywood to Santa Monica, in Los Angeles), the same chain stores, and so on, from one part of the metropolis to another. This has been celebrated variously as the "polycentric" metropolis or "urban village." It is evident that most of these activities have lower central-place thresholds than elite consumption, and that the middle classes have increased in numbers and purchasing power. On this basis, central-place theory cannot tell us much about urbanization today, since the thresholds for these activities are met many times over in today's big cities.

It appears, however, that middle-class consumption has not simply been massified. It has also been fragmented and specialized in certain ways, into subclass lifestyle, age, ethnicity, gender, and other kinds of fragments. Thus, in Los Angeles, there is the rock-music section of Sunset Boulevard, the hip "urban grunge" boutiques on Melrose Avenue, the gay downtown in West Hollywood, innumerable ethnically demarcated villages, the differentiated bourgeois cultures of Brentwood, Beverly Hills, and Westwood, the yuppie culture of Santa Monica, and the bohemias of Venice and East Hollywood. The suburbs are also highly differentiated along all these lines, including the supposedly homogeneous white middle class. Many such fragments consist of goods with lower thresholds, and still others of consumer services such as specialized retail operations, restaurants, clothing stores, music clubs, and so on. These are not only yuppie environments; they display a wide range of class and income characteristics, in addition to their liminal dimensions. They are manifestations of consumer reflexivity, and they reflect both the influences of cross-cultural internationalization that homogenize cities and new forms of relocalization that redifferentiate them. These are also conventionally and relationally defined worlds of consumer–producer action.

The *spectacle* is a particularly important form of consumption that involves a high proportion of service.[60] Spectacles are sometimes deliberate and organized consumer experiences, while at other times they "rise up" from the street, and are not fully organized or internalized by commercial organizations. In big cities, the former has in recent years become more and more reflexive with respect to the latter, reducing the time of imitation and cultural "colonization" of the street by commercial forces. The complex relationship between the two, in the context of increasing reflexivity and increasing fragmentation and diversity of reflexivity, yields our characteristic and confusing impression of both sameness and difference in urban consumption.

Distinctive reflexive cultures—youth, ethnic, gender-based, social-movement- or lifestyle-based—are big inputs into the bottom-up aspect of spectacle creation and the forms of aestheticization to which it gives rise. The commercial recuperation and packaging (*re*presentation) of the experiences generated by these cultures, in goods but also in spectacles (which in turn sell goods), are major parts of the urban economy today. Nowhere is this more important than in the media and entertainment industries. These sectors are perhaps the most dramatic example of the back-and-forth relationship between standardization–cosmopolitanization and destandardization–specificity to which we have alluded many times. On the one hand, the media and entertainment industries use technologies of delivery—for both private electronic consumption of images and sounds and for public consumption of organized spectacles—which are capable of greater and greater economies of scale, but also economies of variety within that scale. On the other hand, there are important, constantly recreated differences in aesthetic sensibility, on both demand and supply sides, for both sorts of services. The film, television, and music complexes of London, Toronto, and Los Angeles are all within the English-speaking world, but they have very different specializations and talents, all the while borrowing elements from each other through cosmopolitan exchange. Differentiation grows more with other cultural factors. It is not possible to get into these complexes and function in them without getting into the conventions and relations that tie the producers to each other, or tie them to particular groups of consumers.

The importance of cities as sites of consumption in general, of collective consumption, and of feedbacks from consumption to production, can only be understood if we are willing to conceive of these activities as worlds of conventionally and relationally structured action, with the action frameworks of specific groups of consumers and producers as the object of analysis. One major dimension of the latter is urbanness in general; another is the specificities of particular cities; for both, there is an ongoing dialectic of homogenization between cities and between urban and nonurban, and their geographical redifferentiation. This dialectic should be a major focus of the geography, economics, and sociology of services.

DEMOGRAPHICS, LABOR MARKETS, AND THE POLARIZATION QUESTION

The theme of urban disorder—inequality, polarization, marginalization—has had a prominent place in recent urban theory, especially in dual-city theories, most of which are linked to one variety or another of global-city theory. This is an enormously complex subject involving labor markets, immigration, education, household and business location, and intricate dynamics of social integration and exclusion. The point to be made here echoes that of previous sections: a theory of urbanization must separate out what is distinctively urban, in manifestation and in cause, in the "polarization turn." Most existing theories are inadequate in this respect.

As has been observed, the combined effects of immigration and the advent of a service economy in cities has not produced greater overall urban income polarization there than in national economies in general (see Table 9.2). Increasing wage inequality is spread across industries and across the landscape. Immigration is, of course, numerically targeted at big cities, and immigrants account for high proportions of low-wage workers in some countries; but much immigration in the past and at present is targeted at smaller cities and even rural areas and increasingly so. Moreover, immigration is not just about low-wage traps; as the literature on ethnic entrepreneurs has shown,[61] there is a strong upward mobility process at work for many groups, and much of their behavior is due to a "push" from their countries of origin, with little "pull" from any existing labor market "demand" structure in the cities of arrival: they create their own niches.

There is still a widespread perception, which cannot be totally unfounded, that big cities contain increasing numbers of poor people, marginalized populations, low-waged workers, and the long-term unemployed. There is, however, a real danger in confusing an urban manifestation of a broader economic dynamic with urban causes of that problem. This is not merely academic hairsplitting: if the problem is in the demographic-occupational-wage structure of economies in general (all strongly underpinned by the requirements of international competition and technological changes) then it is unlikely that *urban* economic development will be able to have much impact on it.[62] Certainly, local economic development programs might have some limited local effects—for example, unionization, upgrading of local industries, etc.—but unless cities have real regulatory power, they are likely to be swamped by national and international labor markets and demographic dynamics.

There are ways in which the characteristics of society in the city seem to be linked to specifically urban causes. There are apparently patterns of poverty and social exclusion that are particularly urban, although it should be remembered that persistent poverty is not, even today, unique to urban areas.[63] Most countries have long had their pockets of persistent poverty, from Appalachia in the United States or the Mezzogiorno in Italy to the Auvergne in France. What seems to be specific to urban areas, across the developed world today, is the association between an economy-wide phenomenon—increasing wage inequality and/or unemployment—and new forms of poverty persistence that are particularly urban and, along with them, new forms of social–spatial isolation— the fortress city[64]—or exclusion in cities.

A similar oppressed economic status, when found predominantly in nonurban areas, sometimes does not lead to the same form of sociospatial exclusion there as in the big city, probably because there are other nonmarket support systems in place.[65] This is part of the split between the city as the site of modernity and smaller towns and the countryside as reservoirs of tradition. Still, there is increasing evidence that the social structures that once clearly demarcated the big city from the rest are breaking down.

These developments suggest that we ask questions about the nature of contemporary modernity. Economic liberalism has been gaining ground in many countries, with privatization and deregulation of economies the order of the day. The new hypermodern economy depends on the rapid movement of goods, services, and persons. Old forms of career stability are now considered to be things of the past. The sociological corollary of this kind of economy is the "risk society," in which the individual must be capable of negotiating a series of life challenges involving risk after risk, from the economic to the social to the personal spheres.

Modernization theory, at least in its American version, always predicted that the psychological and personal "costs" of such flexibility and adaptability would be outweighed by the benefits of personal mobility, choice, and economic enrichment. But it never theorized the possibility that the economic machine would falter durably, leaving significant portions of the population in a position of economic stagnation or even retreat. This is precisely the set of circumstances that has come to be common in the OECD countries over the last few years. Even when the growth machine was working well, there were always certain losers from modernization, and governments attempted to aid them with social welfare safety nets. But these nets are wearing thinner, under budgetary and tax pressures. In the current period, the city seems to concentrate large numbers of people who are cut off from the labor market, not simply temporarily affected by a mismatch of their skills with the new occupational structure. At the same time, families and village structures are practically gone as means of helping individuals to survive and, most critically, to preserve their sense of dignity, pride, and place in this risky world. The effects of this situation are likely to be felt everywhere in our societies, though perhaps most visibly in big cities.

The city undoubtedly enhances these economy- and society-wide dynamics. The urban land nexus[66] creates prices for land due to competition for the best locations, which are often in short supply, precisely because they are "positional goods,"[67] not goods with an expandable supply. It is very possible that the urban land nexus accentuates the dynamics of polarization and exclusion that come from other forces, and hence makes an independent, specifically urban contribution to them. Certain recent studies have shown, for example, that for a given overall growth rate, there are more *spatially* polarized effects (wages and unemployment rates) than in the past, on an *intrametropolitan* scale; this is consistent with the result, reported earlier, that the big cities do not have worse overall income distributions than their national economies, but suggests that these cities are nonetheless producing a certain form of specifically urban socioeconomic polarization.[68]

Moreover, even though many of the impacts of the contemporary economy and social modernization crisis are not caused by cities and are diffused spatially, there is an increasingly convincing body of evidence—from studies of urban poverty, criminality, and marginalization[69]—that certain kinds of troubles cannot largely be reduced either to the economy- or society-wide background factors cited above. Rather, they are the outcomes of specific forms of *local reflexive social action;* cultures of criminality, underclass patterns, certain forms of persistent poverty and exclusion are, at one and the same time, results of things that are "done to" the populations we put in these categories (they are "victims"), and they are also *manufactured, structured, and participated in as part of a reflexively created system of rewards,* in which spatial proximity and intensity of concentration of these actors—their urbanness—plays a role in creating spillovers and feedbacks with respect to economic and social forces. If the work done to date is confirmed, then at least this specific subset of urban distress—the hardcore distressed areas and populations—would need to be addressed not merely by overall economic and social policies, but by specific areally based approaches. These dynamics do not seem to be attributable in any direct way to shifts in the urban-occupational structure, or even straightforwardly to long-term unemployment, though these forces may have been at their origins.

None of this implies that social institutions—such as the welfare state, housing policy, labor market policy, immigration policy, customs and cultures of race relations, labor training, policies toward urban public space, and so on—have no impact on patterns of polarization, exclusion, or integration in the city. The comparative evidence shows that they do.[70] But the relationship between these machine-like external factors and outcomes is not fully straight-forward; social reflexivity is the intermediating process and this is likely to dif-fer from city to city according to the different mix of background factors, and according to the specific mix of conventions and relations constructed by the actors in place, and the evolution of that world of action.[71] This is thus not in any way to blame the victims, but to recognize that these collective dynamics, once in existence, are no longer reducible to their putative external causes, be-cause they are *worlds of action, rooted in their own relations and conventions, constructed by the actors themselves.*

This raises a very thorny general issue for any kind of policy. External factors, such as the economy, location patterns, immigration, race relations, and so on, are certainly important, but they are inadequate mechanical expla-nations of these phenomena, and their reversal, for the populations con-cerned, would itself depend on undoing or altering these action frameworks, not just undoing the external causes. "Victims" are no more machines than are the "elites" of the city: both exist within created worlds of reflexive social action, whether specifically urban or society-wide.

Urban theory, then, has a long road before it in considering the evolution of spheres of social action for its "agglomerated" populations.

CONCLUSION

The city has never been a machine. Indeed, throughout the literature on cities, one can find reflections that recognize, implicitly or explicitly, that the city is a crucible in which the ingredients, once put in the pot together and cooked, often turn out very differently from what we can deduce from their discrete flavors. Yet much urban theory does not want to theorize this dynam-ic, instead stressing expert understanding of the ingredients and not getting too deeply into excessively complex combinations of them. In this respect, it is like most social science, remaining wedded to the notion of society as a set of separable rational-action processes. This epistemological bias, no matter what its political coloration, creates severe limitations for understanding the urban social and economic process today, some of which we have been able to suggest in this chapter.

Recent social, technological, and organizational developments make this more than ever the case, for they have strengthened the role of reflexive action in urban economy and society. Firms, individuals, and other organizations, construct purposive and pragmatic worlds of action—chiseled out by conventions and relations. In the economy, there is more locational separation than ever before between that part of productive activity heavily based on reflexivity and that which is involved in the cognitively and organizationally routinized production of goods and services. Cities get more than their share of the former. This activity can only be fully understood when its constructed collective-action dimensions are taken into account, as well as its machine-like characteristics. The same, we have argued, is true for many forms of consumer behavior, citizen behavior, elite behavior, and nonelite behavior. The worlds of action which make up the city economy and society are hybrids, constrained by the machine-like forces of late modern capitalism, but themselves enabled by the ways that system not only permits, but in certain ways, thrives on social reflexivity, for better and for worse.

NOTES

1. Sassen (1991).
2. Veltz (1995).
3. Castells (1989).
4. A kindred argument has been proposed by Amin and Thrift (1993), in their notion of "institutional thickness" of localities.
5. Giddens (1990); Beck (1992); Lundvall and Johnson (1992).
6. Sassen (1991).
7. Harloe and Fainstein (1994); Mollenkopf and Castells (1992); Fainstein et al. (1987).
8. Pollard and Storper (1996).
9. These are defined empirically in Pollard and Storper (1996).
10. Preteceille (1996).
11. Naponen et al. (1993); Persky and Wiewel (1994).
12. Preteceille (1996); Naponen et al (1993).
13. Chesnais (1994).
14. Much of this analysis of the global–dual city is inspired by long discussions with Edmond Preteceille carried out while coteaching a course on the subject in the winter of 1995 at UCLA. I am grateful for his inputs, but he is not responsible for any of the interpretations, or possible errors, found here.
15. As reported in Jencks (1993).
16. There may be a role for financial capitalism in this, in that the regime of financialized capitalism leaves national governments fewer options for wage regulation, especially in mass-production-oriented tradeable-goods industries. By enforcing a

common pattern of efficiency on them, a pattern based on wage polarization, it can be cited as a cause. This is Chesnais' (1994) analysis. But note that there is nothing particularly urban about this cause nor about the geographical or sectoral distibution of its consequences.

17. Waldinger (1992).

18. Jencks (1993).

19. Friedmann and Wolff (1982); Friedmann (1986, 1993).

20. See the discussion of the geography of enterprise in Sayer and Walker (1992).

21. Thrift (1994a,b).

22. Marchand (1993).

23. Markusen and Gwiasda (1994).

24. Machimura (1992).

25. Dunning (1979).

26. Dunning (1979).

27. Chesnais (1994).

28. Gore (1984).

29. For a theoretical exploration of the issue of whether firms are spatial followers or leaders, see Chapter 8 of this book.

30. Castells (1989, 1992).

31. Castells (1989).

32. Castells (1989, p. 6; 1992).

33. This is becoming a staple of economic history and of the "new" theory of capitalist growth. See, *inter alia*, Mokyr (1988); Landes (1972). The theoretical debate has centered over how to explain "Solow's residual" (Solow, 1957). Recent models that attempt to do this emphasize the accumulation of knowledge as the factor accounting for the residual. See the recent work of Romer (1990) or Lucas (1988).

34. Hounshell (1984).

35. Kennedy (1989).

36. Chesnais (1994); Delaunay and Gadrey (1988).

37. Delaunay and Gadrey (1988); Gadrey (1994); Boulianne et al. (1995), show that pre-existing social relations have determined the spatial pattern of advanced services in Switzerland; Djellal and Gallouj (1995), argue that some services require general benefits of urban location, but others require very specific benefits of local downstream linkages. Jouvaud (1995) also argues that many services are forms of "coproduction," some requiring local "partners" and others having longer-distance relations to their cooperants, and shows the first case to be an empirically important one for the Marseille–Aix region. See also Beyers (1992); Marshall (1988); Coffey and Polese (1987); Daniels and Moulaert (1991); Daniels (1991); O'hUallachain and Reid (1991); Illeris (1989).

38. Lundvall and Johnson (1992); Chesnais (1994); Dosi et al. (1991).

39. What Lundvall (1990) calls "knowing who," "knowing where," and "knowing how."

40. Uncertainty is a central element in the new "cognitive turn" in the study of technological change (Rip, 1991).

41. Technological spillovers: for example, Antonelli (1987, 1995); Jaffe (1986); Jaffe et al. (1993).

42. Pavitt and Patel (1991).

43. As discussed in previous chapters. But see, for recent evidence, Pianta (1996).

44. Castells (1992, p. 2), writes that "the space of flows is not placeless, although its structural logic is . . . ," by which I take him to mean that there is a supraplace force, i.e., an abstract law of development, which makes the space come about, and not the actions of individuals or institutions in real places. This is very similar to Marxist reasoning about the laws of capitalism.

45. Gottman (1989); Pred (1977).

46. I am not going to analyze Castells' extensive comments on social polarization in the information city because his analysis is essentially similar to the global city–dual city model: occupational wage structure in the information economy leads to polarization, combined with the global labor market created by global firms, i.e., immigration. We noted earlier that inequality in general cannot be accounted for by an analysis of the financial services industries, nor can evidence for cities as particular loci of inequality. Castells has a wider sweep, in that he considers the whole economy to be an information economy. But, as we have noted, "informational" is an imprecise characterization of the nature of every sector. The most compelling analysis of increasing wage polarization combines technological unemployment in goods-producing industries, the competitive race fostered by financial capitalism (but not the financial services industries in particular) in the absence of a regulated international financial order, and the aggravation of oversupply of unskilled labor through immigration. This affects whole economies, not just cities. Curiously, its conclusions are closest to Castells, in the sense that "information" does permit drastic reductions in labor demand in many routinized manufacturing and service activities, and reduces the skill content of remaining jobs.

47. This issue is reviewed in Chapter 2 of this book.

48. Scott (1988a).

49. This is Veltz' (1995) analysis of Paris in particular and post-Fordist urban economics in general. A third version of agglomeration theory takes a different approach. It suggests that there are such things as "innovative milieux," places in which embedded social relations permit innovations in products and processes. While not limited to big cities, some versions of milieux theory include big cities. Others, especially of the Italian version, suggest that big cities are unlikely to be innovative milieux because their size discourages the focused social coherence that, it is held, leads local economic actors to maximize innovative potential. See also Chapter 2 of this book.

50. Young (1928), was prescient about the cumulative, endogenous nature of change in the division of labor, due to the way that one change makes necessary practical adjustments in the tasks that surround it. Recently, evolutionary economists have extended and formalized these intuitions, in an explicitly heterodox way. On the more orthodox side, there are also efforts, as in Fujita and Thisse (1995).

51. Again, a long and detailed version of this critique can be found in Chapter 2 of this book.

52. There are extensive discussions of different aspects of the contemporary "learning economy" in Chapters 1 through 8 of this book.

53. The jargon used is "space of representation," from Lefebvre (1991). This expression is also widely used by cultural historians and psychologists (Piaget), and is a subject of much urban literature.

54. Castells (1989).

55. This notion of "relational" capital is an extension of Asanuma's (1989) theory, derived from a study of Japanese industry, of "relational contracting."

56. Someone who has particularly developed the notion of the service as a sort of relation is Gadrey (1994). See also De Bandt and Gadrey (1994).

57. Chesnais (1994, Chap. 8).

58. Of course, using the term "critically reflexive" does not imply any kind of judgment as to whether the results of such reflection are good or bad, right or wrong, in the sense of conventional modernist ideas about "true" versus "false" consciousness. It means, simply, that the act of reflection about the environment, with a view toward strategically acting upon it, is now a more or less explicit part of the action frameworks of individuals and organizations.

59. Christopherson (1994b).

60. Debord (1976).

61. Waldinger (1992).

62. And once again, the literature on wage polarization shows it to be an economy-wide phenomenon, in both sectoral and geographical terms (Harrison and Bluestone, 1992).

63. Jencks (1993).

64. This idea is the principal theme of Wilson (1987).

65. Mingione (1992) also found in much of the American underclass research and French work on exclusion.

66. Readers will recognize the origin of this term in the title of Scott's (1976) book.

67. The term comes from Hirsch (1976).

68. Gregory (1996).

69. Katz (1985); Wacquant (1995).

70. Preteceille (1996).

71. This point is suggested, for the case of immigration, in the work of Todd (1994). He argues that background factors for both immigrants and receiving societies are important. But for each of them, what's really important is the way that such background factors lead to "mentalities" for each. In turn, it is the contact between the two systems that seems to determine the result. We are thus far from the typical descriptions of education levels, occupations, and so on, which are the centerpieces of social scientific explanations of social mobility.

PART V
REGIONAL INSTITUTIONS, TERRITORIAL ORDERS

CHAPTER 10

Institutions of the Learning Economy

DEFINING AN ECONOMIC POLICY PROBLEM

The classical dilemmas of economic policy are still with us. In market economies, the interests of owners in earning a decent rate of return on their investments have somehow to be reconciled with satisfactory levels of demand and political demands for an acceptable distribution of income. The problem, in most of the advanced democratic market countries, is that elites resist using nonmarket means to redistribute income; it costs them money and becomes a disincentive to investment. They prefer distribution of income to be achieved through employment, and employment to be submitted to competitive forces, not mandated by nonmarket agencies such as the state. The current state of ideology (as well as the cost of living), moreover, even in social democratic countries, is such that most people prefer good employment to the most generous dole. Even those countries that might be politically inclined to resolve the problem through expansion of the social welfare apparatus find themselves blocked by strong resistance from their own populations, if they want to tax, and from financial markets, if they want to expand deficits.

Yet most of the market economies of the advanced world have failed in the employment area in recent years. In the western European countries, unemployment rates have been too high for much of the post-1970 period. In the United States, where many jobs have been created, average wages have stagnated in many sectors and declined in manufacturing. In all these countries, there is a troubling growth of low-wage employment and considerable increase in the wage gap between high- and low-wage jobs. The problem of policy, in consequence, has come to be that of employment: how to generate enough of it with decent income levels in a way that is compatible with profitability and growth. Each nation's problem is a variation on this basic theme.

The Marxian formula of balancing productivity gains and wage gains no longer provides the key to resolving the employment problem. Modern management and technology, as well as existing income smoothing institutions, have made the overall rate of growth somewhat independent of workers' incomes; even if wage changes were matched to productivity gains in the national territory, producers would still be able to reduce their wage costs via re-location on a global scale.[1] The Keynesian formula of pumping up expectations is often effective as a means to generating investment and growth, but not full employment. For owners and investors, profitability (especially if we include appreciation of assets) has become possible, except for short recessionary periods, without generating full employment, and is no longer dependent on rates of growth that could generate full employment.[2] Even though it might be socially desirable if Marxian or Keynesian policy formulas were followed on a global scale (equitable global reflation), there are no institutional structures capable of bringing it about, and any nation that attempts it alone will be severely sanctioned by financial markets.

The policy problem is, then, to sustain competitiveness under such conditions, and to do so in a way that deals with the employment problem simultaneously. Competitiveness will refer here to the ability of an economy to hold stable or increasing market shares in an activity while sustaining stable or increasing standards of living for those who participate in it. It must maintain or increase employment and do so in a qualitatively satisfactory way, which for those who are employed means satisfactory incomes.[3]

The conditions of competitiveness and employment creation vary considerably among the major kinds of economic activities today. In any given economy, there are three basic employment trends: creation of high-wage, high-skill jobs, usually in value-intensive industries or activities; creation of low-wage, low-skill jobs; and job loss. The loci of these different trends (for the medium- and high-wage economies) can be broadly described in the following way. Employment losses are concentrated in manufacturing industries producing standardized outputs that are amenable to mechanization and automation. Employment with lower wages is heavily concentrated in the consumer and retail services sector, which is the biggest sector of the whole economy; the exception is management activities in those sectors. Growth in high-wage employment is located in certain occupations, mostly those relying on intellectual labor, found in many sectors, but particularly in advanced producer and financial services, technology-intensive or design-intensive manufacturing, and consumer services with a highly customized output.

Location is a key dimension of these employment dynamics. The first and third categories have a high proportion of tradable outputs, with a highly uneven national and global locational pattern; the second category, retail and consumer services, has tradable management and input functions, but untradable final-output functions; delivery must be close to the customer, thus following the geographical distribution of population and income. For standardized manufactures, the overall downward trend in employment intensity is complicated by the increasing possibility of locational change (relocation), whether to peripheral low-wage regions of advanced countries, or to developing countries. Employment growth in these activities is occurring in a number of developing countries, most spectacularly in East and Southeast Asia. This has to do with the technological content and transactional structure of the production systems for standardized manufactures, which permit easy technological transfer and long-distance linkages to core fabrication and management activities, still located mostly in the rich countries. Not only is employment trending downward in these sectors in the advanced economies, but so are wages, due to locational competition with low-wage areas. World market prices are now dictated by the combination of advanced technology and wages in low-wage areas.

For consumer and retail services, employment is rising as a proportion of the total in most places, but this employment has not proved capable of raising overall real incomes. At the same time that productivity improvements are applied, via increasing automation and computerization, they intersect with the same dynamics that affect standardized, routinized manufacturing activity: the increasing possibility of locational substitution due to the information and telecommunications revolution (for example, the second wave of back offices in retail services).

In contrast to these activities, the employment that could serve as a motor of real incomes is engaged in the production of nonstandardized, nonroutinized goods and services, especially tradables. Such activities, as we have seen, are not easy to come by in this world, where a central logic of competition is precisely to standardize the output and routinize the production process.

COMPETITIVENESS IN THE LEARNING ECONOMY

Theories of competitiveness abound today, as do descriptive monikers for the new economy: postindustrialism, the informational economy, the knowledge-based economy, flexible specialization, post-Fordism. Though each of these labels helps in understanding some dimensions of contemporary economic activity, the logic of the most advanced forms of economic competition— those capable of generating high-wage employment—can best be described as that of learning. Those firms, sectors, regions and nations that can learn faster or better (higher quality or cheaper for a given quality) become competitive because their knowledge is scarce and therefore cannot be immediately imitated by new entrants or transferred, via codified and formal channels, to competitor firms, regions, or nations. The price–cost margin of such activities can rise, while market shares increase; the resulting rents can alleviate downward wage pressure. In this respect, such activities are promising for high-wage areas. But the key defining condition of this happy picture is that these activities are only temporarily immune to relocation or to substitution by competitors. Economies must therefore be equipped to keep outrunning the powerful forces of standardization and imitation in the world economy. Once they are imitated or their outputs standardized, then there are downward wage and employment pressures. They must become moving targets by continuing to learn.[4]

The notion of a learning economy rejects the central arguments of postindustrialism: learning concerns manufacturing, which continues to matter, as well as services. Learning can concern low-technology industries, which can generate high-wage jobs, as well as high-technology sectors. Still, learning-based activities, although central to the direct objective of generating high-wage, high-skill "knowledge-intensive" employment, are never going to account for the majority of output or employment in any given economy. Other kinds of activities (locally serving activities, scale-based production, etc.) will continue to embody high proportions of employment. But core learning activities have propulsive effects on economies in a number of ways: technological spillover effects can widen and lengthen the wealth-producing properties of learning (both upstream and downstream, and horizontally into technologically complementary activities), while the quasirents earned from imperfect competition can be channeled through the producing economy in the form of wages, investment, and cumulative advantage.

Contemporary economic development strategies must therefore be geared toward installing and sustaining activities embodying this propulsive dynamic. In certain cases, they will become strategic, export-oriented, trade-specialization sectors for an economy, the source of foreign-exchange earnings and key to market invasion, much in the way affirmed by the new trade theory.[5] But the learning economy is not merely an offensive strategy; in the presence of increasingly open markets, local production can be defended in certain sectors by upgrading it continuously (adopting productivity and design improvements that are found in potential invader-competitors), as well as by attempting to differentiate the local industry through endogenous forms of learning for differentiation.

To say that the learning economy is necessary to high-wage employment generation is not to claim that it represents a complete economic strategy. All the traditional tasks also remain necessary: balancing production and consumption; finding the right mix between export-oriented and locally serving activity; ongoing productivity improvements; and balanced reallocation of labor. But these traditional tasks of long-term economic management are by themselves no longer sufficient to generate adequate quantities of high-quality employment. That is the role of the learning economy.

LEARNING ECONOMIES AS COHERENT WORLDS OF PRODUCTION

For any given set of products–technologies–markets, and any given set of actors, the various conventions and relations have to fit together; they must be internally coherent. What does internal coherence imply? Certainly not that only those sets of conventional–relational (CR) transactions that lead to an optimal a priori equilibrium resource allocation are viable. There are many different mixes of performance that can be stable, at different levels of wages, profits, growth, adeptness at adjustment, and so on. The existence of multiple equilibria means that there is no single universal criterion of internal coherence (i.e., no single economically feasible practice).[6] Internal coherence thus means that for any given learning-based production system, the ensemble of CR involved defines a common context of interpretation for those actors, which permits them to coordinate coherently with other actors in that context. These common contexts operate across systems that we have termed "worlds" of production, in that they are frameworks of action for the economic agents involved. [7]

The unit of accounting of coherence is, ultimately, the product—whether it be intermediate or final—for the product must pass the external test. There are several organizational subdivisions of the economy that correspond to products.[8] Some are "smaller" than (upstream of), the final-output sector, such as capital goods industries; others are "bigger" than final-output sectors, in that they are essential to a number of such sectors but have wide competencies: these are Perrouxian technological spaces. These different organizational subdivisions of the modern economy, which define systems in which sets of conventions and relations, must be mutually coherent for economically viable learning to take place.

But in addition, at any given moment, there are external tests to which a given set of conventions is subject. In the current case, we are arguing that this test is one of competitiveness—such that market share and employment levels with high wages are maintained or increased—which in turn is consequent upon learning. Where either internal or external dimensions of coherence are not present, a production system will find itself without successful evolutionary tendencies, blocked in its capacity to generate growth, employment, and income. Within a world of production, to get from blocked evolution to successful learning implies the development of an ensemble of conventions that make up the coherent common context of that world. This context cannot be divided into discrete factors: it comes as a package.[9]

INSTITUTIONS, POLICIES, COLLECTIVE ACTION

World Making: Policy's Dual Objective

The task for policy in a learning economy now becomes clear: ideally, it would support the development of packages of conventions and relations in coherent product-based subdivisions of the economy. Because these conventions and relations must be developed according to such subdivisions, policy must have strategic content; because such conventions and relations must be mutually coherent, generating what we have defined as a common context, policy's task is to support the development of worlds of production. Both these tasks are dynamic ones. The object of policy for technological spaces is not simply to install hardware, but to set the economy on a trajectory of technological learning, so as to outstrip the imitator–competitor economies. Moreover, just as technological learning is the outcome of conventions as well as hardware, the national or regional economy must achieve and keep reachieving conventional and relational coordination of the agents involved in learning. The challenge to policy is thus to establish and maintain not one, but two economic dynamics: the technological trajectory (the mastery of specific spaces in the economy characterized by technological spillovers and complementarities), and the trajectory of conventions, which link and relink agents to each other in a coordinated fashion.

Learning Economies as Institutions: The Problem of Circularity

In democratic societies, policies are implemented by formal, public institutions whose vocations are defined according to the values that society projects as its universals. "Universal" in this context refers to the set of a priori rules or criteria that define the legitimate as procedurally nonarbitrary and in the substantive common interest of the people. Overt, de jure particularism is not legitimate because it does not refer to the common interest and may involve procedural arbitrariness.

All institutions are not public, however, and many are not coterminous with formal organizations. Institutions consist of "persistent and connected sets of rules, formal and informal, that prescribe behavioral roles, constrain activity, and shape expectations"[10] and overlap with conventions. For this reason, institutions cannot be reduced to specific organizations, although the latter may be important in the generation of expectations, preferences, and rules.[11] Common to both public and nonpublic institutions, to formal and nonformal institutions, is their need to give order to expectations and allow actors to coordinate under conditions of uncertainty. In terms of a production system, they have to do this so that coordination is economically successful.

If we accept that enduring structures and patterns of interaction and rule are important, then individual behavior is not necessarily the result of exogenous, classically self-interested preferences, as most economists would assume (methodological individualism; universal, rational interest-based calculus). Rather, the conventions by which people define their interests, form expectations of others, and hence calculate their interactions with others, are extremely varied, according to time, place, and the situation of action: rationality is as much a result of such highly differentiated conventions as the other way around. In the specific case at hand, it may vary according to the "possible world" of productive activity (product), and the version of that world found in a particular place (a real, concrete world).

This means that there is a circular relation between convention and institutions. Institutions have a strong effect, by generating regularity and precedent, in the formation of conventions that people employ to cope with the persistent and pervasive uncertainty of their interactions with other people in the economy. But by the same token, formal organized institutions can only function successfully if the rules, procedures, incentives, and sanctions they establish are integrated into the conventions that guide people's behavior. Even coercion is ultimately a convention, in that if people do not take sanction seriously, it is unlikely that the institution will be able to coerce for long. More commonly, who cannot think of ways in which the common, taken-for-granted ("conventional") wisdom of a large segment of the population causes it to interact in ways that render formal rules inefficacious, from the informal economy to paradoxical and unanticipated effects of economic regulation in land, capital, and industrial markets? In these cases, we can say that formal institutions are not fully consistent with the conventions of the populations they are meant to affect. Successful formal institutions, then, have a hard organizational side, and a "soft" conventional foundation.

Policies intended to create or sustain the learning economy would involve a relationship between public, formal institutions and conventions and relations that are neither fully public nor fully formal. There is a circularity here: formal public institutions, in creating or sustaining worlds of learning, must in effect create or sustain the conventions and relations of the latter. In turn, those formal public institutions can only assist in world making if the people in both institutions—the learning production system and the formal public institution—are coordinated by conventions coherent with that project. This kind of endless circularity cannot be gotten around by any traditional notion such as incentive, compulsion, or formal rule. Even the largest, most financially powerful companies and governments—who possess great power to compel or to incite—have regularly failed with major technological projects, not for lack of intelligence or resources. A successful incentive system is itself a convention, which coordinates expectations of performance and reward under conditions of extreme uncertainty. This problem is different from that found in the contemporary literature on systems of innovation, which are the ensembles of formal institutions said to generate different patterns and rates of innovation (schooling, training, universities, governments, legal frameworks, etc.). Such systems surely shape agents' behaviors over time, but these formal institutions could not work in the absence of underlying conventions (and in part, this is why each nation's system works in some activities and not in others: the relations and conventions are very difficult to imitate from one nation to the next). Thus, there is endless and unavoidable circularity of founding the conventions and relations of which learning systems are composed, and of which the public institutions meant to generate them are built.

Learning Economies as Institutions: The Problem of Indivisibilities

The second major problem has to do with some of the difficulties of collective action identified by the modern political economy of institutions.[12] Institutions, as defined by such political economists, exist in cases where decision making is unavoidably interdependent. Unlike perfect markets, there is no possibility of fully dividing decisions from those of other agents. In terms of learning economies, this refers to cases of concrete relations, which in essence are forms of mutually specific assets, hence indivisible, as well as more classical cases of real, mutually specific assets in technology or capital; it could also refer to temporally interdependent decision making under conditions of uncertainty, a condition we have argued is pervasive in the learning economy. Indivisibilities, to different degrees and at different levels, are thus defining conditions of institutions, including learning systems.

But indivisibilities create all kinds of problems for actors, whether individuals or groups that are smaller than the whole.[13] In the terminology of neoclassical economics, indivisibilities in institutions make it difficult for agents to reveal their preferences in the standard way, through immediate entry and exit from a relation. If a relationship necessarily involves some minimal duration, interaction, or commitment, it may only be intact because it provides minuscule net benefits, or it may be intact because it provides colossal benefits. In any case, the standard measuring rod (revealed preference through price) is not applicable.[14] The implication for the establishment of institutions is very important. Major institutional changes usually require not only that new relationships be established, but that some existing ones be broken up, disrupted. Long-standing relationships are usually not measured in income statistics (or any other welfare statistic) because they fall beyond the measuring rod of money. One of the paradoxes of modern life—that what would appear to benefit the majority on average often meets with huge resistance from surprisingly high numbers of people and groups—seems less mysterious in light of this. To the extent that establishing or strengthening one set of institutions sacrifices other relationships, we can expect it to be very difficult, even if it appears to be clearly beneficial, "as a whole."

Indivisibilities also make it impossible to run traditional experiments, that is, those which yield clear information on cause-and-effect relationships. The conventional wisdom is that experiments fail because there are too many complicating interacting factors, too much "background noise." But it is not the absence of controlled experiments that is the problem (astronomers don't do experiments, but have a reliable understanding of stars, for example).

Rather, the difference is between those situations in which there are large numbers, and those in which there are "scant sets." Systems with indivisibilities and many factors are scant sets; in the case of complex socioeconomic systems, they contain only one member.

One kind of indivisibility is particularly relevant to the problem of institutionalization. Nonexclusive public goods exist when nonpurchasers cannot be excluded; so the "good" is collectively consumed, at least by the relevant population. This is "shared indivisibility." The other, more traditional case is akin to economies of scale, or what we might call "lumpy indivisibility." When a public good, such as a set of conventions, is nonexclusive and shared over the whole group that receives the good, any experiment must involve the whole group and is therefore quite costly. For the same reason, it is not divisible into units that can be counted or straightforwardly measured, and so its value is unknown. And shared indivisibility means, in effect, that there is only one collective "supplier" of the good (the government in the case of the formal institution, the whole social group in the case of the learning production system), and it is impossible to know whether there is an alternative supply that could be better.[15] This does not mean that we abandon analysis to description, but simply that in policy for such systems, it is impossible to know in a scientifically convincing way that what is proposed is reliable.

These problems, very considerable, exist when we try to build or change such indivisible systems. Moreover, soft public goods—webs of relations and conventions, whether externalized or organizational—are inherently harder to bring into being than hard public goods such as infrastructure, because the technical state of knowledge of them leads to uncertainty as to whether they will have any positive function at all. Bridges, airports, and schools are at least observable, contained (nonscant set) technological or bureaucratic systems. Learning economies, worlds of production, are not.

In this regard, indivisibilities mean that the "selection" environments in which evolution of technological and organizational systems takes place, may operate in perverse ways. What appear to be small parts of a system can have big effects on the whole, especially the possibility of blocking realization of a whole, where the other elements appear to be in place. Indivisibilities are frightening for policy.

BUILDING RELATIONS: PRECEDENT, TALK, AND CONFIDENCE

Precedent

Relations and conventions are recursive outcomes of precedents, which act as guides on action, are reinterpreted and reevaluated for their efficacy, and reproduced as conventions when they work to coordinate action under conditions of uncertainty. The problem is that if such precedents do not exist or are not adequate to the kind of learning system which is to be created, deliberate institutions to create them suffer from the circularity identified above. And a learning system is a complex organizational structure with many different actors and transactions between them, hence many different conventions and types of relations, built on precedents that are effectively indivisible, if the learning system is to work. It is probably no accident that considerable recent research reveals the cardinal importance of "soft" factors such as "civic culture,"[16] in the performance of democratic institutions, but that few venture any policy-oriented recommendations on how the lack of such a culture could be redressed. Very unorthodox policy strategies are needed in order to break out of these labyrinthine prisons. Two of these may be labeled, respectively, "talk" and "confidence."

Talk

The circular relation between public institutions and the institutionalized learning economy requires that the parties to public institutions somehow be convinced of the utility of having a public institution help in supporting the conventions and relations that make up the institutionalized learning economy. That is, they must share a convention of the utility of the public institution in some specific domain, before it can even get started. *Talk* between the parties may be one approach. Much has been said about the difference between institutions that function via a combination of loyalty and voice, versus those that rely on exit for adjustment and structure.[17] Talk is upstream of voice, in that there is no institution yet existing in which the channels for voice among loyal parties are already established.

Talk refers to communicative interaction, designed not simply to transmit information and relay preferences, but to achieve mutual understanding.[18] In the case of prospective learning, information from other experiences where learning has worked (on evolution of product markets, on suggested potentials for the parties at hand, given their current resources and skills) can be valuable as a stimulus, even though it cannot be represented as automatically useful or valid in other circumstances. Such information can, however, be used as the valid pretext for talk.

It can immediately be objected that if there is no tradition of communication or, worse, if there is distrust or antipathy, what is the possible basis for talk? The objection is important: it is difficult to stimulate talk, precisely because talk is not free: it takes time and effort, and payoffs are not evident, especially if the history of relations is bad, or relations are satisfactory for those already in them.[19] On the other hand, talk is cheap: it is not that costly and the risks are relatively low. Public institutions thus have a possibility of getting low-cost talk going. Talk alone, however, is unlikely to be sufficient if such fears exist; but rather than bribing the parties with incentives (or at least doing so in more than a temporary way), it would be better to offer them some sort of reinsurance,[20] a safety net (at least partial) for failure, forcing them to reveal the efficacity of talk and their propensity to have confidence. Finally, talk of the sort referred to here means intensive communicative interaction. Shallow contact will not do. Talk is more likely to get going if carried out in low-cost ways where *depth* is also possible (more on this shortly).

Confidence

Precedents that underpin conventions or relations inherently involve confidence, without which single events would be just that, and would have no impact on future expectations. Insofar as conventions and relations involve expectations about how others will interact with you in situations that involve some uncertainty, such confidence involves a measure of vulnerability: it is necessary for interacting agents to place themselves in a position where, should the other not follow precedent, they will suffer a real loss.[21] To have confidence in what others will do is, in this sense, to trust them; not in the metaphysical sense, but in the analytical sense of making oneself vulnerable, on the basis of confidence in the precedent. But how to establish such confidence so as to bring into being precedent, relation, and convention, where they do not exist, or worse where there are histories of mistrust, broken promises, and antagonisms?

Talk may involve the parties in getting the ball rolling on a learning project, but it does not establish confidence in the specific sense that generates precedent and convention. Bribery through special material incentives (subsidies, etc) provided by a public institution to private actors is likely to work only as long as the incentives last; if all actors calculate that the other actors only do what they do because of special incentives, then a convention based on incentives is established and with it, the possibility of lock-in to subsidy. Therefore, if the intention of a policy is to establish learning conventions that are not dependent on permanent subsidies, other approaches will have to be tried, or early incentives will have to be slowly replaced with precedents in other, nonsubsidized forms of making oneself vulnerable.

One method of creating confidence in a sea of nonconfidence is, of course, bureaucracy (hierarchy).[22] It has been found, in economic policy making, that certain projects are amenable to isolation from the overall economic culture, by internalizing them within hierarchical bureaucracies. The military is the model. Defense procurement in the United States, or major indivisible high-technology projects such as the French high-speed train, are carried out by quasimilitary bureaucracies with strong financial incentives and command-and-control authority. But internalization is not a solution for much of the learning economy, precisely because of the openendedness and high degree of risk of much learning, which nobody in society wants to pay to internalize, and where the technological character of the product does not permit near-monopoly (scale economies, extreme indivisibilities).[23] Some other method of building confidence must be used.

Small, repeated, experimental interactions may be useful for this purpose. Experimentation, as a policy device, means actually setting the parties to work in limited relations that facilitate learning and attempting to build up in complexity. It does not mean trying to prove the utility of any general, abstract solution. Most importantly, such experiments must proceed "as if" confidence existed. Small experiments build on the communicative understanding that comes from talk, asking the parties to interact by suspending their fears and doubts. The likelihood of getting the parties to act *as if* confidence existed, as the first step toward establishing real precedents, should logically rise with the degree of knowledge they have about each other. Depth is one dimension: the more I know about you in a specific domain; but breadth is another: the more I know about you in general, through collateral forms of information, the more I will be willing to enter into deep contact. These include: risks of collective sanctions for violating the terms of a relation; reputation effects due to rich information flows; cultural proximity, behavioral norms that shape the anticipations of agents; and frequency of contacts in and outside of the particular business context.[24] Attention has also been called to "institutional thickness" — multiple, partially overlapping, and partially redundant institutions — as a basis for breadth.[25]

Depth has a complicated geography, in that professional interactions, in some cases, have channels involving strong specific long-distance relations and weak local ones, above all in specialized or highly formalized (cosmopolitan) professions. Still, even in such circles, local relations often involve forms of depth not achieved in long-distance, infrequent contacts. Breadth has a more uniformly localist dimension: we are more likely to have information on someone's reputation and to be able to validate it by interpreting it against a context with which we are intimately familiar, in a local context.[26] There is thus some relationship between localness and the mutual knowledge that should allow parties to act as if confidence existed, as a first step toward generating precedent. Talk and confidence—depth aided by confidence due to breadth—while not the province of the locality, are in some cases (certain products, certain worlds of production) more likely to succeed when they are geographically localized. This is not a hard and fast rule, of course, and much more theory and evidence is needed before these relationships can be understood in a policy-relevant fashion.

THE DIMENSIONS OF POLICY

There are many intricate dimensions of talk and confidence building as the vehicles for creating precedent, relation, and convention. Who should talk? What they should talk about? What techniques should be used to facilitate such talk? What small relations should be attempted first? What kind of encouragements should be offered to get the parties to suspend skepticism? The answers will vary not only according to the kind of world that talk is intended to get started, but also according to the starting point of the parties. Some very modest beginnings will be attempted in this section.

Starting Points: Strategic Assessment

It has long been standard practice in industrial policies to carry out strategic assessments of local, regional, or national possibilities (depending on the policy's target). The idea is to eliminate unreasonable goals by assessing the existing state of such factors as technological level, the labor market, infrastructure, market structure, and so on. Such analyses, in practice, vary greatly in quality, and unfortunately there is a high propensity for error, especially excessive optimism (since the assessments are usually paid for by agencies with a vested interest in being in the policy business). Critics of industrial policy claim that this is inherent to such policies, but blanket skepticism is unwarranted, since there are also examples of excellent strategic assessments having led to wise decisions (examples include French high-speed trains, numerical controls developed by the U.S. Army, and the Japanese semiconductor industry as guided by MITI's strategic plan).[27]

Simplifying, we can say that in the 1960s it was possible for many European countries to carry out strategic assessment based on a standard factor input-cost method. The question to be answered was: what factor inputs do we need to create, so as to be combined into an industry at something close to world best practice, and how much will it cost in the national context? In the context of rapid world, and especially European, economic expansion, the main consideration for efficiency was simply to assess whether the industry could find a market enabling it to enjoy optimal scale economies, and in that context, to implement state-of-the-art production technology. Oftentimes, *filière* (commodity chain) analysis was applied to maximize the "local content" of the target industry in the national or regional space.[28]

The demands placed on strategic assessment in the context of the learning economy have become vastly more complex than in the 1960s, but the techniques of assessment have not caught up. It would no longer be possible, for example, to use the same method the French employed to plan Fos-sur-Mer today, because world capacity in virtually every major sector is much closer to saturation, and there is no comfortable time lag during which policy can simply copy the best of what is being done elsewhere. The Brazilians learned this with their market protection law for computers; though it had some considerable positive effects, it failed to encourage competitive computer making in that country, leaving them generations behind the state of the art.[29] Any strategic assessment carried out today must use the existing starting point for the economy in question, but the goal of the policy has to be somehow to catch up to a moving target, a target that will move during the period in which the policy is getting started.

The Product as the Central Unit of Reasoning

Strategic assessment has characteristically been organized around the concept of sector: can we build a computer *industry* or a shipbuilding *industry*? The advent of the learning economy means that standard sectoral–*filière* assessments are no longer adequate to the task. Competition via learning takes place around real products, which do not correspond necessarily to industries–*filières*. The majority of output of our economies is intermediate goods, and social and spatial divisions of labor create all manner of organizational clusters in the economy which do not correspond to final-output sectors, or even to the grand (and now crude) distinctions between consumer and producer goods. Some of the most significant such clusters have to do with cognate intermediate products that go to very different final-output sectors; they also have to do with products that have little concrete resemblance to each other but have parallel or convergent technological trajectories, or technological complementarities.

The upshot is that the principal unit of assessment has to be the product or a technological space of products (the latter defined by spillovers, complementarities, and evolutionary dynamics). This does not mean that traditional sectoral analysis is ignored. Success in a given product generally depends on the existence of a production system that extends upstream and downstream of that product in a *filière*, or spills over to complementary technological spaces; but this is, from an industrial policy perspective, a tactic appropriate in some cases, not a universal goal.[30]

Strategic assessment has to include assessment of the worlds of action that are to be brought about, to which talk and confidence building, as means to establish precedent, are to be applied. The assessment, while depending on expertise, however, cannot be left entirely to the experts. By definition, the talk to which we refer in the previous section can have no hope of setting conventions and relations into motion if it is a mere pretext for ratifying judgments already made by technocrats. Not only is it likely that talk will reveal information to which technocrats otherwise have no access, but it is key to avoiding the circularity problem, where those who talk know that they are talking about something that has already been decided.

Developmental Starting Points

Countries and regions have different starting points: the size of the market; the current technological, infrastructural, and knowledge endowments of the society and economy; the generic image of the country or region; underlying relationships between groups and especially between organized interests; the existing stock of firms and interlinkages between them; and the nature and effectiveness of public administration. Three standard approaches to starting points can be viewed with extreme caution in light of the analysis advanced here.

The first is to reason in terms of grand categories of starting points, the principal ones of which are: big wealthy technologically endowed regions/ countries; small, wealthy, technologically endowed places; big, less-developed or latecomer countries; small, less-developed or latecomer countries; and, underdeveloped/poor countries, regions. These categories have some descriptive utility, but they do not lead anywhere in particular with respect to strategies for product-based technological learning. Their principal categories—size and technology endowments—are most relevant to big, capital- and technology-intensive industries, but even there, many small, rich countries have apparently broken the size rule (Holland with Philips, Sweden with Ericsson) and many big countries have failed in spite of it (France with Thomson and Bull). They are instructive, but only up to a point.

The second, and preferable, approach is to reason in terms of broad categories of products. For products with low barriers to entry—mostly certain products in the Interpersonal or Market Worlds—the experiences of Italy and Germany may be guides. In the Italian cases, traditional skills were deployed in interpersonal industries, to serve a national market in the 1950s and early 1960s. That market was big and relatively fragmented.[31] Smaller countries do not have such big markets, however, and virtually all countries are more open to import competition today than was Italy in the early 1950s. The lesson is that such industries are likely to flourish only where: skills are good enough or highly focused enough that they can contribute something unique to the world market; they can serve a local or national market that is unsatisfied by imports or can do so in a way that passes the indifference test: higher local prices are compensated by better tailoring to local demand (but with open markets and media, the knife-edge problem is sharper and sharper); or where innovative institutional arrangements, such as specification subcontracting,[32] are used to link local producers to order-givers in a way that builds their skills and responsibilities.

For industries with high barriers to entry, whether because of traditional scale concerns or because of high investment in technology, the choice is a very stark one: either go all the way with a major technology policy designed to cover a technological space (for example, Airbus, the Japanese semiconductor policy, U.S. military procurement), or target particular subsectors that have potential for spillovers. It is likely that, in any country, big multinational partners will be necessary and substantial commitments of local resources over long time periods will be required. The only strategies likely to succeed in the latter case are those in which technological branching points (e.g., which model of high-definition television? which system for transmitting mobile telephone calls?) are at hand, and where the risk is taken to develop along one branch rather than another. The optimistic note for this strategic assessment process is that there is rarely a single best world practice for any group of products.[33] Entrants can define products and practices, and they can trace out developmental pathways that continue to redefine such products and practices.

The third approach to strategic assessment is to reason in terms of norms for countries, points toward which we want to move, away from the starting point. This leads to a developmental recipe, in terms of such things as capital institutions, technological infrastructure, political and administrative institutions, entrepreneurship, and so on, which, it is said, will bring about developmental results. This is quite wrong in two respects. One is that among the successful, rich countries and regions, a great diversity of products, and hence worlds of production and accompanying economic practices and institutions, exists. They do not all follow the same rules with respect to the provision of capital, skilling of the workforce, public administration, entrepreneurship, and so on.[34] Even within given sectors, there is a plurality of successful but different models. It is a gross oversimplification, except at the most abstract level (for example, honest versus corrupt public administration; schooling versus no schooling) to try to reduce the development process to a single set of general goals with respect to different starting points. The ending points will be different, too, according to the specialization of the learning economy to be created, and the worlds of production they embody.[35]

Those ending points are defined by assessing what kind of worlds are to be created, that is, the identities and capacities for action and coordination among the participants in the production system. A critical part of the strategic assessment of what is possible in a given time and place is, of course, talk. Technocrats may be able to offer suggestions to the talking parties based on the entry conditions we mentioned above, but they cannot substitute for talk among the parties who ultimately will have to "become" the collective actor of the world of production to be developed.

The New Heterodox Policy Framework

In recent years, the analysis of the economic performance of certain successful industrial systems has prompted inquiry into policies and institutions that could be used to institute such systems. A new heterodox policy framework has emerged. This framework, while having many branches, shares a number of features. It favors policies that are context sensitive, that is, interested in the embeddedness of industrial practices in specific contexts and regions, hence "bottom-up."[36] It is production systems oriented rather than firm oriented in its focus. It has a non-Cartesian element, one that accepts the diversity of underlying technological and institutional situations of different economies. In many ways, it appears well positioned with respect to the foregoing analysis. Key words that describe it include: networks, flexibility, decentralization, cooperation, research and development, human capital, technopoles, and training.

The policies are heterodox because of the kinds of public goods they would provide. In standard public-goods theory, "market failures" sometimes occur and when they do, public goods can be provided to rectify them. Such public goods must have economy-wide application, that is, they must be as *generic* as possible. The new theory also calls for policy to produce public goods, but allows that these goods may be *specific* to technological spaces: it is their developmental properties (evolution along trajectories through learning) that ultimately generalize (via spillovers and complementarities) their benefits to the wider economy and society. [37]

The Heterodox Framework versus Other Approaches

There is hardly consensus about this sort of policy framework. Opposed to it are those whose point of departure is the rapid global transfer and diffusion of certain forms of technology and knowledge (but see our analysis above of the hyperbole involved in many such claims), and the increasing costs (hence entry barriers) of carrying out cutting-edge innovation projects. Their vision is of global technology-based oligopolies in competition in which any national policy would have to reinforce the status of the nation's oligopolistic actors. For the United States, for example, this would mean weakening antitrust laws (which are deemed to have outlived their purpose), either in a soft version to promote collaboration (à la Sematech) or in a hard version, to promote concentration. Complementing this, some argue for neomercantilist trade policies. There may, in some cases, be a role for some such policies, a subject into which it is impossible to enter here. But there is little reason to believe that alone they would generate competitive technological learning and performance: the failures of concentration policy are well documented. Such failures often have to do with the absence of links between the resulting giant firms upstream to an effective national system of innovation and downstream to an effective production community. At most, such strategies can play a limited role in the learning economy; and in some cases they may be harmful. The heterodox policy approach is quite the opposite in that it accepts as a given the openness of the trading system, the insufficiency of size alone, and in some cases, the disadvantages of concentration for competitive learning.

Another approach to policy is that of strengthening systems of innovation (SI), as we discussed in Chapter 5.[38] SI is a heterodox neoinstitutionalist approach to technological innovation. There are many different versions of SI extant at the present time. Almost all (except that of Lundvall[39]) share an emphasis on formal institutions, on scientific–engineering skills, and on the national level of formal institution building. The major nonpublic institutions are firms and research laboratories; the major public ones are universities, government laboratories and procurement programs, and technical education. The heterodox approach differs from the SI approach in emphasis, although they are not in contradiction. The emphasis here is on: the plurality of worlds of production and innovation (science and engineering is only a part of the problem); "small" processes of coordination via convention and relations; the circularity of conventions, relations, and institutions; and hence the necessity for a significant mesoeconomic dimension to policy as well as a systematic national level.

THE DANGERS OF ORTHODOXY

The policy approach described above, like any set of measures that attempts to take a complex analysis of economic reality and create a policy formula based on it, runs the danger of missing its target. An example from an earlier period with a different policy framework may help to understand this point. In the 1950s and 1960s, a theoretical analysis of industrial complexes was used as the theoretical justification for growth-pole strategies in many countries. The results were impressive in certain cases, at the national level (e.g., French industrial planning in the late 1950s), but were almost total failures at the regional level in all places. Later on, growth-pole policies failed at the national level in most developing countries.

These failures were not simply because the external environment changed. There were intellectual flaws in the way growth-pole theory was turned into a formula for policy. There was a technical flaw. Growth poles, as derived from Perroux, were defined as economic spaces (sets of activities linked by dense input–output relations, where stimulating downstream activities would reverberate upstream through a multiplier effect). Perroux was very clear that his intention was to identify economic spaces and not territorial spaces; he actually wanted to break up old regional economies in France in favor of national economic integration. Growth-pole policies, however, frequently transformed these economic spaces into territorial spaces by assuming that input–output linkages could be contained within national or regional spaces. This worked, to some extent, at the national level, when markets were protected (e.g. as in many developing countries using import-substitution regulations). It failed utterly at the regional level, however, because many such input–output relations are not necessarily relations of proximity (installing a downstream activity does not induce upstream development in the same territory). The policy makers, in other words, took a theory and applied it in a technically flawed way, sometimes with disastrous results.

Another and more important flaw was substantive rather than technical. Growth-pole policies often forgot about the heart and soul of the growth-pole theory. Even more clearly than Perroux, the development economists (especially the ECLA School and the Brazilians) understood that the core of any development process was the mastery of technology. Policymakers nonetheless implemented growth poles as if they were merely complexes of input–output relations, somehow assuming that the technological level of a region or a nation could be raised by giving it hardware. This turned out not to be true: one-time advantages most often did not turn into long-term competitiveness.

In order to avoid similar problems in the transformation of the current analysis into policy, both technical and substantive reductionisms must be avoided. This analysis of learning is not inherently about small firms, networking, localism, or flexibility per se; it is rather about adaptive technological learning in a territorial context. The proper goals of such policies are:

- For traditional or small-scale intermediate products, ongoing adaptation of products and processes, especially through product differentiation or moves up the price–quality curve, so as to respond to ongoing and inevitable entry by competitors, whether large firms or other regional systems.
- For scale-intensive or new technology products, moves along the technological frontier, where that frontier is unknown or unknowable. The substantive thrust of any policy must be geared to these substantive goals, as specified in light of particular products and their worlds of production to be developed. New economic institutions and practices are only means to these ends.

The real danger exists, as theory now becomes packaged into policy, that such policies will become detached from this substantive content and necessary procedure of building convention, and instead devolve into mechanical formulas and self-referential content. Three particular tendencies are worrisome.

From Framework to Formula

Networking is now frequently discussed in policy literature as a sort of recipe for any form of communication between firms. This has no necessary relation to the precise conventional forms of interfirm relations that underlie successful worlds of production. Networking has to be a means to realizing a common developmental pathway characterized by learning. The content and shape of a network, as well as the degree of external network, will differ according to the products to be made and the specific way productive activity becomes a world of production.

The provision of *services to firms*, in substantive terms, represents a strong departure from traditional public goods provision. In the latter, public goods are provided where markets fail, due to the free-rider problems that come when such goods are nonexclusive. As a result, public goods are provided that have nonspecific assets: they are nonexclusive. But the provision of concrete, real services to real worlds of production involves public goods with asset specificities and, hence, a certain measure of exclusivity. It will not do to disguise service centers as mere providers of any old, generic public goods, and yet this is the tendency in the literature. Another danger is that service provision will be turned into a pretext for doing almost anything that supports local firms with no substantive criteria for assessing the purpose of these services. Indeed, some services can have perverse effects. Modernization services, for example, can be used by some firms to distance themselves from local competitors and thereby to "exit" from their local interdependencies. Many technological extension services are premised on the principle of survival of the fittest, not collective learning. Initially positive effects can then be followed by catastrophe (for example, the French *plan textile*). Services for learning, in other words, only work when the goal is clear and when the services are consistent with the conventions of the world of production to be assisted, as understood by the participants themselves through talk.

Perhaps the most pernicious element of the current policy debate is the category of *small firms* as a goal. Small firms do play essential roles in many successful worlds of production. But smallness is not a goal, nor is there necessarily any commonality among firms merely because they are small. A small firm in a high-technology industry, whose products are evaluated according to their scientific–technological content, has virtually nothing to do with a small-firm subcontractor to a major garment producer: their underlying conventions of work, product markets, interfirm relations, etc. are totally different.

Finally, the category of *localism* has become important in the heterodox framework, because of its theoretical recognition of the agglomeration and territorial embeddedness or specificity of conventions in many learning-based production systems. The problem is that localism cannot be an end in itself: the territoriality of relations that go into learning is, in all cases, highly complex. If the strength of a particular local economy (one that corresponds to the jurisdictions of public institutions) is to be promoted, it is better to focus on learning and its conventional underpinnings than directly on localism. At its worst, localism could lead to an artificial closing off of the production system, reducing its flexibility and hindering the development of conventions that go beyond local borders but ultimately strengthen the local economy.

The Dangers of Cooperation

Nowhere is the danger greater than in the sudden stress on "cooperation" as a key to world-class economic performance. Cooperation was, correctly, discovered as a dimension of certain kinds of highly successful industrial systems, principally in Italy and Germany, and its discovery has prompted a necessary corrective to the stress on competitive atomistic interaction of most economic thinking. But it is fully contradictory with the notions of sectoral diversity and the plurality of ways of successfully organizing modern production (the plurality of "worlds" in other words) to hold up cooperation as a model for behavior in all cases. There are worlds of production where particular, conventionally rooted forms of cooperative coordination can be useful, but there is no general model of cooperation for all industries in all places.

Boilerplate Approaches to the Learning Economy

The transformation of this new heterodox thinking about economic development into an all-purpose formula is dangerous as well. Porter's[40] "diamond" of development is perhaps the best known and certainly the most widely employed of such policy formulas. The framework has two main problems. The first is that it is superficial: for the most part, it restates the obvious *outcomes* of success as observed in many places (the four points of the diamond). It then "reverse engineers" these outcomes, claiming that they were causes of success. But of course this does not follow. Attempting to create success by installing outcomes has always been the downfall of industrial policies; the fact that Porter has based his model on an admittedly more sophisticated analysis of real-world experiences does not prevent the result from being equally prone to failure. Second, by abstracting across a wide variety of cases, that is, preferring an extensive form of reasoning to an intensive one, it turns a great diversity of experiences into a single formula, with potentially great errors (for example, all success is based on high levels of domestic intrasectoral competition, etc.). The record already shows that "intangible factors play a central role in distinguishing cases of success in the new policy framework from dramatic failures."[41]

Scientism and Prescriptive Rationality[42]

Many of the problems described above stem from the tendency of analysts to seek determinate causes of industrial performance and for policymakers to extend that via prescriptive rationality. One of the greatest ironies observable at the present time is the transformation of an analysis explicitly inspired by "non-Cartesian" and "context and contingency sensitive" epistemologies into an all-purpose technocratic formula for development. The "architecture" of a production system and of public, organized institutions is only interesting insofar as it helps understand the frameworks of action that make production possible; the objects (technologies, tools, infrastructures) are themselves the outcomes of human practices and exist to facilitate such practices; rules, skills, and formal roles depend for their efficacity on the identities of agents. The problem with much policy-oriented analysis is that it tends to reduce its vision to architecture, objects, rules, skills, and roles, and to prescribe changes in them. Not only does this ignore the substantive object of analysis, but by attempting technocratically to prescribe behavior for the agents of the system, it has a high risk of failure.

The Entrepreneurial State: "Laboratories of Democracy"

The third great danger is that heterodoxy will be used as a pretext for a neo-conservative retreat of the national state from its appropriate duties, and the installation of a system of ferocious and destructive interregional competition. In recent years, the turn to the region in the United States was stimulated essentially by a retreat of the federal government from the economic development field. In a nation in which industrial and regional policy have always been quite weak by comparison to Western Europe, this left a policy vacuum that many states and localities attempted to fill. In some cases, small tentative steps toward the support of regionally based clusters of firms have been taken, and certain elements of the policy framework described above have been set into place. But in many of the American cases, they resemble only superficially the framework discussed here; instead, what has been done is to set up public-sector centers for delivering services to individual firms on a local basis (often "pay as you go"), where the collective and coordinative aspect of world building has no place in the effort. These "laboratories of democracy"[43] are often nothing more than effective privatization and atomization of industrial policy.[44] And recent federal programs, notably the Clinton Technology Policy, duplicate these problems by making federal resources available only via proposal-based interfirm competition.[45]

The attempted devolution and decentralization of industrial policy in certain areas of the European Union has a different starting point, of course. Many European nations have long had or activist policy frameworks and highly centralized states. It has become imperative to allow more initiative at the regional level. France, for good reason, is now more than a decade into her experiment with administrative and policy decentralization. Still, the results are mixed, in part because formal devolution of decision making does not in and of itself lead to the creation of capacities for action at the regional or local level.[46]

In the United States, a more worrisome form of localism in economic policy is known as the "entrepreneurial" state.[47] The locality and its governmental agencies are viewed as collective entrepreneurs in competition with each other. In practice, this often means simply attempting competitively to lower the price of labor, taxes, etc., so as to attract inward investment. But even when it involves such politically correct measures as stimulating firm start-ups, the ideology of interplace competition serves to block out any fruitful discussion of the need for higher levels of government to set certain ground rules (such as on interplace price competition) and to provide certain kinds of services (for example, national education policies, infrastructure, and other generic public goods). The danger exists that the European Union's principle of subsidiarity will be reduced to savage interplace price–cost competition.

This points out that subsidiarity in economic policy needs to have certain kinds of boundaries, and that what is to be built at subnational levels is not entrepreneurial states but what we might call—taking our cue from the East Asian development literature—"developmental states." These distinctly activist, strategically oriented, systematic state efforts differ entirely from the notion of state entrepreneurialism and are much more consistent with the analysis developed in this chapter.[48]

DRAWING THE THREADS TOGETHER

The preceding analysis can now be summarized. The institutions of the new economy consist of a complex circular relationship between specific, convention-bound, learning-oriented production systems—worlds of production—which are themselves institutions, and various kinds of formal, organized institutions, notably firms, public governmental institutions, and other organizations such as universities, unions, and trade associations. Any policy framework that involves the creation of public institutions to build or sustain the institution of the learning economy has to be based on ways to cut into this circle, and must reject the traditional logic of "public = institution" versus "private = noninstitution."

We identified four major steps in the economic strategy in the new economy. The first is strategic assessment. The technical dimension is the determination of what kinds of products, where the product is the essential unit of analysis, and not the sector or the input–output system, are susceptible to being mastered in the economy at hand, where mastery is defined as ongoing competitive technological learning. There is a complex interaction between the product as a technology—a knowledge field—and its associated process technology. Just as products evolve through learning, so do processes, and both have dynamic parallels and complementarities that spill over their boundaries at a given moment.

However, strategic assessment is not only a technocratic task. Learning depends on the conventions that define collective identities of the actors in the production system by giving them access to a common context of coordination. Without this context, learning will fail, no matter how good the hardware is. The context cannot be produced by plans, nor bought by subsidies; in order to know whether the strategy is possible, it has to be known whether there is any reason to expect actors to go along. The circular relationship described here can only be broken into by talk. Talk is a necessary element in, and component of, strategic assessment.

The second step is the definition of the capacities for action and identities of actors that are associated with the world(s) of production to be assisted by policy. Each world—a specific, local or national concretization of interpersonal, market, intellectual, or industrial action and coordination—involves conventions, which coordinate interfirm relations, markets, and labor markets. These are the substantive goals, the specific (and differentiated) end points of policy. They, too, can only be defined through the difficult and clumsy exercise of talk, in concert with analysis.

The third step is the implementation of specific versions of heterodox mesoeconomic policies, whose content is defined by combination of technical assessment and social process, especially talk. The substantive method of heterodox policies is not to attempt the construction of learning-based worlds of production from whole cloth, but rather to try to create precedents that build confidence and hence make possible the deepening and widening of conventions. Small experiments are one logical way to proceed.

Finally, and only at the end of this long and "soft" process, can the need for further formal institution building be realistically assessed and practically undertaken, the latter on the basis of confidence–precedent (and hopefully success in learning), and consequently emerging collective identities. There are other dimensions of formal institutions—those having to do with macrocompetition rules, banking, education, and so on—that are not considered in this analysis. They, too, require links to the substantive concerns elaborated here. For example, education policies in different countries favor very different kinds of economic action, and push them down different routes of specialization. Some decisions about institutional structures at these levels can be taken with respect to strictly generic concerns (universal values of the society; inputs to any kind of modern economic activity); but a surprising number involve more concrete visions of the particular kind of productive economy and collective action that is desired. Here we have merely laid out the fragments of this way of thinking about the problem—

the problem of constructing coherent conventions and frameworks of action in the learning economy.

NOTES

1. Leamer (1994).

2. Petit (1993).

3. This is the definition that was developed by the Berkeley Roundtable on the International Economy, for the U.S. Competitiveness Council. See, for example, Tyson (1987).

4. The appellation "learning economy" has considerable and important differences with other concepts applied to the "new economy" of the post-1970 period. Its central emphasis is on *time* in sustaining a desirable form of imperfect competition, characterized by ongoing product-based learning. It generates temporary non-substitutability (scarcity) of key inputs, especially labor and human relations. It should be stressed that the term learning as used henceforth refers specifically to product-based technological learning (PBTL). This definition stresses the usefulness of technological change in adapting the product, which is the principal vector of competition. Learning may enhance product differentiation at any given moment, or it may take the principal form of constantly adapting the configuration of products and processes so as to *anticipate* the competition. Such product adaptation may involve many upstream forms of technological change, but in and of themselves, unsystematic forms of technological change will not be adequate to generate competitiveness. PBTL is quite different—analytically speaking—from technological imitation in production processes (such modernization being the main subject of management literatures, even those that now use fashionable terms such as "learning," "knowledge," or "innovative").

5. Krugman (1990).

6. In recent years, the evolutionary school of economic thought has shown that firms have more latitude of decision making than is claimed by orthodox economic thought. There is a "loose" selection environment for disciplining those choices, not a perfectly tight optimizing mechanism of the market. So the firm is, in a sense, liberated to be a creative or satisficing agent. For an illustration of different approaches to profitability in the loose selection environment, see Chapter 4 of this book.

Our analysis complements that of evolutionary economics by showing that the firm copes with its "freedom" by using routines that permit it to reduce what would otherwise be an overwhelmingly complex, vast choice set. In the analysis advanced here, such routines are carried out in part by relational and conventional transactions, whether inside the firm or between the firm and its environment. The important theoretical point is that the firm, though freer in an economic sense than admitted by neoclassical analysis, can only proceed in reality by "binding" itself to the environment through CR transactions. Such CR binding redefines the firm's margin of maneuver in ways not imagined either by neoclassical economics, with its singular focus on markets, or evolutionary economics, with its focus on the firm. One dimension of the margin of maneuver is our second defining characteristic of learning systems: sets of CR transactions must be coherent; and this in turn implies that webs of CR transactions have qualities of indivisibility (see below for further discussion).

7. Storper and Salais (1997).

8. Sayer and Walker (1992).

9. We test this proposition that coherent sets of conventions exist in Storper and Salais (1997, Chap. 4).

10. Keohane (1993).

11. Wolfe (1994).

12. Over the past several decades, economists and political scientists have attempted to come up with a unified social science, applying mostly economic analysis to problems of collective action and institution formation. See, *inter alia*, Arrow (1951); North (1981); Olson (1971); Buchanan and Tullock (1965).

There are many problems with such a "positive political economy," notably its behavioral assumptions (rationality, individualism, exogenous preferences) and its inability to come to grips with the pervasive successful existence of institutions and collective action in reality, in the sense that we define them above as conventions and relations that work (see Storper and Salais, 1997, Chap. 13, for an extended discussion). But it has made significant advances in analyzing the difficulties of reconciling individual interests and the establishment of formal institutions: it has complemented traditional economic theories of why markets fail with newer analyses of why institutions tend to fail. In its concentration on the failures of public institutions, it has gotten something of a right-wing name, but this does not obviate some of the essential analytical lessons that can be drawn about the difficulty of establishing institutions, which are salient to the learning economy as institution. What follows is necessarily highly summary and too brief to do justice to the literature.

13. Olson (1990).

14. Olson (1990, p. 220).

15. Some of these problems do not apply to learning-based systems that exist in fact. In those systems, the actors caught up in concrete relations and conventions have passed entry tests, and hence are part of what is an exclusive or, at least, semi-exclusive group. Their social identities are as members of the indivisible collectivity. They may complain about what they perceive as problematical dimensions of the indivisible web in which they are caught, but the fact that they do not exit, and that the system continues to learn in an economically competitive way, implies that they are not willing to pay the costs of severing existing relations, abandoning existing conventions for the unknown.

16. Putnam (1992); Doeringer and Terkla (1990).

17. Hirschman (1970).

18. Lundvall (1990) relies in part on Habermas (1976).

19. Hirschman (1970).

20. Sabel (1993).

21. Lorenz (1992).

22. This is the basic assumption of modern transactions-cost economics; see note 2 above.

23. There is a detailed study of French successes and failures in Storper and Salais (1997, Chap. 6).

24. Haas-Lorenz (1994).

25. Amin and Thrift (1993).

26. In general, the literature treats the function of reputation as a form of cross-

check on behavior. It multiplies the probability of getting caught, and multiplies the consequences of getting caught. See the papers in Gambetta (1988).

27. Ergas (1992).

28. Salomon (1985).

29. Schmitz and Cassiolato (1992).

30. This is meant as a deliberate critique of the "diamond" found in Porter (1990).

31. Becattini (1975); and Nuti (1989).

32. Gereffi and Fonda (1992).

33. Even Porter (1990) admits this. See also Wade (1990).

34. As in Nelson (1993).

35. Zysman (1994).

36. Amin (1994).

37. I argue this point in greater detail in Storper (1995b); a similar argument may be found in Romer (1993a,b)

38. Nelson (1993).

39. Edquist and Lundvall (1993). See also Storper (1995b) and Weder and Grubel (1995).

40. Porter (1990).

41. Doeringer and Terkla (1990); Ettlinger (1994).

42. Amin (1994).

43. Osborne (1990).

44. Sternberg (1992).

45. Storper (1995b).

46. There is a detailed analysis of decentralization in Storper and Salais (1997, Chap. 11).

47. Maier (1994); Eisinger (1988).

48. Wade (1990).

CHAPTER 11

Conclusion

TECHNOLOGY, FIRM STRATEGIES, AND TERRITORIAL ORDER

TERRITORY AND ECONOMIC DEVELOPMENT AT THE END OF THE 20TH CENTURY

The preceding chapters have put territorially bounded economies in the "foreground" and the overall order into which they fit in the background, in an effort to concentrate on how territories are a central organizational level of contemporary capitalism. Now, it is necessary to speculate about how such territories are being articulated into a broader order, and some of the dilemmas this poses for the process of economic development. To do so, we first need to remind ourselves of some of the broad issues facing territories in the process of economic development today. We are going to view this issue by foregrounding one of the three parts of holy trinity—the firm—as an agent with great power to shape the relationships between territories.

This conclusion will be deliberately speculative in its tone, and it will sketch what is very complex subject matter very briefly, as a way of trying to sharpen certain questions that follow from the analysis offered in the preceding 10 chapters. What it loses in empirical detail it hopefully gains in ability to focus attention on certain key issues.

The Developmental Problematic: Technological Variety and Imitation

The problem of territorial economic development has been discussed from a number of standpoints in previous chapters. All are dependent on the central dynamic around which competition turns, and with it the mobilization of resources and possibility for accumulation of wealth. This dynamic is the *opening up and closing down of variety* in technologies and techniques. Firms try to open up variety in order to benefit from quasirents, and they imitate each other, and hence close down variety, in order to compress costs and open up their price–cost margins.

Variety is essentially closed down through one form of globalization, that of markets: through a combination of variety-reducing globalization of elements of products and local adaptation of products. Variety in techniques is reduced through an accelerated rate of technical diffusion and the resulting convergence of certain technical structures of production (though not of organizational structures).

Variety is opened through the sectoral and subsectoral (products or product groups) specializations of nations and regions, to which we have made frequent allusion in previous chapters. There is little tendency toward convergence in this area. Much international trade is interproduct technology trade, due to the existence of *absolute* advantages. To put it another way, "the geography of variety creation is highly variegated." There is also a kind of variety "inside" of the technical convergence referred to above: there is geographical specificity and differentiation in the absorption and diffusion of technologies, because the ability of systems of innovation to borrow remains highly variable. In addition, local adaptation of technology occurs, through the choice of technique. These latter two processes are responsible for an important share of the geographical distribution of intra- and interbranch *competitive* (Ricardian) advantage. Together, they are responsible for the structured conditions that drive big and small firms' behaviors in generating patterns of export and trade, whether between regions of the same country, or internationally (though only the latter is readily measurable).

Firm strategies are the way that firms carry out this opening and closing. Big firms have a variety of possible "models" by which they attempt to manage these two goals, in part due to sectoral specialization, but not entirely. There is real choice or margin of maneuver for firms, as we have pointed out in our analyses of the conventional bases of production organization and of efficiency.

This model used by a firm— essentially a cognitive representation of what the firm is to do—is subject to a complex interaction with the institutions found in the various territories in which the firm wishes to operate. There is much discussion in the literature about the order and degree of causality in the firms–territories interaction: do firms impose their wills, modifying territorial institutions, habits, and conventions as they wish? Or do the latter constrain, select, and shape how firms, especially the biggest ones, organize themselves? Previous chapters have suggested that there is some complex dance of mutual constraint and coevolution, where both firms and territories are subject to temporal and spatial path dependencies that are intertwined with each other.

What are the main empirical forms of such interactions which seem to be emerging today? To see this, we need to look at current firm strategies and emerging territorial orders, that is, ways in which territories meet the economic needs of firms.

FIRMS AND THEIR IMAGES OF THE ECONOMIC PROCESS

Most of the management literature is fond of the concept of "strategy," which is a managerial version of the economist's concept of "decisionmaking," in that it contains the notion of a series of microeconomic, rational decision parameters as its foundation; the management literature, however, deals more empirically and realistically with such things as markets and products. Sociologists emphasize the notion of organizational structure and dynamics, that is, the internal imperatives of the organization, as the basis for what it can undertake strategically.

It follows from the analysis in this book that we prefer something rather different, which draws from theories of action. As "constructivist" approaches in the sociology of organizations have suggested,[1] firms construct collective images, models, and conceptions, which both filter their possible responses to given decision parameters and integrate the ways they deal with these parameters by arranging them in some kind of order, in which a perfect optimum is neither attainable nor sought. This construction, in many ways, precedes such parameters by filtering information and determining interpretations of it. Such images are sedimented into conventions between actors and into networks, as has recently been suggested by actor–network theory.[2] External competitive conditions, in other words, are not decisive, as in standard economic models, because they are suggestive of what must be done.

In the contemporary era, there are three big key words that seem to figure prominently in the construction of "what must be done" by firms: flexibility, innovation, and some combination of involvement and coordination. They are all well known in the management literature. The first and third are the means to the second, we are told: in order to innovate, a firm must be flexible and it must involve and coordinate its central actors. Yet, flexibility and involvement/coordination are also said to coexist only with great difficulty, and sometimes thought to be mutually exclusive. This is why, in the academic literature on the subject of new models of firms and production systems,[3] these interrelations are oftentimes modeled as a sort of knife-edge equilibrium, a balancing act; the question then becomes how to find the balance point and stay on it. Do we privilege the management of uncertainty, or opt for staying power inside the market or in the external environment (for example, a market)? Thus, do we privilege flexibility in order to avoid lock-in, in the presence of rapidly shifting external conditions, or opt for long-term cumulative advantage and tolerate the potential costs of maintaining it even when conditions shift rapidly and cause us certain financial losses? The literature searches for the organizational structures that correspond to the point at which the firm wants to place itself on a function of tradeoffs: networks, partnerships, and other functional forms which are said to realize the right mixture and balance.[4] Since these are hard and complex tradeoffs to manage, and because there is sectoral variety, there are many possible constructions of how to compete, which have appeared recently in management practice and which, we shall suggest, have important and durable effects on territory, while also being bounded and constrained by what exists in territories.

There appear to be four major current models for dealing with these tradeoffs.[5] The first might be called Lean Management I.[6] The major goal of management is to avoid the risk associated with fixed costs; the principal method of so doing is subcontracting or buying out, where the lead firm retains control over intellectual property, trademarks, marketing, and sometimes, over final product preparation. The second can be called Lean Management II, wherein downward cost pressure is central to management as well. In this case, however, the firm may find certain obstacles to externalization.[7] These might include traditional reasons for not wanting to externalize, such as information asymmetries, problems with perfecting intellectual property, asset specificity, and the like, or may be due to the need of the firm to innovate in certain areas in which it must also continuously cut costs, something that is not always reconcilable with the kinds of contracts the firm would execute with external suppliers whose role it is to cut costs. Thus, the second form of lean management is the "performance-based, internally decentralized organization," where certain forms of internal autonomy are used to assign responsibility to internal operating units for meeting these, often very difficult, performance standards.

The next two firm strategies are fundamentally different from the lean models, in that their principal goal is not to cut costs, but to maximize the synergies of resources inside the firm, under the assumption that efficiency may come from something in addition to cost compression. In the case of Managed Coherence I, the firm is organized according to an internal matrix, which combines vertical coordination of major functions within the firm (research, production, etc.), but permits considerable regional "horizontal" autonomy to the divisions of the firm organized to serve different market areas. The firm's strategy is thus to enjoy considerable economies of scale along vertical lines, as a way of achieving both cost and organizational efficiencies in certain tasks, while allowing divisions to remain close to market needs, both in order to take the pulse of the market and to differentiate outputs for specific markets. Perhaps the strongest contrast with the first model (Lean Management I), where the firm minimizes its internal and external commitments, is Managed Coherence II, or what has been called the "communitarian" firm. The firm organizes itself to a great extent around an internal structure that is cemented by loyalty and long-term commitments, and an external supplier and partner structure that involves a certain degree of loyalty and reciprocity, in both economic and informational senses, between the members of the transactional network. The strong ties that bind both levels of the production system should be sufficiently flexible that they also permit redeployment for flexibility.[8]

Some theories claim that there is a determinate relationship between each model and certain kinds of products: a straightforward efficiency match between how the firm is organized and what kinds of products it makes. This would be consistent with transactions-cost economics, as well as with most of the contemporary institutional economics to which it has given rise. Lean Management I would be appropriate for consumer nondurables (buyer-driven commodity chains),[9] where the major goal of the firm is absorption of relatively standardized techniques that are widely diffused; Lean Management II would correspond to certain kinds of high technology and services, insofar as it allows for the creation of certain kinds of techniques and the diffusion of technologies and techniques already in existence); Managed Coherence I is said to be found largely in consumer durables with high fixed costs, high coordination requirements in the production system, and continuous adaptation; and Managed Coherence II in certain parts of the high-technology industries and services, that is, those where the main activity is to create new kinds of knowledge, new kinds of products. One can easily recognize in these management models, respectively, the Market World, a combination of Market and Industrial Worlds, the Industrial World, and a combination of Interpersonal and Intellectual Worlds.

The evidence on how each of these models performs with respect to innovation, risk aversion, and coping with various forms of uncertainty is quite mixed; in a given sector, we can often find firms following different models and there does not seem to be a one-to-one correspondence between the model adopted and the performance of the firm. Nonetheless, it seems that the two lean management models are becoming the dominant "metaconceptions" or metalanguages of firms, even when, paradoxically, those same firms in practice may rely in part on other principles (syncretisms of practices, in other words) according to their specific product mixes or other considerations.

Why are these two constructions emerging as the dominant points of reference for firms, and not managed coherence, or other possible constructions? Pierre Veltz[10] argues that much of this is due to something that has been totally ignored in the management and economics literature: a *deficit* of positive constructions about how to manage a complex organization under the economic conditions of the late 20th century. In other words, in spite of the thousands of books turned out by professors of management and business consultants, and studied in depth in the most prestigious business schools of the western world, firms have adopted a kind of *minimalist pragmatic* in their conceptions of what do do, a kind of failure to develop alternative, positive constructions about what is to be done.

There are many possible reasons for this, some of which have been the subject of discussion in the literature. It seems unlikely that these models simply emerged as the one, single, best and optimal solution to the "objective" problem of what is to be done. In contrast, some suggest that this minimalism is a construction that derives from Anglo–American economic thought. This may well be possible, in that the notion of a "science" of the firm and of management originated in that world. If so, then this particular construction of what the firm is and what it can do has been diffusing through mimetic behavior among the principal firms of the world, on the job between managers, and within the world of the professional intellectuals who train managers. This brings us directly to the specific territoriality of mimetic behavior in the generation of firm strategies today.

THE TERRITORIALITY OF FIRM STRATEGIES

Such global mimetic behavior with respect to this minimalist pragmatics is a force for convergence in how firms do what they do. But why the particular lean management model? It seems a logical extension of Veltz' proposition that, instead of a well-thought-out project of global liberalism on the part of firms, the international imitation and diffusion of minimalist firm pragmatics has become a standard, quite simply, in the absence of something better; a kind of default model. It may well be that the international think tanks have a project of global liberalism, but the world of firm strategies and that of global economic policy are only partially overlapping.

What was initially a construction, however, is likely now becoming a set of real, "objective" constraints on what firms can envisage doing, because it is becoming firmly inscribed, via convention, into so many "small" behaviors of managers and firms that it is coming to have external economies, and hence to be locked-in, as a feature of the external world in which any firm must operate. That is, the fact that so many firms and their managers expect to conduct themselves according to these principles is now a principal formative element of the environment in which any other firm must operate; hence, it becomes a self-fulfilling prophecy, via lock-in through external economies.

The Territorial Consequences of Firm Strategies

These external economies are not simply economic in nature; they are, to an important degree, territorial. The path dependencies of the firm's model are in many ways due to its territoriality, in the sense that the supply structure of territorial institutions and conventions—its relational assets—become part and parcel of how the firm operates. We can see this by looking at another set of stylized facts about territories today, several different ideal types of territory that correspond to the ideal-type firm strategies described above.

Firms that lack good models of the future—especially Lean Management I—tend to adopt an "exit model" of territorial behavior. *Such firms can only survive if there are territories that offer them conditions that correspond to their strategy.* Firms adopting these strategies have two principal sorts of territorial behavior. On the one hand, they seek the possibility of delocalization (relocation, disinvestment) without paying a strong price for exit, as in thinly populated regions that seek inward investment, as a condition of making such investments in the first place, or they download the responsibility for this onto their external suppliers and subcontractors. On the other hand, these firms, and their external suppliers, may locate in more densely developed regions, such as metropolitan agglomerations, seeking the flexibility and specialization advantages to be found in such economic systems, but these agglomerations will then tend to have a specific conventional and institutional character, a pure version of what we described as the Market World: the agglomeration becomes a massive turnover and risk-spreading system for making and breaking external links with other firms, where the law of large numbers is central. It conforms very much to the vision of transactions-cost economics, where the rule of behavior is moral hazard.[11]

At the opposite end of the spectrum of possible organizational forms of the territorial economy is the highly regulated territorial socioeconomy.[12] Huge costs are imposed on the firm's external flexibility, as when a firm hires, fires, invests or relocates. The economic rationale of this type of policy on the part of the state that carries it out is to force the firm to assume the full social costs of its decisions, either by making it compensate the state for the external (social) effects of what it does, or by encouraging the firm to internalize such effects (keep workers and redeploy them; reconvert production activities in situ, etc.) by making the penalties more onerous than the benefits of exit.

Vestiges of this sort of policy exist today, mostly in continental Europe. Major policy debates have taken place about the efficacy and appropriateness of this type of state–market relationship. Many governments—led first of all by the American and British, but now including many others—and international institutions have concluded that the fiscal and incentive policies of states must allow firms greater "flexibility," of which territorial and labor market entry and exit are key features.

Less recognized is that there is now a *scarcity* of firms who subscribe to a management model, such as the bounded-communitarian firm, which would be consistent with these state–market relations under current conditions. Although the policymakers and economists tend to emphasize the inherent flexibility-limiting nature of such state policies, in many ways they are simply reflecting the *lost art* of this style of management, the disappearance of such firm strategies. Communitarian firm strategies would have to have much longer time horizons than do lean management strategies; therefore, even if medium-term efficiencies of the two strategies could be similar (and there is much evidence that they can be, and even that communitarian strategies can surpass those of lean management), the short-term of the lean management approach will tend to drive out the medium term of communitarian strategies. That is, they will inflict such negative consequences on territories pursuing a highly regulated socioeconomy policy that these territories will, in all likelihood, reshape themselves to accommodate greater flexibility of entry and exit. The result is that highly regulated territorial socioeconomies are disappearing, as are the corresponding types of firm strategies. All the more striking is that, occasionally, leading corporate executives write articles or make speeches calling for a move in the direction of more structured territory–firm relationships, greater loyalty, and so on; and these same executives lament the impossibility of carrying out such strategies in a world that is now increasingly locked into the easy entry and exit model. The point, then, is that territories and firms coevolve and the problem for policy today is no longer to attempt to impose greater costs for entry and exit, but to work with firms to evolve a new sort of compatibility. In any case, such compatibility would not be the old policy of severe fiscal penalties for factor mobility, but something that would combine a certain degree of territorial loyalty with the flexibility necessary for innovation and adjustment, henceforth partially internalized at the territorial level. That is the next model.

A number of authors have studied political systems that provide actors with strong means of expressing needs and preferences without this being accomplished through the sanction of exit; in Hirschman's[13] terms, they combine voice and loyalty. Loyalty does not mean that there is no sanction of exit, whether from a given relationship or from the region, through disinvestment, but rather that this is not the first or the predominant way of doing things. Instead, there is a widely held convention, and procedural tools that accompany it, for expressing needs within some territorially identified community of economic actors and a tendency to use this as first recourse. In the field of regional economic development, these features are said to exist in systems such as those of NEC Italy, which we examined in Chapter 6.

The economics of such modes of participation are quite complex. Ideally, voice mechanisms permit a degree of flexibility that is otherwise only obtained through exit and entry, but with very different consequences, because voice is exercised by existing groups within the production community on their behalf. Thus, it is designed to permit them to adapt to changing circumstances, and to do so with staying power, without disintegrating. The problem, as is well known in the economic literature on institutions,[14] is that voice can also be used to protect positions and monopoly rents, creating institutional sclerosis. So voice and loyalty exist in a sort of knife-edge relationship to economic performance. Their performance is determined by the detailed kinds of conventions and institutional arrangements by which they are exercised.

Voice and loyalty, as the basis of a territorial political economy, must achieve some mix of quasi-internalization[15] of economic resources at the regional scale, unlike the communitarian model, which pushes for firms to internalize, or the exit model, which allows full externalization. Regional and sectoral institutions and conventions permit firms to be flexible by externalizing certain resources into the regional environment in a way that they are not lost. The counterpart, for the firm, is that it can quasiexternalize such resources into the regional environment. That is, firms can be open systems, but regional economies can be quasiopen systems, without firm openness creating intolerable social costs for the regional economy. Regional institutions for efficiently training and moving labor through a fluid interfirm regional environment, or for assisting firms to cooperate in innovation, or in diffusing techniques that come from outside, are examples of this strategy, in which firms participate in the operation of such institutions through voice, but in return can permit themselves greater loyalty to the region, because of the economic advantages created by these practices. We suggested some of the contours of such regional and sectoral institutions in the previous chapter. These are difficult sorts of institutions, conventions, and relations to create and maintain, as we point out in Chapter 10, but the economic and social benefits are considerable.

A TERRITORIAL ORDER BASED ON EXIT?

The first and last of these territorial types certainly exist today. The latter are often cited as exemplary cases of learning-based, socially balanced, regional economic development. The problem is that they are in relatively short supply. From the standpoint of the transnational firm, it is quite possible to use lean management as the overall model of how to operate, and simultaneously to enjoy the benefits of operating in both the first and third kinds of territory. The danger, then, is that the overall, dominant coevolutionary trajectory of firms and territorial economies is increasingly that of lean management and easy entry and exit territories. Therefore, the fact that learning-oriented regional success stories exist in a wider environment leads to a perverse result: in organizational terms, the proliferation of *lean learners*, and in territorial terms, a strong split between exit territories and voice-and-loyalty territories. *This is the new core-periphery pattern in economic geography.*

The paradox is that this may be far from optimal. For one, the abundance of territories that organize themselves for easy entry and exit—what Lynn Mytelka calls "locational tournaments"[16]—may permit firms to enjoy a kind of à la carte menu of cost-minimizing locations, and therefore may be fatally attractive to them. The recent case of Mercedes in Alabama, where total subsidies amounted to almost $400,000 per job, has put that state's public sector in financial peril, and has provoked a debate, even in the ultraliberal United States, about the need to set some ground rules for interterritorial competition.[17] But this geography may not even be optimal for firms themselves; the latter may simply be engaging in organizational and territorial mimetic behavior, and creating situations in which the territorial resources (conventions, relations, and institutions) no longer exist to do things any other way, in which moral hazard is the way of doing business and short-term cost compression by competitors in these environments "drives out" any other strategies before they can bear fruit. One can ask, for example, whether this emerging territorial order permits too much spatial fragmentation of firm operations, in which firms sacrifice advantages of proximity that would lead to other forms of efficiency, such as greater learning. It has, for example, been shown that the American military–industrial complex was constructed in the postwar period on the basis of a distinctive geography: the Gunbelt.[18] The geography of the Gunbelt—the Southwest and Pacific Coast of the United States—was largely politically generated, and it appears to have pulled apart (in geographical terms) the preexisting agglomerations of high-technology producers in the Northeast and Midwest, via the political geography of prime contracting. This not only had very severe economic effects on those communities; it may have resulted in an overall rate and direction of technological learning that was not optimal. If we generalize this lesson to the current era of economic competition between regions, sometimes at a world scale, it may behoove us to consider the erosion of certain proximity effects as a negative and unintended consequence of the emerging territorial order and its coevolutionary intertwinement with firm strategies.

This sort of outcome has a different evolutionary dynamic from the firm–territory interaction in the early postwar period. In the heyday of postwar growth, firms developed their management models and territorial policy had to supply, at national and regional levels, the missing resources needed by firms. This time around, firms may be victims of their own success in globalizing; their choices are now, for many kinds of production, so vast as to offer them an "out," the possibility of not developing more effective, positive strategies for dealing with learning and uncertainty. Here we return to the notion that many of them are engaging in minimalist firm pragmatics.

Hence, it cannot be said that lean learning firms are not "embedded" in territories, as is claimed in some of the literature. In light of what we have said above, there is a kind of territorial "embeddedness of nonembeddedness," that is, exit-based territorial development. What firms do is inherently tied up with what territories do, and vice-versa. Any analysis that sees this as a one-way relation is only analyzing half the picture: coevolution is the appropriate object of our attention.

One of the principal questions in economic geography today has to do with the frontier zone between agglomeration and dispersion. This is a complex theoretical and empirical area. It appears that certain forms of decentralization of industry are occurring, which weaken traditional agglomerative forces in certain industries; yet they are not classical processes of dispersion. On one hand, there are vast polycentric metropolitan tissues, such as Southern California, where the advantages of location may now spread over wide areas; and it may be possible that certain kinds of agglomeration economies are now more regional than they are local. In order to spread out within the metropolitan tissue, however, firms must make certain kinds of organizational adjustments: greater internalization than would otherwise be the case but not as much as if they were to quit the region altogether for a classic locational dispersion; or, perhaps, substitution of logistical efficiencies that permit them to operate linkages at metropolitan scale rather than local scale. On the other hand, some of these processes may be operating at the system-of-city level, where the linkages are now stretched between agglomerations at considerable distance from each other. In both these cases, firms are neither anchored as strongly as most of our stories of agglomeration economies would tend to suggest (there is more locational substitution possible), but nor are they as free as classical conceptions of dispersion would claim. They are a major new territorial "gray zone," a new borderland where specificities and flows are both operating, in varying measure. The margin of maneuver for firms and for territorial policies would have a different character in these places than in territorialized economies or flow economies. Indeed, in a speculative vein, it may be the case that certain rapidly growing metropolitan areas in the United States are gray zone economies, where some of the old rules about embeddedness and specificity are being bent in new directions, but not in the ways that flow economy theories would suggest.

To say that the emerging order is not optimal is not, by the same token, to claim that it cannot work. The absence of better territorial supply structures, such as those we argued for in the previous chapter, may be making for an increasingly lean world, but not necessarily one that cannot function. This is perhaps one of the most important large-scale collective action problems that faces the capitalist world at the end of the 20th century: how to create a territorial order in which the possibilities for social and economic development, which we know to exist in learning regions, are not mere islands floating in a sea of lean management and rapid entry and exit. The analysis presented in this book cautions very strongly against the belief that this problem can be resolved principally at the level of high-level policy interventions, such as international trade and investment rules, macroeconomic policy, and national labor-market policy. Appropriate reforms are certainly necessary in these areas in order to stem the damage from unlimited exit and generalized locational tournaments, but these reforms alone, without the painstaking work of developing, in tandem, the bases of conventions and relations of learning in regions and in firms, will fall flat. A territorial order that could assure the bases of sound economic and social development in the 21st century must therefore be built simultaneously and synergetically, from the bottom up, in firms and communities, and in the houses of parliament and international think tanks.

NOTES

1. Zucker (1987).
2. Callon (1992); Latour (1993).
3. Foray (1990); Best (1990).
4. Much the same has been said about territories and their institutions: how to get the right mix between flexibilty and what's needed for building up resources with long gestation periods, while keeping territorially bound externalities, which take a long time to build up, together.
5. I owe much of my thinking about firm models to my colleague, Pierre Veltz, Director of the LATTS Laboratory at the École des Ponts et Chaussées in France. He is, however, entirely absolved of responsibility for what follows. His recent book (Veltz, 1995) also has an extensive and somewhat different discussion of this issue.
6. There is, of course, a huge literature on "lean management," "hollowing out," and, more critically "lean and mean." See Harrison (1994).
7. See our earlier discussions of externalization in Chapters 1, 2, 3, and 5, drawing on the New Institutional Economics and the many reflections it has spawned in recent decades.
8. The reader will easily recognize certain economic models of the Japanese firm, as can be found in Dore (1987) or Aoki (1991).
9. Gereffi and Korzeniewicz (1994).
10. Veltz (1996).
11. This is also Veltz's argument for the contemporary Paris agglomeration as an economic system. A different analysis of the Paris region can be found in Storper and Salais (1997). This vision overlaps partly with that of the transactional agglomeration that is modeled in Scott (1988a, 1993).
12. For analysis of the territorialized socioeconomy, see Amin (1994). For socioeconomics in general, see the extensive new literature on this subject. Without using this terminology, much of the recent literature on industrial districts, industrial restructuring, and corporatism explores very much the same concerns.
13. Hirschman (1970).
14. North (1981); Olsen (1971); Moe (1987).
15. I believe that the lineage of this term comes from Aldo Enrietti's (1983) work on "quasiintegration." But I am looking at the problem not from the standpoint of the firm, but the region.
16. Mytelka (1996).
17. See, for example, the *International Herald Tribune*, Monday September 2, 1996, p. 1.
18. Markusen et al. (1991).

References

Aglietta, M. 1976. *A Theory of Capitalist Regulation*. London: New Left Books.

Albert, M. 1992. *Capitalismes contre Capitalismes*. Paris: Seuil.

Alt, J., and Schepsle, J., eds. 1990. *Perspectives on Positive Political Economy*. Cambridge, U.K.: Cambridge University Press.

Amendola, M., and Gaffard, J. L. 1990. *La Dynamique Economique de l'Innovation*. Paris: Economica.

Amendola, G., Guerrieri, P., and Padoan, P. C. 1992. "International Patterns of Technological Accumulation and Trade." *Journal of International and Comparative Economics 1:* 173–197.

Amin, A. 1994. "Socioeconomics, Democracy, and Economic Policy." Paper delivered to the Innis Centennial Conference, University of Toronto, September.

Amin, A., and Robbins, K. 1990. "Flexible Specialisation and Small Firms in Italy: Myths and Realities." In F. Pyke, G. Becattini, and W. Sengenberger, eds. *Industrial Districts and Inter-Firm Cooperation in Italy*. Geneva: ILO, pp. 185–219.

Amin, A., and Thrift, N. 1992. "Neo-Marshallian Nodes in Global Networks." *International Journal of Urban and Regional Research 16:* 571–587.

Amin, A., and Thrift, N. 1993. "Globalization, Institutional Thickness and Local Prospects." *Revue d'Economie Régionale et Urbaine 3:* 405–430.

Amin, A., and Thrift, N. 1994. "Institutional Issues for the European Regions: From Markets and Plans to Powers of Association." Paper delivered to the European Science Foundation RURE Program Conference, Rome, March.

Andersen, E. S. 1992. "Approaching National Systems of Innovation from the Production and Linkage Structure." In B. A. Lundvall, ed., *National Systems of Innovation*. London: Pinter, pp. 68–92.

Anderson, B. 1982. *Imagined Communities*. London: Verso.

Angel, D. P. 1989. "The Labor Market for Engineers in the U.S. Semiconductor Industry." *Economic Geography 65*(2): 99–112.

Angel, D. 1994. *Restructuring for Innovation: The Remaking of the U.S. Semiconductor Industry*. New York: Guilford Press.

Antonelli, C. 1987. "The Determinants of the Distribution of Innovative Activity in a Metropolitan Area: the Case of Turin." *Regional Studies 21*(2): 85–94.

Antonelli, C. 1995. *The Economics of Localized Technological Change and Industrial Dynamics*. Dordrecht, The Netherlands: Kluwer.

Aoki, M. 1989. *Information, Incentives and Bargaining in the Japanese Economy*., Stanford, CA: Stanford University Press.

Aoki, M., 1990. "Toward an Economic Model of the Japanese Firm." *Journal of Economic Literature 28*(1): 1–27.

Arato, J., and Cohen, A. 1992. *Civil Society and Political Theory*. Cambridge, MA: MIT Press.

Ardigo, A., and Donati, P. 1976. *Famiglia e Industrializzazione*. Milan: Franco Angeli.

Arrow, K. J. 1951. *Social Choice and Individual Values*. Cambridge U.K.: Cambridge University Press.

Arrow, K. J. 1962. "The Economic Implications of Learning by Doing." *Review of Economic Studies 29:* 155–173.

Arthur, W. B. 1989. "Competing Technologies, Increasing Returns and Lock-in by Historical Events." *Economic Journal 99:* 116–131.

Arthur, W. B., 1990a. "Positive Feedbacks in the Economy" *Scientific American*, February, 9–19.

Arthur, W. B. 1990b. "Silicon Valley Locational Clusters: When Do Increasing Returns Imply Monopoly?" *Mathematical Social Sciences 19:* 235–251.

Asanuma, B. 1989. "Manufacturer–Supplier Relationships in Japan and the Concept of Relation-Specific Skill." *Journal of the Japanese and International Economies 3:* 1–30.

Audretsch, D. B. and Vivarelli, M. 1994. "Small Firms and R&D Spillovers: Evidence from Italy." *Revue d'Economie Industrielle 67:* 225–238.

Axelrod, R., 1984. *The Evolution of Cooperation*. New York: Basic Books.

Aydalot, P., ed. 1986. *Milieux Innovateurs en Europe*. Paris: Presses Universitaires de France.

Aydalot, P., and Keeble, D., eds. 1988. *High Technology Industries and Innovative Environments: The European Experience*. London: Routledge.

Badaracco, J., Jr. 1988. "The Changing Form of the Corporation." In J. Meyer and J. Gustafson, eds., *The US Business Corporation: An Institution in Transition*. Cambridge, MA: Ballinger.

Bagnasco, A. 1977. *Tre Italie*. Bologna: Il Mulino.

Balestri, A. 1982. "Industrial Organization in the Manufacture of Fashion Goods: Prato, 1950–1980." University of Lancaster, MA thesis in Economics.

Balestri, A. 1991. *La Produzione di Impianti e Macchinari Tessile nell'Area Pratese*. Prato: Unione Industriale Pratese.

Ballance, R. H. 1987. *International Industry and Business: Structural Change, Industrial Policy and Industry Strategies*. London: Allen and Unwin.

Barbagli, M., Cappcchi, V. and Cobalti, A. 1988. *La Mobilità Sociale in Emilia Romagna*. Bologna: Il Mulino.

Barca, F. 1989. "Modèle de Spécialisation Flexible des PME et Ecart de Rémunération." In M. Maruani and C. Romani, eds., *La Flexibilité en Italie*. Paris: Syros, pp. 239–251.

Bass, S. 1993. "Growth Pole Theory and the Technopolis: Prelude to a Study of Japan's Technopolis Program." University of California at Los Angeles, seminar paper, urban planning.

Bass, S. J. 1995. "Creating High Technology Growth Poles: Science Park Development in Japan." University of California at Los Angeles, PhD proposal in regional development.

Baumont, C., and Huriot, J. M. 1995. "Effets d'Agglomeration, Economie Urbaine, et Economie Industrielle." Colloquium Industrial Dynamics, Territorial Dynamics, Toulouse.

Becattini, G. 1975. *Lo Sviluppo Economico della Toscana*. Florence: Guaraldi.

Becattini, G. 1978. "The Development of Light Industry in Tuscany: An Interpretation." *Economic Notes, Monte dei Paschi di Siena* 7(2–3): 107– 123.

Becattini, G., ed. 1987. *Mercato e Forze Locali.* Bologna: Il Mulino.

Becattini, G. 1989. "Riflessione sul Distretto Industriale Marshalliano come Concetto Socio-Economico." *Stato e Mercato 25:* 111–128.

Becattini, G. 1991. "Per una Lettura Sistematica dei Distretti Industriali Marshalliani." University of Florence, Deptartment of Economics, paper.

Beck, U. 1992. *Risk Society: Towards a New Modernity.* London: Sage.

Beck, U., Giddens, A., and Lash, S. 1994. *Reflexive Modernization.* Cambridge, MA: Polity Press.

Beije, P. 1991. "The Economic Arena for Management of Innovation Networks." Paper presented at the international seminar, "New Frontiers in Science and Engineering in a European Perspective," Paris, 27–29 May.

Belis-Bourgouignan, M. C., and Carrincazeaux, C. 1996. "Dynamique de Proximite dans les Processus d'Innovation: Une Analyse Sectorielle Comparative." Colloquium Industrial Dynamics, Spatial Dynamics, Toulouse, August.

Bellah, R., Madsen, R., Sullivan, W., Swidler, A., and Tipton, S. 1985. *Habits of the Heart: Individualism and Commitment in American Life.* Berkeley: University of California Press.

Bellandi, M. 1986. "The Marshallian Industrial District." Florence: University of Florence, Marshallian Studies #1.

Bellandi, M. 1989. "Capacità Innovativa Diffusa e Distretti Industriali." Florence: University of Florence, Deptartment of Economics, Marshallian Studies Series.

Bellandi, M. 1995. *Economie di Scala e Organizzazione Industriale.* Milan: Franco Angeli.

Bellandi, M., and Trigilia, C. 1990. "Come Cambia un Distretto Industriale: l'Industria Tessile di Prato." Florence: Universita degli Studi di Firenze, Economics, working paper.

Bellet, M. 1995. "Espace, Marché et Proximité: à Propos de Quelques Apports Récents." Paper delivered to conference on Industrial Dynamics, Territorial Dynamics, Toulouse.

Berardi, D., and Romagnoli, M. 1984. *L'area Pratese: Tra Crisi e Mutamento.* Prato: Consorzio Centro Studi.

Berger, S. 1981. "The Petite Bourgeoisie." In S. Berger and M. Piore eds., *Dualism and Discontinuity in Industrial Societies.* New York: Cambridge University Press.

Berger, P., and Luckman, T. 1966. *The Social Construction of Reality.* London: Allen Lane.

Best, M. 1990. *The New Competition: Institutions of Industrial Restructuring.* Cambridge, Polity Press.

Beyers, W. B. 1992. "Producer Services and Metropolitan Growth and Development." In E. S. Mills and J. F. McDonald, eds., *Sources of Metropolitan Growth.* New Brunswick, NJ: Center for Urban Policy Research.

Bianchi, P. 1992. "Levels of Policy and the Nature of Post-Fordist Competition." In M. Storper and A. J. Scott, eds., *Pathways to Industrialization and Regional Development.* London: Routledge, pp. 303–315.

Bianchi, P., Giordano, M. G., and Pasquini, F. 1988. "Industrial Policy in Italy at a Local Level." Paper presented to the Regional Science Association, 28th Regional Congress, Stockholm, August.

Bloch, R. 1993. "The Making of an Outer City: Industry, Culture and Land in Oakland County, Michigan." University of California at Los Angeles, PhD dissertation in Urban Planning.

Bluestone, B., and Harrison, B. 1982. *The Deindustrialization of America*. New York: Basic Books.

Boissonade, P. 1931. *Le socialisme de l'Etat*. Paris: Champion.

Boltanski, L., and Thevenot, L. 1991. *De la Justification*. Paris: Gallimard.

Bordogna, L. 1987. "Strategies of Flexibility: Enterprises, Trade Unions, Local Governments: The Case of Montedison Petrochemical Plan in Ferrara." Colloquium, New Technologies and New Forms of Industrial Relations, MIT Endicott House, February.

Bouba-Olga, O. 1995. "Changements Techniques et Territoires: Un Modèle Évolutionniste Spatialisé." Poitiers: University of Poitiers.

Boulianne, L. M., Decoutère, S., Bailly, M. S., Rey, M. 1995. "Services aux Entreprises et Structuration Urbaine: l'Exemple de la Suisse Romane." Paper presented to colloquium, Industrial Dynamics, Spatial Dynamics, Toulouse, 30 August.

Bourdieu, P. 1989. *La noblesse de l'Etat*. Paris: Minuit.

Bourdieu, P. and Delsaut, Y. 1975. "Le Couturier et Sa Griffe." *Actes de la Recherche en Sciences Sociales, 1:* 3–22.

Boyer, R. 1992. *La Théorie de la Régulation*. Paris: Economica.

Bramanti, A., Maggioni, M. 1994. "The Dynamics of Milieux: From Governance Structures to Network Analysis." Milan: Dynamis (Istituto di Ricerca sulla Dinamica dei Sistemi Economici, Milan), *5:* 32 pp.

Breheny, M. J. and McQuaid, R. 1988. *The Development of High Technology Industries: An International Survey*. London: Routledge.

Bridge (The). "Italian Textile Workers: Innovation and New Industrial Relations." Rome: The Bridge Association.

Brunet, R. 1986. *Le redeploiement industriel*. Montpellier: GIP/RECLUS.

Brusco, S. 1982. "The Emilian Model: Productive Decentralization and Social Integration." *Cambridge Journal of Economics 6:* 167–184.

Brusco, S., and Pezzini, M. 1990. "Small Scale Enterprise in the Ideology of the Italian Left." In G. Becattini and F. Pyke, eds., *Industrial Districts and Inter-Firm Cooperation in Italy*.

Brutti, P. 1990. "Industrial Districts: the Point of View of the Unions." ILO, Conference on Industrial Districts and Local Economic Regeneration, Geneva, 18–19 October.

Bucaille, A., and Beauregard, B. 1987. *PMI: Enjeux Régionaux et Internationaux*. Paris: Economica.

Buchanan, J., and Tullock, G. 1965. *The Calculus of Consent*. Ann Arbor: University of Michigan Press.

Bursi, T. 1982. *Il Settore Meccano-Ceramico nel Comprensorio della Ceramica: Struttura e Processo de Crescita*. Milan: Franco Angeli.

Bursi, T. 1989. *Piccola e Media Impresa e Politiche di Adattamento: Il Distretti della Maglieria di Carpi*. Milan: Franco Angeli.

Callon, M. 1986. "Eléments pour une Sociologie de la Traduction." *L'année Sociologique 36:* 169–208.

Callon, M. 1992. "Variété et Irréversibilité dans les Réseaux de Conception et d'Adoption des Techniques." In D. Foray and C. Freeman, eds. *Technologie et Richesse des Nations.* Paris: Economica, pp. 275–324.

Camagni, R., ed. 1991. *Innovation Networks: Spatial Perspectives.* London: Belhaven Press;

Cappecchi, V. 1990a. "L'industrializzazione a Bologna nel Novecento: Dagli Inizi del Secolo alla Fine della Seconda Guerra Mondiale." *Storia Illustrata di Bologna* 18/V, pp. 341–360.

Cappecchi, V. 1990b. "L'industrializzazione a Bologna nel Novecento: dal Secondo Dopoguerra ad Oggi." *Storia Illustrata di Bologna* 9/V, pp. 161–180.

Carboni, C. 1991. *Lavoro Informale ed Economia Diffusa: Costanti e Trasformazione Recenti.* Rome: Ed. Lavoro.

Carnoy, M. 1993. "Multinations in a Changing World Economy. Whither the Nation State?" In M. Carnoy, M. Castells, S. Cohen, and F. H. Cardoso, eds., *The New Global Economy in the Information Age.* University Park, PA: Pennsylvania State University Press, pp. 45–96.

Carroué, L. 1984. "l'Électronique Professionnel en Région Parisienne." *Analyse de l'Espace 3/4:* 22–44.

Castells, M. 1989. *The Informational City.* Oxford: Basil Blackwell.

Castells, M. 1992. "The Space of Flows: Elements of a Theory of Urbanism in the Informational Society." Princeton: Princeton Papers in Architecture.

Castillo, J. J., ed. 1991. "Neofordismo o Especialisacion Flexible? Las Pequeñas y Medianas Empresas en el Contexto Europeo." *Sociologia del Trabajo*, special issue, 257 pp.

Caves, R. 1982. *Multinational Enterprise and Economic Analysis.* Cambridge: Cambridge University Press.

Centre d'Etudes de l'Emploi, 1987. "Les entreprises et Leurs Produits." *Cahiers du Centre d'Etudes de l'Emploi, 30.*

Chandler, A. 1966. *Strategy and Structure: Chapters in the History of the Industrial Enterprise.* Cambridge, MA: MIT Press

Chandler, A. 1977. *The Visible Hand: the Managerial Revolution in American Business.* Cambridge, MA: Harvard University Press.

Chandler, C. 1995. "Electronic Communications Media, New Product Teams, and the Learning Economy." University of California at Los Angeles, paper prepared for course in regional development, spring.

Chesnais, F. 1994. *La Mondialisation du Capital.* Paris: Syros.

Choffel, P., Cuneo, P., and Kramarz, F. 1988. "Des Trajéctoires Marqués par la Structure de l'Entreprise." *Economie et Statistique 213*, September.

Christopherson, S., and Storper, M. 1986. "The City as Studio; the World as Back Lot: the Impacts of Vertical Disintegration on the Motion Picture Industry." *Society and Space 4*(3): 305–320.

Christopherson, S. and Storper, M. 1989. "The Effects of Flexible Specialization on Industrial Politics and the Labor Market: the Motion Picture Industry." *Industrial and Labor Relations Review 42*(3): 331–347.

Christopherson, S. 1994a. "Rules as Resources in Investment and Location Decisions." Paper presented at the Innis Centennial Conference University of Toronto, Toronto, September.

Christopherson, S. 1994b. "The Fortress City: Privatized Space, Consumer Citizenship." In A. Amin, ed., *Post Fordism: A Reader.* Oxford: Blackwell, pp. 409–427.

Coase, R. 1937. "The Nature of the Firm." *Economica 4:* 386–405.

Coffey, W., and Polese, M. 1987. "Intrafirm Trade in Business Services: Implications for the Location of Office-Based Activities." *Papers of the Regional Science Association 62:* 71–80.

Cohen, S., and Zysman, J. 1984. *Manufacturing Matters.* New York: Basic Books.

Cohendet, P., and Llerena, P. eds. 1989. *Flexibilité, Information, et Décision.* Paris: Economica.

Coleman, J. S. 1988. "Social Capital in the Creation of Human Capital." *American Journal of Sociology 94,* supplement S95–S120.

Coleman, J. R. 1990. *Foundations of Social Theory.* Cambridge, MA: Belknap Press of Harvard University.

Colombo, M. G., Mariotti, S., and Mutinelli, M. 1991. "The Internationalisation of the Italian Economy." Prepared for CEE-FAST, Dossier Prospective no. 2. Milan: Politecnico di Milano.

Cooke, P., and K. Morgan. 1990. *Learning through Networking: Regional Innovation and the Lessons of Baden-Wurttemburg.* Cardiff: University of Wales.

Cooke, P., and Morgan, K. 1991. "The Network Paradigm: New Departures in Corporate and Regional Development." Paper presented at international conference on Europe after Maastricht, Lemnos, Greece, 2–5 September.

Coriat, B. 1990. *l'Atelier et le Robot.* Paris: Christian Bourgois.

Coriat, B. 1991. *Penser à l'Envers.* Paris: Christian Bourgois.

Crozier, M., and Friedberg, E. 1977. *l'Acteur et le Système.* Paris: Seuil.

Cusumano, M. 1985. *The Japanese Automobile Industry.* Cambridge: Harvard University Press.

Daniels, P., ed. 1991. *Services and Metropolitan Development.* London: Routledge.

Daniels, P., and Moulaert, F. eds., 1991. *The Changing Geography of Advanced Producer Services.* London: Belhaven Press.

David, P. A. 1975. *Technical Choice, Innovation, and Economic Growth.* London: Cambridge University Press.

De Bandt, J., and Gadrey, J. 1994. *Relations de Marché, Relations de Services.* Paris: CNRS Editions.

De Bresson, C., and Amesse, F. 1991. "Networks of Innovators: A Review and Introduction to the Issue." *Research Policy 20:* 363–379

de Maria, R., and Scarpitti, L. 1992. " Networks, Industrial Districts, and their Socio-Economic Framework." Boulder, Colorado: Aspen Institute, 1–3 July.

de Vet, J. M. 1990. "Innovation and New Firm Formation in Southern California's Medical Device Industry." University of California at Los Angeles, Department of Geography, M.A. thesis.

de Vet, J. 1993. "Globalization and Local and Regional Competitiveness." *STI Review 13:* 89–121.

Debord, G. 1976. *La Société du Spectacle.* Paris: Editions Lebovici.

Decoutere, S., Boulianne, L., Bailly, A., Maillat, D., Rey, M, 1995. "Services aux Entreprises et Structuration Urbaine: l'Exemple de la Suisse Romande." Paper presented to the French Regional Science Conference, Toulouse, August.

Dei Ottati, G. 1987. "Distretto Industriale, Problemi della Transazione e Mercato Communitario: Prime Considerazione." *Economia e Politica Industriale 51:* 93–122.

Dei Ottati, G. 1990. "l'Agricoltura nel Distretto Pratese: Da Sostegno dello Sviluppo Industriale ad Attivita di Consumo." *La Questione Agraria 38:* 113–145.

Dei Ottati, G. 1991. "Prato: 1944–1963: Reconstruction and Transformation of a Local System of Production," In *La Toscana nel Secondo Dopoguerra*. Milan: Franco Angeli, pp. 155–171.

Dei Ottati, G. 1992. "Trust, Interlinking Transactions, and Credit in the Industrial District." *Cambridge Journal of Economics*, December.

del Monte, A., and Esposito, F. 1989. "Flexibility and Industrial Organization Theory." Paper prepared for the Conference, "Recent Developments in the Theory of Industrial Organization." Naples, 28–29 April.

Delaunay, J., and Gadrey, J. 1988. *Les Enjeux de la Société des Services*. Paris: Presses de la Fondation Nationale des Sciences Politiques.

Dertouzos, M., Lester, R., and Solow, R. 1990. *Made in America: Regaining the Competitive Edge*. Cambridge, MA: MIT Press.

di Lellio, A. 1987. "Changing Citizenship in 'High Tech' Communities: the Case of Dallas and Grenoble." Paper delivered to the International Sociological Association Conference on Technology, Restructuring and Urban–Regional Development, Dubrovnik, June.

Di Maggio, P. 1986. "Structural Analysis of Organizational Fields: A Block Model Approach." In B. Stand and L. Cummings, eds., *Research in Organizational Behavior 8*: pp. 335–370.

Di Maggio, P. 1991. "Constructing an Organizational Field as a Professional Project: US Art Museums, 1920–1940." In W. W. Powell, and P. DiMaggio, eds., *The New Institutionalism in Organizational Analysis*. Chicago: University of Chicago Press, pp. 267–292.

Dicken, P. 1988. *Global Shift: Industrial Change in a Turbulent World*. London: Chapman.

Djellal, F. and Gallouj, C. 1995. "Innovation et Développement Régional: Le Cas des Firmes de Conseil en Rechnologie d'Information." Paper presented to the French Regional Science Association Conference, Toulouse, August.

Doeringer, P., and Terkla, D. 1990. "How Intangible Features Contribute to Economic Development: Lessons from a Mature Local Economy." *World Development 18*: 1295–1308.

Dollar, D. 1986. "Technological Innovation, Capital Mobility, and the Product Cycle in North–South Trade." *American Economic Review 76*: 177–190.

Dore, R. 1987. *Flexible Rigidities*. Stanford: Stanford University Press.

Dosi, G. 1987. "Institutions and Markets in a Dynamic World." Brighton: SPRU Discussion Paper No. 32.

Dosi, G. 1988. "Sources, Procedures, and Microeconomic Effects of Innovation." *Journal of Economic Literature 25*: 1120–1171.

Dosi, G., and Orsenigo, L. 1985. "Order and Change: An Exploration of Markets, Institutions and Technology in Industrial Dynamics." Brighton: SPRU Discussion Paper No. 22.

Dosi, G., Pavitt, K., and Soete, L. 1991. *The Economics of Technical Change and International Trade*. New York: New York University Press.

Dosi, G. and Salvatore, R. 1992. "The Structure of Industrial Production and the Boundaries between Firms and Markets." In M. Storper and A. J. Scott, eds., *Pathways to Industrialization and Regional Development*. London: Routledge, pp. 171–193.

Douglas, P. H. 1976. "The Cobb–Douglas Production Function, Once Again: Its Testing, and Some New Empirical Values." *Journal of Political Economy 84*: 903–915.

Dubini, P. and Aldrich, H. 1991. "Personal and Extended Networks are Essential to the Entrepreneurial Process." *Journal of Business Venturing 6:* 305–313.

Dunning, J. H. 1979. "Explaining Changing Patterns of International Production: in Defense of the Eclectic Theory." *Oxford Bulletin of Economics and Statistics 41:* 269–295.

Dunning, J. H. 1988. *Multinationals, Technology, and Competitiveness.* London: Unwin Hyman.

Dunning, J. H. 1992. "The Global Economy, Domestic Governance Strategies, and Transnational Corporations: Interaction and Policy Implications." *Transnational Corporations 1*(3): 7–45, December.

Dupuy, C., and Gilly, J. P. eds. 1992. "Dynamique Industrielle, Dynamique Territoriale, et Stratégies des Groupes." Toulouse: Institut d'Economie Régionale de Toulouse.

Dupuy, C., and Gilly, J. P. 1995a. "Les Stratégies Territoriales des Grandes Groupes." In Rallet and Torre, eds., *Economie Industrielle et Economie Spatiale.* Paris: Economica, pp. 129–146.

Dupuy, C., and Gilly, J. P. 1995b. "Apprentissage Organisationnel et Dynamiques Territoriales: Une Nouvelle Approche des Rapports entre Groupes Industriels et Systemes Locaux d'Innovation." Colloquium Industrial Dynamics, Spatial Dynamics, Toulouse, August.

Edquist, C., and Lundvall, B.A. 1992. "Comparing the Danish and Swedish Systems of Innovation." In R. Nelson, ed., *National Systems of Innovation.* New York: Oxford, pp. 265–308.

Eisenger, P. 1988. *The Rise of the Entrepreneurial State.* Madison: University of Wisconsin Press.

Elster, J. 1984. *Ulysses and the Sirens.* New York: Cambridge University Press.

Enany, A. 1991. "The Biotechnology Complex in San Diego." University of California at Los Angeles, seminar paper in urban planning.

Enrietti, A. 1983. "Industria Automobilistica: La 'Quasi-Integrazione Verticale' come Modello Interpretativo dela Rapporti tra le Imprese." *Economia e Politica Industriale 38:* 39–72.

Ergas, H. 1992. "The Failures of Mission-Oriented Technology Policies." Paper delivered to the International Conference on Systems of Innovation, Bologna, October.

Ernste, H., and Jaeger, C. eds. 1989. *Information Society and Spatial Structure.* London: Belhaven.

Ettlinger, N. 1994. "The Localization of Development in Comparative Perspective." *Economic Geography 70*(2): 144–166.

Eymard-Duvernay, F. 1987. "Les entreprises et leurs modèles." *Cahiers du Centre d'Etudes de l'Emploi 30:* 5–27.

Fainstein, N., Fainstein, S., and Schwartz, A. 1987. "How New York Remained a Global City, 1940–87." In R. Beauregard, ed., *Atop the Urban Hierarchy.* New York: Rowman and Littlefield.

Favereau, O., 1993. "l'Incompltude N'Est Pas le Problème, C'est la Solution." Paper presented to colloquium on Limited Rationality and the Constitution of the Collective, Cerisy, France, June.

Favereau, O. 1994. "Règles, Organisation, et Apprentissage Collectif: Un Paradigme non Standard pour Trois théories Hétérodoxes." In A. Orlean, ed., *l'Analyse Économique des Conventions*. Paris: Presses Universitaires de France.

Feldman, M. 1993. "An Examination of the Geography of Innovation." *Industrial and Corporate Change 2*(3): 451–470.

Feldman, M., and Florida, R. 1994. "The Geographic Sources of Innovation: Technological Infrastructure and Product Innovation in the United States." *Annals of the Association of American Geographers 84*(2): 210–229.

Fishlow, A. 1965. *American Railroads and the Transformation of the Ante-Bellum Economy*. Cambridge, MA: Harvard University Press.

Foray, D. 1990. "The Secrets of Industry Are in the Air: Eléments pour un cadre d'analyse du Phénomène du Réseau d'Innovateurs." *Research Policy 20*(5): 393–405.

Forlai, L. and Bertini, S. 1989. *Evoluzione e Prospettive del Distretto Pratese*. Bologna: NOMISMA.

Frank, R., and Cook, P. J. 1995. *The Winner-Take-All Society*. New York: the Free Press.

Freeman, C. 1991. "Networks of Innovators: A Synthesis of Research Issues." *Research Policy 20:* 499–514

Friedmann, J. 1986. "The World City Hypothesis." *Development and Change 17*(1): 69–84.

Friedmann, J. 1993. "Where We Stand: A Decade of World City Research." Paper presented to the Conference on World Cities in a World System, Sterling, Virginia, 1–3 April.

Friedmann, J., and Wolff, G. 1982. "World City Formation: An Agenda for Research and Action." *International Journal of Urban and Regional Research 6*(3): 309–344.

Frobel, F., Heinrichs, J., and Kreye, O. 1980. *The New International Division of Labor*. New York: Cambridge University Press.

Fua, G. 1983. "Rural Industrialization in Later Developed Countries: the Case of Northeast and Central Italy." *Banca Nazionale del Lavoro Quarterly Review 147*, 351–377.

Fua, G. 1985. "Les Voies Diverses du Développement en Europe." *Annales Economies, Sociétés, Civilisations 3:* 579–603.

Fua, G., and Zacchia, C. eds. 1973. *Industrializzazione senza Fratture*. Bologna: Il Mulino.

Fujita, M., and Thisse, J. F. 1995. "Economic Geography: Old Problems and New Perspectives." Paris: Ecole Nationale des Ponts et Chaussées, CERAS, paper.

Furtado, C. 1963. *Formação Econômica do Brasil*. Brasilia: Universidade de Brasilia Editor.

Gadrey, J. 1994. "The Embeddedness of Service Products in Value Systems." *Journal of Socio-Economics 23*(3): 161–171.

Gaffard, J. L. 1990. "Sunk Costs and the Creation of Technology." OECD/TEP Conference on Technology and Competitiveness, Paris (La Vilette), 27–29 June.

Gambetta, D., ed. 1988. *Trust*. New York: Oxford University Press.

Ganne, B. 1992. "Industrial Development and Local Industrial Systems in Post-war France." In M. Storper and A. J. Scott, eds., *Pathways to Industrialization and Regional Development*. London: Routledge, pp. 216–229.

Gauthier, D. 1993. "The Aerospace Industry in Southern California between the Wars." University of California at Los Angeles: M.A. thesis.

Gereffi, G., and Fonda, S. 1992. "Regional Paths of Development." *Annual Review of Sociology 18:* 419–448.

Gereffi, G., and Korzeniewicz, M. eds. 1994. *Commodity Chains and Global Capitalism.* Westport, CT: Praeger.

Gerstenberger, N. 1990. "Reshaping Industrial Structures." OECD Colloquium, Technology-Employment Programme (TEP). Paris, June. (La Villette).

Gertler, M. 1988. "The Limits to Flexibility: Comments on the Post-Fordist Vision of Production and its Geography." *Transactions of the Institute of British Geographers 17:* 259–278.

Gertler, M. 1993. "Implementing Advanced Manufacturing Technologies in Mature Industrial Regions: Toward a Social Model of Technology Production." *Regional Studies 27*(7): 665–680.

Gertler, M. 1995. "Being There: Proximity, Organization and Culture in the Development and Adoption of Advanced Manufacturing Technologies." *Economic Geography 71:* 1–26.

Giddens, A. 1990. *The Consequences of Modernity.* Cambridge, MA: Polity Press.

Giddens, A. 1994. *Between Left and Right.* Cambridge, MA: Polity Press.

Giovannini, P. 1987. "La Società Toscana e le sue Trasformazioni." Florence: Istituto Gramsci Toscano, Verso una Riflessione sul Modello Toscano di Sviluppo. (Acts of a Seminar Held in Florence, April, pp. 31–52.)

Glasmeier, A. 1986. "The Structure, Location and Role of High Technology Industries in US Regional Development." Berkeley: Department of City and Regional Planning, Ph.D. dissertation.

Glickman, N. and Woodward, D. 1989. *The New Competitors: How Foreign Investors are Changing the US Economy.* New York: Basic Books.

Golich, V. 1992. "From Competition to Collaboration: The Challenge of Commercial-class Aircraft Manufacturing." *International Organization 46*(4), Autumn, 899–934.

Gollop, F., and Monahan, J. 1982. "From Homogeneity to Heterogeneity: an Index of Diversification." Washington DC: US Bureau of the Census.

Goncourt, E. de, 1982. *La Femme au XVIIIème Siècle.* Paris: Flammarion. (Originally published 1862)

Gordon, R. 1990. "Systèmes de Production, Réseaux Industriels, et Régions: Les Transformations dans l'Organisation Sociale et Spatiale de l'Innovation." *Révue d'Economie Industrielle 51:* 304–339.

Gore, C. 1984. *Regions in Question.* London: Methuen.

Gottman, J. 1989. "What are Cities Becoming the Centers of?" In R. Knight and G. Gappert, eds., *Cities in a Global Society.* Newbury Park, CA: Sage.

Grabher, G. 1993. "Rediscovering the Social in the Economics of Interfirm Relationships." In G. Grabher, ed., *The Embedded Firm.* London: Routledge.

Grandinetti, R., and Rullani, E. 1994. "Sunk Internationalisation: Small Firms and Global Knowledge." *Révue d'Economie Industrielle 67:* 255–280.

Granovetter, M. 1985. "Economic Action and Social Structure: the Problem of Embeddedness." *American Journal of Sociology 93*(3): 481–510.

Granovetter, M. 1988. "The Sociological and Economic Approaches to Labor Market Analysis: A Social Structural View." In G. Farkas and P. England, eds., *Industries, Firms and Jobs: Sociological and Economic Approaches.* New York, Plenum Press.

Greenaway, D., and Milner, C. 1986. *The Economics of Intra-Industry Trade.* Oxford: Basil Blackwell.

Griliches, Z. 1991. "The Search for R&D Spillovers." Cambridge, MA: NBER Working Papers #3768.

Grossman, G., and Helpman, E. 1991. *Innovation and Growth in the Global Economy.* Cambridge, MA: MIT Press.

Haas-Lorenz, S. 1994. "Apprentissage et Proximité Géographique dans une Perspective Évolutionniste." Doctoral thesis, Economics, University of Aix-Marseille, Aix-en-Provence.

Habermas, J. 1971. *Knowledge and Human Interests.* London: Heinemann.

Hakansson, H., ed. 1987. "Industrial Technological Development: A Network Approach." London: Croom Helm.

Hakansson, H. 1989. *Corporate Technological Behavior: Cooperation and Networks.* New York: Routledge.

Hakansson, H. 1994. "Economics of Technological Relationships." In O. Grandstrand, ed., *Economics of Technology.* Amsterdam: Elsevier Science pp. 253–270.

Hakansson, H., and Johanson, J. 1993. "The Network as a Governance Structure: Interfirm Cooperation beyond Markets and Hierarchies." In G. Grabher, ed., *The Embedded Firm.* London: Routledge, pp. 35–51.

Hampton, B. 1970. *History of the American Film Industry: From its Beginnings to 1931.* New York: Dover.

Harloe, M., and Fainstein, S. 1992. *Divided Cities.* Oxford: Blackwell.

Harrison, B. 1989. "Concentration without Centralization: the Changing Morphology of Small Firm Industrial Districts in the Third Italy." Paper presented to the International Symposium on Local Employment, National Institute of Employment and Social Research, Tokyo.

Harrison, B. 1994. *Lean and Mean: The Resurrection of Corporate Power in an Age of Flexibility.* New York: Basic Books.

Harrison, B., and Bluestone, B. 1991. *The Great U-Turn.* New York: Basic Books.

Hartz, L. 1955. *The Liberal Tradition in America.* New York: Harcourt, Brace.

Herrigel, G. 1995. *Reconceptualizing the Sources of German Industrial Power.* New York: Cambridge University Press.

Hickmann, R. 1989. "The Job Creation Process: Implications for Regional Economic Development." Paris: Report to the Ministry of Employment and Social Affairs.

Hill, R. 1989. "Comparing Transnational Production Systems: The Automobile Industry in the USA and Japan." *International Journal of Urban and Regional Research* *13*(3).

Hirsch, F. 1976. *Social Limits to Growth.* Cambridge, MA: Harvard University Press.

Hirschman, A.O. 1977. *The Passions and the Interests.* Princeton, NJ: Princeton University Press.

Hirschman, A. O. 1970. *Exit, Voice, and Loyalty: Responses to Decline in Firms, Organizations and States.* Cambridge: Harvard University Press.

Hirst, P., and Zeitlin, J., 1992. "Flexible Specialization versus Post-Fordism: Theory, Evidence, and Policy Implications." In M. Storper and A. J. Scott, eds., *Pathways to Industrialization and Regional Development.* London: Routledge, pp. 70–115.

Hodgson, G. M. 1988. *Economics and Institutions.* Cambridge, MA: Polity Press.

Hodgson, G. M. 1993. *Economics and Evolution.* New York: Cambridge University Press.

Holmes, J. 1992. "The Organization and Locational Structure of Production Subcontracting." In M. Scott and A. J. Storper, eds., *Pathways to Industrialization and Regional Development.* London: Routledge, pp. 80–106.

Hounshell, D. 1984. *The American System of Mass Production.* Baltimore: Johns Hopkins University Press.

Hyman, R., and Streeck, W., eds. 1988. *New Technologies and Industrial Relations.* Oxford: Basil Blackwell.

Hymer, S. 1976. *The International Operations of National Firms: A Study of Direct Foreign Investment.* Cambridge, MA: MIT Press.

Illeris, S. 1989. *Services and Regions in Europe.* Aldershot, U.K.: Avebury.

Jaffe, A. 1986. "Technological Opportunity and Spillovers of R&D: Evidence from Firms' Patents, Profits and Market Value." *American Economic Review 76:* 984–1001.

Jaffe, A. 1989. "Real Effects of Academic Research." *American Economic Review LXXIX:* 957–970.

Jaffe, A., Trachtenberg, M., Henderson, R. 1993. "Geographic Localization of Knowledge Spillovers as Evidenced by Patent Citations." *Quarterly Journal of Economics:* 577–598.

Jaikumar, R. 1986. "Post Industrial Manufacturing." *Harvard Business Review 113*(6): 69–76.

Jencks, C. 1993. *Rethinking Social Policy.* New York: Harper Perennial.

Joas, H. 1995. *The Creativity of Action.* Cambridge, MA: Polity Press.

Johansen, J., and Mattson, L. G. 1987. "Interorganizational Relations in Industrial Systems: A Network Approach Compared with the Transaction Cost Approach." *International Studies of Management and Organization XVII*(1): 34–48.

Jouvaud, M. 1995. "Localisation des Services aux Entreprises: Combinaisons des Facteurs et Types d'Activités." Paper presented to the French Regional Science Association Conference, Toulouse, August.

Julius, de A. 1990. *Global Companies and Public Policy.* London: Pinter.

Kaldor, N. 1970. "The Case for Regional Policies." *Scottish Journal of Political Economy 17*(3): 337–348.

Kaldor, N. 1972. "The Irrelevance of Equilibrium Economics." *Economic Journal 82:* 1237–1255.

Katz, J. 1994. *Seductions of Crime.* New York: Basic Books.

Katz, M. 1989. *The Undeserving Poor.* New York: Pantheon.

Katz, M. 1995. *Improving Poor People.* Princeton, NJ: Princeton University Press.

Kenney, M., and Florida, R. 1990. *The Breakthrough Illusion.* New York: Basic Books.

Kennedy, P. M. 1989. *The Rise and Fall of the Great Powers.* New York: Vintage.

Keohane, R. 1993. International Institutions: Two Approaches." In J. G. Ruggie, ed., *Multilateralism Matters: The Theory and Praxis of Institutional Form.* New York: Oxford.

Kertzer, D. 1984. *Family Life in Central Italy, 1880–1910: Sharecropping, Wage Labor, and Coresidence.* New Brunswick, NJ: Rutgers University Press.

Knight, F. 1921. *Risk, Uncertainty, and Profit.* New York: Augustus Kelley.

Kreps, D. 1990. "Corporate Culture and Economic Theory." In J. Alt and K. Shepsle, eds., *Perspectives on Positive Political Economy.* Cambridge, U.K.: Cambridge University Press.

Krugman, P. 1990. *Rethinking International Trade.* Cambridge, MA: MIT Press.

Krugman, P. 1991a. "History versus Expectations." *Quarterly Journal of Economics CVI*(2): 957–970.

Krugman, P. 1991b. "Increasing Returns and Economic Geography." *Journal of Political Economy 99*(3): 483–499.

Krugman, P. 1992. *Geography and Trade*. Cambridge, MA: MIT Press.

Krugman, P. 1995. *Development, Geography, and Economic Theory*. Cambridge, MA: MIT Press.

Lafay, G., and Herzog, C. 1989. *Commerce International: La Fin des Avantages Acquis*. Paris: Economica.

Landes, D. 1970. *The Unbound Prometheus*. London: Cambridge University Press.

Langlois, R. ed. 1993. *Economics as a Process*. Cambridge, U.K.: Cambridge University Press.

Lassini, A. 1985. *Gli Interventi Regionali per i Servizi alle Imprese*. Milan: Franco Angeli.

Latour, B. 1993. *We Have Never Been Modern*. Hemel Hempstead, U.K.: Harvester Wheatsheaf.

Latour, A. 1961. *Magiciens de la Mode*. Paris: Juilliard.

Lazerson, M. 1989. "A New Phoenix: the Return of the Putting-Out Mode of Production." ILO Workshop on Industrial Districts, Florence, April.

Lazerson, M. 1990. "Subcontracting in the Modena Knitwear Industry." In F. Pyke, G. Becattini, and W. Sengenberger, eds., *Industrial Districts and Interfirm Cooperation in Italy*. Geneva: ILO, pp. 108–133.

Leamer, E. 1994. "Third World Imports and the Unskilled in the West." University of California at Los Angeles, Conference on the World Trading System after the Uruguay Round, December.

Leborgne, D., and Lipietz, A. 1992. "Conceptual Fallacies and Open Issues in Post-Fordism." In M. Storper and A. J. Scott, eds., *Pathways to Industrialization and Regional Development*. London: Routledge, pp. 332–348.

Leborgne, D., and Lipietz, A. 1993. "New Technologies and New Modes of Regulation: Some Spatial Implications." *Environment and Planning D: Society and Space 6*: 263–280.

LeBras, H., and Todd, E. 1981. *Les Deux France*. Paris: Seuil.

Lecoq, B. 1993a. "Proximité et Rationalité Économique." *Révue d'Economie Régionale et Urbaine 3:* 469–488.

Lecoq, B. 1993b. "Dynamique industrielle, Histoire et Localisation: Alfred Marshall Révisité." *Révue Franaise d'Economie VIII*(4): 196–223.

Lefebvre, H. 1991. *The Production of Space*. Oxford: Blackwell.

Leontief, W. 1953. *Studies in the Structure of the American Economy*. New York: Oxford University Press.

Le Play, F. 1879. *Les Ouvriers Européens*. Tours: Mame.

Levinthal, D. A., and March, J. G. 1993. "The Myopia of Learning." *Strategic Management Journal 14:* 95–112.

Lewis, D. 1969. *Convention: A Philosophical Study*. Cambridge: Harvard University Press.

Liebenstein, H. 1976. *Beyond Economic Man: A New Foundation for Microeconomics*. Cambridge, MA: Harvard University Press.

Lipovetsky, G. 1987. "l'Empire de l'Éphémère: La Mode et Son Destin dans les Sociétés Modernes." Paris: Gallimard.

Llerena, P. 1993. "Décentralisation des Apprentissages, Théorie de la Firme et Evaluation." Paper presented to colloquium on Limitations of Rationality and Constitution of the Collective, Cerisy, France.

Lorenz, E.1984. "Neither Friends nor Strangers: Informal Networks and Subcontracting Relations in French Industry." In D. Gambetta, ed., *Trust*. New York: Oxford University Press, pp. 134–158.

Lorenz, E. 1991. "Historical Dependency, Conventions, and the Competitive Decline of the British Shipbuilding Industry." Paper presented to the Annual Conference of the Economic History Association, Boulder, 27–29 September.

Lorenz, E. 1992. "Trust and the Theory of Industrial Districts." In M. Storper and A. J. Scott, eds., *Pathways to Industrialization and Regional Development*. London: Routledge.

Lucas, R. E. 1988. "On the Mechanics of Economic Development." *Journal of Monetary Economics 22:* 3–42.

Lundvall, B. A. 1988. "Innovation as an Interactive Process: from User–Producer Interaction to Naional Systems of Innovation." In G. Dosi, et al., eds., *Technology and Economic Theory*. London: Pinter, pp. 349–369.

Lundvall, B. A. 1990. "User–Producer Interactions and Technological Change." Paper presented to the OECD-TEP Conference, Paris (La Villette), June.

Lundvall, B. A. 1992. *National Systems of Innovation: Toward a theory of Innovation and Interactive Learning*. London: Pinter.

Lundvall, B. A. 1993. "Explaining Interfirm cooperation and Innovation: Limits of the Transactions-Costs Approach." In G. Grabher, ed., *The Embedded Firm*. London: Routledge.

Lundvall, B. A., and Johnson, B. 1992. "The Learning Economy," Paper presented to the European Association for Evolutionary Political Economy conference, Paris November 4–6.

Lung, Y., and Mair, A. 1992. "La géographie du juste-à-temps: faux espoirs et vraies questions." Paper presented to the Regional Science Association European section. Lovain-la-Neuve, 25–28 August.

Luria, D.1988. "Automation, Markets and Scale: Can 'Flexible Niching' Modernize the Frostbelt?" Paper written for the Michigan Industrial Modernization Project, Ann Arbor, MI.

Machimura, T. 1992. "The Urban Restructuring Process in Tokyo in the 1980s: Transforming Tokyo into a World City." *International Journal of Urban and Regional Research 16*(1): 114–128.

MacIntyre, A. 1988. *Whose Justice? Which Rationality?* Notre Dame, IN: University of Notre Dame Press.

Maier, M. 1994. "Post Fordist City Politics." In A. Amin, ed., *Post-Fordism: A Reader*. Oxford: Basil Blackwell.

Maillat, D., Crévoisier, O., and Lecoq, B. 1990. "Innovation and Territorial Dynamism." Paper for workshop "Flexible Specialisation in Europe," Zurich 25–26 October.

Maillat, M., Quévit, M., and Senn, L. eds. 1993. *Milieux Innovateurs et Réseaux d'Innovation: Un Défi pour le Développement Régional*. Neuchâtel: EDES.

Maillat, D., Lecoq, B., Nemeti, F., and Pfister, M. 1995. "Technology District and Innovation: the Case of the Swiss Jura Arc." *Regional Studies 29:* 251–263.

Malecki, E. J. 1984. "Technology and Regional Development: A Survey." *APA Journal 50*(3): 262–266.

Mansfield, E. 1972. "The Contribution of R&D to Economic Growth in the United States." *Science 175:* 477–486.

Marchand, B. 1993. *Paris: Histoire d'une Ville*. Paris: Seuil.

Mariti, P., and Smiley, R. H.1983. "Cooperative Agreements and the Organization of Industry." *Journal of Industrial Economics XXXI*(4): 437–451.

Markusen, A. 1985. *Regions: the Economics and Politics of Territory*. Totowa, NJ: Rowman and Littlefield.

Markusen, A. 1986. *Profit Cycles, Oligopoly, and Regional Development*. Cambridge, MA: MIT Press.

Markusen, A., and Gwiasda, V. 1994. "Multipolarity and the Layering of Functions in World Cities." *International Journal of Urban and Regional Research 18*(3): 167–193.

Markusen, A. R., Hall, P., Campbell, S., and Deitrick, S. 1991. *The Rise of the Gunbelt: the Military Remapping of Industrial America*. New York: Oxford University Press.

Markusen, A. R., Hall, P., and Glasmeier, A. 1986. *High Tech America: The What, How, Where and Why of the Sunrise Industries*. Boston: Allen and Unwin.

Marsden, D. 1986. *The End of Economic Man? Custom and Competition in Labor Markets*. New York: St. Martin's Press.

Marshall, A. 1919. *Industry and Trade*. London: Macmillan.

Marshall, J. N. 1988. *Services and Uneven Development*. Oxford: Oxford University Press.

Martin, R., and Sunley, P. 1996. "Paul Krugman's Geographical Economics and Its Implications for Regional Development Theory: A Critical Assessment." *Economic Geography 72*(3): 259–292.

Maskell, P., and Malmberg, A. 1995. "Localised Learning and Industrial Competitiveness," Paper presented to Regional Studies European Conference on "Regional Futures," Gothenburg, 6–9 May.

Massey, D. B., and Meegan, R. 1982. *The Anatomy of Job Loss*. New York: Methuen.

Massey, D. B. 1984. *Spatial Divisions of Labour*. New York: Routledge.

Mathis, J., Mazier, J., and Rivaud-Danset, D. 1988. *La Compétitivité Industrielle*. Paris: Dunod.

Maurice, M., Sellier, F., and Silvestre, J. J. 1986. *The Social Foundations of Industrial Power: A Comparison of France and Germany*. Cambridge, MA: MIT Press.

McCombie, J. S. L. 1981. "What Still Remains of Kaldor's Laws?" *Economic Journal 91*: 206–216.

McCombie, J. S. L., and de Ridder, J. R. 1984. "The Verdoorn Law Controversy: Some New Empirical Evidence Using US State Data." *Oxford Economic Papers 36*(2).

Millon-Delsol, C. 1992. *l'État Subsidiaire*. Paris: Presses Universitaires de France.

Mingione, E. 1992. *Fragmented Societies*. Oxford: Blackwell.

Moe, T. 1987. "Interests, Institutions, and Positive Theory." *Studies in American Political Development 2*: 236–299.

Mokyr, J. 1988. *The Lever of Riches*. New York: Oxford University Press.

Mollenkopf, J., and Castells, M. 1992. *Dual City: Restructuring New York*. New York: Russell Sage Foundation.

Molotch, H. 1975. "The City as a Growth Machine." *American Sociological Review 82*: 226–238.

Montagne-Villette, S. 1987. "l'Industrie de Prêt-à-Porter en France." Paris: University of Paris IV, doctoral thesis.

Moore, B. 1966. *Social Origins of Dictatorship and Democracy*. Boston: Beacon.

Mowery, D., ed. 1988. *International Collaborative Ventures in Manufacturing*. Cambridge, MA: Ballinger.

Mytelka, L. K. 1990. *Strategic Partnerships and the World Economy*. London: Pinter.

Mytelka, L. K. 1996. "Locational Tournaments, Strategic Partnerships and the State." Paper delivered to European Management and Organization in Transition Conference, Durham, June 27–29.

Naponen, H., Graham, J., and Markusen, A. 1993. *Trading Industries; Trading Regions.* New York: Guilford Press.

Nelson, R. R. 1987. *Understanding Technical Change as an Evolutionary Process.* Amsterdam: North-Holland. (The F. De Vries Lectures in Economics)

Nelson, R. R. ed. 1992. *National Systems of Innovation.* New York: Oxford.

Nelson, R., and Winter, S. 1982. *An Evolutionary Theory of Economic Change.* Cambridge, MA: Harvard University Press.

Nicolas, B. 1996. "Structures d'Organisation et Paradigmes Sectoriels: Le Cas des Studios de Cinema en France et au Royaume-Uni, 1895–1995." Paris: Doctoral thesis at the Ecole Polytechnique, Social Sciences, Specialization in Management.

Nohria, N., and Eccles, R. 1992. *Networks and Organizations: Structure, Form and Action.* Boston: Harvard Business School Press.

North, D. 1981. *Structure and Change in Economic History.* New York: Norton.

Norton, R., and Rees, J. 1979. "The Product Cycle and the Spatial Decentralization of American Manufacturing." *Regional Studies 13:* 141–151.

Nuti, F. 1990. "I Distretti Manifatturiera." Bologna: Department of Economics, University of Bologna, report for the CNR Study on Sistema delle Imprese.

OECD. 1992. *Background Report Concerning the Technology/Economy (TEP) Programme.* Paris: Organization for Cooperation and Development.

OECD. 1993. *Territorial Development and Structural Change: A New Perspective on Adjustment and Reform.* Paris: Organization for Cooperation and Development.

Ohmae, K. 1993. "The Rise of the Region State." *Foreign Affairs* 78–87.

Olson, M. 1971. *The Logic of Collective Action: Public Goods and the Theory of Groups.* Cambridge, MA: Harvard University Press.

Olson, M. 1990. "Towards a Unified View of Economics and Other Social Sciences." In J. Alt and K. Shepsle, eds., *Perspectives on Positive Political Economy.* Cambridge, U.K.: Cambridge University Press.

Onida, F. 1980. "Esportazioni et Struttura Industriale dell'Italia negli anni 70." *Economia Italiana 1:* 97–139.

Orléan, A. 1994. *Bayesian Interactions and Collective Dynamics of Opinion: Herd Behavior and Mimetic Contagion.* Paris: Centre de Recherche en Epistemologie Appliquée.

Osborne, D., and Gaebler, T. 1993. *Reinventing Government: How the Entrepreneurial Spirit is Transforming the Public Sector.* New York: Plume.

O'hUallachain, B., and Reid, N. 1991. "The Location and Growth of Business and Professional Services in American Metropolitan Areas, 1976–1986." *Annals of the Association of American Geographers 81:* 254–70.

Pace, R. 1995. "Endogenous Organizational Change and External Economies of Scale." Dayton, University of Dayton, ms.

Paci, M. 1973. *Mercato del Lavoro e Classi Sociali in Italia.* Bologna: Il Mulino.

Paci, M. 1980. *Famiglia e Mercato del Lavoro in un'Economia Periferica.* Milan: Franco Angeli.

Paloscia, R. 1991. "Agriculture and Diffused Manufacturing in the Terza Italia: A Tuscan Case Study." In S. Whatmore et al., eds. *Rural Enterprise: Shifting Perspectives on Small-Scale Production.* London: D. Fulton, pp. 34–57.

Patel, P., and Pavitt, K. 1992. "Europe's Technological Performance." Brighton: SPRU, University of Sussex, paper.

Pavitt, K. 1984. "Sectoral Patterns of Technical Change: Toward a Taxonomy and a Theory." *Research Policy 13*.

Pavitt, K., and Patel, P. 1991. "Large Firms in the Production of the World's Technology: an Important Case of Non-Globalisation." *Journal of International Business Studies, First Quarter,* 1–21.

Perrin, J. C. 1993. "Pour une Révision de la Science Régionale: l'Approche en Termes de Milieu." Centre d'Economie Régionale, University of Aix-Marseille, Aix-en-Provence, *148*(3).

Perroux, F. 1950a. "Les Espaces Economiques." *Economie Appliquée, 1*(1): 25–244 .

Perroux, F. 1950b. "Economic Space: Theory and Applications." *Quarterly Journal of Economics 64*(1): 89–104.

Perroux, F. 1955. "Note sur les Poles de Croissance." *Economie Appliquée 1*(2): 302–320.

Persky, J., and Wiewel, W. 1994. "The Growing Localness of the Global City." *Economic Geography 70*(2): 129–143.

Perulli, P. 1987. "Flexibility Strategies: Employers, Trade Unions and Local Government: The Case of Modena Industrial Districts." Contribution to colloquium, "New Technologies and New Forms of Industrial Relations," MIT Conference Center, Endicott House, Cambridge, MA.

Pesce, A. 1990. "Un'Altra Emilia Romagna: elementi per una storia sociale della differenza sessuale." In *Commissione per la Realizzazione della Parita Fra Uomo e Donna, Regione Emilia Romagna.* Un'altra Emiglia Romagna, Milan: Franco Angeli, pp. 17–130.

Petit, P. 1993. "Are Full Employment Policies Passé?" Paper delivered to the Annual Meeting of the American Economics Association. Anaheim, CA.

Pianta, M. 1996. "Globalisation of Technology, Specialisation, and Performance: A Sectoral Analysis of OECD Countries." Paper presented at CEPREMAP, ARCH Seminar. Paris, February.

Piore, M., and Sabel, C. 1984. *The Second Industrial Divide.* New York: Basic Books.

Piore, M. 1989. "Some Further Notes on Technological Trajectories." Paper for colloquium, "Reversibilités et Irreversibilités dans les Modes de Croissance: Institutions, Techniques, et Économie," Paris, 21–23 June 1989.

Piore, M. [n.d.], "Work, Labor and Action in a System of Flexible Specialization." Cambridge, MA: MIT, unpublished paper.

Pitman, B. 1992. University of California at Los Angeles, Ph.D. thesis in Urban Planning.

Planque, B. 1990. "Note sur la Notion de Réseau d'Innovation: Réseaux Contractuels et Réseaux Conventionnels." Aix-en-Provence: University of Aix-Marseille, Centre d'Economie Régionale, paper.

Pollard, J., and Storper, M. 1996. "A Tale of Twelve Cities: Metropolitan Employment Change in Dynamic Industries in the 1980s." *Economic Geography 72*(1): 1–22.

Porter, M. 1990. *The Competitive Advantage of Nations.* London: Macmillan.

Powell, W. W. 1987. "Hybrid Organizational Arrangements: New Form or Transitional Arrangement?" *California Management Review 30:* 67–87.

Powell, W.W. 1990, "Neither Market nor Hierarchy: Network Forms of Organization." *Research in Organizational Behavior 12:* 295–336.

Pred, A. 1977. *City Systems in Advanced Economies.* Cambridge, MA: Harvard University Press.

Preteceille, E. 1996. "Division Sociale de l'Espace et Globalisation." *Sociétés Contemporaines 22:* 1–37.

Prevost, J. C. 1957. *Le dandyisme en France, 1817–1839.* Paris: Flammarion.

Putnam, D. (with Nanetti, R. and Leonardi, R.). 1993. *Making Democracy Work: Civic Culture and Regional Government in Contemporary Italy.* Princeton, NJ: Princeton University Press.

Rallet, A. 1993. "Choix de Proximité et Processus d'Innovation Technologique." *Révue d'Economie Régionale et Urbaine 3:* 365–386.

Rallet, A. 1995. "Interactions Spatiales et Dynamique de Proximité: Bilan et Perspectives." Paper delivered to colloquium, Industrial Dynamics, Territorial Dynamics. Toulouse, August.

Rallet, A., and Torre, A. eds. 1995. *Economie Industrielle et Economie Spatiale.* Paris: Economica.

Ramo, S. 1988. *The Business of Science.* New York: Hill and Wang.

Reich, R. 1990. "Who Is Us?" *Harvard Business Review* January–February: 53–64.

Reich, R. 1991. *The Work of Nations: Preparing Ourselves for Twenty-First Century Capitalism.* New York: Alfred Knopf.

Research Policy. 1992. (C. De Bresson and R. Walker, eds.). Special issue on "Networks of Innovators," *20*(5).

Révue Economique. 1989. "l'Économie des Conventions: Numéro Special." *40*(2), March.

Rey, G. 1989. "Profile and Analysis, 1981–85." In E. Goodman, and J. Bamford, eds. *Small Firms and Industrial Districts in Italy.* London: Routledge, pp. 69–93.

Richardson, G. B. 1972. "The Organisation of Industry." *Economic Journal 82:* 883–896.

Richardson, H. 1973. *Regional Growth Theory.* London: Macmillan.

Rip, A. 1991. "A Cognitive Approach to Technology Policy." Paper presented to the symposium, "New Frontiers in Science and Engineering." Paris, 27–29 May.

Ritaine, E. 1989. "La Modernité Localisée? Leçons Italiennes sur le Developpement Régional." *Révue Française de Science Politique 39*(2): 155–177.

Romer, P. M. 1986. "Increasing Returns and Long-Run Growth." *Journal of Political Economy 94*(5): 1002–1037.

Romer, P. M. 1990. "Endogenous Technological Change," *Journal of Political Economy 98*(5): S71–S101.

Romer, P. M. 1987. "Growth Based on Increasing Returns due to Specialization." *AEA, Papers and Proceedings 77*(2): 56–62.

Romer, P. M. 1993a. "Implementing a National Technology Strategy with Self-Organizing Industry Investment Boards." Paper Prepared for the June 1993 Meeting of the Brookings Panel on Microeconomics. Washington, DC.

Romer, P. M. 1993b. "Two Strategies for Economic Development: Using Ideas and Producing Ideas." Proceedings of the World Bank Annual Conference on Development Economics, 1992, Washington, DC.

Rosenberg, N. 1972. *Technology and American Economic Growth.* New York: Harper and Row.

Rosenberg, N. 1982. *Inside the Black Box: Technology and Economics.* New York: Cambridge University Press.

Rosenfeld, S. 1992. *Competitive Manufacturing: New Strategies for Regional Development.* New Brunswick, NJ: Center for Urban Policy Research.

Rowthorn, R. 1975a. "What Remains of Kaldor's Laws?" *Economic Journal 85:* 10–19.

Rowthorn, R. 1975b. "A Reply to Lord Kaldor's Comment." *Economic Journal 85:* 897–901.

Russo, M. 1986, "Technical Change and the Industrial District: the Role of Interfirm Relations in the Growth and Transformation of Ceramic Tile Production in Italy," *Research Policy 14:* 329–343.

Russo, M. 1995. "Units of Investigation for Local Economic Development Policies." Modena: University of Modena, Department of Economic Policy, Materiali di Discussione, #106.

Sabel, C. 1988. "The Resurgence of Regional Economies." In P. Hirst and J. Zeitlin, eds., *Reversing Industrial Decline,* Oxford: Berg, pp. 17–20

Sabel, C. 1993, "Constitutional Ordering in Historical Context." In F. Scharpf, ed., *Games in Hierarchies and Networks.* Boulder, CO: Westview Press.

Sabel,C., Kern, H., and Herrigel, G. 1989. "Collaborative Manufacturing: New Supplier Relations in the Automobile Industry and the Redefinition of Industrial Co-operation." Cambridge, MA: MIT, paper.

Sabel, C., and Zeitlin, J. 1985. "Historical Alternatives to Mass Production: Politics, Markets and Technology in Nineteenth Century Industrialization." *Past and Present 108:* 133–176.

Salais, R. 1989. "L'Analyse Économique des Conventions du Travail." *Révue Economique 40*(2): 199–240.

Salais, R., and Storper, M. 1992. "The Four Worlds of Contemporary Industry." *Cambridge Journal of Economics 16:* 169–193.

Salais, R., and Storper, M. 1993. *Les Mondes de Production.* Paris: Editions de l'Ecole des Hautes Etudes en Sciences Sociales.

Salvestrini, A. 1965. *I Moderati Toscani e la Classe Dirigente Italiana, 1859–1876.* Florence: Olschki.

Sassen, S. 1991. *Global Cities: New York, London, Tokyo.* Princeton, NJ: Princeton University Press.

Saxenian, A. 1988. "Regional Networks and the Resurgence of Silicon Valley," Berkeley: Institute of Urban and Regional Development Working Paper # 508.

Saxenian, A. 1991. "Contrasting Patterns of Business Organization in Silicon Valley." Berkeley: Institute of Urban and Regional Development, Working Paper #535.

Saxenian, A. 1994. *Regional Advantage: Culture and Competition in Silicon Valley and Route 128.* Cambridge, MA: Harvard University Press.

Sayer, R., and Walker, R. 1992. *The New Social Economy.* Oxford: Blackwell.

Scarpitti, L., and Trigilia. C. 1987. "Strategies of Flexibility: Firms, Unions and Local Governments: The Case of Prato." Contribution to colloquium on New Technologies and New Forms of Industrial Relations, MIT Conference Center, Endicott House, Cambridge, MA.

Schmitz, H., and Cassiolato, J., eds. 1992. *High Tech for Industrial Development: Lessons from the Brazilian Experience in Electronics and Automation.* London: Routledge.

Schwartz, M., and Romo, F. 1992. "The Structural Embeddedness of Business Decisions." Stony Brook, NY: SUNY, Deptartment of Sociology, paper.

Schwartz, M., and Romo, F. 1993. "The Rise and Fall of Detroit: How the Automobile Industry Destroyed its Capacity to Compete." Stony Brook NY: SUNY, Department of Sociology, manuscript.

Scitovsky, T. 1952. "Two Concepts of External Economies." *Economic Journal LXII:* 54–67.

Scott, A. J. 1976. *The Urban Land Nexus and the State.* London: Pion.

Scott, A. J. 1986. "High Technology Industry and Territorial Development: the Rise of the Orange County Complex, 1955–1984," *Urban Geography 7:* 3– 45.

Scott, A. 1988a. *Metropolis: From the Division of Labor to Urban Form.* Berkeley: University of California Press.

Scott, A. J. 1988b. *New Industrial Spaces.* London: Pion.

Scott A. J. 1990. "The Aircraft Industry in Southern California, the Early Years." University of California Los Angeles: Papers in Economic and Human Geography 2.

Scott, A. J. 1993. Technopolis: *High Technology Industry and Regional Development in Southern California.* Berkeley: University of California Press.

Scott, A. J. 1996. "Regional Motors of the Global Economy." *Futures 28*(5): 391–411.

Scott, A. J., and Kwok E. C. 1989. "Interfirm Subcontracting and Locational Agglomeration: A Case Study of the Printed Circuits Industry in Southern California." *Regional Studies 23*(5): 405–416.

Scott, A. J., and Storper, M. eds. 1986. *Production, Work, Territory.* London: Allen and Unwin.

Scott A. J., and Storper, M. 1987. "High Technology Industry and Regional Development: A Theoretical Critique and Reconstruction." *International Social Science Journal 112:* 215–232.

Scott, A. J., and Storper, M. 1991. "Regional Development Reconsidered," In H. Ernste and V. Meier, eds., *Regional Development and Contemporary Industrial Response: Expanding Flexible Specialisation.* London: Belhaven, pp. 3–24.

Scranton, P. 1985. *Figured Tapestry.* New York: Cambridge University Press.

Searle, J. 1977. *Speech Acts.* London: Cambridge University Press.

Segrestin, D. 1985. "Le Phénomène Corporatiste: Essai sur l'Avenir des Systèmes Professionnels Fermés en France." Paris: Fayard.

Seravalli, G. 1992. "Subcontractors' Relationships: A Suggested Research Outline." Berkeley: University of California, Insitute for Urban and Regional Development, Working Paper.

Sforzi, F. 1990. "The Quantitative Importance of Marshallian Industrial Districts in the Italian Economy."In F. Pyke, G. Becattini, and W. Sengenberger, eds., *Industrial Districts and Interfirm Cooperation in Italy.* Geneva: International Institute of Labor Studies, pp. 75–107.

Simon, H. A. 1979. *Models of Thought.* New Haven: Yale University Press.

Simon, P. 1931. *Monographie sur une Industrie de Luxe: la Haute Couture.* Paris: Scuil.

Solinas, G. 1982. "Labor Market Segmentation and Workers' Careers: The Case of the Italian Knitwear Industry." *Cambridge Journal of Economics 6:* 331–352.

Solow, R. M. 1957. "Technical Change and the Aggregate Production Function." *Review of Economics and Statistics 39:* 312–320.

Soskice, D. 1993. "Innovation Strategies of Companies: A Comparative Institutional Explanation of Cross-Country Differences." Wissenschaftszentrum Berlin, paper, July.

Spender, J. C. 1989. *Industry Recipe: An Enquiry into the Nature and Sources of Managerial Judgement.* Oxford: Basil Blackwell.

Sraffa, P. 1960. *Production of Commodities by Means of Commodities.* Cambridge, U.K.: Cambridge University Press.

Sternberg, E. 1992. *Photonic Technology and Industrial Policy: US Responses to Technological Change.* Albany, NY: SUNY Press.

Stigler, G. 1951. "The Division of Labor is Limited by the Extent of the Market." *Journal of Political Economy 69:* 213–225.

Stoffaes, C. 1983. *Politique Industrielle.* Paris: Droit.

Storper, M. 1982. "The Spatial Division of Labor: Technology, the Labor Process, and the Location of Industries." University of California, Berkeley: Ph.D. dissertation.

Storper, M. 1985, "Oligopoly and the Product Cycle." *Economic Geography 61*(3): 260–282.

Storper, M. 1989. "The Transition to Flexible Specialization in the US Film Industry: External Economies, the Division of Labor, and the Crossing of Industrial Divides." *Cambridge Journal of Economics 13:* 273–305.

Storper, M. 1992. "The Limits to Globalization: Technology Districts and International Trade," *Economic Geography 68*(1): 60–93.

Storper, M. 1995a. "The Resurgence of Regional Economies, Ten Years Later." *European Urban and Regional Studies 2*(3): 191–221.

Storper, M. 1995b. "Regional Technology Coalitions: An Essential Dimension of National Technology Policy." *Research Policy 24:* 895–911.

Storper, M. and Christopherson, S., 1987, "Flexible Specialization and Regional Industrial Agglomerations." *Annals of the Association of American Geographers,* 77.

Storper, M., and Harrison, B. 1991. "Flexibility, Hierarchy and Regional Development: the Changing Structures of Production Systems and their Forms of Governance in the 1990s." *Research Policy 21:* 407–422.

Storper, M., and R. Salais. 1992. "The Division of Labor and Industrial Diversity: Flexibility and Mass Production in the French Automobile Industry." *International Review of Applied Economics 6*(1): 1–37.

Storper, M., and Salais, R. 1997. *Worlds of Production: the Action Frameworks of the Economy.* Cambridge, MA: Harvard University Press.

Storper, M., and Scott, A. 1989. "The Geographical Foundations and Social Regulation of Flexible Production Complexes." In J. Wolch and M. Dear, eds., *The Power of Geography; How Territory Shapes Social Life.* London: Unwin Hyman, pp. 21–40.

Storper, M., and Scott, A. J. 1990. "Work Organization and Local Labor Markets in an Era of Flexible Production." *International Labour Review 129*(5): 573–591.

Storper, M., and Scott, A. J. 1995. "The Wealth of Regions: Market Forces and Policy Imperatives in Local and Global Context." *Futures 27*(5): 505–526.

Storper, M., and R. Walker. 1989. *The Capitalist Imperative: Territory, Technology, and Industrial Growth.* Oxford: Basil Blackwell.

Stowsky, J. 1987. "The Weakest Link: Semiconductor Production Equipment, Linkages, and the Limits to International Trade." Berkeley: UC Berkeley, BRIE, Working Paper 27.

Suleiman, E. 1979. *Les élites en France. Grands corps et grandes écoles.* Paris: Seuil.

Thévenot, L, 1986, "Economie et Formes Conventionnelles." In R. Salais and L. Thévenot, eds., *Le Travail: Marchs, Règles, Conventions.* Paris: Economica, pp. 195–217.

Thirlwall, A. P. 1980. "Rowthorn's Interpretation of Kaldor's Laws." *Economic Journal* 90: 386–388.

Thisse, J. F. 1992. "Espace et Concurrence: Une Cohabitation Difficile?" In P. H. Derycke, ed., *Espace et Dynamiques Territoriales*. Paris: Economica.

Thorelli, H. B. 1986. "Networks: Between Markets and Hierarchies." *Strategic Management Journal* 7: 37–51.

Thrift, N. J. 1994a. "A Phantom State? The Detraditionalisation of Money, the International Financial System, and International Financial Centers." University of California at Los Angeles: Paper given to the UCLA Center for Social Theory and Comparative History, Annual Colloquium Series, 6 June.

Thrift, N. J. 1994b. "On the Social and Cultural Determinants of International Financial Centres." In S. Corbridge, R. Martin, and N. J. Thrift, eds., *Money, Space and Power*. Oxford: Blackwell.

Tinacci-Mosello, M. 1983. "Modernità e Tradizione di un Sistema Industriale Locale: il Modello Pratese della 'Fabbrica Diffusa' e la sua Evoluzione Storica." Florence: Acts of the 23rd Italian Geographical Congress 2(2): 294–305.

Tinacci-Mosello, M. 1989. "Innovative Capacity of Industrial Districts." Florence: University of Florence, Department of Economics, Discussion Paper 59.

Todd, E. 1994. *Le Destin des Immigrés*. Paris: Seuil.

Todtling, F. 1992. "The Uneven Landscape of Innovation Poles: Local Embeddedness and Global Networks." University of Vienna, IIR, 46.

Tolliday, S., and Zeitlin, J. 1988. "Between Fordism and Flexibility: the Automobile Industry and its Workers, Past, Present and Future." *Archiv für social Geschichte XXCI-II*: 153–171.

Tolomelli, C. ed. 1993. *Le Politiche Industriale Regionali: Experienze, Soggetti, Modelli*. Bologna: CLUEB.

Torre, A. 1995. "Dynamiques Locales et Coordination des Acteurs." Colloquium, Industrial Dynamics, Spatial Dynamics, Toulouse August.

Trigilia, C. 1985. "La Regolazione Localistica: Economia e Politica nell'Aree di Piccola Imprese." *Stato e Mercato 14*: 181–228.

Trigilia, C. 1986a. "Small Firm Development and Political Subcultures in Italy." *European Sociological Review 2*: 161–175.

Trigilia, C. 1986b. *Grandi Partiti e Piccole Imprese*. Bologna: Il Mulino.

Trigilia, C.1990. "Italian Industrial Districts: Neither Myth nor Interlude." Papier delivered to conference on Industrial Districts and Local Economic Regeneration, Geneva, Oct. 18–19.

Tyson, L. 1987. *Creating Advantage: Strategic Policy for National Competitiveness*. Berkeley, CA: University of California, BRIE.

Tyson, L. 1990. *Who's Bashing Whom? Trade Conflict in High Technology Industries*. Washington, DC: Institute for International Economics.

Tyson, L. 1991. "They Are Not Us." *The American Prospect*, Winter.

Veltz, P. 1993. "De l'Économie des Coûts à l'Économie de l'Organisation." Paris: Ecole des Ponts et Chaussées, LATTS, working paper.

Veltz, P. 1995. *Mondialisation, Villes, et Territoires: L'économie de l'Archipel*. Paris: Presses Universitaires de France.

Vernon, R. 1966. "International Investment and International Trade in the Product Cycle." *Quarterly Journal of Economics 80*: 190–207.

Vernon, R. 1974. "The Location of Economic Activity." In Dunning, J. ed., *Economic Analysis and the Multinational Enterprise.* London: Allen and Unwin.

Vernon, R. 1979. "The Product Cycle Hypothesis in a New International Environment." *Oxford Bulletin of Economics and Statistics 4:* 255–167.

von Hippel, E. 1987. "Cooperation between Rivals: Informal Know-How Trading," *Research Policy 16:* 291–302.

von Hippel, E. 1988. *The Sources of Innovation.* New York: Oxford University Press.

von Hippel, E. 1994. "Sticky Information and the Locus of Problem Solving: Implications for Innovation." *Management Science 49*(4): 429–439.

Wacquant, L. 1995. "The Rise of Advanced Marginalty: Notes on Its Nature and Its Implications." *Acta Sociologica.*

Wade, R. 1990. *Governing the Market: Economic Theory and the Role of Government in East Asian Industrialization.* Princeton, NJ: Princeton University Press.

Waldinger, R. 1992. "Taking Care of the Guests: the Impact of Immigrants on Services." *International Journal of Urban and Regional Research 16*(1).

Waterman, D. 1982. "The Structural Development of the Motion Picture Industry." *American Economist XVI*(1).

Weder, R., and Grubel, H. G. 1994. "The New Growth Theory and Coasean Economics: Institutions to Capture Externalities." *Weltwirtschaftliches Archiv:* 488–513

Williams, K., Cutler, T., Williams J., and Haslam, C. 1987. "The End of Mass Production?" *Economy and Society 16*(3): 405–439.

Williamson, O. 1975. *Markets and Hierarchies: Analysis and Antitrust Implications.* New York: Free Press.

Williamson, O. 1985. *The Economic Institutions of Capitalism.* New York: Basic Books.

Williamson, O. 1990. "The Firm as a Nexus of Treaties," In M. Aoki, B. Gustafsson, and O. Williamson, eds., *The Firm as Nexus of Treaties.* Newbury Park, CA: Sage Publications, pp. 1–25.

Wilson, W. J. 1987. *The Truly Disadvantaged.* Chicago: University of Chicago Press.

Wolfe, D. 1994. "The Institutions of the New Economy." Toronto, University of Toronto, Deptartment of Political Science, manuscript.

Young, A. 1928. "Increasing Returns and Economic Progress." *Economic Journal 38:* 527–542.

Zucker, L. G. 1987. "Institutional Theories of Organization." *Annual Review of Sociology 13:* 443–464.

Zucker, L. G. 1988. "Where Do Institutional Patterns Come From? Organizations as Actors in Social Systems." In L. Zucker, ed., *Institutional Patterns and Organizations.* Cambridge, MA: Ballinger, pp. 23–49.

Zysman, J. 1995. "National Roots of a 'Global' Economy." *Révue d'Economie Industrielle 71*(1): 107–122.

Index